Computational Intelligence
in Theory and Practice

Advances in Soft Computing

Editor-in-chief
Prof. Janusz Kacprzyk
Systems Research Institute
Polish Academy of Sciences
ul. Newelska 6
01-447 Warsaw, Poland
E-mail: kacprzyk@ibspan.waw.pl
http://www.springer.de/cgi-bin/search-bock.pl?series=4240

Esko Turunen
Mathematics Behind Fuzzy Logic
1999. ISBN 3-7908-1221-8

Robert Fullér
Introduction to Neuro-Fuzzy Systems
2000. ISBN 3-7908-1256-0

Robert John and Ralph Birkenhead (Eds.)
Soft Computing Techniques and Applications
2000. ISBN 3-7908-1257-9

Mieczysław Kłopotek, Maciej Michalewicz and Sławomir T. Wierzchoń (Eds.)
Intelligent Information Systems
2000. ISBN 3-7908-1309-5

Peter Sinčák, Ján Vaščák, Vladimír Kvasnička and Radko Mesiar (Eds.)
The State of the Art in Computational Intelligence
2000. ISBN 3-7908-1322-2

Bernd Reusch · Karl-Heinz Temme
Editors

Computational Intelligence in Theory and Practice

With 39 Figures
and 5 Tables

Springer-Verlag Berlin Heidelberg GmbH

Prof. Dr. Bernd Reusch
Dr. Karl-Heinz Temme
University of Dortmund
Otto-Hahn-Straße 16
44227 Dortmund
Germany

ISSN 1615-3871
ISBN 978-3-7908-1357-9

Cataloging-in-Publication Data applied for
Die Deutsche Bibliothek – CIP-Einheitsaufnahme
Computational intelligence in theory and practice: with 5 tables / Bernd Reusch; Karl-Heinz Temme ed. – Springer-Verlag Berlin Heidelberg, 2001
(Advances in soft computing)
ISBN 978-3-7908-1357-9 ISBN 978-3-7908-1831-4 (eBook)
DOI 10.1007/978-3-7908-1831-4

Originally published by Physica-Verlag Heidelberg New York in 2001

Hardcover Design: Erich Kirchner, Heidelberg

SPIN 10789143 88/2202-5 4 3 2 1 0 – Printed on acid-free paper

Preface

Computational Intelligence with its roots in Fuzzy Logic, Neural Networks and Evolutionary Algorithms has become an important research and application field in computer science in the last decade. Methodologies from these areas and combinations of them enable users from engineering, business, medicine and many more branches to capture and process vague, incomplete, uncertain and imprecise data and knowledge. Many algorithms and tools have been developed to solve problems in the realms of high and low level control, information processing, diagnostics, decision support, classification, optimisation and many more.

This development would not have been possible without an interactive play of theory and practice. A good example is the conference series of the Dortmund Fuzzy Days, first time held in 1991, now the 6th event in 1999, initially intended for scientists and practitioners for discussions on the theory and application of fuzzy logic alone, synergetic links with neural networks and later with evolutionary algorithms were included and the conference envolved gradually to embrace the full spectrum of Computational Intelligence.

This book tries to show the impact and feedback between theory and applications of Computational Intelligence, highlighted on selected examples. They are taken from the 25th Anniversary Colloquium of Chair Informatik I, University of Dortmund, celebrated during Wintersemester 1997/98 with invited talks of many outstanding researchers from Europe and Canada.

This book is partitioned into four chapters:

Fuzzy Logic Theory

Rough Sets

Fuzzy Clustering

Fuzzy Data Models and Bases

Out of the broad field of Fuzzy Logic Theory selected topics are targeted. They show how theory results can support for example case-based decisions, applications of many valued logic or selection of operators (here t-norms) in fuzzy systems.

Rough sets are an alternative method to represent uncertain knowledge. In practical applications they support evaluation of uncertain statements but in algebraic theory there are many open questions, which are investigated.

Fuzzy Clustering is a very good example to illustrate how method of one branch of Computational Intelligence (here Fuzzy Logic) are applied to solve a particular class of problems, and on the other hand methods of other branches (here Genetic Algorithms) are used for optimization. With focus on clustering and classification general ideas and case studies are presented.

The introduction of fuzzy models into data bases has risen many questions in respect to representation, querying and retrieval. Three papers give insight into solutions.

The editors wish to thank all authors who contributed to this book as well as those who gave their talks during the Anniversary Colloquium.

Dortmund, December 2000

Bernd Reusch Karl-Heinz Temme

Contents

3 Fuzzy Clustering

4 Fuzzy Data Models and Bases

A Fuzzy Set Approach to Case-Based Decision

Didier Dubois and Henri Prade*

Institut de Recherche en Informatique de Toulouse (IRIT) – CNRS
Université Paul Sabatier, 118 route de Narbonne
31062 Toulouse Cedex 4, France

Abstract. This paper is an attempt at providing a fuzzy set-based approach to case-based decision. Case-based decision consists in selecting an action to be applied to a current problem on the basis of a set of cases storing the results of various actions applied to similar, previously encountered, problems. Recently, Gilboa and Schmeidler have presented an axiomatic justification of a counterpart of the expected utility used in decision under uncertainty, where similarity degrees play a role somewhat analogous to probability, and have proposed to apply it to case-based decision. This proposal resembles Sugeno's approach to fuzzy control. The relation between the two approaches is investigated. Besides, another approach, based on possibility and necessity measures, is presented and discussed. The idea is to favor actions which have never given bad results in problems similar to the current problem. A much more permissive view considers all the actions which have given good results (at least once) in a similar problem.

Keywords. Case-based decision, similarity, gradual rule, possibility theory

1 Introduction

Analogical reasoning, and more particularly, case-based reasoning is pervasive in the way humans handle practical problems. It is based on the idea that if two problems are similar with respect to a set X of attributes describing them, they should, or at least may, still be similar with respect to other attribute(s) Y pertaining to them. Then, we can take advantage of past experience about problems which are similar (with respect to X) to a current problem in order to infer a plausible value for Y in the current problem. Case-based reasoning is now a very active research area in Artificial Intelligence (Kolodner [12]). Nevertheless, there has been rather few attempts at formalizing case-based reasoning. A proposal was made by Davies and Russell [2] who use acknowledged functional dependencies

---

* This paper first appeared in the unpublished proceedings of the Second European Workshop on Fuzzy Decision Analysis and Neural Networks for Management, Planning and Optimization (EFDAN'97), R. Felix (ed.), June 10 - 11, 1997, Dortmund, Germany, pages 1 - 9.

from attributes X to Y for controlling the inference process. However, this framework is very restrictive since inference is possible only if there is a perfect identity between the X-values describing the two problems, and if it is known that when the X-values are equal, the Y-values should be equal (i.e., that the functional dependency "X determines Y" holds). Then, it may be tempting to allow for a graded assessment of similarity between problems and to take advantage of "fuzzy" functional dependencies, as suggested in (Léa Sombé [13]). This idea will be briefly investigated in Section 2, where "strong" dependencies expressing that the value of X (fuzzily) determines the value of Y, are contrasted with "weak" dependencies stating only that if the X-values are similar, it is *possible* that the Y-values are similar.

Besides, Gilboa and Schmeidler [11] have recently proposed an axiomatized approach to case-based decision, where a similarity-based counterpart of expected utility is justified. Interestingly enough, the decision procedure they advocate looks somewhat similar to Sugeno and Nishida [16] approach to fuzzy rule-based control, where a control value is computed by interpolation between values recommended by fuzzy rules, on the basis of the degrees of matching of the current situation with these rules.

In Section 3, Gilboa and Schmeidler's proposal is recalled and its relationship with fuzzy control techniques is discussed in relation with the strong modelling of fuzzy functional dependencies. Then, Section 4 proposes another approach to case-based decision more in agreement with the weak dependency view.

2 Fuzzy Functional Dependencies in Case-Based Reasoning

This section outlines the fuzzy logic framework for case-based reasoning proposed by Dubois, et al. [3]. Let M denote a memory of experienced cases represented by pairs (s_i,t_i) for $i = 1,n$, where s_i denotes a problem description and t_i the associated outcome (solution). The current problem will be denoted by s_0 and its intended solution by t_0.

A fuzzy functional dependency (e.g., Raju and Majumdar [15]) of the form "the more similar s_1 and s_2, the more similar t_1 and t_2" where (s_1,t_1) and (s_2,t_2) are cases of M, can be modelled by the constraint

$$\forall (s_1,t_1),(s_2,t_2) \in M,\ S(s_1,s_2) \leq T(t_1,t_2) \tag{1}$$

where S and T are fuzzy proximity relations (they range on [0,1]). In this paper, we use the notations $S(s_1,s_2)$ and $T(t_1,t_2)$ for denoting the degrees of similarity for simplicity, rather than using the notations $\mu_S(s_1,s_2)$ and $\mu_T(t_1,t_2)$ commonly used in the fuzzy set literature where they distinguish between a fuzzy set F and its membership function μ_F. Thus, in all the paper, we write F(u) instead of $\mu_F(u)$. S and T are supposed to be symmetric ($\forall s_1, s_2, S(s_1,s_2) = S(s_2,s_1), T(t_1,t_2) = T(t_2,t_1)$), and reflexive ($\forall s_1, S(s_1,s_1) = 1, T(t_1,t_1) = 1$). According to (1), the similarity of s_1 and s_2 constrains the similarity of t_1 and t_2 at a minimum level, i.e., $S(s_1,s_2)$ is a lower bound of $T(t_1,t_2)$. In particular if $S(s_1,s_2) = 1$ then $T(t_1,t_2)$ should be 1 also. Expression (1) corresponds to the representation of a gradual rule [5]. In particular, $\forall \alpha \in (0,1]$, we have

$$(s_1,s_2) \in S_\alpha \Rightarrow (t_1,t_2) \in T_\alpha$$

where $S_\alpha = \{(s,s'), S(s,s') \geq \alpha\}$ is the α-cut of S and T_α is similarly defined. So it expresses that when s_1 and s_2 are close, t_1 and t_2 should be at least as close. Moreover, if T is such that $T(t_1,t_2) = 1 \Leftrightarrow t_1 = t_2$, then the classical functional dependency $s_1 = s_2 \Rightarrow t_1 = t_2$ is a consequence of (1) using the reflexivity of S. Constraint (1) is then clearly stronger than a classical functional dependency in this case, since the above implication holds for any α-cut.

Let us know examine how (1) is used in the case-based inference process. Let $(s,t) \in M$, we have for the current situation s_0

$$S(s,s_0) \leq T(t,t_0)$$

where t_0 is unknown. Thus, the constraint defines a set of possible values for t_0, namely $\{t_0, S(s,s_0) \leq T(t,t_0)\}$. Since, it applies for any (s,t) in M, we obtain the following set E of possible values for t_0

$$E = \bigcap_{(s,t)\in M} \{t' \in \mathcal{T} \mid S(s,s_0) \leq T(t,t')\}. \qquad (2)$$

Note that E may be empty if T is not permissive enough. It can be shown that the non-emptiness of E can be guaranteed by the logical coherence (in the sense of (Dubois, Prade and Ughetto [10])) of the set of fuzzy gradual rules "the more s_0 is S-similar to s_i the more t_0 should be T-similar to t_i for each case $(s_i,t_i)\in M$.

The requirement that the value of s uniquely determines the value of t, or at least that when s_i and s_j are close, t_i and t_j should be close also, may be felt to be too strong in some practical applications where M may for instance simultaneously include cases like (s,t) and (s,t') with t much different from t'. Indeed two very similar second-hand cars might be sold at different prices, for instance. In such a case, we suggest to use a weaker version of the principle underlying case-based reasoning, stating that "the more similar s_1 and s_2, the more *possible* t_1 and t_2 are similar". The formal expression of this principle requires the clarification of the intended meaning of 'possible' in the above rule.

Rules of the form "the more X is A, the more possible Y is B" correspond to a particular kind of fuzzy rules called "possibility rules" (Dubois and Prade [9]). They express that "the more X is A, the more possible B is a range for Y", which can be understood as "$\forall$u, if X = u, it is possible at least at the degree A(u) that Y lies in B". When B is an ordinary subset, it clearly expresses that i) if $v \in B$, v is possible for Y at least at the level A(u) if X = u, and ii) if $v \notin B$, nothing is said about the minimum possibility level of value v for Y. It leads to the following constraint on the conditional possibility distribution $\pi_{Y|X}$ representing the rule

$$\forall\, u \in U, \forall\, v \in V, \min(A(u), B(v)) \leq \pi_{Y|X}(v,u).$$

See Dubois and Prade [7] for a full justification of its semantics when both A and B are fuzzy. This model of fuzzy rule is close to Mamdani [14]'s original proposal in fuzzy logic-based control.

Since we apply the principle "the more similar are s and s_0 (in the sense of S), the more possible is that t and t_0 are similar (in the sense of T)", the fuzzy set of possible values t' for t_0 is given by

$$\pi_{t_0}(t') \geq \min(S(s,s_0), T(t,t')).$$

As it can be seen, what is obtained is the fuzzy set of values t' T-similar to t, "truncated" by the global degree $S(s,s_0)$ of similarity of s and s_0. Since it applies to all the pairs $(s,t) \in M$, we obtain the following fuzzy set E of possible values t' for t_0 ($E(t') = \pi_{t_0}(t')$)

$$E(t') = \max_{(s,t)\in M} \min(S(s,s_0), T(t,t')). \qquad (3)$$

3 Gilboa and Schmeidler's Approach

Computing the result of a case-based inference is not only a matter of retrieving similar relevant cases, even if no adaptation is to be performed, as shown by the case-based decision paradigm. Recently, Gilboa and Schmeidler [11] have advocated a similarity-based approach to decision where a case is described as a triple (problem, act, result) and where a decision-maker's non-negative utility function u assigns a numerical value u(r) to a result r. When faced with a new situation s_0, the decision-maker is supposed to choose an act *a* which maximizes a counterpart of classical expected utility used in decision under uncertainty, namely

$$U_{s_0,M}(a) = \Sigma_{(s,a,r)\in M}\ S(s_0,s) \cdot u(r) \qquad (4)$$

where S is a non-negative function which estimates the similarity of situations, here the similarity of the current situation s_0 against already encountered ones stored in the memory M. Moreover it is assumed that $\forall s, \forall a, \exists! r$ such that (s, a, r) $\in$ M (i.e., results are uniquely determined by the act applied to the context of a given problem), and $\forall s, \exists! a$ such that (s, a, r) $\in$ M and $u(r) \neq 0$ (i.e., it means that only the best act in context s is stored in the memory). Gilboa and Schmeidler [11] give an axiomatic derivation of this U-maximization, within a formal model.

In order to relate the case-based reasoning framework of the previous section to the above approach to decision problems, we consider the triples (s, a, r) as cases ((s,a), r) and we assume $S((s,a), (s_0,a)) = S(s,s_0)$. Under a rather special hypothesis on the contents of M, it is then possible to retrieve (4) by applying the approach of Section 2 in the deterministic case. Indeed let us try to estimate the utility $u(r_0)$ attached to the act *a* applied to the current problem description s_0. Then (2) yields

$$E_a = \bigcap_{(s,a,r)\in M} \{u(r') \mid S(s,s_0) \leq T(u(r), u(r'))\}. \qquad (5)$$

Using results in the Appendix, it can be checked that under the hypothesis that M and S are such that for s_0, $\exists!(s_1,s_2)$ such that $(s_1, a, r_1) \in M$, $(s_2, a, r_2) \in M$, $S(s_0,s_1) > 0$, $S(s_0,s_2) > 0$ and moreover that $S(s_0,s_1) + S(s_0,s_2) = 1$, then E_a contains only one element e_a equal to

$$e_a = \frac{\sum_{(s,a,r)\in M} S(s,s_0) \cdot u(r)}{\sum_{(s,a,r)\in M} S(s,s_0)} \qquad (6)$$

where we recognize (4) up to a normalization factor depending on the act *a*. An appropriate choice of T in (5) is also required in order to have (5) reduced to the value (6). See Appendix. This shows that for particular S and T, (5) embeds a linear interpolation mechanism. One way of satisfying the requirement of the above hypothesis when the problems s in M can be linearly ordered, is in fact to assume that a different S, say S_s, is associated with the neighborhood of each problem s, in such a way that S(s,s') decreases to 0 when s' goes away from s and coincide with one of the two closest neighbors of s in M. Moreover we have to enforce

$S_{s_1}(s_0,s_1) + S_{s_2}(s_0,s_2) = 1.$

Note that (4) is also akin to the fuzzy vote procedure used by Bensana et al. [1] for selecting a (scheduling) decision b in a situation s_0 from a set of rules if s is $S^{(i)}$ then the recommended act is $a^{(i)}$ with weight $w^{(i)}$ (where $w^{(i)}$ can be viewed as the utility of the result of the act $a^{(i)}$) as the one maximizing an index of the form

$$U(a) = \sum_{i:a=a^{(i)}} S^{(i)}(s_0) \cdot w^{(i)} \qquad (7)$$

where $S^{(i)}$ is a fuzzy set describing a fuzzy class of situations.

At the reasoning level, the above decision procedures make use of similarity notions which can be viewed as the amount of "stretching" of the typical situation described in the condition part of the rule (i.e., the tolerance expressed by $S^{(i)}$ for extending the range of use of the rule) to encompass the current problem s_0.

Although (4) looks like an expected utility expression where probabilities are replaced by similarity degrees, its intuitive interpretation is quite different from the decision under uncertainty situation. First, note that there is no constraint on the sum $\Sigma_s S(s,s_0)$, in particular it has not to sum to 1 (in (6) the normalizing factor depends on act *a*). The idea is rather to look for acts that in several similar situations had results with a high utility. However, a drawback of (4) is it unability to distinguish between the two following types of "extreme" situations

(i) For act a_1, $\exists!$ s^* such that $S(s_0,s^*)$ is high, $u(r^*)$ is *high* and $(s^*, a_1, r^*) \in M$ and $S(s_0,s)$ is zero for any other s such that $(s, a, r) \in M$;

(ii) For act a_2, $\exists$ $s_1, \ldots, s_n$, with n sufficiently large, such that $S(s_0,s_i)$ is high for $i = 1,n$ and $u(r_i)$ is *low* but non-zero where $(s_i, a_2, r_i) \in M$, while $S(s_0,s)$ is zero for any other s such that $(s, a, r) \in M$

and we may have $U_{s_0,M}(a_1) < U_{s_0,M}(a_2)$.

But, it may look strange to prefer act a_2, which always gave rather poor results in situations similar to s_0, to act a_1, which gave a very good result in a situation quite similar to s_0 (even if this situation is unique). Moreover (4) somewhat compensates between good results r and bad results r' attached to the same act *a* for distinct problems s and s' which are both similar to s_0 (if we have both (s, a, r) and (s', a, r') in M).

4 An Alternative Approach

Another idea is to look for acts which for similar problems always gave good results. Then, for a given act *a*, we are interested in computing a degree of inclusion of the fuzzy set of problems which are similar to s_0 and where act *a* was experienced, into the fuzzy set of situations where act *a* led to good results.

The function u, like S, is now supposed to range on the real interval [0,1], with the following interpretations: $S(s,s') = 1$ means perfect similarity of s and s', $S(s,s') = 0$ means that s and s' are not at all similar as previously, while $u(r) = 1$

means that the result r is among the best ones, and $u(r) = 0$ means that r is among the worst ones. Thus, the fuzzy set of situations similar to s_0 is represented by $S(s_0) = \{s_0\} \circ S$, and u is the membership function of the fuzzy set of good results. The following degree of inclusion enables us to select the act(s) *a*, if any, which for problems similar to s_0 always gave good results:

$$U_{*s_0,M}(a) = \min_{(s,r):\ (s,a,r)\in M} S(s,s_0) \rightarrow u(r) \tag{8}$$

where $\rightarrow$is a multiple-valued implication connective (i.e., $x \rightarrow y$ increases with y, decreases with x, and coincides with material implication on $\{0,1\}$). Assume that

- $U_{*s_0,M}(a) = 1$ only if

$$\{s, (s, a, r) \in M, S(s,s_0) > 0\} \subseteq \{s, (s, a, r) \in M \text{ and } u(r) = 1\}$$

- $U_{*s_0,M}(a) = 0$ as soon as $\exists s$, $S(s,s_0) = 1$, $(s, a, r) \in M$ and $u(r) = 0$.

This leads to choose an implication $x \rightarrow y$ of the form $x \rightarrow y = n(x) \perp y$ where n is an involutive negation function and $\perp$ a disjunction operation. In case of a purely ordinal interpretation of [0,1] where only the ordering of the levels is meaningful, we are led to use $x \rightarrow y = \max(1 - x, y)$,[1] i.e.,

$$U_{*s_0,M}(a) = \min_{(s,r):\ (s,a,r)\in M} \max(u(r), 1 - S(s,s_0)) \tag{9}$$

which expresses that the existence of a case (s, a, r) in M does not penalize act *a* w.r.t. s_0, if r is a good result, or if s is not similar to s_0.

$U_{*s_0,M}$ is a rather drastic criterium since it requires that in *all* the problems similar to s_0, act *a* led in good results. A more "optimistic" behaviour can consist in selecting all the acts which led to a good result for at least one problem similar to s_0, i.e., the dual criteria

$$U^*_{s_0,M}(a) = \max_{(s,r):\ (s,a,r)\in M} \min(u(r), S(s,s_0)). \tag{10}$$

Thus $U^*_{s_0,M}(a)$ is maximum as soon as there exists a case corresponding to a problem completely similar to s_0 where the act *a* led to an excellent result. Note that

$$U^*_{s_0,M}(a) \geq U_{*s_0,M}(a), \tag{11}$$

---

[1] Since $\max(1 - x, y) = 1$ if and only if $y = 1$ whenever $x > 0$. On an ordinal scale, $1 - (\cdot)$ is replaced by the order-reversing function of the scale.

provided that the fuzzy set $S(\cdot, s_0)$ of situations s which are similar to s_0 and where act a was already experienced (i.e., such that $\exists$ r and $(s, a, r) \in M$ for the considered act a), is a normalized fuzzy set. Indeed when

$$h_S(s_0) = \max_{s:\ (s,a,r)\in M} S(s,s_0) < 1,$$

it means that act a was never experienced on a situation completely similar to s_0. In particular when $\{s, (s, a, r) \in M, S(s,s_0) > 0\} = \emptyset$, $U_{*s_0,M}(a) = 1$ using (9) and this is not satisfactory. It suggests to modify (9) into

$$U_{*s_0,M}(a) = \min(h_S(s_0), \min_{(s,r):\ (s,a,r)\in M} \max(u(r), 1 - S^*(s,s_0)) \qquad (12)$$

where $S^*(\cdot, s_0)$ is a renormalized version of $S(\cdot, s_0)$ (for instance, $S^*(s,s_0) = S(s,s_0) / h_S(s_0)$ with $h_S(s_0) \neq 0$). The rationale behind (12) is that our willingness to apply act a to s_0 is upper bounded by the existence of situations completely similar to s_0 where act a was experienced. Moreover $S(\cdot, s_0)$ is renormalized in order to obtain a meaningful degree of inclusion. Thus, (12) corresponds to the expression of the compound condition "there exists situations similar to s_0 where act a was used and the situations *which are the most similar to* s_0 are among the situations where act a led to good results". Note that the similarity is no longer estimated in an absolute manner, but in a relative way, hence the normalization. However with (12), the inequality (11) is not guaranteed, except if we change $S(\cdot, s_0)$ into $S^*(\cdot, s_0)$ in (10) also. Besides, it would be natural to have the optimistic evaluation all the greater as the act a was never applied to situations similar to s_0 in the past (indeed in this case, the lack of information should benefit to act a). This leads to modify (10) into

$$U^*_{s_0,M}(a) = \max(1 - h_S(s_0), \max_{(s,r):\ (s,a,r)\in M} \min(S(s,s_0), u(r))). \qquad (13)$$

Using (12) and (13), the inequality (11) is preserved. Moreover when $h_S(s_0) = 1$ (i.e., the set of situations similar to s_0 is normalized), (9) and (10) are retrieved. Note that we have $U^*_{s_0,M}(a) = 1$ and $U_{*s_0,M}(a) = 0$, in two different situations:

i) act a was experienced in situations completely similar to s_0 and both excellent and very bad results were obtained according to the considered cases;

ii) act a has never been applied to a situation somewhat similar to s_0.

Note that, this contrasts with $U_{s_0,M}$ defined by (4) which gives a non-zero result in the first case and is zero in the second case. However, $U_{(s_0,M)}$ cannot always distinguish between acts which always gave good results and acts which sometimes failed.

Interestingly enough, (9) can be viewed as the counterpart of qualitative utilities recently introduced in decision making under uncertainty (Dubois and Prade [8]), just as (4) may be seen as a counterpart of the classical expected utility.

We might also think of applying the approach proposed in Section 2 based on weak functional dependencies. This point of view leads to estimate the utility of act *a* for problem s_0 as the fuzzy set E_a of possible values t' defined as

$$E_a(t') = \max_{(s,a,r)\in M} \min(S(s,s_0), T(u(r), t')), \tag{14}$$

by application of a weak dependency rule stating that an act *a* applied to similar situations possibly yields results with similar values (which requires the knowledge of the relation T). When T is the identity (which expresses that the value of the result of an act remains unchanged when applied to situations which are somewhat similar), (14) can be simplified into

$$E_a(t') = \max_{s:\ (s,a,r)\in M \text{ and } u(r) = t'} S(s,s_0). \tag{15}$$

Thus, (9) and (10) can be also viewed as pessimistic and optimistic scalar summaries (in a sense which is to be clarified), of the fuzzy set of values whose membership function is given by (15). Indeed (9) and (10) are weighted median operations; see (Dubois and Prade [5]).

5 Concluding remarks

This is short note is clearly preliminary. A deeper study is necessary for understanding when the different case-based decision methods which have been suggested can be applied.

Besides, it is possible in practice to make $U_{*s_0,M}$ as defined in Section 4 less drastic by only requiring that for *most* cases (rather than all) where *a* is present, the obtained results are good when the situation is similar to s_0, thus allowing for a few exceptions. This is a topic for further research.

References

[1] Bensana E., Bel G. and Dubois D., (OPAL: A multi-knowledge-based system for industrial job-shop scheduling, Int. J. of Prod. Res., Vol. 26, 1988, pp. 795-819.

[2] Davies T.R. and Russell S.J., A logical approach to reasoning by analogy, Proc. of the 10th Inter. Joint Conf. on Artificial Intelligence (IJCAI'87), Milano, Italy, Aug. 23-28, 1987, pp. 264-270.

[3] Dubois D. Esteva F. Garcia P. Godo L. Lopez de Mantaras R. Prade H., Fuzzy Modeling of Case-Based Reasoning and Decision. In Case-Based Reasoning Research and Development (ICCBR-97), Edited by D. B. Leake R. Plaza, LNAI 1266, Springer Verlag, Berlin, 599-610, 1997.

[4] Dubois D., Grabisch M. and Prade H., Gradual rules and the approximation of control laws, in: Theoretical Aspects of Fuzzy Control, Edited H.T. Nguyen, M. Sugeno, R. Tong and R.R. Yager, Wiley, New York, 1995, pp. 147-181.

[5] Dubois D. and Prade H., Théorie des Possibilités — Applications à la Représentation des Connaissances en Informatique, (2nd edition) Masson, Paris, 1987.

[6] Dubois D. and Prade H., Gradual inference rules in approximate reasoning, Information Sciences, Vol. 61, 1992, pp. 103-122.

[7] Dubois D. and Prade H., Fuzzy rules in knowledge-based systems —Modelling gradedness, uncertainty and preference—, in: An Introduction to Fuzzy Logic Applications in Intelligent Systems, Edited by R.R. Yager and L.A. Zadeh, Kluwer Academic Publ., Dordrecht, 1992, pp. 45-68.

[8] Dubois D. and Prade H., Possibility theory as a basis for qualitative decision theory, Proc. of the 14th Inter. Joint Conf. on Artificial Intelligence (IJCAI'95), Montréal, Canada, Aug. 20-25, 1995, pp. 1924-1930.

[9] Dubois D. and Prade H., What are fuzzy rules and how to use them, Fuzzy Sets and Systems, Vol. 84, 1996, pp. 169-185.

[10] Dubois D., Prade H. and Ughetto L., Coherence of fuzzy knowledge bases, Proc. of the 5th IEEE Inter. Conf. on Fuzzy Systems (FUZZ-IEEE'96), New Orleans, LO, Sept. 8-11, 1996, IEEE Press, 1996, pp. 1858-1864.

[11] Gilboa I. and Schmeidler D., Case-based decision theory, The Quarterly J. of Economics, August 1995, pp. 607-639.

[12] Kolodner J., Case-Based Reasoning, Morgan Kaufmann, San Mateo, CA, 1993.

[13] Léa Sombé (Group), Reasoning by analogy, in: Reasoning Under Incomplete Information in Artificial Intelligence, Edited by Léa Sombé, Wiley, New York, 1990, pp. 418-424.

[14] Mamdani E.H., Application of fuzzy logic to approximate reasoning using linguistic systems, IEEE Trans. Comput., Vol. 26, 1977, pp. 1182-1191.

[15] Raju K.V.S.V.N. and Majumdar A.K., Fuzzy functional dependencies and lossless join decomposition of fuzzy relational database systems, ACM

Trans. on Database Systems, Vol. 13, No. 2, 1988, pp. 129-166.

[16] Sugeno M. and Nishida M., Fuzzy control of model car, Fuzzy Sets and Systems, Vol. 16, 1985, pp. 103-113.

[17] Zadeh L.A., Similarity relations and fuzzy orderings, Information Sciences, 1971, pp. 177-200.

[18] Zadeh L.A., A theory of approximate reasoning, in: Machine Intelligence, Vol. 9, Edited by J.E. Hayes, D. Michie and L.I. Mikulich, Elsevier, New York, 1979, pp. 149-194.

Appendix: Fuzzy Gradual Rules and Sugeno and Nishida's Interpolation Method

Sugeno and Nishida [16]'s method starts from rules with non-fuzzy conclusion parts of the form "if X is $A^{(i)}$ then Y = $b^{(i)}(x)$ (we do not deal here with compound conditions for simplicity), and computes the output y as the weighted sum

$$y = \frac{\sum_i A^{(i)}(x).b^{(i)}(x)}{\sum_i A^{(i)}(x)} \qquad \text{(I)}$$

which indeed looks like an interpolation. When $b^{(i)}(x)$ does not depend on x, this result can be obtained by applying Zadeh [18]'s approximate reasoning combination and projection approach viewing the rules as *gradual rules* expressing that "the closer X is to $a^{(i)}$, the closer Y is to $b^{(i)}$", i.e., modelling them as inequality constraints of the form $A^{(i)}(u) \leq B^{(i)}(v)$. Then the subset of V obtained by combining the results of the rules for the input $X = x_0$ is given by $\min_{i=1,n} A^{(i)}(x_0) \rightarrow B^{(i)}(v)$ where the implication defined by $a \rightarrow b = 1$ if $a \leq b$ and $a \rightarrow b = 0$ if $a > b$ encodes the above interpretation of the rules. When the $A^{(i)}$'s and $B^{(i)}$'s make suitable fuzzy partitions of U and V respectively (it guarantees that $\forall u, \sum_i A^{(i)}(u) = 1$), which is in particular the case with the usual partitions made of triangular membership functions as in Figure A.1, it can be shown that the fuzzy subset of V which is thus obtained is nothing but the singleton {y} computed by Sugeno's method (I). Let us explain the situation in more details.

Let us consider a collection of gradual rules of the form "the closer X is to a_i, the closer Y is to b_i" where (a_i,b_i), i = 1,n are pairs of *scalar* values and $a_1 < a_2 < a_3$ ... The first problem is to represent "close to a_i", by means of a fuzzy set A_i. It seems natural to assume that $A_i(a_{i-1}) = A_i(a_{i+1}) = 0$ since there are special rules adapted to the cases $X = a_{i-1}$, $X = a_{i+1}$. Moreover if $u \neq a_i$, then $A_i(u) < 1$ for $u \in (a_{i-1},a_{i+1})$, since information is only available for $u = a_i$. Hence A_i should be a fuzzy interval with support (a_{i-1},a_{i+1}) and core $\{a_i\}$. Besides, by symmetry, since the closer x is to a_{i-1}, the farther it is from a_i, A_{i-1} should decrease when A_i increases, and

$$A_i\left(\frac{a_i + a_{i+1}}{2}\right) = A_{i-1}\left(\frac{a_{i-1} + a_i}{2}\right) = 0.5.$$

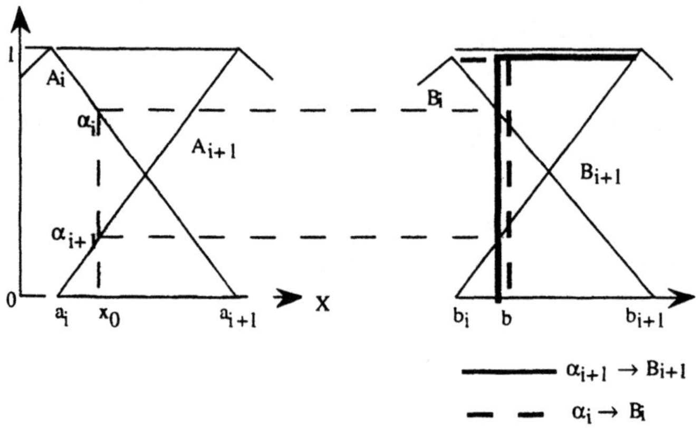

Fig. A.1. The core of $(\alpha_i \to B_i) \cap (\alpha_{i+1} \to B_{i+1})$ is the result of a linear interpolation

The simplest way of achieving this is to let

$$\forall\, u \in [a_{i-1},a_i],\ A_{i-1}(u) + A_i(u) = 1$$

an example of which are triangular-shaped fuzzy sets as in Figure A.1. Clearly the conclusion parts of the rules should involve fuzzy sets B_i whose meaning is "close to b_i", with similar convention. In other words, each rule is understood as "the more X is A_i, the more Y is B_i", i.e., here "the closer X is to a_i, the closer Y is to b_i". In that case the output associated with the precise input X = a, where $a_{i-1} < a < a_i$, is :

$$B = (\alpha_{i-1} \to B_{i-1}) \cap (\alpha_i \to B_i) = (B_{i-1})_{\alpha_{i-1}} \cap (B_i)_{\alpha_i}$$

where $\alpha \to B$ corresponds to the level cut B_α, and $\to$ is the implication defined above and $\alpha_{i-1} = A_{i-1}(a)$, $\alpha_i = A_i(a)$ with $\alpha_{i-1} + \alpha_i = 1$. Then it can be easily proved (without the assumption of a triangular shape) that there exists a unique value y = b such that B(b) = 1, which exactly corresponds to the result of a linear interpolation, i.e., we have $b = \alpha_{i-1} \cdot b_{i-1} + \alpha_i \cdot b_i$. See Figure A.1. It is a theoretical justification for Sugeno and Nishida [16]'s inference method where the conclusion parts of the rules are precise values b_i and where a linear interpolation is performed on the basis of the degrees of matching $\alpha_i = A_i(a)$. Hence reasoning with gradual rules does model interpolation, linear interpolation being retrieved as a particular case. The more complicated case of gradual rules with compound conditions, i.e., rules of the form "the more X_1 is A_1, ..., and the more X_n is A_n, the more Y is B" is studied in details in (Dubois, Grabisch and Prade [4]). In general, the interpolation result does not precisely scale up to several input variables, and, in case of coherence, an interpolating interval is retrieved instead of a point value.

Proof Theory of Many-Valued Logic and Linear Optimization

Reiner Hähnle

Institute for Logic, Complexitiy and Deduction Systems
Department of Computer Science
University of Karlsruhe, D-76128 Karlsruhe
reiner@ira.uka.de
http://i12www.ira.uka.de/~reiner

Abstract. A simple reduction of two-valued logic to certain linear integer programs is well-known for a long time. This relationship can be extended to any finite-valued and to a large class of infinite-valued logics, for instance to Łukasiewicz and Gödel logics. The resulting reduction is deterministic and has linear cost which makes it feasible to implement satisfiability checking in such logics via linear optimization methods. The reduction is based on semantic tableau methods that are enriched by certain arithmetic constraints. This technique is principally applicable to non-arithmetic constraints as well which opens a general approach to non-classical deduction.

1 Introduction

The intention of this paper is not mainly to prove new results, rather, known results in the proof theory[1] of many-valued logic are connected with linear optimization. This connection can be seen as part of an ongoing research programme that aims to establish links between many-valued logic and further disciplines such as functional analysis [25,21], algebra [6,5], coding theory [23], geometry [26], and circuit design [29,14,13] (see Fig. 1).

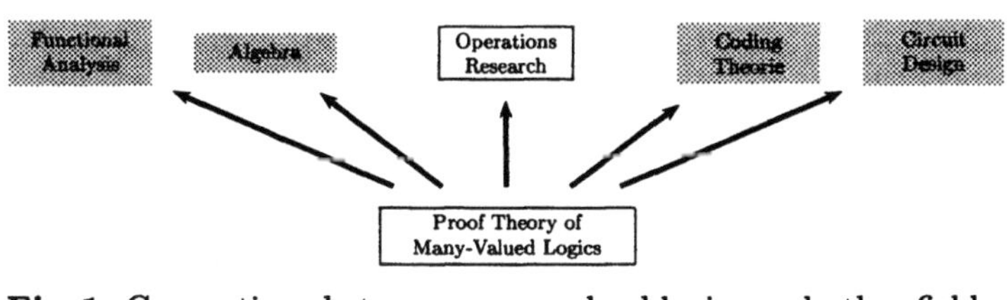

Fig. 1. Connections between many-valued logics and other fields

---

* This contribution is a slightly modified and abridged version of [13]. Included with permission of Springer-Verlag, Heidelberg.

[1] In this article I always mean proof theory in the tradition of Gentzen, not of Frege or Hilbert.

These connections provide the possibility for fruitful interaction between the mentioned disciplines, however, they are not widely known among researchers in either area. Once familiar with the others' terminology, I believe that the respective communities can greatly benefit from each other.

One reason for the lack of interaction is that while some relationships are well-known and straightforward in the two-valued case, the connection becomes a lot deeper and interesting in the many-valued case. Another is the familiar phenomenon of different communities talking different languages.

Hence, one purpose of this paper is to present some recently discovered results, in this case between many-valued logic and optimization [10], in a self-contained and easily accessible style. The second goal is to point out explicitly several spots, where proof theory and linear optimization could benefit from each other.

2 The Basics

All I want to tell in this paper can be told at the propositional level. Thus I deal only with propositional many-valued logics.

2.1 Many-Valued Logic: Syntax

Definition 1. Let Σ be a **propositional signature**, that is, a denumerable set of propositional variables $\{p_0, p_1, \dots\}$. Σ is also called the set of **atomic formulas** (or **atoms** for short).

Definition 2. A **propositional language** is a pair $\mathbf{L} = \langle \Theta, \alpha \rangle$, where Θ is a finite or denumerable set of **logical connectives** and $\alpha : \Theta \to \mathbb{N}$ defines the arity of each connective. Connectives with arity 0 are called **logical constants**. The set L_Σ of **L-formulas** over Σ is inductively defined as follows:

1. $\Sigma \subseteq L_\Sigma$.
2. If $\theta \in \Theta$ and $\alpha(\theta) = 0$ then $\theta \in L_\Sigma$.
3. If $\phi_1, \dots, \phi_m \in L_\Sigma$, $\theta \in \Theta$ and $\alpha(\theta) = m$ then $\theta(\phi_1, \dots, \phi_m) \in L_\Sigma$.

Remark 1. A propositional language $\langle \Theta, \alpha \rangle$ with a finite set of connectives $\Theta = \{\theta_1, \dots, \theta_r\}$ is denoted $\langle \theta_1/\alpha(\theta_1), \dots, \theta_r/\alpha(\theta_r) \rangle$. Moreover, the usual conventions on bracketing for well-known connective symbols (which are assumed to have the usual precedence order) are being made. For binary connectives, infix notation is used.

Example 1. Following Mundici [24], the language of **Łukasiewicz** logic is given by $\mathbf{L}_{\text{Luk}} = \langle \neg/1, \oplus/2, \odot/2 \rangle$. Examples of $\mathbf{L}_{\text{Luk}}$-formulas are: $(p \odot q) \oplus ((p \oplus q) \odot r)$, $(\neg p \odot \neg q) \oplus ((\neg p \oplus \neg q) \odot \neg r)$.

2.2 Many-Valued Logic: Semantics

Definition 3. The **set of truth values** N is either the unit interval on the rational numbers, denoted with $[0, 1]$, or it is a finite set of rational numbers of the form $\{0, \frac{1}{n-1}, \ldots, \frac{n-2}{n-1}, 1\}$, where $2 \leq n \in \mathbb{N}$. In either case $|N|$ denotes the cardinality of N, in particular, $|[0, 1]| = \aleph_0$.

It is stressed that fractional numbers are used to represent truth values merely because they are convenient to define several well-known logics. If nothing else is said, no use is made of their special properties, in particular, truth values are assumed to be unordered if not stated otherwise. Let $\mathcal{P}^+(N)$ denote the non-empty subsets of a truth value set N.

Definition 4. Let ϕ be a formula and $S \in \mathcal{P}^+(N)$. Then the expression $S\,\phi$ is called a **signed formula**. If p is an atomic formula, then $S\,p$ is a **signed literal**. A signed formula that is not a literal is a **complex signed formula**.

Informally, a signed formula states that it takes on truth values contained in its sign, see Def. 9 below.

Definition 5. If $\mathbf{L} = \langle \Theta, \alpha \rangle$ is a propositional language then call a pair $\mathbf{A} = \langle N, A \rangle$, where N is a set of truth values and A assigns to each $\theta \in \Theta$ a function[2] $A(\theta) : N^{\alpha(\theta)} \to N$ a **(propositional) matrix** for $\mathbf{L}$. The **range** $\mathrm{rg}(\theta)$ of a connective θ is defined as the range of the function $A(\theta)$:

$$\mathrm{rg}(\theta) = \{A(\theta)(i_1, \ldots, i_{\alpha(\theta)}) \mid i_1, \ldots, i_{\alpha(\theta)} \in N\}\ .$$

Definition 6. A pair $\mathcal{L} = \langle \mathbf{L}, \mathbf{A} \rangle$ consisting of a propositional language and a matrix for it is called **many-valued** or **$|N|$-valued propositional logic**.

If no confusion can arise I use the same symbol for θ and $A(\theta)$. Moreover, with each formula ϕ of a many-valued logic containing variables $\{p_1, \ldots, p_k\}$ a function $f_\phi : N^k \to N$ is associated in a natural way: f_{p_i} is the projection to the i-th component and $f_{\theta(\phi_1, \ldots, \phi_{\alpha(\theta)})} = A(\theta)(f_{\phi_1}, \ldots, f_{\phi_{\alpha(\theta)}})$ otherwise (cf. Definition 7 below). Again, normally the same symbol is used for ϕ and f_ϕ.

Sometimes a logic is equipped with a non-empty subset D of the set of truth values called the **designated truth values** which play the rôle of the truth values which are considered to affirm satisfability.

Example 2. Let N be arbitrary and $n = |N|$. Then define the family of n-valued Łukasiewicz logics to be the propositional logics with language $\mathbf{L}_{\mathbf{Luk}}$, designated truth values $D = \{1\}$, and the matrix given by:

$$\neg i = 1 - i \tag{1}$$

$$i \oplus j = \min\{1, i + j\} \tag{2}$$

$$i \odot j = \max\{1, i + j - 1\} \tag{3}$$

[2] If $\alpha(\theta) = 0$ then the usual convention $A(\theta) \in N$ is made.

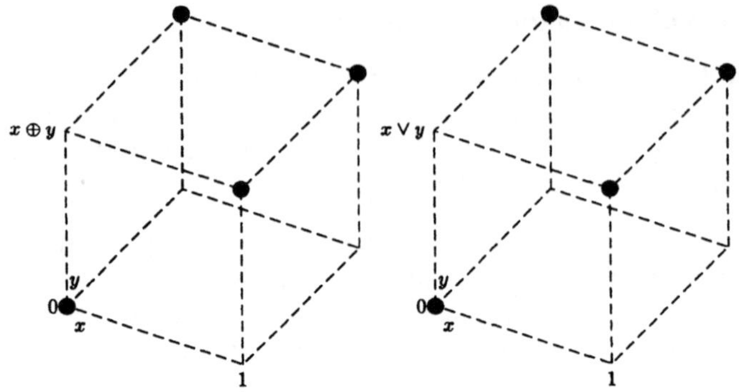

Fig. 2. Functions $x \oplus y$ and $x \vee y$ on $N = \{0, 1\}$

The family of n-valued Kleene logics relative to the language $\mathbf{L}_{\mathrm{Kle}}$ is defined by

$$\neg i = 1 - i \tag{4}$$

$$i \vee j = \max\{i, j\} \tag{5}$$

$$i \wedge j = \min\{i, j\} \tag{6}$$

The family of n-valued Gödel logics relative to the language $\mathbf{L}_{\mathrm{G}}$ is defined by

$$\neg_{\mathrm{G}} i = \begin{cases} 1 \text{ if } i = 0 \\ 0 \text{ otherwise} \end{cases} \tag{7}$$

$$i \rightarrow_{\mathrm{G}} j = \begin{cases} 1 \text{ if } i \leq j \\ j \text{ otherwise} \end{cases} \tag{8}$$

In each case $\min, \max, +, -, \leq$ are interpreted wrt the natural order on N. In Figs. 2, 3, and 5, respectively, the functions of Łukasiewicz sum and Kleene disjunction in two-valued, three-valued, and infinite-valued logic, are shown. In the two-valued case (Fig. 2) both functions are identical and reduce to classical disjunction. In the three-valued case (Fig. 3) they differ only in the highlighted function value while only from the infinite-valued connectives (Fig. 5) their completely different nature is obvious. Figure 7 shows the matrix of infinite-valued Gödel logic.

Definition 7. Let $\mathcal{L}$ be a propositional logic; a **(propositional) (Σ-)interpretation** is a function $\mathbf{I} : \Sigma \rightarrow N$. $\mathbf{I}$ is extended to $\phi \in L_\Sigma$ as usual:

1. If ϕ is a logical constant then $\mathbf{I}(\phi) = A(\phi)$.
2. If $\phi = \theta(\phi_1, \ldots, \phi_r)$, then $\mathbf{I}(\theta(\phi_1, \ldots, \phi_r)) = A(\theta)(\mathbf{I}(\phi_1), \ldots, \mathbf{I}(\phi_r))$.

Definition 8. Let $S \subseteq N$. A formula ϕ is said to be S-**satisfiable** iff there is an interpretation $\mathbf{I}$ such that $\mathbf{I}(\phi) \in S$. When this is the case $\mathbf{I}$ is a S-**model** of ϕ. ϕ is a S-**tautology**, in symbols $\models \phi$, iff every interpretation S-satisfies ϕ.

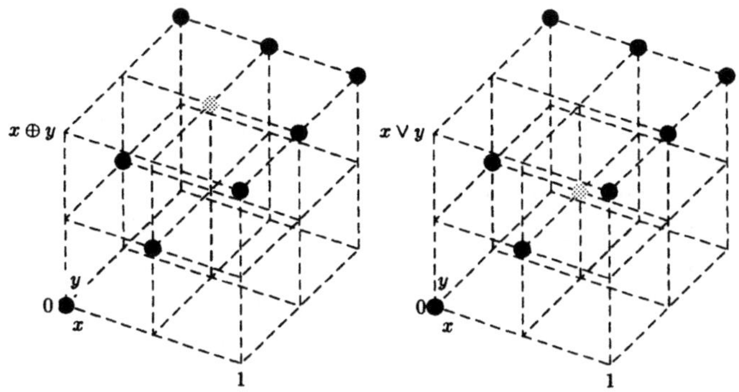

Fig. 3. Functions $x \oplus y$ and $x \vee y$ on $N = \{0, \frac{1}{2}, 1\}$

Definition 9. A signed formula $S\ \phi$ is **satisfiable** iff $\mathbf{I}(\phi) \in S$ for some $\mathbf{I}$.

Definition 10. Let $S \subseteq N$. A formula ψ is a **logical** S**-consequence** of ϕ, in symbols $\phi \models \psi$ iff every S-model of ϕ is an S-model of ψ. ϕ and ψ are **logically** S**-equivalent** iff each is a logical S-consequence of the other.

If a logic is equipped with designated truth values D, and if D is obvious from the context, one simply says **satisfiable** instead of D-satisfiable, **model** instead of D-model etc. If $N = \{0, 1\}$ and $D = \{1\}$ then, of course, all notions collapse to the standard ones of classical logic.

2.3 Representation of Finite-Valued Connectives

In the present subsection I state and prove a fundamental result regarding the representation of finite-valued connectives or, equivalently, of functions over finite domains. The result is straightforward, but nevertheless it constitutes the theoretical basis of tableaux and sequent calculi for finite-valued propositional logics.

As is the case for other non-classical logics, proof calculi for deduction in MVL can be roughly divided into two classes:

Internal calculi: the objects constructed during a proof are expressed in the same language as the goal to be proven; a typical example are Hilbert type calculi.

External calculi: formal proofs are over an *extended* language that may involve elements from the semantics such as designators for truth values, worlds or even non-logical expressions such as constraints; a typical example are signed semantic tableaux.

Purists among proof theorists often only accept calculi of the first kind and regard the second option as "cheating". On the other hand, if a uniform and computationally efficient treatment of deduction is desired, there seems to be no alternative to external calculi.

A somewhat extreme position of gaining a classical logic approach to deduction in non-classical logic would be to formulate the "external" elements in the second approach as a meta theory in classical logic. For a wide range of logics this is even possible within first-order logic. The "meta theory" of finite-valued logic in particular can always be captured without having to move to a higher-order stage.[3] On the other hand, classical *propositional* logic is too weak for an adequate representation of most many-valued semantics.

It turns out that in the case of infinite-valued logic even signed formulas are not enough which leads to incorporating linear arithmetic constraints and, ultimately, to a reduction of infinite-valued deduction to mixed integer programming. Later we will see that mixed integer programming is in a certain sense an adequate formalism to handle infinite-valued logic. Let us start with the finite-valued case.

Theorem 1. *Let N be finite, $n = |N|$, $\mathbf{S} \subseteq \mathcal{P}^+(N)$ a family of truth values satisfying*

For all $i \in N$ there are $S_1, \ldots, S_k \in \mathbf{S}$ such that $\bigcap_{j=1}^k S_j = \{i\}$. (9)

If $\phi = S\,\theta(\phi_1, \ldots, \phi_m)$ ($m \geq 1$, $S \in \mathbf{S}$) is a signed formula from an n-valued logic $\mathcal{L} = \langle \mathbf{L}, A\rangle$ such that $S \cap rg(\theta) \neq \emptyset$, then there are numbers $M_1, M_2 \leq n^m$, index sets $I_1, \ldots, I_{M_1}, J_1, \ldots, J_{M_2} \subseteq \{1, \ldots, m\}$, and signs $S_{rs}, S_{kl} \in \mathbf{S}$ with $1 \leq r \leq M_1$, $1 \leq k \leq M_2$ and $s \in I_r$, $l \in J_k$ such that

$$\phi \text{ is satisfiable iff } \bigvee_{r=1}^{M_1} \bigwedge_{s \in I_r} (S_{rs}\,\phi_s \text{ is satisfiable})$$
$$\text{iff } \bigwedge_{k=1}^{M_2} \bigvee_{l \in J_k} (S_{kl}\,\phi_l \text{ is satisfiable}),$$

*where $\bigvee$ and $\bigwedge$ denote classical meta disjunction and conjunction, respectively, and have their usual meaning. Call the first expression a **sets-as-signs DNF representation** of ϕ, the second a **sets-as-signs CNF representation** of ϕ.*

This theorem is proved in many places for the case $S \in \mathbf{S} = \{\{i\} \,|\, i \in N\}$, for instance, in [28,34,4,36,1]. The general case was first handled in [8], see also [9].

Observe that for guaranteeing the existence of DNF/CNF representations "enough" signs must be available: $\mathbf{S}$ has to satisfy (9). A linear number of signs is sufficient as $\mathbf{S} = \{\{i\} \,|\, i \in N\}$ clearly satisfies (9), but the choice of $\mathbf{S}$ has a considerable impact on the **size** (i.e. the numbers M_1 and M_2) of the resulting representations. This topic is further discussed in [9].

Example 3. Below are DNF, resp., CNF representations of a signed formula in three-valued Łukasiewicz logic. The representations are denoted like rules

[3] This is not necessarily true for infinite-valued logic, see [30].

to enhance readability. CNF representations use double horizontal bars to distinguish them from DNF representations.

$$\begin{array}{c|c} \multicolumn{2}{c}{\{0,\frac{1}{2}\}\,\phi \oplus \psi} \\ \hline \{0,\frac{1}{2}\}\,\phi & \{0\}\,\phi \\ \{0\}\,\psi & \{0,\frac{1}{2}\}\,\psi \end{array} \qquad \begin{array}{c|c|c} \multicolumn{3}{c}{\{0,\frac{1}{2}\}\,\phi \oplus \psi} \\ \hline\hline \{0,\frac{1}{2}\}\,\phi & \{0\}\,\phi & \\ & \{0\}\,\psi & \{0,\frac{1}{2}\}\,\psi \end{array} \tag{10}$$

2.4 Many-Valued Deduction Based on Clause Form Representations

The significance of Theorem 1 is that it directly gives rise to rules in generic sequent and tableau calculi for finite-valued logics. In fact DNF representations are identified with those rules:

Definition 11. If $\bigvee_{r=1}^{M} \bigwedge_{s \in I_r} S_{rs} \phi_s$ is a sets-as-signs DNF representation of $\phi = S\,\theta(\phi_1, \dots, \phi_m)$ $(m \geq 1)$, then a **many-valued sets-as-signs tableau rule** for ϕ is defined as

$$\begin{array}{c|c|c} \multicolumn{3}{c}{S\,\theta(\phi_1, \dots, \phi_m)} \\ \hline C_1 & \cdots & C_M \end{array} ,$$

where $C_r = \{S_{rs}\,\phi_s \mid s \in I_r\}$. The C_r are called **extensions** of the rule.

The notion of a tableau for a signed formula $S\,\phi$ is defined exactly as in the classical case [33,7], but with respect to many-valued sets-as-signs rules.

Definition 12. One defines a **many-valued sets-as-signs tableau** for a finite set of signed formulas Φ as a directed tree labeled with signed formulas and constructed as follows:

1. A linear tree whose labels are exactly the formulas in Φ is a many-valued sets-as-signs tableau for Φ.
2. If $\mathbf{T}$ is a many-valued sets-as-signs tableau for Φ, ϕ a complex signed formula occurring on a branch B of $\mathbf{T}$, and $C_1, \dots, C_M$ the extensions of a sets-as-signs tableau rule for ϕ, then a many-valued sets-as-signs tableau for Φ is obtained from $\mathbf{T}$ by extending B with $|M|$ many new linear branches, where the labels of the r-th branch are exactly the members of C_r.
3. No other tree is a many-valued sets-as-signs tableau for Φ.

Some care must be spent on the definition of closure:

Definition 13. Let $\mathbf{T}$ be a many-valued sets-as-signs tableau and B one of its branches. B is **closed** iff one of the following conditions holds:

1. There are signed formulas $S_1\,\phi, \dots, S_r\,\phi$ on B such that $\bigcap_{i=1}^{r} S_i = \emptyset$. In this case one says that (the set of signed formulas on) B is **inconsistent**.[4]

[4] Just as in classical logic it is sufficient to restrict the definition to the case when ϕ is atomic. Accordingly one says that B is **atomically inconsistent**.

2. There is a signed formula $S\,\theta(\phi_1, \ldots, \phi_m)$ $(m \geq 0)$ on B such that $S \cap \mathrm{rg}(\theta) = \emptyset$.

T is closed iff each of its branches is closed. A branch that is not closed is called **open**.

Theorem 2 ([8]). *Let ϕ be a formula in a finite-valued logic and $S \in \mathcal{P}^+(N)$. Then ϕ is S-valid iff there exists a finite, closed many-valued sets-as-signs tableau for $(N\backslash S)\,\phi$.*

As in classical logic it is sufficient to apply each rule at most once to each complex formula on a branch. Therefore, many-valued sets-as-signs tableaux can assumed to be finite.

We saw that recursive application of DNF representations to all complex subformulas of a signed formula yields a tableau procedure. The usual semantics of a tableau is that the disjunction over the conjunction of the formulas in its branches is satisfiable, thus corresponding to a classical DNF over the signed formulas occurring on its branches. Hence, a DNF over signed literals can be computed by identifying its (conjunctive) clauses with the signed literals occurring on an open branch of a fully expanded tableau.

Just in the same way a CNF over signed literals can be computed for a given signed formula using CNF representations instead of DNF representations. Once a CNF over signed literals has been obtained, generalized versions of resolution [1,11], of the Davis-Putnam-Loveland procedure [12], etc. can be employed for a deductive treatment of many-valued logic.

One problem of DNF and CNF representations is that their size (the numbers M_1 and M_2 in Theorem 1) depends on the cardinality of the truth value set of the underlying logic. If a logic has more than a few truth values, then the resulting tableaux and CNFs become intolerably large in the worst case. The bad news is that the worst case is in fact achieved for some well-known and important connectives, for example, Łukasiewicz sum (2) and product (3).

In classical logic the growth at least of CNFs can be kept within polynomial bounds with so-called ***structure preserving CNF transformations*** [35,27]. The basic idea is to use a polynomial size transformation of a complex formula ϕ into a satisfiability equivalent formula $\bigwedge_i \phi_i$ such that each ϕ_i is of constantly bounded depth. As a consequence, the CNF of $\bigwedge_i \phi_i$ and, therefore, of ϕ, has polynomial size. Such a transformation can be easily described. In the following, $p\{q/r\}$ stands for simultaneous replacement of each occurrence of r in p with q.

For each proper complex subformula ψ of ϕ:
replace ϕ with $\phi\{p_\psi/\psi\} \wedge (p_\psi \leftrightarrow \psi)$, where p_ψ is a new atom. (11)

The result is a formula of the form $p_\phi \wedge \bigwedge_\psi (p_\psi \leftrightarrow \psi)$. Thus each complex subformula ψ is replaced by its ***abbreviation*** or ***definition*** p_ψ. Each equivalence of the form $p_\psi \leftrightarrow \psi$ says that p_ψ is equivalent to the subformula it abbreviates. The CNF of each equivalence is of constant length: all proper complex subformulas in ψ were themselves abbreviated, hence all the ψ contain exactly one connective. Finally, as the number of complex subformulas is linear (in the size of ϕ), the CNF of $p_\phi \wedge \bigwedge_\psi (p_\psi \leftrightarrow \psi)$ is polynomial in the size of ϕ. Exactly the same technique can be used in the many-valued case (let ϕ be a signed formula):

$$\begin{array}{l}\text{For each unsigned proper complex subformula } \psi \text{ of } \phi\text{:}\\ \text{replace } \phi \text{ with } \phi\{p_\psi/\psi\} \wedge \{1\}(p_\psi \Leftrightarrow \psi)\text{, where } p_\psi \text{ is a new atom.}\end{array} \tag{12}$$

Here, $\Leftrightarrow$ is a connective playing a similar rôle as classical equivalence and which is definable in Łukasiewicz logic (and, similarly, in many other logics) as $p \Leftrightarrow q = (\neg p \oplus q) \wedge (p \oplus \neg q)$ or explicitly given as:

$$i \Leftrightarrow j = \min\{1, 1 - i + j, 1 + i - j\} \tag{13}$$

3 Satisfiability in Many-Valued Logic as Mixed Integer Programming

3.1 Limits of Clause Form Representations

Even if one uses a polynomial size CNF transformation Theorem 1 still cannot be used as a basis for deduction in the infinite-valued case. Although it is possible to generalize it to an infinite number of truth values, the resulting representations become infinite as well, thus leading to infinitely branching tableau, resp., translation rules already for formulas with only one connective.

The reason for these difficulties is that so far classical propositional logic plus signs as a meta language was used to characterize many-valued connectives. This is very desirable from a deductive point of view, because one can make use of all the deductive machinery available in classical logic, but the approach is limited: classical propositional logic is simply to poor to yield straightforward finite characterizations of infinite-valued logics (later we will see better why this is so).

The extension of classical logic I have in mind to solve the current problems is best motivated with an example. Let us have a look at Łukasiewicz sum with three truth values depicted as the solid spheres in the left part of Fig. 3 on page 5. A signed formula of the form $S\,\phi \oplus \psi$ defines a subset of this function (seen as a relation). A CNF/DNF representation of the signed formula uses intersections/unions of rectangular areas to build the required subset, schematically displayed in the left part of Fig. 4.

The DNF/CNF representation obviously is not independent of the cardinality of the truth value set. In particular, when using this technique for infinite-valued functions an infinite number of rectangles is required in the worst case.

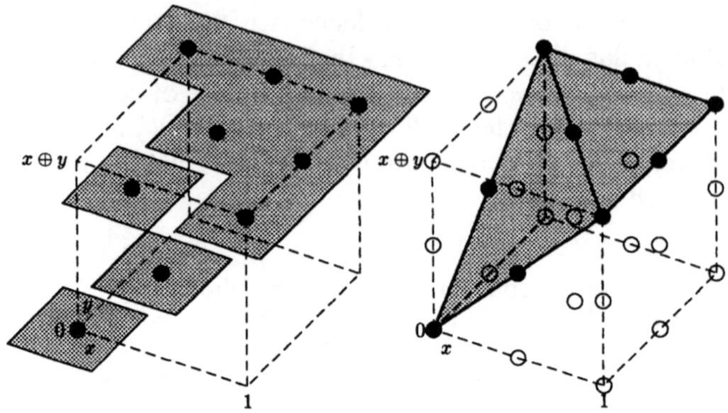

Fig. 4. Two ways of representing $x \oplus y$ over $\{0, \frac{1}{2}, 1\}$

Looking at $\oplus$ over $N = [0, 1]$ (left part of Fig. 5), on the other hand, suggests a quite different way of representation which is much less dependent on the number of truth values: to represent $\oplus$ over, say, $N' = \{0, \frac{1}{2}, 1\}$ simply intersect $\oplus$ over $N = [0, 1]$ with $(N')^3$. This is illustrated in the right part of Fig. 4, where the spheres represent $(N')^3$ of which the solid ones belong to $\oplus$. The question now is how $\oplus$ or, more generally, how an arbitrary many-valued function can be represented.

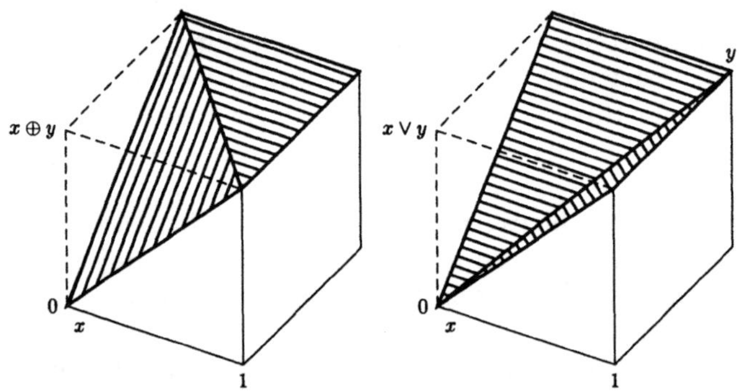

Fig. 5. Functions $x \oplus y$ and $x \vee y$ on $N = [0, 1]$

3.2 McNaughton's Theorem

It turns out that for Łukasiewicz logic there is a classical solution to the representation problem which gives a clue on how to proceed for other logics as well.

Definition 14. A function $f : [0,1]^k \to [0,1]$ is a **McNaughton function** if

1. f is continuous wrt the natural topology of $[0,1]^k$ and
2. it is **piecewise linear with integral coefficients** i.e. there is a finite number of linear polynomials $p_i(x_1, \dots, x_k)$ with integral coefficients such that for each $\boldsymbol{x} \in [0,1]^k$ there is an i with $p_i(\boldsymbol{x}) = f(\boldsymbol{x})$.

Theorem 3 ([20]).

1. *If $\phi \in \mathbf{L}_{Luk}$ then f_ϕ is a McNaughton function.*
2. *Let $f : [0,1]^k \to [0,1]$ be a McNaughton function. Then there is a formula $\phi \in \mathbf{L}_{Luk}$ such that $f = f_\phi$.*

The second part of the theorem is the hard one. It gives a deep characterization of infinite-valued Łukasiewicz logic. The first part of the theorem is easy to prove, for instance, by noting that $f_{\neg x}$, $f_{x \oplus y}$, and $f_{x \odot y}$ are McNaughton functions by definition (1)–(3). A straightforward induction yields the result. The number of polynomials required for f in the second part of the theorem is in general exponential in the number of connectives of ϕ.

3.3 Mixed Integer Programming

In this subsection some bare facts and definitions about Mixed Integer Programming (MIP) are given. As a background reading, for example, [31,19] is recommended.

It is a well known fact (see, for example, [16,19]) that propositional classical CNF formulas correspond to certain 0-1 integer programs. More precisely, given a set Φ of classical clauses over the signature Σ one transforms each clause

$$p_1 \vee \cdots \vee p_k \vee \neg p_{k+1} \vee \cdots \vee \neg p_{k+m} \tag{14}$$

into a linear inequation

$$\sum_{i=1}^{k} p_i - \sum_{j=k+1}^{m} p_j \geq 1 - m \tag{15}$$

Here, the variables from Σ are interpreted as *polynomial variables* ranging over $\{0,1\}$. It is easy to see that the resulting set of inequations is solvable iff Φ is satisfiable.

With the expression **linear inequation** I mean in the following always a term of the form $a_1p_1 + \cdots + a_mp_m \geq c$, where $a_1p_1 + \cdots + a_mp_m$ is a linear polynomial over $\{p_1, \dots, p_m\}$ with integral coefficients, where the variables p_i either run over $\{0,1\}$ or over N (N is as in Definition 3), and c is an integer. $a_1p_1 + \cdots + a_mp_m$ is called **linear term**.

Definition 15. Let $\mathbf{J}$ be a finite set of linear inequations and K a linear term. Let Σ be the set of variables occurring in $\mathbf{J}$ and K. Assume N is finite. Then $\langle \mathbf{J}, K \rangle$ is a **(bounded) integer program** (IP) with **cost function** K.[5] If N is infinite, then one has a **(bounded) 0-1 mixed integer program** (MIP). When all variables in Σ run over infinite N, the result is a **(bounded) linear program** (LP).

A variable assignment $\sigma : \Sigma \to \{0, 1\} \cup N$ that respects the type of each variable and such that all inequations in $\mathbf{J}\sigma$ are satisfied is called a **feasible solution** of $\langle \mathbf{J}, K \rangle$. A variable assignment to σ such that the value of K is minimal among all feasible solutions is called an **optimal solution.** $\langle \mathbf{J}, K \rangle$ is **feasible** iff there are feasible solutions.

In the following, when I speak of (M)IP/LPs, only the set of inequations $\mathbf{J}$ is meant. If there is a cost function as well, it will be explicitly mentioned.

Definition 16. Let $M \subseteq [0, 1]^k$. M is **MIP-representable** if there is an MIP $\mathbf{J}$ with variables $\Sigma' = \{x_1, \dots, x_k\}$ over $[0, 1]$ and variables Σ'' over $\{0, 1\}$ such that

$$M = \{\boldsymbol{x} \mid \boldsymbol{x} \text{ is feasible solution of } \mathbf{J}\sigma \text{ for some } \sigma : \Sigma'' \to \{0, 1\}\} .$$

A many-valued logic is **MIP-representable** iff for all its connectives θ the function $A(\theta)$ (viewed as a $\alpha(\theta) + 1$-ary relation) is MIP-representable. The variable in a (relational) MIP-representation of a function that holds the function value is called **output variable**, the variables that hold the function arguments are called **argument variables**.

All finite-valued logics are obviously MIP-representable.

Proposition 1 (see [31]). *Each of the problems to check whether a 0-1 MIP (resp., an IP) has feasible solutions and to find an optimal/feasible solution is NP-complete. The problem to check whether an LP has feasible solutions and to find an optimal/feasible solution is in P.*

3.4 McNaughton Functions and MIP-Representations

McNaughton's Theorem can be generalized in a way most important from the deductive point of view:

Theorem 4 (Generic MIP version of McNaugthon's Theorem).

1. *If $\phi(\mathbf{p})$ is a formula of an MIP-representable logic then there is an MIP $\mathbf{J}_\phi$ with argument variables $\mathbf{p}$ and output variable y whose feasible solutions restricted to $(\mathbf{p}, y)$ are the function $f_\phi(\mathbf{p})$. Moreover, the size of $\mathbf{J}_\phi$ is linear in the size of ϕ.*

---

[5] The adjective *integer* is justified, because the elements of N can w.l.o.g. assumed to be of the form $\{0, 1, \dots, n-1\}$.

2. *Let* **J** *be an MIP over variables* Σ. *Then there is a* Σ*-formula* $\phi_{\mathbf{J}} \in \mathbf{L}_{Luk}$ *which is satisfiable iff* **J** *is feasible.*

The first part of the theorem now is non-trivial to prove. In return, it provides a direct way to perform deduction in MIP-representable infinite-valued logics. The second part of the theorem simply says that there is a "backend" to McNaughton's result that allows to go from MIP to McNaughton functions. We will see that MIPs in fact are captured quite naturally by McNaughton functions.

Before plunging into the proof of Theorem 4, let us apply it first to Łukasiewicz logic.

Proposition 2. *Infinite-valued Łukasiewicz logic is MIP-representable.*

Proof. An MIP-representation of $\oplus$ is given by the following MIP, where x and y are argument variables, i is output variable and z is an additional 0-1-variable.

$$\begin{array}{llcr} (i) & x + y + z - i & \geq & 0 \\ (ii) & -x - y + z + i & \geq & 0 \\ (iii) & x + y - z & \geq & 0 \\ (iv) & -x - y + z & \geq & -1 \\ (v) & \quad\quad\; - z + i & \geq & 0 \end{array} \tag{16}$$

To see this, first set $z = 0$. Then the polynomial $p_1(x, y) = i = x + y$ is defined by (i,ii), inequations (iii,v) are trivially satisfied, and (iv) i.e. $x+y \leq 1$ determines the area in which p_1 equals $\oplus$. This is the part of the function depicted on the left in Fig. 5 with vertical hatches.

Similarly, if $z = 1$ the polynomial $p_2(x, y) = i = 1$ is given by (v), inequations (i,ii,iv) are trivially satisfied, and (iii) i.e. $x + y \geq 1$ determines the area in which p_2 equals $\oplus$. This is the part of the function depicted on the left in Fig. 5 with horizontal hatches. An MIP-representation of $\neg$ is straightforward:

$$\begin{array}{rcr} -x - i & \geq & -1 \\ x + i & \geq & 1 \end{array}$$

Łukasiewicz product $\odot$ is handled by duality: $x \odot y = \neg(\neg x \oplus \neg y)$. □

Theorem 4 applied to Łukasiewicz logic guarantees the existence of MIP-representations of arbitrary formulas ϕ. They can be found with the following method which at the same time is a

Proof of Theorem 4.1. Assume we have an MIP-representation of $A(\theta)$ with output variable y_ψ and argument variables $x_{\phi_1}, \ldots, x_{\phi_k}$ for each complex subformula $\psi = \theta(\phi_1, \ldots, \phi_k)$ of ϕ (as provided by Proposition 2 in the case of Łukasiewicz logic).

Now connect the MIPs for each proper complex subformula ψ of ϕ by adding equations of the form $x_\psi = y_\psi$; furthermore, add equations $x_p = p$ for each propositional variable p of ϕ and obtain an MIP-representation of f_ϕ with output variable y_ϕ and argument variables p. The size of each MIP is constant and depends only on the connective θ and the number of all MIPs is proportional to the number of complex subformulas in ϕ, hence it is linear in the size of ϕ. □

Here, the same technique as in structure preserving CNF transformations is used: by explicitly naming output variables they can be connected to many occurrences of corresponding argument variables.

Given its MIP-representation it is easy to check, say, $[c, d]$-satisfiability of a many-valued formula ϕ for given $0 \leq c \leq d \leq 1$: simply add the constraint $c \leq y_\phi \leq d$, where y_ϕ is the output variable of ϕ and test the resulting MIP for feasibility. This is a notable improvement on the procedure given in [10], where cost functions were required.

From Theorem 4.1 and Proposition 1 immediately follows (answering an open question raised in [10, p. 256]):

Corollary 1. *The $[c, d]$-satisfability problem of any MIP-representable logic for $0 \leq c \leq d \leq 1$ is in NP.*

A straightforward and concise implementation of a satisfiability checker for infinite-valued Łukasiewicz logic based on these ideas is displayed in Fig. 6. It is written in Eclipse Prolog and can solve textbook examples within fractions of a second. To use it, issue a query such as

```
:- sat(I, plus(neg(atom(P)),atom(P))), I $< 1.
```

The answer is "no" indicating that there is no interpretation such that $\neg p \oplus p$ evaluates to a truth value smaller than 1, in other words, it is a $\{1\}$-tautology.

The MIP-representation of $\oplus$ in (16) seemed to drop from the sky. How can MIP-representations be computed systematically?

One possibility, is to employ *disjunctive programming* [2,19] techniques as developed in Operations Research (OR). These give means to combine arbitrary polyhedra disjunctively from their MIP-representations.

Theorem 5 ([19]). *Let $M^1, \dots, M^t$ be polyhedra in $[0,1]^k$ with MIP-representations $\mathbf{A}^i\boldsymbol{x}^i + \mathbf{B}^i\boldsymbol{y}^i \geq \mathbf{h}^i$, where in each MIP $\boldsymbol{x}^i$ are $[0,1]$-variables and $\boldsymbol{y}^i$ are $\{0,1\}$-variables. Then the following MIP (where the m_i are new $\{0,1\}$-variables) is feasible iff $\boldsymbol{x} \in (M^1 \cup \dots \cup M^t)$:*

$$
\begin{array}{lllr}
\mathbf{A}^i\boldsymbol{x}^i & + \mathbf{B}^i\boldsymbol{y}^i - & \mathbf{h}^i m^i & \geq 0 \quad (i = 1, \dots, t) \\
 & & m^1 + \dots + m^t & = 1 \\
-x_j + x_j^1 + \dots + x_j^t & & & = 0 \quad (j = 1, \dots, k)
\end{array}
$$

```
:- lib(r).                  % load constraint solver

sat(I,plus(Phi,Psi)) :-
    sat(X,Phi),             % Connect X, Phi
    sat(Y,Psi),             % Connect Y, Psi
    truth_var(X),           % X is in [0,1]
    truth_var(Y),           % Y is in [0,1]
    truth_var(I),           % I is in [0,1]
    control_var(Z),         % Z is in {0,1}
    X + Y + Z $>= I,        % (i)
    X + Y - Z $<= I,        % (ii)
    X + Y - Z $>= 0,        % (iii) see (14)
    X + Y - Z $<= 1,        % (iv)
            I $>= Z.        % (v)

sat(I,neg(Phi))          :- sat(1-I,Phi).

sat(I,atom(P))           :- I $= P.

control_var(0).
control_var(1).

truth_var(X)             :- 0 $<= X, X $<= 1.
```

Fig. 6. A satisfiability checker for infinite-valued Łukasiewicz logic implemented in Eclipse Prolog

This theorem can be used to compute an MIP-representation such as the one of $\oplus$ in (16): MIP-representations of the convex regions whose union constitute $\oplus$ are obvious from the right part of Fig. 4 – use $x_3^1 = x_1^1 + x_2^1$ and $x_3^2 = 1$. Then apply the theorem to these.

The freshly introduced variables such as the m^i (which play the same rôle as z in (16) are called *control variables*, because they control which disjunction is being selected. Let us close this subsection with a

Proof sketch of Theorem 4.2. It suffices to construct a McNaughton function which vanishes iff **J** is feasible. To this end, first decompose **J** into a finite union of feasible LPs [19, p. 12]. Each of them describes an m-dimensional convex polyhedron P. Embed this polyhedron into $[0,1]^{m+1}$ via $(x_1, \dots, x_m) \mapsto (x_1, \dots, x_m, 0)$. Now construct piecewise linear, continous functions with integral coefficients $f_P : [0,1]^m \to [0,1]$ by connecting each corner of P to its nearest point in $\{0,1\}^m \times \{1\}$. This is possible, because the P are convex. The f_P can obviously be represented by linear polynomials with integral coefficients effectively computed from (the corners of) P. By construction, the f_P are continuous and hence a McNaughton function.

Finally, for each f_P let ϕ_{f_P} be a Łukasiewicz formula as supplied by McNaughton's Theorem. Kleene conjunction $\wedge$ (6) is definable in Łukasiewicz logic and computes the minimum of two truth values, thus the formula $\bigwedge_{f_P} \phi_{f_P}$ takes on the truth value 0 iff the original MIP is feasible. □

McNaughton's Theorem and its variant Theorem 4.2 express that MIP is captured naturally by Łukasiewicz logic. Earlier I mentioned that classical logic corresponds to IPs of the form (15). Thus the difference between Łukasiewicz logic and classical logic is analogous to that between MIPs and IPs of a very special kind. There is no easy transition between the latter which explains why classical logic is not suitable as a meta language for expressing Łukasiewicz logic.

Another aspect of Theorem 4.2 is the following: if every MIP can be expressed as an infinite-valued Łukasiewicz logic formula which in turn can be express through an MIP, then the use of the reduction from many-valued logic to MIP developed here seems to be confined to (sublogics of) Łukasiewicz logic. This is not quite true, however: first, it can be used for *any* finite-valued logic $\mathcal{L}$ without the detour of expressing $\mathcal{L}$ in infinite-valued Łukasiewicz logic; second, even if a connective is definable in Łukasiewicz logic, its definition might be very long, whereas its MIP-representation might be short (note that the Corollary does not follow from Theorem 4.2 – part 1 of the theorem is required for that); and, most importantly, in the following section I demonstrate that the logics captured by the MIP approach can be extended beyond Łukasiewicz logic.

3.5 Limits and Extensions of MIP-Representability

The contraposition of Theorem 4.2 yields that functions that are not definable in Łukasiewicz logic cannot be MIP-representable. Let us look at the reasons why MIP-representability may fail for a function f (see [19] for an in-depth discussion).

First, f might be not linear or have irrational coefficients. Or infinitely many linear polynomials are required to represent it. Finally, f can be an open set. For example, it might be not continuous, but composed of finitely many piecewise linear polynomials with integral coefficients. In this case, however, it might be possible to represent f by MIPs with ***strict inequalities.***

A typical example of this situation are Gödel's connectives (see (7, 8) and Fig. 7) which are not continuous.[6] To represent them ***strict*** linear inequalities or linear ***disequations*** are needed. An algorithmic treatment of strict inequalities is sometimes possible with so-called transposition theorems [31, p. 94f] which relate strict to non-strict inequalities. More efficient are modified constraint solvers that can directly handle disequations [15,18].

It is easy to prove that the strict MIP feasibility is still in NP. If one defines **strictly MIP-representable logics** as MIP-representable logics,

[6] It is well-known that Gödel's connectives cannot be expressed in Łukasiewicz logic, so this was to be expected.

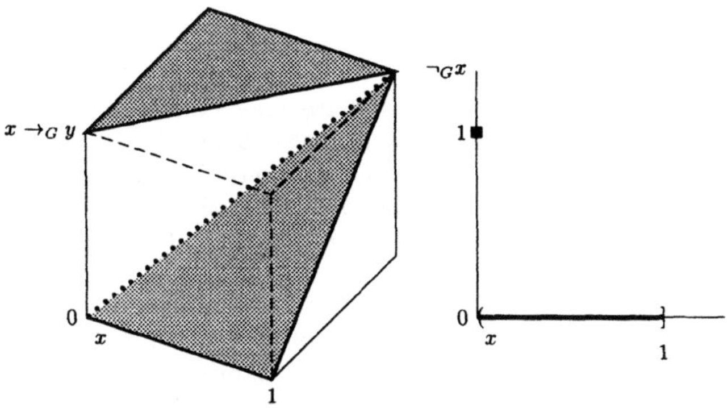

Fig. 7. Functions $x \to_G y$ and $\neg_G x$ on $N = [0, 1]$

where also strict inequations are allowed in the MIP representation, then one has immediately:

Theorem 6. *The $[c, d]$-satisfability problem of any strictly MIP-representable logic for $0 \leq c \leq d \leq 1$ is in NP.*

It is known that the satisfiability problems of Łukasiewicz [22] and of Gödel logic [Matthias Baaz, 1996: Personal Communication] are in NP, but the new technique works even if connectives from both logics are present and it works for altogether different logics as well.

For other interesting, but totally different uses of (M)IP in connection with logic, see [17,3].

4 Conclusion

Acknowledgments I would like to thank Prof. Dr. Reusch and his staff for inviting me to the anniversary colloquium of Informatik Lehrstuhl I, University of Dortmund. Support obtained from EC COST Action No 15 *Many-Valued Logic for Computer Science Applications* is gratefully acknowledged.

References

1. M. Baaz and C. G. Fermüller. Resolution-based theorem proving for many-valued logics. *Journal of Symbolic Computation*, 19(4):353–391, Apr. 1995.
2. E. Balas. Disjunctive programming. *Annals of Discrete Mathematics*, 5(Discrete Optimization II):3–51, 1979. Proc. of the Advanced Research Institute on Discrete Optimization and Systems Applications of the Systems Science Panel of NATO and of the Discrete Optimization Symposium , Canada 1977. Edited by P. L. Hammer, E. L. Johnson, and B. H. Korte.

3. C. Bell, A. Nerode, R. Ng, and V. Subrahmanian. Mixed integer programming methods for computing nonmonotonic deductive databases. *Journal of the ACM*, 41(6):1178–1215, Nov. 1994.
4. W. A. Carnielli. Systematization of finite many-valued logics through the method of tableaux. *Journal of Symbolic Logic*, 52(2):473–493, June 1987.
5. R. Cignoli and D. Mundici. An invitation to Chang's MV algebras. In M. Droste and R. Göbel, editors, *Advances in algebra and model theory: selected surveys presented at conferences in Essen, 1994 and Dresden, 1995*, number 9 in Algebra, logic and applications. Gordon & Breach, Amsterdam, 1997.
6. R. L. O. Cignoli, I. M. L. D'Ottaviano, and D. Mundici. *Álgebras das Lógicas de Łukasiewicz (in Portuguese)*, volume 12 of *Coleção CLE*. Centro de Lógica, Epistemologiae História da Ciênca, Unicamp, Campinas, Brazil, 1995.
7. M. C. Fitting. *First-Order Logic and Automated Theorem Proving*. Springer-Verlag, New York, second edition, 1996.
8. R. Hähnle. Towards an efficient tableau proof procedure for multiple-valued logics. In E. Börger, H. Kleine Büning, M. M. Richter, and W. Schönfeld, editors, *Selected Papers from Computer Science Logic, CSL'90, Heidelberg, Germany*, volume 533 of *LNCS*, pages 248–260. Springer-Verlag, 1991.
9. R. Hähnle. *Automated Deduction in Multiple-Valued Logics*, volume 10 of *International Series of Monographs on Computer Science*. Oxford University Press, 1994.
10. R. Hähnle. Many-valued logic and mixed integer programming. *Annals of Mathematics and Artificial Intelligence*, 12(3,4):231–264, Dec. 1994.
11. R. Hähnle. Short conjunctive normal forms in finitely-valued logics. *Journal of Logic and Computation*, 4(6):905–927, 1994.
12. R. Hähnle. Exploiting data dependencies in many-valued logics. *Journal of Applied Non-Classical Logics*, 6(1):49–69, 1996.
13. R. Hähnle. Proof theory of many-valued logic—linear optimization—logic design: Connections and interactions. *Soft Computing—A Fusion of Foundations, Methodologies and Applications*, 1(3):107–119, Sept. 1997.
14. R. Hähnle and W. Kernig. Verification of switch level designs with many-valued logic. In A. Voronkov, editor, *Proc. LPAR'93, St. Petersburg, Russia*, volume 698 of *LNCS*, pages 158–169. Springer-Verlag, 1993.
15. P. V. Hentenryck and T. Graf. Standard Forms for Rational Linear Arithmetics in Constraint Logic Programming. *Annals of Mathematics and Artificial Intelligence*, 5(2–4), 1992.
16. J. N. Hooker. A quantitative approach to logical inference. *Decision Support Systems*, 4:45–69, 1988.
17. J. N. Hooker. New methods for computing inferences in first order logic. *Annals of Operations Research*, 43(1–4):479–492, Oct. 1993. Selected Papers of Applied Mathematical Programming and Modelling, APMOD91.
18. J. L. Imbert and P. V. Hentenryck. Efficient Handling of Disequations in CLP over Linear Rational Arithmetics. In F. Benhamou and A. Colmerauer, editors, *Constraint Logic Programming: Selected Research*, pages 49–71. MIT Press, 1993.
19. R. G. Jeroslow. *Logic-Based Decision Support. Mixed Integer Model Formulation*. Elsevier, Amsterdam, 1988.
20. R. McNaughton. A theorem about infinite-valued sentential logic. *Journal of Symbolic Logic*, 16(1):1–13, 1951.

21. D. Mundici. Interpretation of AF C*-algebras in Łukasiewicz sentential calculus. *Journal of Functional Analysis*, 65:15–63, 1986.
22. D. Mundici. Satisfiability in many-valued sentential logic is NP-complete. *Theoretical Computer Science*, 52:145–153, 1987.
23. D. Mundici. Algebras of Ulam's games with lies. In *Proceedings SILFS International Congress, Viareggio*, 1990.
24. D. Mundici. A constructive proof of McNaughton's Theorem in infinite-valued logic. *Journal of Symbolic Logic*, 59(2):596–602, June 1994.
25. D. Mundici and G. Panti. Extending addition in Elliott's local semigroup. *Journal of Functional Analysis*, 171:461–472, 1993.
26. G. Panti. A geometric proof of the completeness of the Łukasiewicz calculus. *Journal of Symbolic Logic*, 60(2):563–578, June 1995.
27. D. A. Plaisted and S. Greenbaum. A structure-preserving clause form translation. *Journal of Symbolic Computation*, 2:293–304, 1986.
28. G. Rousseau. Sequents in many valued logic I. *Fundamenta Mathematicæ*, LX:23–33, 1967.
29. T. Sasao. Multiple-valued decomposition of generalized Boolean functions and the complexity of programmable logic arrays. *IEEE Transactions on Computers*, C-30:635–643, Sept. 1981.
30. B. Scarpellini. Die Nichtaxiomatisierbarkeit des unendlichwertigen Prädikatenkalküls von Łukasiewicz. *Journal of Symbolic Logic*, 27(2):159–170, June 1962.
31. A. Schrijver. *Theory of Linear and Integer Programming.* Wiley-Interscience Series in Discrete Mathematics. John Wiley & Sons, 1986.
32. J. Siekmann and G. Wrightson, editors. *Automation of Reasoning: Classical Papers in Computational Logic 1967–1970*, volume 2. Springer-Verlag, 1983.
33. R. M. Smullyan. *First-Order Logic.* Dover Publications, New York, second corrected edition, 1995. First published 1968 by Springer-Verlag.
34. M. Takahashi. Many-valued logics of extended Gentzen style I. *Science Reports of the Tokyo Kyoiku Daigaku, Section A*, 9(231):95–116, 1967. MR 37.39, Zbl 172.8.
35. G. Tseitin. On the complexity of proofs in propositional logics. *Seminars in Mathematics*, 8, 1970. Reprinted in [32].
36. R. Zach. Proof theory of finite-valued logics. Master's thesis, Institut für Algebra und Diskrete Mathematik, TU Wien, Sept. 1993. Available as Technical Report TUW-E185.2-Z.1-93.

Triangular Norms – An Overview

Radko Mesiar

Department of Mathematics
Slovak University of Technology, Radlinského 11,
813368 Bratislava, Slovakia
and MÚSAV, Štefánikova 49
81473 Bratislava, Slovakia

Abstract. Historical development of triangular norms theory is recalled. Basic properties of t-norms are discussed. Several examples are included. Then we discuss the algebraic properties of t-norms. Different construction methods including latest ones are described. A special attention is paid to the representation of continuous t-norms. Some related operations and fields of applications are discussed, too. An exhaustive bibliography is included.

Keywords: generator, ordinal sum, triangular norm

1. Historical Overview

The notion of a triangular norm (t-norm for short) appeared for the first time in Menger's paper [35] in 1942. Menger tried to generalize the classical metric spaces replacing the real-valued metric by a metric with values in the space of distribution functions on R^+. In order to formulate properly the triangle inequality, he introduced a special class of two-place functions on the unit square called triangular norms. However, the associativity was not required by Menger as well as his boundary conditions were essentially weaker than those for nowadays t-norms. The present axioms for t-norms (commutativity, associativity, monotonicity, neutral element 1) were stated by Schweizer and Sklar [49] in 1958, where, e. g., the associativity was a consequence of a proper formulation of polygonal inequality. The dual operations, the triangular conorms (t-conorms for short), were introduced by Schweizer and Sklar [50] in 1960. Let $\mathbf{T}: [0, 1]^2 \to [0, 1]$ be a t-norm. Then the function $\mathbf{S}: [0, 1]^2 \to [0, 1]$, $\mathbf{S}(x, y) = 1 - \mathbf{T}(1 - x, 1 - y)$, is called a dual t-conorm (note that in the original Schweizer – Sklar notation **S** for t-conorms is hidden the use of the notion "s-norms"). Because of the duality between t-norms and t-conorms, all results concerning t-norms can be reformulated for t-conorms, and vice-versa. Note, however, that t-conorms may be introduced independently of t-norms by a similar set of axioms, with the only difference in the neutral element, which is 0 for t-conorms, while 1 for t-norms.

Further developments of the theory of t-norms were strongly influenced by Ling [32] in 1965. She characterized the continuous t-norms as ordinal sums and Archimedean continuous t-norms as t-norms generated by continuous additive generators. In Ling's paper, the two main sources for t-norms appeared for the first time. Namely, she applied the results from semi-group theory (Faucett [12], Mostert and Shields [42]) as well as those from the functional equations domain (Aczél [2] and even Abel [1]).

The development of t-norms was done in its beginnings mostly in the framework of probabilistic metric spaces. Note, e. g., that special t-norms, so-called copulas, are used to define properly a joint probability distribution from two given marginal probability distributions. Another impulses came from the other fields where t-norms or related operation became important. This is, e. g., the case of information theory. Kampé de Fériet [24] in 1969 formulated a composition law for information measures, which is an isomorphic transformation of a t-norm.

In 1974, Sugeno [54] introduced the fuzzy measure theory. His λ-measures are based on special t-conorms. In this streaming, Weber [60] introduced so called $\perp$-decomposable measures, where $\perp$ is a t-conorm.

One of the major fields of applications of t-norms is the area of fuzzy sets and fuzzy logic. Even in his seminal paper from 1965, Zadeh [63] sketched the use of other operations for fuzzy intersection (union) then min (max). With respect to MV-logic (many-valued logic), we can even go back to 1930 to Lukasiewicz [34] (note that the Lukasiewicz t-norm T_L was not mentioned explicitly in [34], however, it could be derived from the implication operator introduced by Lukasiewicz in [34]). The first explicit traces of the use of t-norms in the fuzzy sets and fuzzy logic framework go back to 1980, see e. g. Dubois [10], Klement [27].

Triangular norms are described in several monographs in special chapters. The deepest results on t-norms can be found in the book of Schweizer and Sklar [52] from 1983. Among several recent books containing t-norm chapters, recall e. g., Lowen [33] or Nguyen and Walker [43]. However, till now there is no monograph devoted properly to triangular norms. A monograph prepared by Klement, Mesiar and Pap will hopefully cover this gap.

2. Basic Definitions and Properties

First, we recall the definition of a t-norm from [49, 50].

Definition 2.1 A triangular norm is a binary operation on the unit interval, i. e., a function $\mathbf{T}: [0,1]^2 \to [0, 1]$ such that for all x, y, z $\in$ [0, 1] the following four axioms are satisfied:

$\mathbf{T}(x, y) = \mathbf{T}(y, x)$	commutativity	(1)
$\mathbf{T}(x, \mathbf{T}(y, z)) = \mathbf{T}(\mathbf{T}(x, y), z)$	associativity	(2)
$\mathbf{T}(x, y) \le \mathbf{T}(x, z)$ whenever $y \le z$	monotonicity	(3)
$\mathbf{T}(x, 1) = x$	boundary condition	(4).

Remember that t-norms play the role of the intersection in the fuzzy set theory, generalizing the classical intersection operator on Cantorian sets (which is commutative, associative, monotone and fulfills the boundary condition $A \cap X = A$, X being the given universe of discour).
The couple ([0, 1], **T**) is a (fully ordered) semigroup with neutral element 1 and annihilator 0. On the other hand, **T** is a special two-place real function, which is a solution of functional equation (2). Therefore we can naturally extend the usual order on reals to a partial order on t-norms. Namely, given two t-norms $\mathbf{T}_1$ and $\mathbf{T}_2$, we say that $\mathbf{T}_1$ is weaker than $\mathbf{T}_2$, $\mathbf{T}_1 \leq \mathbf{T}_2$, if for all $x, y \in [0, 1]$ it is $\mathbf{T}_1(x, y) \leq \mathbf{T}_2(x, y)$. Due to (1) and (4), for any t-norm **T** and any $x \in [0, 1]$ we have $\mathbf{T}(x, 1) = \mathbf{T}(1, x) = x$. Further, (1), (3) and (4) immediately ensures

$$0 \leq \mathbf{T}(x, 0) = \mathbf{T}(0, x) \leq \mathbf{T}(0, 1) = 0, \text{ i. e., } \mathbf{T}(x, 0) = \mathbf{T}(0, x) = 0.$$

Hence, all t-norms coincide on the boundaries of the unit square $[0, 1]^2$. Two t-norms may differ only on the open square $]0, 1[^2$. Applying (3) and (4), we get $\mathbf{T}(x, y) \leq \mathbf{T}(x, 1) = x$ for any $x, y \in [0, 1]$. Similarly $\mathbf{T}(x, y) \leq y$, i. e., $\mathbf{T}(x, y) \leq \mathit{min}(x, y)$. It easy to check that the above upper bound of all t-norms, $\mathbf{T}_M(x, y) = \mathit{min}(x, y)$, fulfills the axioms (1) – (4) and therefore it is the strongest t-norm. On the other hand, for all $x, y \in]0, 1[$ we have $0 \leq \mathbf{T}(x, y)$. Again, the lower bound of all t-norms, $\mathbf{T}_W(x, y) = 0$ whenever $\mathit{max}(x, y) < 1$ (and obviously $\mathbf{T}_W(x, y) = \mathit{min}(x, y)$ whenever $\mathit{max}(x, y) = 1$) is a t-norm. It is called the drastic product and for any t-norm **T** we have

$$\mathbf{T}_W \leq \mathbf{T} \leq \mathbf{T}_M. \tag{5}$$

Recall the probabilistic origin of triangular norms. Let P be a probability measure on some measurable space and let A, B be two events. Knowing P(A) and P(B), what can we say about $P(A \cap B)$? If the events A and B are stochastically independent then $P(A \cap B) = P(A)\,P(B)$. Inspired by the product composition of probabilities, put $\mathbf{T}_P(x, y) = xy$, $x, y \in [0, 1]$. It is evident that $\mathbf{T}_P$ is a t-norm! Product is the third basic triangular norm. Continue in the example with $P(A \cap B)$. If no information about the relationship of the events A and B is known, we can only estimate that

$$\mathit{max}(0, P(A) + P(B) - 1) \leq P(A \cap B) \leq \mathit{min}(P(A), P(B)).$$

The right-hand side of the above inequalities corresponds to the strongest t-norm $\mathbf{T}_M$. Concerning the left-hand side, define

$$\mathbf{T}_L(x, y) = \mathit{max}(0, x + y - 1) \qquad x, y \in [0, 1].$$

The properties (1), (3), (4) are obviously fulfilled by $\mathbf{T}_L$. To see the associativity, we have
$\mathbf{T}_L(x, \mathbf{T}_L(y, z)) = \mathit{max}(0, x + \mathit{max}(0, y + z - 1) - 1) = \mathit{max}(0, x + y + z - 2) = \mathit{max}(0, z + x + y - 2) = \mathbf{T}_L(z, \mathbf{T}_L(x, y)) = \mathbf{T}_L(\mathbf{T}_L(x, y), z)$. $\mathbf{T}_L$ is therefore a t-norm, namely the fourth basic t-norm. It is called the Lukasiewicz t-norm based on the paper of Lukasiewicz [34] from 1930, where he introduced an implication in 3-valued logic which leads to the formula describing $\mathbf{T}_L$. Note that the next inequality is valid:

$$\mathbf{T}_W < \mathbf{T}_L < \mathbf{T}_P < \mathbf{T}_M.$$

The continuity of a t-norm **T** corresponds to the continuity of a two-place real function. Among the four basic t-norms, $\mathbf{T}_M$, $\mathbf{T}_L$ and $\mathbf{T}_P$ are continuous, while the continuity of T_W is violated on the upper and right boundary of the unit square. The following propositions show that the joint continuity of a t-norm can be replaced by the continuity of all partial mappings with fixed first coordinate.

Proposition 2.1. T is continuous if and only if each partial mapping

$$T(x,.): [0,1] \to [0,1]$$

is continuous, $x \in [0, 1]$.

Similarly we can introduce the lower and the upper continuity of t-norms.

Proposition 2.2. The following statements are equivalent:

i) T is upper continuous

ii) $T\left(\inf_n (x_n), \inf_m (y_m)\right) = \inf_{n,m} T(x_n, y_m)$

iii) each partial mapping T(x, .) is right-continuous.

Due to the above results, the upper continuous t-norms are called also right-continuous. Similarly, the lower continuous t-norms are called left-continuous.

Proposition 2.3 The following statements are equivalent:

i) T is lower continuous

ii) $T\left(\sup_n (x_n), \sup_m (y_m)\right) = \sup_{n,m} T(x_n, y_m)$

iii) each partial mapping T(x, .) is left-continuous.

The weakest t-norm T_W is an example of a right-continuous t-norm which is not continuous. The following example (nilpotent minimum T_{NM}, see [13]) shows a non-continuous t-norm which is left-continuous:

$$T_{NM}(x,y) = \begin{cases} 0 & \text{if } x+y \le 1 \\ \min(x,y) & \text{otherwise} \end{cases}. \tag{6}$$

3. Other Examples of T-Norms

Several parameterized families of t-norms have been introduced in the literature. We recall some of them. All of these families are monotone and continuous in the index parameter.

Example 3.1 Schweizer and Sklar [51] introduced a family of t-norms containing all four basic t-norms $\left(T_\lambda^{ss}\right)_{\lambda \in [-\infty,\infty]}$ given by

$$\mathbf{T}_\lambda^{ss}(x,y)=\begin{cases}\mathbf{T}_M(x,y) & \lambda=-\infty\\ \left(x^\lambda+y^\lambda-1\right)^{\frac{1}{\lambda}} & \lambda\in]-\infty,0[\\ \mathbf{T}_P(x,y) & \lambda=0\\ \left(\max\left(0,x^\lambda+y^\lambda-1\right)\right)^{\frac{1}{\lambda}} & \lambda\in]0,\infty[\\ \mathbf{T}_W(x,y) & \lambda=+\infty\end{cases}$$

where $\mathbf{T}_1^{ss}=\mathbf{T}_L$.

Example 3.2 A characterization of the conjunctions in [0, 1]-valued logics, which can be represented in a rational form (i. e., $\mathbf{T}=\frac{P}{Q}$ where P and Q are polynomials), is due to Hamacher [22]. The corresponding conjunctions from the Hamacher family of t-norms $\left(\mathbf{T}_\lambda^H\right)_{\lambda\in[0,+\infty[}$ are given by

$$\mathbf{T}_\lambda^H(x,y)=\frac{xy}{\lambda+(1-\lambda)(x+y-xy)}$$

up to the case x = y = λ = 0 (in which case obviously $\mathbf{T}_0^H(0,0)=0$). $\mathbf{T}_0^H$ is called the Hamacher product. The dual t-conorm $\mathbf{S}_2^H$ given by $\mathbf{S}_2^H(x,y)=\frac{x+y}{1+xy}$ is known as the Einstein sum.

Example 3.3 The investigations of the associativity of functions G fulfilling the functional equation

$$F(x, y) + G(x, y) = x + y,\ x, y \in [0, 1]$$

where F is a special associative function on the unit square, have led to the Frank family of t-norms [17], $\left(\mathbf{T}_\lambda^F\right)_{\lambda\in[0,\infty]}$. Note that this family is also called a family of fundamental t-norms [6] and that fuzzy intersections and fuzzy unions based on the Frank t-norms and t-conorms generalize the usual valuation property of crisp sets to the fuzzy sets,

$$\mu_{A\cap B}+\mu_{A\cup B}=\mu_A+\mu_B\,.$$

We have

$$\mathbf{T}_\lambda^F(x,y)=\begin{cases}\mathbf{T}_M(x,y) & \lambda=0\\ \mathbf{T}_P(x,y) & \lambda=1\\ \mathbf{T}_L(x,y) & \lambda=\infty\\ \log_\lambda\left(1+\frac{\left(\lambda^x-1\right)\left(\lambda^y-1\right)}{\lambda-1}\right) & \text{otherwise}\end{cases}.$$

Example 3.4. The following family $\left(T_\lambda^Y\right)_{\lambda\in[0,\infty]}$ was proposed by Yager [61] for modelling the intersection of fuzzy sets:

$$T_\lambda^Y(x,y)=\begin{cases}T_W(x,y) & \lambda=0\\ T_M(x,y) & \lambda=\infty\\ max\left(0,1-\left((1-x)^\lambda+(1-y)^\lambda\right)\right)^{\frac{1}{\lambda}} & \text{otherwise}\end{cases}$$

Several peculiar t-norms can be recalled, too. For example, Klement [28] introduced a (Borel) non-measurable t-norm. Budinčevič and Kurilič [5] introduced a family of t-norms with dense subset of discontinuity points. We give an example. For x, y ∈]0, 1[let

$$x=\sum_{n=1}^{\infty}\frac{1}{2^{x_n}} \text{ and } y=\sum_{n=1}^{\infty}\frac{1}{2^{y_n}}$$

be the unique dyadic representation of x and y, respectively (note that if a finite dyadic representation is possible, too, we choose always the infinite one). Then T_{BK}: $[0, 1]^2 \to [0, 1]$ fulfilling on the unit square boundaries the t-norms requirements and on the open unit square given by

$$T_{BK}(x,y)=\sum_{n=1}^{\infty}\frac{1}{2^{x_n+y_n-1}} \tag{7}$$

is a t-norm. Each point (x, y) ∈ $]0, 1[^2$ where at least one coordinate admits also a finite dyadic representation (i.e., it is a dyadic rational) is a discontinuity point of T_{BK}. Note that a modofications T^* of T_{BK} given (on the half open unit square $]0,1]^2$) by $T^*(x, y) = \sum_{n=1}^{\infty}\frac{1}{2^{x_n+y_n-n}}$ is a left - continuous t-norm with dense subset of discontinuity points. More details about specific properties of the t-norm T^* can be found in [53].

4. Algebraic Properties of T-Norms

The semigroup features of t-norms allow to introduce several algebraic notions into the t-norm theory.

Definition 4.1. Let T be a t-norm.

(i) An element x ∈ [0, 1] is called an idempotent of T if T(x, x) = x. The set of all idempotents of T will be denoted as ID_T.

(ii) An element x ∈]0, 1[is called a nilpotent element of T if there exists some n∈ N such that

$$x^{(n)_T}=0, \text{ where } x^{(1)_T}=x,\ x^{(n)_T}=T(x^{(n-1)_T},x),\ n=2,3,\cdots.$$

The set of all nilpotent elements of $\mathbf{T}$ will be denoted as NIL_T.

(iii) An element $x \in]0, 1[$ is called a zero divizor of $\mathbf{T}$ if there exist some $y \in]0,1[$ such that $\mathbf{T}(x, y) = 0$. The set of all zero divizors of $\mathbf{T}$ will be denoted as ZD_T.

It is immediate that 0 and 1 are trivial idempotents of any t-norm $\mathbf{T}$, i. e., $ID_T \supset \{0, 1\}$. Further, $ID_T = [0, 1]$ if and only if $\mathbf{T} = \mathbf{T_M}$ is the strongest t-norm. Note that $ID_{T_{NM}} = \{0\} \cup]\frac{1}{2}, 1]$, while for $\mathbf{T_P}$, $\mathbf{T_L}$, $\mathbf{T_W}$, $\mathbf{T_{KB}}$ only trivial idempotents exist. Each nilpotent element is a zero divizor, $NIL_T \subset ZD_T$. Vice versa, if x is a zero divizor of $\mathbf{T}$, then $\min(x, y)$ is a nilpotent element of $\mathbf{T}$, where $y \in]0, 1[$ is an element such that $\mathbf{T}(x, y) = 0$. No nilpotent element can be an idempotent. If $\mathbf{T}$ is continuous then also zero divizors cannot be idempotents. We have, e. g.,

$$NIL_{T_W} = NIL_{T_L} =]0,1[\,, NIL_{T_{NM}} =]\,0, \frac{1}{2}\,], NIL_{T_P} = NIL_{T_M} = NIL_{T_{BK}} = \emptyset$$

$$ZD_{T_W} = ZD_{T_L} = ZD_{T_{NM}} =]\,0, 1\,], ZD_{T_P} = ZD_{T_M} = ZD_{T_{BK}} = \emptyset$$

Some other immediate results:

(1) if x is an idempotent element then $x^{(n)_T} = x$ for all $n \in N$ and consequently no $y \ge x$ can be a nilpotent element; more $\mathbf{T}(x, y) = x$ for all $y \ge x$.

(2) if x is a nilpotent element (zero divizor) then any y, $0 < y < x$, is also a nilpotent element (zero divizor). Consequently, $NIL_T =]0, t[$ or $]0, t]$ for some $t \in [0, 1]$, similarly $ZD_T =]0, v[$ or $]0, v]$, $1 \ge v \ge t$.

A t-norm $\mathbf{T}$ may have additional algebraic properties which may highly influence its behaviour.

Definition 4.2. Let $\mathbf{T}$ be a t-norm. Then

(i) $\mathbf{T}$ is called Archimedean if for all $x, y \in]0, 1[$ there exists an $n \in N$ such that $x^{(n)_T} < y$

(ii) $\mathbf{T}$ is said to be strictly monotone if $\mathbf{T}(x, y) < \mathbf{T}(x, z)$ whenever $x \neq 0$ and $y < z$

(iii) $\mathbf{T}$ is called strict if it is continuous and strictly monotone

(iv) $\mathbf{T}$ is called nilpotent if it is continuous and $NIL_T =]0, 1[$.

Recall that strictness of $\mathbf{T}$ ensures $NIL_T = \emptyset$. Among previous examples of t-norms, $\mathbf{T_P}$ is strict, and Archimedean. $\mathbf{T_L}$ is nilpotent and Archimedean. $\mathbf{T_W}$ is Archimedean, $NIL_{T_W} =]0,1[$, but $\mathbf{T_W}$ is not nilpotent (continuity is violated). $\mathbf{T_{BK}}$ is strictly monotone but not Archimedean! We summarize some of the relationships and results concerning the introduced algebraic properties.

Proposition 4.1. T is Archimedean if and only if $\lim_{n\to\infty} x^{(n)_T} = 0$ for all $x \in\ ]0,1[$.
Consequently, if T is Archimedean and without nilpotent elements, then T is strictly monotone, opposite not being true (take T_{BK}).

Proposition 4.2. For continuous t-norms, the followings are equivalent:
(i) T is strictly monotone.
(ii) T satisfies the cancellation law, i. e. if $T(x, y) = T(x, z)$ and $x > 0$, then $y = z$.
(iii) for any $x \in\ ]0, 1[$, $\{ x^{(n)_T} \}$ is strictly decreasing.

In general, strict monotonicity implies the cancellation law and the cancellation law implies the strict monotonicity of $\{ x^{(n)_T} \}$ for all $x \in\ ]0, 1[$. However, the latter property does not ensure the strict monotonicity. Define, e. g.,

$T(x, y) = xy \qquad$ if $x, y \le \frac{1}{2}$,

$T(x, y) = \frac{1}{2} + \frac{1}{2}(2x-1)(2y-1) \qquad$ if $x, y > \frac{1}{2}$, and

$T(x, y) = \min(x, y)$ in all remaining cases. Then T is a t-norm which is not strictly monotone (and hence cancellation law is violated), however, for any $x \in\ ]0,1[$, $\{ x^{(n)_T} \}$ is strictly decreasing.
Now, we will show that T_{BK} is not Archimedean though it is strictly monotone.

Put $T = T_{BK}$. For $x \in\ ]0, 1[$, $x = \sum_{i=1}^{\infty} \frac{1}{2^{x_i}}$, it is $x^{(n)_T} = \sum_{i=1}^{\infty} \frac{1}{2^{n x_i - n + 1}}$, see [5].

If $x_1 > 1$, i. e., $x \in\ ]0, \frac{1}{2}]$, then $n x_1 + n + 1 \to +\infty$ and consequently $x^{(n)_T} \to 0$.

For example, $\left(\frac{1}{2}\right)^{(n)_T} = \sum_{i=1}^{\infty} \frac{1}{2^{in+1}} = \frac{1}{2.(2^n - 1)}$. On the other side, if $x > \frac{1}{2}$ then

$x_1 = 1$ but $x_2 > 1$, $n x_2 - n + 1 \to +\infty$, and consequently $x^{(n)_T} \to \frac{1}{2}$. It is evident that all sequences $\{ x^{(n)_T} \}$, $x \in\ ]0, 1[$, are strictly decreasing, i. e., T_{BK} is strictly monotone but not Archimedean.

Proposition 4.3. If T is Archimedean then $T(x, x) < x$ for all $x \in\ ]0, 1[$ but not vice - versa. If T is continuous, then the followings are equivalent:
(i) T is Archimedean.
(ii) $T(x, x) < x$ for all $x \in\ ]0, 1[$.
(iii) T is strict or nilpotent.

5. Some Construction Methods

The main problem in construction of a t-norm is the associativity property. Therefore mostly the semigroup methods are used for constructing t-norms. First of all, t-norms can be obtained by isomorphism from special semigroups on the real line.

Proposition 5. 1. Let f: $[0, 1] \to [0, \infty]$ be a decreasing bijection. Take the semigroup $([0, \infty], +)$. Let the corresponding isomorphic semigroup be $([0,1],*)$ with $x * y = f^{-1}(f(x) + f(y))$. Then $*$ corresponds to a strict t-norm **T**, $\mathbf{T}(x, y) = x * y$.

For a strict t-norm **T** derived by means of the function f the notation $\mathbf{T}^{(f)}$ is used and f is called an additive generator of $\mathbf{T}^{(f)}$.

Recall that, e. g., $\mathbf{T_P} = \mathbf{T}^{(f)}$ with $f(x) = -log(x)$. However, $g = cf$ with $c > 0$ implies $\mathbf{T}^{(g)} = \mathbf{T}^{(f)}$, i. e., an additive generator is not unique! Put $f(x) = \frac{1}{x} - 1$, $x \in [0, 1]$. Then the corresponding strict t-norm $\mathbf{T}^{(f)}$ is just the Hamacher product $\mathbf{T}_0^{\mathrm{H}}$.

Proposition 5.2. Let f: $[0, 1] \to [0, k]$, $k \in]0, \infty[$, be a decreasing bijection. Take the semigroup $([0, k], \oplus)$, where $u \oplus v = min(k, u + v)$, $u, v \in [0, k]$. The corresponding f-isomorphic semigroup $([0, 1], *)$ induces the nilpotent t-norm $\mathbf{T}^{(f)}$, $\mathbf{T}^{(f)}(x, y) = x * y = f^{-1}(f(x) \oplus f(y)) = f^{-1}(min(k, f(x) + f(y)) = f^{(-1)}(f(x) + f(y))$.
Here $f^{(-1)} : [0, \infty] \to [0, 1]$ is so called pseudo-inverse of f, defined by

$$f^{(-1)}(t) = sup\,(x \in [0, 1]; f(x) > t) = f^{-1}(min\,(f(0), t)).$$

Again $\mathbf{T}^{(f)} = \mathbf{T}^{(cf)}$ for $c > 0$ (note only that cf acts on the semigroup $([0, ck], \oplus)$). Therefore we can always start from $k = 1$, i. e., f: $[0, 1] \to [0, 1]$, and then f is called a normed additive generator. Put, e. g., $f_\lambda(x) = (1 - x)^\lambda$, $\lambda \in]0, \infty[$. Then the corresponding t-norms are Yager's t-norms, $\mathbf{T}^{(f_\lambda)} = \mathbf{T}_\lambda^{\mathrm{Y}}$. Especially, for $f(x) = 1 - x$ we get $\mathbf{T}^{(f)} = \mathbf{T_L}$ the Lukasiewicz t-norm.
However, we can start from a non-connected real semigroup. For example, take the semigroup $(\{0\} \cup]1, \infty], +)$, h: $[0, 1] \to \{0\} \cup]1, \infty]$,

$$h(x) = \begin{cases} 0 & x = 1 \\ -log\frac{x}{2} & x < 1 \end{cases}.$$

Then the corresponding t-norm $\mathbf{T}^{(h)}$ is defined by

$$\mathbf{T}^{(h)}(x, y) = \begin{cases} min(x, y) & \text{if } max(x, y) = 1 \\ \frac{xy}{2} & \text{otherwise} \end{cases}.$$

Note that $\mathbf{T}^{(h)}$ is strictly monotone, Archimedean, but not strict (it is only right-continuous but not continuous). In general, we have the following result:

Theorem 5. 1. Let f: $[0, 1] \to [0, \infty]$ be a strictly decreasing function whose range is relatively closed under addition, i. e., u, v $\in$ Range (f) $\Rightarrow$ u + v $\in$ Range (f) or u + v > $f(0^+)$, and which satisfies $f(1) = 0$. Then the two-place function $\mathbf{T}^{(f)}$: $[0, 1]^2 \to [0, 1]$ defined by

$$\mathbf{T}^{(f)}(x, y) = f^{(-1)}(f(x) + f(y)),$$

is a t-norm.

The function f in the above theorem is called an additive generator of $\mathbf{T}^{(f)}$. It is evident that due to the Archimedean property of reals each $\mathbf{T}^{(f)}$ constructed by means of Theorem 5.1. is an Archimedean t-norm (the opposite is an open problem yet). It is continuous only if f is continuous (see Proposition 5.1., 5.2.). It is right-continuous if f is right-continuous, see e. g. above introduced $\mathbf{T}^{(h)}$ (the opposite not being true). Left-continuity (it is enough in point 1 for f, in point (1, 1) for $\mathbf{T}^{(f)}$) immediately brings the total continuity. Note that even $\mathbf{T}_W$ has an additive generator - take, e. g.

$$f(x) = \begin{cases} 0 & x = 1 \\ 2 - x & x < 1 \end{cases}$$

or

$$g(x) = \begin{cases} 0 & x = 1 \\ 2 - x & x \in]\frac{1}{2}, 1[\\ 2 - \frac{x}{2} & x \in \left[0, \frac{1}{2}\right] \end{cases}$$

Then $\mathbf{T}^{(f)} = \mathbf{T}_W$ (this was remarked already by Ling [32]). More, also $\mathbf{T}^{(g)} = \mathbf{T}_W$. Note that g is not right-continuous while $\mathbf{T}^{(g)} = \mathbf{T}_W$ is. More, f and g are examples of two different additive generators with $f(0) = g(0)$ generating the same t-norm $\mathbf{T}^{(f)} = \mathbf{T}^{(g)} = \mathbf{T}_W$. However, if $\mathbf{T}$ is continuous or strictly monotone then $\mathbf{T}^{(f)} = \mathbf{T}^{(g)}$ only if $g = cf$. Note that Theorem 5.1. gives only sufficient condition on f to be an additive generator of a t-norm $\mathbf{T}^{(f)}$. There are also additive generators not fitting Theorem 5.1., see [57]. However, in such case the resulting t-norm $\mathbf{T}^{(f)}$ need not be Archimedean!

If one prefers, the multiplicative generators may be introduced as well. However, due to the isomorphism between ([0, ∞], +) and ([0, 1], .), no new t-norms can be obtained.

Another possibility is to start from a given t-norm **T**. Based on the results from [52], see also [56], we have introduced (together with Klement and Pap) the following construction method.

Theorem 5. 2. Let φ: $[0, 1] \to [0, 1]$ be a non-decreasing function and let **T** be a t-norm such that for all x, y $\in$ [0, 1] we have

$$\varphi \circ \varphi^{-1} (\mathbf{T}(\varphi(x), \varphi(y))) = \mathbf{T}(\varphi(x), \varphi(y)), \tag{8}$$

where $\varphi^{(-1)} : [0, 1] \to [0, 1]$ is the pseudo-inverse of φ given by

$$\varphi^{(-1)}(t) = sup\ (x \in [0, 1]; \varphi(x) < t).$$

Then the function $\mathbf{T}_{[\varphi]} : [0, 1]^2 \to [0, 1]$ given by

$$\mathbf{T}_{[\varphi]}(x, y) = \begin{cases} min(x, y) & max(x, y) = 1 \\ \varphi^{(-1)}(\mathbf{T}(\varphi(x), \varphi(y))) & \text{otherwise} \end{cases} \tag{9}$$

is a t-norm.

Note that the condition (8) is fulfilled if $\varphi \circ \varphi^{(-1)} \circ \varphi = \varphi$ and $\mathbf{T}(\varphi(x), \varphi(y)) \in \mathrm{Range}(\varphi) \cup [0, \varphi(0^+)]$. A sufficient condition for this is, e. g., the injectivity (or right-continuity) of φ and Range(φ) being an interval. It is evident that if φ is a bijection, then $\mathbf{T}_{[\varphi]}$ given by (9) is simply a t-norm isomorphic with **T**. For the basic four t-norms, we have some interesting properties concerning the isomorphic t-norms.

Proposition 5. 3.

(i) Let **T** be t-norm. Then $\mathbf{T}_{[\varphi]} = \mathbf{T}$ for any increasing bijection φ if and only if **T** is either $\mathbf{T_M}$ or $\mathbf{T_W}$.

(ii) $\mathbf{T_P} = (\mathbf{T_P})_{[\varphi]}$ if and only if $\varphi(x) = x^p$, $p > 0$.

(iii) $\mathbf{T_L} = (\mathbf{T_L})_{[\varphi]}$ if and only if $\varphi(x) = x$.

The isomorphism φ preserve the properties of given **T**. So, e. g., if **T** is i) continuous, ii) non-continuous, iii) strict, iv) non-strict, v) nilpotent, vi) non-nilpotent, vii) Archimedean, viii) non-Archimedean, ix) without zero-divizors, x) with zero-divizors, all of these properties are fulfilled also by $\mathbf{T}_{[\varphi]}$ whenever φ is an isomorphism. However, in general, **T** having any of properties among i) - x), there may exist non-decreasing function φ fitting Theorem 5.2. such that $\mathbf{T}_{[\varphi]}$ does not fulfill the corresponding property (then clearly φ cannot be an isomorphism). Take, e. g., $\varphi(x) = 2^{x-1}$, $x \in [0, 1]$. Then $(\mathbf{T_P})_{[\varphi]} = \mathbf{T_L}$, i. e., starting from a strict t-norm we have got a nilpotent one.

Take, e. g., $\varphi(x) = min\ (2x, 1)$, $x \in [0, 1]$. Then

$$(\mathbf{T_W})_{[\varphi]}(x, y) = \begin{cases} 0 & (x, y) \in [0, \frac{1}{2}[^2 \\ \frac{1}{2} & (x, y) \in [\frac{1}{2}, 1[^2 \\ min(x, y) & \text{otherwise} \end{cases} \tag{10}$$

Starting from an Archimedean t-norm $\mathbf{T_W}$, we have got a non-Archimedean t-norm $(\mathbf{T_W})_{[\varphi]}$ with idempotent element $\frac{1}{2}$.

The last construction method we want to mention goes back to the semigroup construction methods of Climescu [8] and Clifford [7].

Theorem 5. 3. Let ($]\alpha_k, \beta_k[$) $_{k\in K}$ be a disjoint system of open subintervals of [0,1] and let $(T_k)_{k\in K}$ be a system of t-norms. Then the two-place function
$T: [0, 1]^2 \to [0, 1]$
defined by

$$T(x, y) = \\ = \begin{cases} \alpha_k + (\beta_k - \alpha_k)T\left(\dfrac{x-\alpha_k}{\beta_k-\alpha_k}, \dfrac{y-\alpha_k}{\beta_k-\alpha_k}\right) & \text{if } (x,y)\in[\alpha_k,\beta_k] \text{for some } k\in K \\ min(x,y) & \text{otherwise} \end{cases}$$

is a t-norm. **T** is called an ordinal sum with summands $<\alpha_k, \beta_k, T_k>$, $k \in K$, and the notation $T \approx (<\alpha_k, \beta_k, T_k>, k \in K)$ is used.
As an example, recall the t-norm $(T_W)_{[\varphi]}$ given by (10), which is, indeed, an ordinal sum, $(T_W)_{[\varphi]} \approx (<0, \frac{1}{2}, T_W>, <\frac{1}{2}, 1, T_W>)$. Note that each t-norm T can be represented as $T \approx (<0,1,T>)$. If this is the only ordinal sum representation then T is called ordinaly irreducible. As an example, t-norms T_P, T_L, T_W, T_{NM}, T_{BK} are ordinaly irreducible.
On the other hand, $T_M \approx (<\alpha, \beta, T_M>)$ for any $]\alpha, \beta[\subset [0, 1]$ (even $T_M \approx \emptyset$!).
Among the class of continuous t-norms, only strict and nilpotent t-norms are ordinaly irreducible. The representation of continuous t-norms is the topic of the next section.

6. Continuous Triangular Norms

The largest class of t-norms which structure is perfectly known is just the class of all continuous t-norms. The results of this section are based on the results of Aczél [2, 3], Mostert and Schields [42], Ling [32].

Theorem 6.1. Let **T** be a continuous Archimedean t-norm. Then there is a continuous additive generator f: $[0, 1] \to [0, \infty]$ so that for all x, y $\in$ [0, 1], $T(x,y) = f^{(-1)}(f(x) + f(y)) = f^{-1}(min\,(f(0), f(x) + f(y)))$. **T** is strict if and only if $f(0) = +\infty$, otherwise **T** is nilpotent.

Theorem 6. 1. together with Proposition 5. 1. and 5. 2. shows that continuous Archimedean t-norms are exactly those t-norms which are generated by a continuous additive generator. Therefore each strict t-norm is isomorphic with another strict t-norm (e. g., with T_P). Especially, let T_1 and T_2 be strict t-norms with additive generators f_1 and f_2, respectively. Then φ: $[0, 1] \to [0, 1]$ defined by

$\varphi = f_1^{-1} \circ f_2$ is an increasing bijection and $(\mathbf{T}_1)_{[\varphi]} = \mathbf{T}_2$. Recall that also $c_1.f_1$, $c_1 > 0$, is a generator of $\mathbf{T}_1$, and similarly $c_2.f_2$, $c_2 > 0$, generates $\mathbf{T}_2$. Consequently, the isomorphism φ between $\mathbf{T}_1$ and $\mathbf{T}_2$ of two strict t-norms is not unique (see also Proposition 5. 3. (ii)). Namely, η: [0, 1] → [0, 1] defined by $\eta = (c_1.f_1)^{-1} \circ (c_2.f_2)$, i. e., $\eta(x) = f_1^{-1}(\frac{c_2}{c_1} f_2(x)) = f_1^{-1}(d\, f_2(x))$, is another isomorphism between $\mathbf{T}_1$ and $\mathbf{T}_2$ whenever $d \neq 1$, i. e., $c_1 \neq c_2$.

For two nilpotent t-norms $\mathbf{T}_1$ and $\mathbf{T}_2$ we have a slightly modified result. Any two nilpotent t-norms are isomorphic (and especially isomorphic with $\mathbf{T}_L$), but the corresponding isomorphism is unique, see also Proposition 5.3. (iii). Namely, if two normed generators f_1 and f_2 (which are unique!) generate the nilpotent t-norms $\mathbf{T}_1$ and $\mathbf{T}_2$, respectively, then the corresponding isomorphism is $\varphi = f_1^{-1} \circ f_2$.
For a general continuous t-norm **T** we have the following characterization.

Theorem 6. 2. Let **T** be a continuous t-norm. Then $\mathbf{ID_T}$ is a closed subset of [0, 1] and its complement $[0, 1] \setminus \mathbf{ID_T}$ can be uniquely represented as a union of disjoint open intervals (perhaps empty union), $[0, 1] \setminus \mathbf{ID_T} = \bigcup_{k \in K}]\alpha_k, \beta_k[$. Further, **T** is an ordinal sum with Archimedean summands, i. e. , $\mathbf{T} = (<\alpha_k, \beta_k, \mathbf{T}_k>, k \in K)$, where each $\mathbf{T}_k$, $k \in K$, is either strict or nilpotent t-norm.

Note that in the case of continuous t-norms, their commutativity follows from the other axioms [42].
Due to Theorem 6. 1., any $\mathbf{T}_k$ in Theorem 6. 2. can be generated by means of some continuous additive generator f_k: [0, 1] → [0, ∞], $k \in K$. Put h_k: $[\alpha_k, \beta_k] \to [0, \infty]$, $k \in K$, $h_k = f_k \circ \tau_k$, where τ_k: $[\alpha_k, \beta_k] \to [0, 1]$ is the increasing affine bijection, $\tau_k(x) = \dfrac{x - \alpha_k}{\beta_k - \alpha_k}$. Then any continuous t-norm **T** characterized by Theorem 6. 2. can be represented in the next form, $\mathbf{T} \approx (<\alpha_k, \beta_k, h_k>, k \in K)$,

$$\mathbf{T}(x, y) = \begin{cases} h_k^{(-1)}(h_k(x) + h_k(y)) & (x, y) \in [\alpha_k, \beta_k]^2 \text{ for some } k \in K \\ min(x, y) & \text{otherwise} \end{cases},$$

where h_k: $[\alpha_k, \beta_k] \to [0, \infty]$ is continuous and strictly decreasing mapping with $h_k(\beta_k) = 0$, and $h_k^{(-1)}$: $[0, \infty] \to [\alpha_k, \beta_k]$, $h_k^{(-1)}(t) = h_k^{-1}(\, min(h_k(\alpha_k), t)\,)$. Among several interesting results on continuous t-norms, recall the following ones.

Proposition 6. 1. [47] For a given t-norm **T** and $n \in N$, put $\mathbf{T}^{(n)}$: [0, 1] → [0, 1], $\mathbf{T}^{(n)}(x) = x^{(n)}_{\mathbf{T}}$. Then a continuous t-norm **T** is of Hadžič - type, i. e., the functional sequence $\{\mathbf{T}^{(n)}\}_{n \in N}$ is uniformly continuous in point 1, if and only if $\sup(\mathbf{ID_T} \setminus \{1\}) = 1$.

Proposition 6. 2. [9]. Let f be an additive generator of a continuous t-norm **T** and let $\lambda \in]0,\infty[$. Then f^{λ} is also an additive generator and it generates some t-norm $\mathbf{T}_\lambda$. More,

$$\lim_{\lambda \to 0^+} \mathbf{T}_\lambda = \mathbf{T}_W$$

and .

$$\lim_{\lambda \to \infty} \mathbf{T}_\lambda = \mathbf{T}_M$$

Proposition 6. 3. [23] Let $\{\mathbf{T}_n\}_{n\in N}$, **T** be continuous Archimedean t-norms. Then $\lim_{n\to\infty} \mathbf{T}_n = \mathbf{T}$ if and only if there exist additive generators $\{f_n\}_{n\in N}$, f, generating the corresponding t-norms, such that
$\lim_{n\to\infty} f_n(x) = f(x)$ for all $x \in]0, 1]$.

Note that the strict t-norms may converge also to a nilpotent t-norm (which is, e. g., the case of Frank family). However, each generator of a strict t-norm has value $+\infty$ in point 0, while each generator of a nilpotent t-norm is finite in 0.

Proposition 6.2. is important from approximation point of view, showing that $\mathbf{T}_M$ (which has no additive generator) can be approximated by generated t-norms. More, this approximation is uniform! Due to the results of Fodor and Jenei [16], the same holds true for an arbitrary continuous t-norm.

Proposition 6. 4. Let **T** be a continuous t-norm. Then for any $\varepsilon > 0$ there is a continuous additive generator f_ε generating a continuous Archimedean t-norm $\mathbf{T}_\varepsilon$ such that for all $x, y \in [0,1]$ it is $|\mathbf{T}(x, y) - \mathbf{T}_\varepsilon(x, y)| < \varepsilon$.

Another interesting result concerns the ordering of t-norms. For two continuous Archimedean t-norms $\mathbf{T}_1$ and $\mathbf{T}_2$ with additive generators f_1 and f_2, respectively, the relationship $\mathbf{T}_1 \le \mathbf{T}_2$ is equivalent to the subadditivity of the composite function $h = f_1 \circ f_2^{-1}$ [53]. Several sufficient conditions ensuring $\mathbf{T}_1 \le \mathbf{T}_2$ (e. g., the monotonicity of $\frac{f_1'}{f_2'}$) , as well as the comparison of t-norms in the general continuous case, can be found in [30].
Several interesting results concern the diagonal of a continuous t-norm **T**. Recall, e. g., the famous open problem from [52]:
let **T** be a t-norm and let $\mathbf{T}^{(2)} = \delta$ (diagonal of **T**) be a continuous function, is **T** necessarily continuous?

It is known, that two different continuous t-norms can coincide on diagonal [26, 39]. The only exception is the strongest t-norm $\mathbf{T}_M$. However, strict t-norm **T** is uniquely determined by its diagonal $\mathbf{T}^{(2)}$ and the opposite diagonal $\mathbf{T}(x, 1 - x)$, $x \in [0, 1]$, see [4]. For an exhaustive overview of other results and properties we recommend the prepared monograph of Klement, Mesiar and Pap, and a special issue of the journal Fuzzy Sets and Systems devoted to t-norms (in preparation, guest editors B. De Baets and R. Mesiar).

7. Related Operations and Fields of Applications

In the last section, we sketch some of the related operations and their properties, as well as some of the fields of applications of t-norms (and related operations). Recall the t-conorms, which were not treated till now due to their duality with t-norms. Triangular norms and conorms are widely used in the fuzzy set theory as a basis of fuzzy intersection and union, respectively. However, not all properties of intersection and union on crisp sets may be extended to the fuzzy framework. So, for example, the idempotency $A \cap A = A$ (or $A \cup A = A$) of crisp set case leads to the only possible t-norm, namely $\mathbf{T_M}$ (t-conorm, $\mathbf{S_M} = max$, dual to $\mathbf{T_M}$), in the fuzzy set framework. But then law of non-contradiction $A \cap A^c = \varnothing$ (the excluded middle law $A \cup A^c = X$) is violated for any proper fuzzy subset. Vice versa, we can ensure the validity of both above mentioned laws. Take, e. g., the Lukasiewicz t-norm $\mathbf{T_L}$ as a basis of fuzzy intersection, its dual $\mathbf{S_L}$, $\mathbf{S_L}(x, y) = min(1, x + y)$ as a basis of fuzzy union, and the standard negation n, $n(x) = 1 - x$, $x \in [0, 1]$, as a basis of fuzzy complementation. Then for any fuzzy subset A of the universe X we have $A \cap A^c = \varnothing$ and $A \cup A^c = X$. However, in the last case the idempotency $A \cap A = A$ and $A \cup A = A$ holds only if A is a crisp set. For an overview we recommend [18, 33, 44, 64].

Another field of applications of t-norms is the fuzzy logic area (i. e., many-valued logic with [0, 1] interval as truth-values range). Here, t-norms play the role of a fuzzy conjunction while t-conorms model the fuzzy disjunction. The negation is modeled by several types of non-increasing mappings $[0, 1] \to [0, 1]$. In any kind of logic we need some kind of implication. Fuzzy logic implications are mostly closely connected with t-norms and t-conorms (in a similar way as the standard implication is connected with conjunction and disjunction). Having only a t-norm $\mathbf{T}$, we can derive a residual implicator $R_\mathbf{T}: [0,1]^2 \to [0, 1]$,

$$R_\mathbf{T}(x, y) = sup(z \in [0, 1]; \mathbf{T}(x, z) \le y).$$

$R_\mathbf{T}$ is an extension of the standard crisp implication, however, a backward derivation of the starting t-norm is possible only in the case when $\mathbf{T}$ is a left-continuous t-norm. Therefore the fuzzy logic conjunctions exploit usualy the left-continuous t-norm only. More, so called Φ-operators introduced by Pedrycz [48], $\varphi: [0, 1]^2 \to [0, 1]$,

(Φ1) $\quad \varphi(x, y) \le \varphi(x, z)$ whenever $y \le z$

(Φ2) $\quad \mathbf{T}(x, \varphi(x, y)) \le y$

(Φ3) $\quad y \le \varphi(x, \mathbf{T}(x, y))$,

exist only if $\mathbf{T}$ is left-continuous and in that case $\varphi = R_\mathbf{T}$. For more details about fuzzy logic connectives we refer to [18,21, 44].

Triangular conorms were used as a composition rule in the fuzzy measure theory [46, 54, 58, 60]. In general, the non-additive measure theory uses as a composition rule some binary operation $\oplus:[a, b]^2 \rightarrow [a, b]$ (a pseudo-addition) which is monotone, associative, continuous and a is its neutral element. But then $\oplus$ fulfilles all axioms for continuous t-norms (up to the domain and range). As far as the commutativity is the consequence of the other axioms of $\oplus$, $\oplus$ is isomorphic with a continuous t-norm), and therefore it has an ordinal sum structure. For building up an integral, one needs some kind of multiplication. Among several types of pseudo-multiplications, recall, e. g., the PAN-multiplication $\otimes$: $[0, \infty]^2 \rightarrow [0, \infty]$, which is associative, commutative, distributive with respect to given PAN-addition $\oplus$, monotone, and it has a neutral element e, see [41, 58]. The PAN-multiplication $\otimes$ is isomorphic to some uni-norm **U** [15, 29, 62], i. e., an associative, monotone, commutative binary operation on [0, 1] with neutral element u. Note that **U** = **T** is a t-norm if u = 1, **U** = **S** is a t-conorm if u = 0, and if $u \in]0, 1[$, then $\mathbf{U} \mid [0, u]^2$ acts as a t-norm while $\mathbf{U} \mid [u, 1]^2$ acts as a t-conorm. For more details about pseudo-additions, pseudo-multiplications and uni-norms we recommend [15, 29, 46, 55, 60, 62]. An alternative approach, concerning the measures of fuzzy sets, is treated in [6]. Here the key role is played by the Frank t-norms stressing the validity of the valuation property of fuzzy intersections and fuzzy unions.
Among other fields of applications of t-norms and related operations, we cannot omit the area of probability theory, and especially the probabilistic metric spaces [47, 52]. Recall also the information theory [24, 25], multi-criteria decision making [14, 19], aggregation operators [11, 29, 31], etc.

Acknowledgment
The work on this overview was supported by University Dortmund, Dept. Informatics I, and by grant VEGA 1/4064/97

References

1. N. H. Abel. Untersuchungen der Funktionen zweier unabhängigen veränderlichen Größen x und y wie *f (x, y)*, welche die Eigenschaft haben, daß *f (z, f x, y))* eine symmetrische Funktion von x, y und z ist. *J. Reine Angew. Math.*,1:11-15, 1826.
2. J. Aczél. Sur les opérations definies pour des nombres réels. *Bull. Soc. Math. France,* 76:59-64, 1949.
3. J. Aczél. *Lectures on Functional Equations and their Applications.* Academic Press, New York, 1966.

4. J. P. Bézivin and M. S. Tomás. On the determination of strict t-norms on some diagonal segments. *Aequat. Math.*, 45:239-245, 1993.
5. M. Budinčevič and M. KuriliČ. A family of strict and discontinuous triangular norms. *Fuzzy Sets and Systems* 95: 381-384, 1998.
6. D. Butnariu and E. P. Klement. *Triangular Norm-Based Measures and Games with Fuzzy Coalitions.* Kluwer, Dordrecht,1993
7. H. Clifford. Naturally totally ordered commutative semigroups. *Amer. J. Math.*, 76:631-646, 1954.
8. C. Climescu. Sur l'équation fonctionelle de l'associativité. *Bull. École Polytechnique Iassy*,1:1-16, 1946.
9. J. Dombi. A general class of fuzzy operators, De Morgan class of fuzzy operators and fuzziness measures induced by fuzzy operators. *Fuzzy Sets and Systems,* 8:149-163,1982.
10. D. Dubois. Triangular norms for fuzzy sets. In: E. P. Klement, editor, *Proceedings Second Intern. Sem. on Fuzzy Set Theory,* Linz, 39-68,1980.
11. D. Dubois and H. Prade. A review of fuzzy set aggregation connectives. *Inf. Sci.,* 36:85- 121, 1985.
12. W. M. Faucett. Compact semigroups irreducibly connected between two idempotents. *Proc. Amer. Math. Soc.*, 6:741-747, 1955.
13. J. C. Fodor. Contrapositive symmetry of fuzzy implications. *Fuzzy Sets and Systems,* 69: 141 – 156, 1995
14. J. C. Fodor and M. Roubens. *Fuzzy Preference Modelling and Multi-Criteria Decision Support*, Kluwer, Dordrecht, 1994
15. J. C. Fodor, R. R. Yager, and A. Rybalov. Structure of uni-norms. *Int. J. Uncertainty, Fuzziness and Knowledge-Based Systems*, 5: 411 – 427, 1997
16. J. C. Fodor, S. Jenei. On continuous triangular norms. *Fuzzy Sets and Systems,* (in press)
17. M. J. Frank. On the simultaneous associativity of F(x, y) and x + y - F(x, y). *Aequat.* Math.,19:194-226, 1979.
18. S. Gottwald. *Fuzzy Sets and Fuzzy Logic. Foundations and Applications - from a Mathematical Point of View.* Vieweg, Braunschweig-Wiesbaden, 1993.
19. M. Grabisch. Fuzzy integral in multicriteria decision making. *Fuzzy Sets and Systems,* 69:279-298, 1995.
20. M. Grabisch, T. Murofushi, M. Sugeno. Fuzzy measure of fuzzy events defined by fuzzy integral. *Fuzzy Sets and Systems*, 50: 293 – 313, 1992
21. P. Hájek, L. Godo, and F. Esteva. A complete many-valued logic with product-conjunction. *Archive Math. Logic,* 35:191-208, 1996

22. H. Hamacher. *Über logische Aggregationen nicht-binär explizierter Entscheidungskriterien.* Rita G. Fischer Verlag, Frankfurt,1978

23. S. Jenei. On Archimedean triangular norms. *Fuzzy Sets and Systems,* (in press)

24. J. Kampé de Fériet. Mesures de l'information par un ensemble d'observateurs. *C. R. Acad. Sci. Paris, Série A,* 269:1081-1085, 1969.

25. J. Kampé de Fériet, B. Forte, and P. Benvenuti. Forme génerale de l'opération de composition continue d'une information. *C. R. Acad. Sci. Paris, Série A,* 269:529-534, 1969.

26. J. C. Kimberling. On a class of associative functions. *Publ. Math. Debrecen,* 20:21-39,1973

27. E. P. Klement. Some remarks on t-norms, fuzzy σ-algebras and fuzzy measures. In E. P. Klement, editor, *Proceedings Second Intern. Sem. on Fuzzy Set Theory, Linz,* 125- 142,1980

28. E. P. Klement. Characterization of fuzzy measures constructed by means of triangular norms. *J. Math. Anal. Appl.,* 86:345-358, 1982.

29. E. P. Klement, R. Mesiar, and E. Pap. On the relationship of associative compensatory operators to triangular norms and conorms. Int. J. *Uncertainty, Fuzziness and Knowledge-Based Systems,* 4:129-144, 1996

30. E. P. Klement, R. Mesiar, and E. Pap. A characterization of the ordering of continuous t-norms. *Fuzzy Sets and Systems,* 86: 189 – 195, 1997

31. A. Kolesárová, M. Komorníková. Triangular norm-based iterative compensatory operators. *Fuzzy Sets and Systems,* to appear.

32. C. Ling. Representation of associative functions. *Publ. Math. Debrecen,* 12:189-212, 1965

33. R. Lowen. *Fuzzy Sets Theory.* Kluwer, Dordrecht, 1997

34. J. Lukasiewicz. Bemerkungen zu mehrwertigen Systemen des Aussagenkalküls. *Comptes Rendus Séances Société des Sciences et Lettres Varsovie cl. III,* 23:51-77, 1930

35. K. Menger. Statistical metrics. *Proc. Nat. Acad. Sci.,* U.S.A., 8:535-537, 1942

36. R. Mesiar. Fundamental triangular norm based tribes and measures. *J. Math. Anal. Appl.,* 177: 633 – 640, 1993

37. R. Mesiar. Choquet-like integrals. *J. Math. Anal. Appl.,*194:477-488, 1995

38. R. Mesiar and M. Navara. T_s-tribes and T_s-measures. *J. Math. Anal. Appl.,* 201:91-102, 1996

39. R. Mesiar, M. Navara. Diagonals of continuous t-norms. *Fuzzy Sets and Systems,* to appear

40. R. Mesiar, E. Pap. Different interpretations of triangulars norms. *Fuzzy Sets and Systems,* (in press)
41. R. Mesiar and J. Rybárik. Pan-operations structure. *Fuzzy Sets and Systems*, 74: 365 – 369, 1995
42. P. S. Mostert and A. L. Shields. On the structure of semigroups on a compact manifold with boundary. *Ann. Math.*, 65:117-143, 1957
43. N. T. Nguyen, H. Walker. *A First Course in Fuzzy Logic*. CRC Press, Boca Raton, 1997
44. V. Novák. *Fuzzy Sets and Their Applications*. A. Hilger, Bristol, 1989
45. B. Paalman-de Miranda. *Topological Semigroups*, volume 11 of Mathematical Centre Tracts. Matematisch Centrum, Amsterdam,1970
46. E. Pap. *Null-Additive Set Functions*. Kluwer and Ister Science, Dordrecht and Bratislava,1995
47. E. Pap, O. Hadžič, and R. Mesiar. A fixed point theorem in probabilistic metric spaces. *J. Math. Anal. Appl.*, 202: 433 – 449, 1996.
48. W. Pedrycz. *Fuzzy Control and Fuzzy Systems*. Dept. Math., Delft Univ. of Technology, Report 82, 14, 1982
49. B. Schweizer and A. Sklar. Espaces métriques aléatoires. *C. R. Acad. Sci. Paris, Série* A, 247:2092-2094, 1958.
50. B. Schweizer and A. Sklar. Statistical metric spaces. *Pacific J. Math.*,10:313-334,1960.
51. B. Schweizer and A. Sklar. Associative functions and abstract semigroups. *Publ. Math. Debrecen*,10:69-81, 1963
52. B. Schweizer and A. Sklar. *Probabilistic Metric Spaces*. North-Holland, Amsterdam,1983
53. D. Smutná: On a peculiar t-norm. *Busefal*, to appear.
54. M. Sugeno. *Theory of fuzzy integrals and its applications*. PhD thesis, Tokyo Institute of Technology, 1974
55. M. Sugeno and T. Murofushi. Pseudo-additive measures and integrals. *J. Math. Anal. Appl.*,122:197-222, 1987
56. P. Viceník. A note to a construction of t-norms by means of a pseudo-inverse of a monotone functions. *Fuzzy Sets and Systems*, to appear
57. P. Viceník: A note to generators of t-norms. *Busefal*, to appear.
58. Z. Wang and G. J. Klir. *Fuzzy Measure Theory*. Plenum Press, New York,1992
59. S. Weber. A general concept of fuzzy connectives, negations and implications based on t-norms and t-conorms. *Fuzzy Sets and Systems*, 11:115-134, 1983
60. S. Weber. Decomposable measures and integrals for Archimedean t-conorms. *J. Math. Anal. Appl.*,101:114-138, 1984.

61. R. R. Yager. On a general class of fuzzy connectives. *Fuzzy Sets and Systems,* 4:235-242, 1980
62. R. R. Yager and A. Rybalov. Uninorm aggregation operators. *Fuzzy Sets* and *Systems,* 80:111-120, 1996
63. L. A. Zadeh. Fuzzy sets. *Inform. Control,* 8:338-353,1965
64. H.-J. Zimmermann. *Fuzzy Set Theory and Its Applications.* Kluwer, Dordrecht,1991

A First View on the Alternatives of Fuzzy Set Theory

E.E. Kerre

Department of Applied Mathematics & Computer Science
University Gent, Krijgslaan 281 – S9
B9000 Gent, Belgium

Abstract. During many centuries probability theory and error calculus have been the only models to treat imprecision and uncertainty. In the past three decennia however a lot of new models have been introduced for handling incomplete information. Undoubtly fuzzy set theory initiated by Zadeh [1] in 1965 plays the central role. Besides this widely applied theory, many other models pretending to be competitive with fuzzy set theory have been launched: rough set theory, flou set theory, L-flou set theory, intuitionistic set theory ... Allthough we are convinced that freedom and openness in research has be be respected in a degree as large as possible we will warn for increasing the number of alternatives to a degree that introduces confusion and hence diminishes the trust in our models, especially for new practitioners. As I already mentioned in a previous paper [2], time has come to clean up the existing material, to summarize the relevant theoretical models and indicate their relevance by means of convicting concrete examples, by which I do not mean the stipulation in a superficial way of some possible areas of application but indeed the description of real situations and the solution of real problems. In this talk we will focuss on several alternative theories and try to indicate their mutual relationships and their relationships to earlier existing mathematical models.
We will start with a short overview of the basic operations on the class of fuzzy sets and indicate the loss of structure (in this case a Kleene algebra) comparing to the Boolean algebra of (crisp) set theory. Secondly we will briefly outline Goguen's [3] extension to L-fuzzy set theory where L denotes a complete lattice. Next we will introduce the structure of Gentilhomme's flou set theory as well as its extension to n-flou sets and L-flou sets as given by Negoïta and Ralescu [5]. In the last model L denotes a complete lattice satisfying some supplementary condition (L):
(L)($8A$ L)($8a$ 2 L)($a <$ sup$A$) ($9b$ 2 A)(a b))
For an extensive treatment of such lattices, the so-called kite-tail lattices, we refer to [6]. The sixth model that will presented is the theory of twofold fuzzy sets as introduced by Dubois and Prade [7] in 1987. Finally Pawlak's [8] rough set theory will be briefly described.
In the second part of this paper we will outline some links between the models mentioned above. In particular it will be shown that:

1. Fuzzy set theory is an extension of flou set theory.
2. L-fuzzy set theory is equivalent to L-flou set theory for L a complete lattice satisfying the supplementary condition (L).

3. f0, 1g-flou set theory is equivalent to set theory.
4. f0, $\frac{1}{2}$, 1g-flou set theory is equivalent to flou set theory.
5. [0, 1]-flou set theory is equivalent to fuzzy set theory.
6. Twofold fuzzy set theory extends flou set theory.
7. Twofold fuzzy set theory is equivalent to fuzzy set theory.
8. Flou set theory extends rough set theory.

1.1 A survey of different models of imprecision and uncertainty

Starting from an arbitrary universe X, every crisp property P formulated about the elements of this universe, partitions it into two disjoint subclasses, i.e., the set A of elements of X that satisfy P and the set co$A$ of elements of X that don't satisfy P. The powerclass $\mathcal{P}(X)$, i.e., the class of all subsets A of X that correspond to the different crisp properties that can be formulated about X, can be provided with the binary set-theoretic operations of union and intersection and with the unary set-theoretic operation of complementation. It is well-known that the structure $(\mathcal{P}(X), \cup, \cap, \text{co})$ constitutes a Boolean algebra, i.e. a complemented, bounded distributive lattice, considered as an order structure. or as an algebraic structure satisfying the famous mutually independent Huntington axioms for A, B, C arbitrary elements of $\mathcal{P}(X)$:

B.1 $A \cup B = B \cup A$ B.1' $A \cap B = B \cap A$
commutative laws
B.2 $A \cup (B \cap C) = (A \cup B) \cap (A \cup C)$ B.2' $A \cap (B \cup C) = (A \cap B) \cup (A \cap C)$
distributive laws
B.3 $A \cup \emptyset = A$ B.3' $A \cap X = A$
neutral elements
B.4 $A \cup \text{co}A = X$ B.4' $A \cap \text{co}A = \emptyset$
complementation laws

The orderrelation $\subseteq$ (inclusion) and the algebraic operations ($\cup$ and $\cap$) are related by:
$A \subseteq B \Leftrightarrow A \cup B = B \Leftrightarrow A \cap B = A$
Note that the complementation axiom B.4 relies on the law of the excluded middle and B.4' on the law of contradiction.
However starting from an arbitrary universe not every property formulated about its elements will be crisp. On the contrary many properties are imprecise because they are described by means of fuzzy predicates such as large, high, low, young, ...
At the same time propositions may be uncertain since their truth or falsity cannot be claimed. Classically there are two ways to represent uncertainty: probability theory and error calculus. As extensively argued in Zadeh [9], the

longstanding tradition in science to treat any kind of uncertainty with probability theory can be questioned. Classical probability theory is insufficiently expressing to serve as the language of uncertainty. It has no facilities to describe fuzzy predicates such as young, small, much larger than ..., fuzzy quantifiers such as most, many, about one third ..., fuzzy probabilities such as likely, not very likely ..., and fuzzy truth values such as very true, more-or-less false ...

In this section we will outline some of the many new theories that have been developed during the last three decennia in order to model imprecision and uncertainty.

1.1.1 Fuzzy set theory in Zadeh's sense

A fuzzy set on a universe X is a mapping from X into the unit interval $[0, 1]$. The value $A(x)$ of A in $x \in X$ is called the degree of membership of x in A. The following notions related to a fuzzy set A on X will be used in the sequel:

- the support of A defined as:
  $\text{supp}A = \{x|x \in X \text{ and } A(x) > 0\}$
- the core or kernel of A defined as:
  $\text{core}A = \{x|x \in X \text{ and } A(x) = 1\}$
- the weak α-level ($\alpha \in]0, 1]$) of A defined as:
  $A_\alpha = \{x|x \in X \text{ and } A(x) \geq \alpha\}$
- the strong α-level ($\alpha \in [0, 1[$) of A defined as:
  $A_{\overline{\alpha}} = \{x|x \in X \text{ and } A(x) > \alpha\}$

The class of all fuzzy sets on X will be denoted as $\mathcal{F}(X)$. Following Zadeh $\mathcal{F}(X)$ can be endowed with two binary operations union ($\cup$) and intersection ($\cap$) and one unary operation (pseudo-) complementation co defined as for $A \in \mathcal{F}(X), B \in \mathcal{F}(X)$:
$\text{co}A(x) = 1 - A(x), \forall x \in X$
$A \cup B(x) = \max(A(x), B(x)), \forall x \in X$
$A \cap B(x) = \min(A(x), B(x)), \forall x \in X$
or, more generally, for an arbitrary family $(A_j)_{j2\,J}$ of elements of $\mathcal{F}(X)$:
$\cup_{j2\,J} A_j(x) = \sup_{j2\,J} A_j(x)$
$\cap_{j2\,J} A_j(x) = \inf_{j2\,J} A_j(x)$
The class $\mathcal{F}(X)$ can be endowed with a partial order relation $\subseteq$:
$A \subseteq B \Leftrightarrow (\forall x \in X)(A(x) \leq B(x))$
that is compatible with the extended (fuzzy) union and intersection, i.e.,
$A \subseteq B \Leftrightarrow A \cup B = B \Leftrightarrow A \cap B = A$
The Zadeh class of fuzzy sets $(\mathcal{F}(X), \cup, \cap, \text{co})$ no longer constitutes a Boolean algebra as $(\mathcal{P}(X), \cup, \cap, \text{co})$ does but only reveals the structure of a Morgan algebra, i.e., a bounded, distributive lattice satisfying the supplementary properties:

(M1) $\text{co}(\text{co}A) = A$ (co is involutive)
(M2) $\text{co}(A \cup B) = \text{co}A \cap \text{co}B$
$\text{co}(A \cap B) = \text{co}A \cup \text{co}B$ (de Morgan laws)
(M3) $\text{co}\emptyset = X$, $\text{co}X = \emptyset$

Moreover $(\mathcal{F}(X), \cup, \cap, \text{co})$ satisfies:
$A \cap \text{co}A \subseteq B \cup \text{co}B$
for arbitrary fuzzy sets A and B on X. Hence $(\mathcal{F}(X), \cup, \cap, \text{co})$ is a Kleene algebra. In particular we can state that $(\mathcal{F}(X), \cup, \cap)$is a complete lattice. The main deviations from the "crisp" power class are:

(D.1) Only a weakened law of contradiction holds:
$A \cap \text{co}A \subseteq k_{0.5}$
where $k_{0.5}$ is the constant $X - \{0.5\}$ mapping, i.e., a partial overlap between a fuzzy set and its complement remains possible.

(D.2) Only a weakened law of excluded middle holds:
$k_{0.5} \subseteq A \cup \text{co}A$
i.e., a fuzzy set and its complement not necessarily fill up the universe completely.

(D.3) $A \cap B = \emptyset \Rightarrow A \subseteq \text{co}B$
but not the reverse implication.

(D.4) $A \cup B = X \Rightarrow \text{co}A \subseteq B$
but not the reverse implication.

The deviation (D.3) has had a great impact on the fuzzification of notions involving disjoint sets. For an illustration of this impact we refer to Kerre [10]. Now consider the following mapping:

$$\Phi_1 : \mathcal{P}(X) \to \mathcal{F}(X)$$
$$A \mapsto \chi_A, \quad \forall A \in \mathcal{P}(X)$$

where χ_A denotes the characteristic mapping of A defined as: $\chi_A(x) = 1 \Leftrightarrow x \in A, \forall x \in X$.
It is easily verified that Φ_1 is an injective mapping satisfying for arbitrary A and B in $\mathcal{P}(X)$:

$\Phi_1(A \cup B) = \Phi_1(A) \cup \Phi_1(B)$
$\Phi_1(A \cap B) = \Phi_1(A) \cap \Phi_1(B)$
$\Phi_1(\text{co}A) = \text{co}\Phi_1(A)$
$A \subseteq B \Leftrightarrow \Phi_1(A) \subseteq \Phi_1(B)$

Hence Φ_1 is an embedding of $(\mathcal{P}(X), \cup, \cap, \text{co})$ into $(\mathcal{F}(X), \cup, \cap, \text{co})$ and in this way fuzzy set theory (in Zadeh's sense) may be seen as a natural extension of set theory.

1.1.2 Fuzzy set theory in Schweizer-Sklar's sense

Already very soon after Zadeh's creation of fuzzy set theory researchers became aware of the fact that maximum and minimum are not the only possible operations to generalize crisp union and intersection. Indeed triangular norms and conorms as introduced by Schweizer and Sklar [11] in the framework of probabilistic metric spaces became very popular in the fuzzy litterature. A triangular norm T (resp. conorm S) is a $[0,1]^2 - [0,1]$ mapping satisfying commutativity, associativity, non-decreasingness and the boundary condition $(\forall x \in [0,1])(T(x,1) = x)$ (resp. $(\forall x \in [0,1])(S(x,0) = x)$). Well-known popular choices of triangular norms are

- the minimum operator: $M(x,y) = \min(x,y)$
- the algebraic product: $P(x,y) = xy$
- the Lukasiewicz norm: $\mathcal{L}(x,y) = \max(0, x+y-1)$
- the drastic norm:

$$\begin{aligned} Z(x,y) &= x \text{ if } y = 1 \\ &= y \text{ if } x = 1 \\ &= 0 \text{ elsewhere.} \end{aligned}$$

To every triangular conorm S and triangular norm T there corresponds a fuzzy set-theoretic union $\cup_S$ and intersection $\cap_T$ defined as:

$A \cup_S B(x) = S(A(x), B(x)), \forall x \in X$

$A \cap_T B(x) = T(A(x), B(x)), \forall x \in X$

for A and B fuzzy sets on X.

A general complementation co_c for fuzzy sets can be defined by means of a $[0,1] - [0,1]$ mapping c that satisfies the boundary conditions $c(0) = 1, c(1) = 0$ and some other properties such as monotonicity, continuity and involution:

$(\text{co}_c A)(x) = c(A(x)), \forall x \in X$

for A a fuzzy set on X.

For a good description of such a c-operator we refer to Klir and Folger [12]. Each choice of the binary operators S, T and the unary operator c gives rise to an alternative structure $(\mathcal{F}(X), \cup_S, \cap_T, \text{co}_c)$ called STc-fuzzy set theory. All these theories extend (crisp) set theory. Indeed the injective mapping Φ_1 as introduced in the previous section satisfies the following properties for arbitrary crisp subsets A and B of X:

$\Phi_1(A \cup B) = \Phi_1(A) \cup_S \Phi_1(B)$

$\Phi_1(A \cap B) = \Phi_1(A) \cap_T \Phi_1(B)$

$\Phi_1(\text{co}A) = \text{co}_c \Phi_1(A)$

The properties of the structure $(\mathcal{F}(X), \cup_S, \cap_T, \text{co}_c)$ heavily depend on the choice of the operators S, T and c involved.

For an extensive outline of fuzzy set theory based on the Lukasiewicz norm and its dual conorm the bounded sum we refer to Guinan et al [13]. For a similar overview of fuzzy set theory based on the algebraic product and its dual conorm the probabilistic sum we refer to Kerre [14].

1.1.3 *L*-fuzzy set therory in Goguen's sense

As pointed out by Goguen [3] there may be situations in which it is not possible to use the totally ordered unit interval to represent degrees of membership. The major part of those situations may be captured using a complete lattice $(L, \leq)$ as an evaluation set. So Goguen defined an L-fuzzy set on a universe X as a $X - L$ mapping. The class of L-fuzzy sets on X will be

denoted as $\mathcal{F}_L(X)$. A pointwise application of the lattice operations sup and inf on L leads to the introduction of binary operations on $\mathcal{F}_L(X)$. For A and B elements of $\mathcal{F}_L(X)$ we define:
$A \cup B(x) = \sup(A(x), B(x)), \forall x \in X$
$A \cap B(x) = \inf(A(x), B(x)), \forall x \in X$
and, more generally, for an arbitrary family $(A_j)_{j2\,J}$ of L-fuzzy sets on X, we have
$\cup_{j2\,J} A_j(x) = \sup_{j2\,J} A_j(x)$
$\cap_{j2\,J} A_j(x) = \inf_{j2\,J} A_j(x)$
which are meaningfull because of the completeness of the lattice $(L, \leq)$.
It is easy to check that $(\mathcal{F}(X), \cup, \cap)$ constitutes a complete lattice with smallest element the constant $X - \{0\}$ mapping and greatest element the constant $X - \{1\}$ mapping where $0, 1$ denote the identities of L. The mapping Φ_1^0 defined as:

$$\begin{aligned} \Phi_1^0 : \mathcal{P}(X) &\to \mathcal{F}_L(X) \\ A &\mapsto \chi_A, \forall A \in \mathcal{P}(X) \end{aligned}$$

is an injection satisfying for every A and B in $\mathcal{P}(X)$:
$\Phi_1^0(A \cup B) = \Phi_1^0(A) \cup \Phi_1^0(B)$
$\Phi_1^0(A \cap B) = \Phi_1^0(A) \cap \Phi_1^0(B)$
and hence L-fuzzy set theory may be viewed as an extension of set theory.

Remark. The notions of triangular norm and conorm may be extended to lattices in an obvious way. However we want to warn for diversity when the extension of the drastic norm is considered. Indeed, first consider a bounded chain $(C, \leq)$ such as the unit interval $([0, 1], \leq)$ and the two $C^2 - C$ mappings Z_1 and Z_2 defined as:

$$\begin{aligned} Z_1(x, y) &= y && \text{if } x = 1_C \\ &= x && \text{if } y = 1_C \\ &= 0_C && \text{elsewhere} \\ Z_2(x, y) &= \min(x, y) && \text{if } \max(x, y) = 1_C \\ &= 0_C && \text{elsewhere} \end{aligned}$$

It is easily verified that Z_1 and Z_2 both are t-norms and moreover $Z_1 = Z_2$ holds.
Secondly consider a bounded distributive lattice $(L, \leq)$ and consider the $L^2 - L$ mappings Z_1^0 and Z_2^0 defined as:

$$\begin{aligned} Z_1^0(x, y) &= y && \text{if } x = 1_L \\ &= x && \text{if } y = 1_L \\ &= 0_L && \text{elsewhere} \\ Z_2^0(x, y) &= \inf(x, y) && \text{if } \sup(x, y) = 1_L \\ &= 0_L && \text{elsewhere} \end{aligned}$$

Then it can be verified that Z_1^0 and Z_2^0 both are t-norms but generally $Z_1^0 \leq Z_2^0$ and not $Z_1^0 = Z_2^0$ holds. However as one of my graduate students noticed, distributivity is necessary to prove that Z_2^0 is indeed a

t-norm. So thirdly consider the above mappings Z_1^0 and Z_2^0 in a bounded, non-distributive lattice $(L, \leq)$ then one has : Z_1^0 is a t-norm, $Z_1^0 \leq Z_2^0$ but Z_2^0 is not necessarily a t-norm, because the associativity property does not always hold. The following counterexample has been given by B. De Baets. Consider $L = \{0_L, \alpha, \beta, \gamma, \delta, \varepsilon, 1_L\}$ and covering relation $<<$ given by:
$<<= \{(0_L, \varepsilon), (\varepsilon, \delta), (\varepsilon, \gamma), (\delta, \alpha), (\delta, \beta), (\alpha, 1_L), (\beta, 1_L), (\gamma, 1_L)\}$
It is easily verified that $(L, \leq)$ is a bounded, non-distributive lattice satisfying
$Z_2^0(\alpha, Z_2^0(\beta, \gamma)) = 0_L$
$Z_2^0(Z_2^0(\alpha, \beta), \gamma) = \varepsilon$
and hence Z_2^0 is not associative.

1.1.4 Flou set theory in Gentilhomme's sense

Flou sets stem from linguistic considerations of Gentilhomme [4] about the vocabulary of a natural language (French in his case). He observed that starting from some kernel such as "agree" one can form other "words" by adding prefixes such as "re", "dis", "un", "ir" and/or by adding suffixes such as "abl", "able", "ably", "ment", ... Some of the combinations result in acceptable words (agreement, disagreeably), other combinations are certainly unusual (iragreement) and sometimes there will be combinations that sound acceptable but nevertheless one cannot find in a dictionary for example. These considerations lead Gentilhomme to the partitioning of a universe into three classes: the class of central elements i.e., those elements that certainly satisfy a given predicate, secondly the class of peripherical elements i.e., the doubtful elements and thirdly the class of non-elements, i.e., those elements that certainly don't satisfy the given predicate. More formally a flou set in a universe X is an ordered pair (E, F) of subsets of X such that $E \subseteq F$; E is called the certain zone, F the maximal zone and $F \backslash E$ the flou region. The class of all flou sets in a universe X will be denoted as $\mathcal{F}l(X)$, hence:
$\mathcal{F}l(X) = \{(E, F) | E \in \mathcal{P}(X) \text{ and } F \in \mathcal{P}(X) \text{ and } E \subseteq F\}$
The class $\mathcal{F}l(X)$ may be endowed with two binary and one unary operation in the following way:
$(E, F) \cup (E^0, F^0) = (E \cup E^0, F \cup F^0)$
$(E, F) \cap (E^0, F^0) = (E \cap E^0, F \cap F^0)$
It is easily checked that $(\mathcal{F}l(X), \cup, \cap)$ constitutes a complete lattice. Moreover $(\mathcal{F}l(X), \cup, \cap, \text{co})$ is a Kleene algebra with smallest element $(\emptyset, \emptyset)$ and greatest element (X, X). The presence of uncertainty is reflected in a violation of the law of excluded middle and the law of contradiction, i.e.:
$(E, F) \cup \text{co}(E, F) \neq (X, X)$
$(E, F) \cap \text{co}(E, F) \neq (\emptyset, \emptyset)$
as soon as $E \neq F$.
The mapping Φ_2 defined as:

$$\begin{aligned} \Phi_2 \colon \mathcal{P}(X) &\to \mathcal{F}l(X) \\ E &\mapsto (E, E), \forall E \in \mathcal{P}(X) \end{aligned}$$

is an injection satisfying for every A and B in $\mathcal{P}(X)$:

$$\Phi_2(A \cup B) = \Phi_2(A) \cup \Phi_2(B)$$
$$\Phi_2(A \cap B) = \Phi_2(A) \cap \Phi_2(B)$$
$$\Phi_2(\text{co}A) = \text{co}\Phi_2(A)$$

and hence flou set theory extends set theory.

1.1.5 n-flou set theory in Negoita-Ralescu's sense

Already in 1975 Negoita and Ralescu have extended Gentilhomme's concept to n-flou sets. A n-flou set in a universe $X (n \geq 2)$ is a n-tuple $(E_1, E_2, \ldots, E_n)$ of nested subsets of X i.e., $E_1 \subseteq E_2 \subseteq \ldots \subseteq E_n \subseteq X$. The class of n-flou sets in a universe X will be denoted as $\mathcal{F}l_n(X)$.
Note that $\mathcal{F}l_2(X) = \mathcal{F}l(X)$ holds. The class $\mathcal{F}l(X)$ can be endowed with the following binary and unary operations:
$(E_1, E_2, \ldots, E_n) \cup (E_1^0, E_2^0, \ldots, E_n^0) = (E_1 \cup E_1^0, E_2 \cup E_2^0, \ldots, E_n \cup E_n^0)$
$(E_1, E_2, \ldots, E_n) \cap (E_1^0, E_2^0, \ldots, E_n^0) = (E_1 \cap E_1^0, E_2 \cap E_2^0, \ldots, E_n \cap E_n^0)$
$\text{co}(E_1, E_2, \ldots, E_n) = (\text{co}E_n, \text{co}E_{n\ 1}, \ldots, \text{co}E_1)$
Straightforward verifications lead to the conclusion that $(\mathcal{F}l_n(X), \cup, \cap)$ is a complete lattice and moreover that $(\mathcal{F}l_n(X), \cup, \cap, \text{co})$ is a Kleene algebra with smallest element $(\emptyset, \emptyset, \ldots, \emptyset)$ and greatest element $(X, X, \ldots, X)$.
The mapping Φ_2^0 defined as:

$$\Phi_2^0 \colon \mathcal{P}(X) \to \mathcal{F}l_n(X)$$
$$E \quad \mapsto (E, E, \ldots, E), \forall E \in \mathcal{P}(X)$$

is an injection satisfying for every A and B in $\mathcal{P}(X)$.
$\Phi_2^0(A \cup B) = \Phi_2^0(A) \cup \Phi_2^0(B)$
$\Phi_2^0(A \cap B) = \Phi_2^0(A) \cap \Phi_2^0(B)$
$\Phi_2^0(\text{co}A) = \text{co}\Phi_2^0(A)$
and hence n-flou set theory extends set theory.

1.1.6 *L*-flou set theory in the sense of Negoita and Ralescu.

In a successful attempt to link fuzzy set theory and flou set theory Negoita and Ralescu [5] have introduced the higher concept of L-flou sets and they have compared this concept with Goguen's L-fuzzy set theory. In this section $(L, \leq)$ will represent a complete lattice with identities $0, 1$ and satisfying the supplementary condition $(\mathcal{L})$:
$(\forall A \subseteq L)(\forall a \in L)(a < \text{sup}A \Rightarrow (\exists b \in A)(a \leq b))$
A L-flou set in X is a $L - \mathcal{P}(X)$ mapping i.e., a family of subsets of X indexed with L, $(E_\alpha)_{\alpha 2\, L}$, satisfying the conditions:

(C1) $E_0 = \emptyset$

(C2) $E_{\sup\limits_{i2\, I} \alpha_i} = \cup_{i2\, I} E_{\alpha_i}$ for any family $(\alpha_i)_{i2\, I}$ in L.

The class of L-flou sets in a universe X will be denoted as $\mathcal{F}l_L(X)$. Using the convention sup$\emptyset = 0$ it is easily shown that property (C1) is an immediate consequence of (C2).
For $L = \{0,1\}$ we obtain $\mathcal{F}l_{f0,1g}(X) \cong \mathcal{P}(X)$, hence $\{0,1\}$ - flou set theory is equivalent to set theory.
For $L = \{0, \frac{1}{2}, 1\}$ we obtain $\mathcal{F}l_{f0,\frac{1}{2},1g}\ (X) \cong \mathcal{F}l(X)$, hence $\{0, \frac{1}{2}, 1\}$ -flou set theory is equivalent to flou set theory.
For $L = \{0, \frac{1}{n}, \frac{2}{n}, \dots, \frac{n\ 1}{n}, 1\}$ we obtain $\mathcal{F}l_{f0,\frac{1}{n},\dots,\frac{n\ 1}{n},1g}(X) \cong \mathcal{F}l_n(X)$, hence $\{0, \frac{1}{n}, \dots, \frac{n\ 1}{n}, 1\}$-flou set theory is equivalent to n-flou set theory.
The class $\mathcal{F}l_L(X)$ of all L-flou sets can be endowed with two binary operations in the following way. The union of two L-flou sets is obtained by pointwise application of the classical union on $\mathcal{P}(X)$, i.e.,
$(E_\alpha)_{\alpha 2\, L} \cup (E^0_\alpha)_{\alpha 2\, L} = (E_\alpha \cup E^0_\alpha)_{\alpha 2\, L}$
A pointwise application of the classical intersection on $\mathcal{P}(X)$ however doesn't lead to an internal operation on $\mathcal{F}l_L(X)$ i.e., $(E_\alpha \cap E^0_\alpha)_{\alpha 2\, L}$ is not necessary an element of $\mathcal{F}l_L(X)$. Negoita and Ralescu solved this problem by a well-known mathematical technique namely defining the intersection of two L-flou sets as the greatest L-flou set that is contained in both L-flou sets i.e., as the union of all L-flou sets that are contained in both L-flou sets. More formally:
$(E_\alpha)_{\alpha 2\, L} \underline{\cap} (E^0_\alpha)_{\alpha 2\, L} = \cup\{f | f \in \mathcal{F}l_L(X) \text{ and } f \subseteq (E_\alpha)_{\alpha 2\, L} \text{ and } f \subseteq (E^0_\alpha)_{\alpha 2\, L}\}$
Negoita and Ralsecu have shown that $(\mathcal{F}l_L(X), \cup, \underline{\cap})$ constitutes a complete lattice.
In order to prove their famous representation theorem they introduced the auxiliary structure $(\mathcal{F}l^0_L(X), \bar{\cup}, \cap)$ as follows:
$A \in \mathcal{F}l^0_L(X)$ iff A is a $L - \mathcal{P}(X)$ mapping $(E_\alpha)_{\alpha 2\, L}$ satisfying the conditions:

(C1') $E_0 = X$
(C2') $E_{\sup\limits_{i2\, I} \alpha_i} = \cap_{i2\, I} E_{\alpha_i}$ for any family $(\alpha_i)_{i2\, I}$ in L.

For $(E_\alpha)_{\alpha 2\, L}$ and $(E^0_\alpha)_{\alpha 2\, L}$ arbitrary elements of $\mathcal{F}l^0_L(X)$ we define binary operations as:
$(E_\alpha)_{\alpha 2\, L} \cap (E^0_\alpha)_{\alpha 2\, L} = (E_\alpha \cap E^0_\alpha)_{\alpha 2\, L}$
$(E_\alpha)_{\alpha 2\, L} \bar{\cup} (E^0_\alpha)_{\alpha 2\, L} = \cap\{f | f \in \mathcal{F}l^0_L(X) \text{ and } (E_\alpha)_{\alpha 2\, L} \subseteq f \text{ and } (E^0_\alpha)_{\alpha 2\, L} \subseteq f\}$
It is easily checked that $(\mathcal{F}l^0_L(X), \bar{\cup}, \cap)$ is a complete lattice.

Remark on the condition $\mathcal{L}$

Before continuing our overview of the models we would like to dwell upon the condition $\mathcal{L}$. Sometimes in the litterature one can find "alternative" forms for this condition. We want to clear out these alternatives. Let $(L, \leq)$ be a complete lattice and consider the following four possible combinations of inequality signs:

($\mathcal{L}$) $(\forall A \subseteq L)(\forall a \in L)(a < \sup A \Rightarrow (\exists b \in A)(a \leq b))$

($\mathcal{L}_1$) $(\forall A \subseteq L)(\forall a \in L)(a \leq \sup A \Rightarrow (\exists b \in A)(a < b))$

($\mathcal{L}_2$) $(\forall A \subseteq L)(\forall a \in L)(a \leq \sup A \Rightarrow (\exists b \in A)(a \leq b))$

($\mathcal{L}_3$) $(\forall A \subseteq L)(\forall a \in L)(a < \sup A \Rightarrow (\exists b \in A)(a < b))$

The following properties can be proved:

1. There is no lattice satisfying $(\mathcal{L}_1)$
2. $(\mathcal{L}_2) \Rightarrow (L, \leq)$ is a chain
3. $(\mathcal{L}_3) \Leftrightarrow (L, \leq)$ is a chain
4. $(\mathcal{L}_3) \Rightarrow (\mathcal{L})$
5. $(L, \leq)$ is a kite-tail lattice $\Rightarrow (\mathcal{L})$
6. In a finite lattice [6]

$(L, \leq)$ is a kite-tail lattice $\Leftrightarrow (\mathcal{L})$
where a kite-tail lattice has been defined in [6] as a finite vertical sum of the lattices 2 and M_2.

1.1.7 Twofold fuzzy set theory in the sense of Dubois and Prade.

Dubois and Prade [7] extended the notion of a flou set to so-called twofold fuzzy sets. A twofold fuzzy set in a universe X is defined as an ordered pair (E, F) of fuzzy sets in X satisfying the supplementary condition: $E \subseteq$ core F or equivalently supp $E \subseteq$ core F since:

$$\begin{aligned} E \subseteq \text{core}F &\Leftrightarrow (\forall x \in X)(E(x) \leq \text{core}F(x)) \\ &\Leftrightarrow (\forall x \in \text{core}F)(E(x) \leq 1) \text{ and} \\ &\quad\ (\forall x \in X \setminus \text{core}F)(E(x) \leq 0) \\ &\Leftrightarrow (\forall x \in X \setminus \text{core}F)(E(x) = 0) \\ &\Leftrightarrow (\forall x)(x \notin \text{core}F \Rightarrow x \notin \text{supp}E) \\ &\Leftrightarrow (\forall x)(x \in \text{supp}E \Rightarrow x \in \text{core}F) \\ &\Leftrightarrow \text{supp}E \subseteq \text{core}F \end{aligned}$$

The class of all twofold fuzzy sets in X is denoted as $\mathcal{TF}(X)$. Hence:
$\mathcal{TF}(X) = \{(E, F) \mid E \in \mathcal{F}(X)$ and $F \in \mathcal{F}(X)$ and supp $E \subseteq \text{core}F\}$. The class $\mathcal{TF}(X)$ has been endowed with two binary and one unary operation as follows:

$(E_1, F_1) \cup (E_2, F_2) = (E_1 \cup E_2, F_1 \cup F_2)$
$(E_1, F_1) \cap (E_2, F_2) = (E_1 \cap E_2, F_1 \cap F_2)$
$\text{co}(E_1, F_1) = (\text{coF}_1, \text{coE}_1)$
for (E_1, F_1) and (E_2, F_2) elements from $\mathcal{TF}(X)$. The operations $\cup$, $\cap$ and co in the right hand sides are the usual union, intersection and complementation of fuzzy sets in Zadeh's sense. It is easily proved that $(\mathcal{TF}(X), \cup, \cap)$ is a complete lattice and moreover that $(\mathcal{TF}(X), \cup, \cap, \text{co})$ constitutes a Kleene algebra.
The mapping Φ_3 defined as:

$$\begin{array}{llll} \Phi_3: & \mathcal{P}(X) & \to & \mathcal{TF}(X) \\ & E & \mapsto & (E,E), \forall E \in \mathcal{P}(X) \end{array}$$

is an injection satisfying for every A and B in $\mathcal{P}(X)$

$$\begin{array}{ll} \Phi_3(A \cup B) & = \Phi_3(A) \cup \Phi_3(B) \\ \Phi_3(A \cap B) & = \Phi_3(A) \cap \Phi_3(B) \\ \Phi_3(\text{co}A) & = \text{co}\Phi_3(A) \end{array}$$

and hence twofold fuzzy set theory extends set theory.

1.1.8 Rough set theory in Pawlak's sense

Just as flou sets, rough sets [8] are introduced as a tool for modelling uncertainty rather then for modelling imprecision. While flou sets were basically founded on the concept of a partial orderrelation (inclusion) rough sets are derived from an equivalence relation. Using such an equivalence relation on a given universe X, a crisp subset A of X is approximated by means of a pair of subsets of X. This approach is quite similar to general topology where the universe is endowed with a topology and a subset A of X is approximated by means of its interior $\text{int}(A)$ and its closure $\text{cl}(A)$.

It is very strange that most papers on rough sets do not mention the definition of a rough set.

In [7] for example one can only read:"a rough set is a collection of objects which cannot be precisely characterized in terms of the values of a set of attributes, while a lower and an upper approximation of the collection can be characterized in terms of these attributes". In [8] rough sets are compared with fuzzy sets, pretending the former notion being wider than the latter one, without any explicit definition of a rough set. In [15] we read:"any set characterized by its lower and upper approximations in an approximation space is called a rough set" which should mean that strictly spoken a rough set is simply a crisp subset. Now let us turn to a proposal for a formal definition of a rough set in some universe.

Let X be a universe and R an equivalence relation on X. The corresponding quotient set X/R partitions X into non-overlapping, nonempty equivalence classes, i.e.

$X/R = \{[x]_R \mid x \in X\}$

where $[x]_R = \{y \mid y \in X \text{ and } xRy\}$.

In fact the equivalence class $[x]_R$ is nothing but the R-afterset of x. The elements of X/R and the empty set are called elementary sets or atoms. Every union of atoms (not only finite ones) is called a composed set with regard to the structure (X, R). The class of composed sets is denoted Com (X, R) and the ordered pair $(X, \text{Com}(X, R))$ is called an approximation space. A rough set on X is an ordered pair of subsets of X approximating a given subset A. More explicitly for every A one defines the lower approximation of A, denoted $\underline{A}$, as:

$\underline{A} = \{x \mid x \in X \text{ and } [x]_R \subseteq A\}$

and the upper approximation of A, denoted $\overline{A}$, as:

$\overline{A} = \{x \mid x \in X \text{ and } [x]_R \cap A \neq \emptyset\}$.
Hence $(\underline{A}, \overline{A})$ constitutes a rough approximation of $A \in \mathcal{P}(X)$. Let's denote the class of rough sets in a universe X corresponding to an equivalence relation R on X as $\mathcal{R}_R(X)$.
We never saw any definition of operations endowed on $\mathcal{R}_R(X)$. We only could find some formulas to calculate the lower and upper approximations of unions and intersections of (crisp) subsets of the universe. Some examples are:

(i) $(\overline{A \cup B}) = \overline{A} \cup \overline{B}$
i.e. the upper approximation of a (finite) union equals the union of the upper approximations.

(ii) $\underline{A} \cup \underline{B} \subseteq \underline{A \cup B}$
i.e. the lower approximation of a (finite) union contains the union of the lower approximations.

(iii) $(\underline{A \cap B}) = \underline{A} \cap \underline{B}$
i.e. the lower approximation of a (finite) intersection equals the intersection of the lower approximations.

(iv) $\overline{A \cap B} \subseteq \overline{A} \cap \overline{B}$
i.e. the upper approximation of a (finite) intersection is contained in the intersection of the upper approximations.

(v) $\overline{\mathrm{co}A} = \mathrm{co}\underline{\mathrm{A}}$ and $\underline{\mathrm{coA}} = \mathrm{co}\overline{\mathrm{A}}$
i.e. the upper (lower) approximation of the complement of a set equals the complement of the lower (upper) approximation of that set.

Remark

Without going into details we want to emphasize here some possible connections between rough set theory and (crisp) relational calculus. Indeed let R be a (crisp) relation from X to Y i.e. $R \subseteq X \times Y$. For $x \in X$ the R - afterset of X is defined as:$xR = \{y \mid (x, y) \in R\}$ and for $y \in Y$ the R-foreset of y is defined as: $Ry = \{x \mid (x, y) \in R\}$. For $A \subseteq X$ the classical direct image of A under R is defined as:
$R(A) = \{y \mid A \cap Ry \neq \emptyset\}$
In [16] we defined the superdirect image of A under R as:
$R^{\triangleright}(A) = \{y \mid \emptyset \subset Ry \subseteq A\}$
Now it is easy to see that if $X = Y$, i.e. R is a binary relation on X and moreover if R is an equivalence relation then for $A \subseteq X$ we obtain:
$R(A) = \overline{A}$
$R^{\triangleright}(A) = \underline{A}$
hence the direct image, respectively the super direct image of A under R, coincides with the upper approximation respectively the lower approximation of A under the equivalence relation R.

1.2 Links between the different models

1.2.1 Fuzzy set theory extends flou set theory

This statement can be formalized in the following proposition.

Proposition 1 *The mapping* Ψ_1 *defined as*

$$\begin{array}{lll} \Psi_1 : \mathcal{F}(X) & \rightarrow & \mathcal{F}l(X) \\ A & \mapsto & (\mathrm{core}A, \mathrm{supp}A), \forall A \in \mathcal{F}(X) \end{array}$$

is a surjective homomorphism between the lattices $(\mathcal{F}(X), \cup, \cap)$ *and* $(\mathcal{F}l(X), \cup, \cap)$.

Note that the mapping Ψ_1 is not injective i.e. different fuzzy sets may have the same flou representation.

1.2.2 L-fuzzy set theory is equivalent to L-flou set theory

This statement can be formalized by means of the following propositions, linking $\mathcal{F}_L(X)$ with $\mathcal{F}l_L(X)$ via $\mathcal{F}l^0_L(X)$. These propositions are due to Negoita and Ralescu [5].

Proposition 2 *The mapping* Φ *defined as:*

$$\begin{array}{lll} \Phi : \mathcal{F}_L(X) & \rightarrow & \mathcal{F}l^0_L(X) \\ A & \mapsto & (A_\alpha)_{\alpha 2\, L}, \forall A \in \mathcal{F}_L(X) \end{array}$$

is an isomorphism between the complete lattices $(\mathcal{F}_L(X), \cup, \cap)$ *and* $(\mathcal{F}l^0_L(X), \overline{\cup}, \cap)$. *in which* L *denotes a complete lattice satisfying condition* $(\mathcal{L})$.

Proposition 3 *The mapping* Ψ *defined as:*

$$\begin{array}{lll} \Psi : \mathcal{F}l^0_L(X) & \rightarrow & \mathcal{F}l_L(X) \\ (E_\alpha)_{\alpha 2\, L} & \mapsto & (\mathrm{co}E_\alpha)_{\alpha 2\, L}, \forall (E_\alpha)_{\alpha 2\, L} \in \mathcal{F}l^0_L(X) \end{array}$$

is a dual isomorphism between the complete lattices $(\mathcal{F}l^0_L(X), \overline{\cup}, \cap)$ *and* $(\mathcal{F}l_L(X), \cup, \sqcap,)$, *i.e.*

$$\Psi((E_\alpha)_{\alpha 2\, L} \overline{\cup} (E^0_\alpha)_{\alpha 2\, L}) = \Psi((E_\alpha)_{\alpha 2\, L}) \sqcap \Psi((E^0_\alpha)_{\alpha 2\, L}).$$

Proposition 4 *The mapping* Ψ_2 *defined as:*

$$\begin{array}{lll} \Psi_2 : \mathcal{F}_L(X) & \rightarrow & \mathcal{F}l_L(X) \\ A & \mapsto & (\mathrm{co}A_\alpha)_{\alpha 2\, L}\ , \forall A \in \mathcal{F}_L(X) \end{array}$$

is a dual isomorphism between the complete lattices $(\mathcal{F}_L(X), \cup, \cap)$ *and* $(\mathcal{F}l_L(X), \cup, \sqcap)$

As a consequence of proposition 3 the following particular cases may be considered:

(i) $L = \{0, 1\}$
In this case we have: $\mathcal{F}l_{\{0,1\}}(X) \cong \mathcal{P}(X)$, i.e. $\{0,1\}$ - flou set theory is equivalent to set theory.

(ii) $L = \{0, \frac{1}{2}, 1\}$
In this case we have: $\mathcal{F}l_{\{0,\frac{1}{2},1\}}(X) \cong \mathcal{F}l(X)$ i.e. $\{0, \frac{1}{2}, 1\}$ - flou set theory is "equivalent" to flou set theory.

(iii) $L = [0, 1]$
In this case we have: $\mathcal{F}l_{[0,1]}(X) \cong \mathcal{F}(X)$, i.e. [0,1] - flou set theory is "equivalent" to fuzzy set theory.

1.2.3 Twofold fuzzy set theory extends flou set theory

From the equality
$\mathcal{TF}(X) = \{(E, F) \mid E \in \mathcal{F}(X)$ and $F \in \mathcal{F}(X)$ and supp $E \subseteq$ core $F\}$ it easily follows that twofold fuzzy sets are a straightforward extension of flou sets. Indeed for $E \in \mathcal{P}(X), F \in \mathcal{P}(X)$ we have supp $E = E$ and core $F = F$ and hence the condition supp $E \subseteq$ core F reduces to $E \subseteq F$. More formally we may write:
$\mathcal{TF}(X) \cap (\mathcal{P}(X) \times \mathcal{P}(X)) = \mathcal{F}l(X)$

Proposition 5 *The mapping Ψ_3 defined as:*
$\Psi_3 : \mathcal{TF}(X) \to \mathcal{F}l(X)$
$(E, F) \mapsto$ *(supp E, core F), $\forall (E, F) \in \mathcal{TF}(X)$*
is a surjective homomorphism between the Kleene algebras $(\mathcal{TF}(X), \cup, \cap, \text{co})$ *and* $(\mathcal{F}l(X), \cup, \cap, \text{co})$.
Note that the mapping Ψ_3 is not injective, i.e. different twofold fuzzy sets may have the same representation.

1.2.4 Twofold fuzzy set theory is equivalent to set theory

In [7] Dubois and Prade stated the following proposition.

Proposition 6 *The mapping Ψ_4 defined as:*
$\Psi_4 : \mathcal{TF}(X) \to \mathcal{F}(X)$
$(E, F) \mapsto \frac{E+F}{2}, \forall (E, F) \in \mathcal{TF}(X)$
is an isomorphism between the Kleene algebras $(\mathcal{TF}(X), \cup, \cap, \text{co})$ *and* $(\mathcal{F}(X), \cup, \cap, \text{co})$.

The arithmetic sum appearing in proposition 6 is defined pointwise, i.e.

$$\frac{E+F}{2}(x) = \frac{E(x)+F(x)}{2}, \forall x \in X.$$

One easily verifies that the inverse mapping $\Psi_4^{\ 1}$ involves two alternative fuzzy set operations namely the bold intersection or the Lukasiewicz t-norm, and the bounded sum:
$\Psi_4^{\ 1}(A) = (A \Cap A, A +_b A), \forall A \in \mathcal{F}(X)$
with: $A \Cap A(x) = \max\ (0, 2A(x) - 1), \forall x \in X$
$A +_b A(x) = \min\ (1, 2A(x)), \forall x \in X.$

1.2.5 Fuzzy set theory extends flou set theory (second extension)

Combining proposition 5 and 6 we obtain a second way of extending flou set theory to fuzzy set theory.

Proposition 7 *The mapping* Ψ_5 *defined as:*

$$\Psi_5 : \mathcal{F}(X) \to \mathcal{F}l(X)$$
$$A \mapsto (\mathrm{suppA} \Cap \mathrm{A}, \mathrm{coreA} +_b \mathrm{A}), \forall \mathrm{A} \in \mathcal{F}(\mathrm{X})$$

is a surjective homomorphism between the Kleene algebras $(\mathcal{F}(X), \cup, \cap, \mathrm{co})$ *and* $(\mathcal{F}l(X), \cup, \cap, \mathrm{co})$.

Now let's compare the two homomorphisms Ψ_1 and Ψ_5. One easiliy verifies the following relationships for $A \in \mathcal{F}(X)$:
core $(A +_b A) = $ supp $(A \Cap A) \cup \{x \mid x \in X \text{ and } A(x) = \frac{1}{2}\}$
core $A \subseteq$ supp $(A \Cap A)$
supp $A \supseteq$ core $(A +_b A)$
co(supp$A$) $\subseteq$ co(core$(A +_b A)$).

Hence, starting with a fuzzy set A we can obtain the flou representation (core A, supp A) by applying the mapping Ψ_1. By applying the mapping Ψ_4 we obtain another flou representation, namely (supp $A \Cap A$, core $A +_b A$). The above formulas indicate that these two flou representations are related to each other in some hybrid way: the certain region of $\Psi_4(A)$ is larger than the certain region of $\Psi_1(A)$, while the maximal zone of $\Psi_4(A)$ is smaller than the maximal zone of $\Psi_1(A)$, or equivalently the flou zone of $\Psi_4(A)$ is smaller than the flou zone of $\Psi_1(A)$. In this way we may call $\Psi_4(A)$ a better flou representation of the fuzzy A than $\Psi_1(A)$.

Conclusion

In this paper we have been given a first overview of theories to model incomplete information and of some possible links between these models. We are aware of the fact that still some theories are missing in the comparison and that not all possible links have been considered. In a further paper we want to report upon the position of Pawlak's rough set theory. In particular we want to search for the relationship of rough set theory with topology, fuzzy topology, fuzzy set theory and twofold fuzzy set theory.

References

[1] L.A. Zadeh, Fuzzy sets, Information Control 8 (1965) 338–353.

[2] E.E. Kerre, A call for crispness in fuzzy set theory. Fuzzy Sets and Systems 29 (1989) 57–65.

[3] J. Goguen, *L*-fuzzy sets. J. Math. Anal. Appl. 18 (1967) 145–174.

[4] Y. Gentilhomme, Les sous-ensembles flous en linguistique, Cahiers de Linguistiques Théoriques et Appliquée V (1968) 47–63.

[5] D. Ralescu, C.V. Negoita. Applications of Fuzzy Sets to Systems Analysis (Birkhauser Verlag, Bazel) 1975.

[6] B. De Baets, E.E. Kerre, Kite-tail lattice and their characterization, Far East Journal of Mathematical Sciences, Vol. 1, n° 1 (1993) 1–12.

[7] D. Dubois, H. Prade, Twofold fuzzy sets and rough sets, some issues in knowledge representation, Fuzzy Sets and Systems (1987) 3–18.

[8] Z. Pawlak, Rough sets and fuzzy sets, Fuzzy Sets and Systems 17 (1985) 99-102.

[9] L.A. Zadeh, Is probability theory sufficient for dealing with uncertainty in A. I.: a negative view. In: Uncertainty in Artificial Intelligence, L.N. Kanal, J.F. Lemmer (eds.), Elsevier Science Publishers B.V.(1986) 103–116.

[10] E.E. Kerre, Characterization of normality in fuzzy topological spaces, Simon Stevin, 53 (1979) 239–248.

[11] B. Schweizer, A. Sklar, Probabilistic Metric Spaces (Elsevier Science, New York) 1983.

[12] G. Klir, T. Folger, Fuzzy Sets, Uncertainty and Information (Prentice Hall, New Jersey) 1988.

[13] D. Guinan, K. Streicher, E.E. Kerre, Set-theoretic properties of the class of fuzzy sets endowed with the bounded sum and the bold intersection. University of Nebraska, Dep. Comp. Sc. and Eng., Report Series, n° 114 (1990), 54 pages.

[14] E.E. Kerre, Basic principles of fuzzy set theory for the representation and manipulation of imprecision and uncertainty. In: Introduction to the Basic Principles of Fuzzy Set Theory and some of its Applications, E.E. Kerre, ed., Communication and Cognition, Gent, second revised edition (1993) 1–158.

[15] S.K.M. Wong, W. Ziarko, Comparison of the probabilistic approximate classification and the fuzzy set model, Fuzzy Sets and Systems 21 (1987) 357–362.

[16] B. De Baets, E. Kerre, A revision of Bandler - Kohout compositions of relations, Mathematica Pannonica 4/1 (1993) 59–78.

Rough Sets and their Applications

Zdzislaw Pawlak

Institute of Theoretical and Applied Informatics
Polish Academy of Sciences, ul. Baltycka 5
44 000 Gliwice, Poland
zpw@ii.pw.edu.pl

Abstract. The paper discusses basic concepts of rough set theory. Starting point of the theory are data tables which are used to define rudiments of the theory: approximations, dependency and reduction of attributes, decision rules and others. Various applications of the theory are outlined and future problems pointed out.

Keywords. Rough sets, fuzzy sets, vagueness, decision tables, decision rules, data mining.

1 Introduction

Rough set theory is a new approach to imperfect knowledge. Particularly it offers a new perspective to vagueness and uncertainty, fundamental issues discussed in modern philosophy, logic and AI. Recently, researcher interested in cognitive sciences, machine learning, data mining and others contributed essentially to this area. The most important contributions, no doubt, are fuzzy set theory and the theory of evidence.

Rough set theory is still another look on vagueness and uncertainty. Although it is somehow related to fuzzy set theory [5, 6, 14, 33, 37, 40, 51, 58, 61, 62, 72, 95, 107, 111, 112] and the evidence theory, [76] it can be viewed as a independent discipline in its own rights.

We witnessed a rapid grow of interest in rough set theory and its application, world wide. Many international workshops, conferences and seminars included rough sets in their programs. Over a thousand papers have been published on rough sets and their applications so far.

Rough set theory hinges on the assumption that every object of the *universe of discourse* has some characteristic features, which are represented by information (knowledge, data) about the object. Objects having the same features are indiscernible. The indiscernibility relation leads to the so called "boundary-line" approach to vagueness, first formulated by father of modern logic, Gotlob Frege [17]. According to Frege "the concept without a sharp boundary", i.e. vague concept, must have boundary-line examples which cannot be classified, neither to the concept nor to its complement. Thus from philosophical point of view rough set theory can be understood as a special case of Frege's idea.

Practically, rough set theory can be seen as a new approach to data analysis, known recently as also data mining. In general, data mining is a methodology for discovering hidden patterns in data. Rough set theory has proved to be useful in data mining, and it "... constitutes a sound basis for data mining applications" [13]. The theory offers mathematical tools to discover hidden patterns in data. It identifies partial or total dependencies (i.e. cause-effect relations) in data bases, eliminates redundant data, gives approach to null values, missing data, dynamic data and others.

Many real life, nontrivial applications of this methodology for knowledge discovery have proved it usefulness. Rough set theory has been successfully applied in many areas. Medicine [57, 59, 68, 77, 78, 79, 92, 93, 97, 100, 101, 102, 103, 106], pharmacology [30, 31], banking, financial and market analysis [3, 19, 20, 82, 83, 84] are areas where rough set approach showed its advantages. Very interesting results have been also obtained in speaker independent speech recognition and acoustics [9, 10, 11, 12, 29]. The rough set approach seems also important for various engineering applications, like machine diagnosis [54], process control [1, 8, 36, 40, 43, 69, 90, 91, 96, 114, 115, 119], material science [28], databases [4, 7, 16, 18, 27, 74, 85] and others [2, 22, 23, 24, 25, 26, 67, 73, 86, 113]. More about applications of rough set theory can be found in [34, 35, 39, 41, 42, 56, 58, 65, 80, 81, 99, 104, 105, 117].

Rough set theory, has also links between Boolean reasoning methods [75], statistics [15, 32, 87, 94], neural networks [44, 45, 46, 48, 49, 50, 52, 53, 88, 110], mathematical morphology [70], mereology [71], just to name few.

The theory is not competitive but rather complementary to other methods and can also be often used jointly with other approaches (e.g. fuzzy sets, genetic algorithms, statistical methods, neural networks etc.)

Rough set theory has been generalized in many ways, but we are going to present in this paper basic concepts of this theory only. Rudiments of rough set theory can be found in [63, 66, 78, 89]. Readers interested in more advanced results are advised to consult suitable literature.

2 Information Tables

The basic concepts of rough set theory can be formulated in quite general terms, but in order to give more intuitive insight into the theory we will start our consideration from *data tables* called *information tables*, *information systems* or *attribute-value systems*. Column of the table are labeled by *attributes*, rows by *objects* and entries of the table are *attribute values*. An example of information table is shown below.

Table 1. An example of an information table

	H	M	T	F
p1	no	yes	high	yes
p2	yes	no	high	yes
p3	yes	yes	v. high	yes
p4	no	yes	normal	no
p5	yes	no	high	no
p6	no	yes	v. high	yes

Columns of the table are labeled by attributes Headache (H), Muscle-pain (M), Temperature (T) and Flu (F) and rows – by patients (objects) *p*1, *p*2, *p*3, *p*4, *p*5 and *p*6.

Each row of the table can be seen as information about specific patient. For example patient *p*2 is characterized in the table by the following attribute-value set

{(Headache, yes), (Muscle-pain, no), (Temperature, high), (Flu, yes)}.

Let us observe that each subset of attributes divides the set of all objects in the table into classes having the same features, i.e. clumps of objects which are indiscernible in view of the available data. For example, in the table patients *p*2, *p*4 and *p*6 are indiscernible with respect to the attribute Headache, since all they have the same value of this attribute. Similarly, patients *p*3 and *p*5 are indiscernible in terms of attributes Headache and Temperature, etc. Thus each subset of attributes induces on the set of objects an equivalence relation, whose equivalence classes form *granules* (*blocks, clusters*) of objects having the same features. These granules will be referred to as *elementary sets,* which are basic building bricks of rough set theory.

Now we present the above concepts formally.

Let $S = (U, A)$ be an information table, where U and A, are finite, non-empty sets called the *universe*, and a set *attributes* respectively. With every attribute $a \in A$ we associate a set V_a of its *values*, called the *domain* of a. Any subset B of A determines a binary relation $I(B)$ on U which will be called an *indiscernibility relation,* and is defined as follows:

$(x, y) \in I(B)$ if and only if $a(x) = a(y)$ for every $a \in A$, where $a(x)$ denotes the value of attribute a for element x.

Obviously $I(B)$ is an equivalence relation. The family of all equivalence classes of $I(B)$, i.e., partition determined by B, will be denoted by $U/I(B)$, or simple U/B; an equivalence class of $I(B)$, i.e., block of the partition U/B, containing x will be denoted by $B(x)$.

If $(x, y) \in I(B)$ we will say that x and y are *B-indiscernible*. Equivalence classes of the relation $I(B)$ (or blocks of the partition U/B) are refereed to as *B-elementary sets.*

In the table patients $p2$, $p3$ and $p5$ are indiscernible with respect to the attribute Headache, patients $p3$ and $p6$ are indiscernible with respect to attributes Muscle-pain and Flu, and patients $p2$ and $p5$ are indiscernible with respect to attributes Headache, Muscle-pain and Temperature. Hence, for example, the attribute Headache generates two elementary sets $\{p2, p3, p5\}$ and $\{p1, p4, p6\}$, whereas the attributes Headache and Muscle-pain form the following elementary sets: $\{p1, p4, p6\}$, $\{p2, p5\}$ and $\{p3\}$.

3 Approximation of Sets

It can be seen from Table 1 that the concept "flu", i.e. the set $\{p1, p2, p3, p6\}$ (or the concept "not flu", i.e. the set $\{p4, p5\}$) cannot be defined in terms of attributes Headache, Muscle-pain and Temperature, because patients $p2$ and $p5$ have the same symptoms, i.e. values of attributes Headache, Muscle-pain and Temperature, but $p2$ has flu and $p5$ has not. Therefore we propose to define two set, called the *lower* and the *upper approximation* of a concept, which can be defined in terms of features contained in the table. The lower approximation of a concept is the set of all objects which can be *surely* classified as belonging to the concept, whereas the upper approximation of set is the set of all objects which *possible* belong to the concept – in view of available data.

Formally approximations are operations on sets defined as follows:

$$B_*(X) = \{x \in U : B(x) \subseteq X\},$$

$$B^*(X) = \{x \in U : B(x) \cap X \neq \emptyset\},$$

which assign to every subset X of the universe U two sets $B_*(X)$ and $B^*(X)$ called the *B-lower* and the *B-upper approximation* of X, respectively.

The set

$$BN_B(X) = B^*(X) - B_*(X)$$

will be referred to as the *B-boundary region* of X.

If the boundary region of X is the empty set, i.e., $BN_B(X) = \emptyset$, then the set X is *crisp* (*exact*) with respect to B; in the opposite case, i.e., if $BN_B(X) \neq \emptyset$, the set X is *rough* (*inexact*) with respect to B.

Rough set can be also characterized numerically by the following coefficient

$$\alpha_B(X) = \frac{card(B_*(X))}{card(B^*(X))},$$

called *accuracy of approximation*. Obviously $0 \leq \alpha_B(X) \leq 1$. If $\alpha_B(X) = 1$, X is *crisp* with respect to B (X is *precise* with respect to B), and otherwise, if $\alpha_B(X) < 1$, X is *rough* with respect to B (X is *vague* with respect to B).

Let us depict above definitions by examples referring to Table 1. Consider the concept "flu", i.e., the set $X = \{p1, p2, p3, p6\}$ and the set of attributes B = {Headache, Muscle-pain, Temperature}. Hence $B_*(X) = \{p1, p3, p6\}$ and $B^*(X) = \{p1, p2, p3, p5, p6\}$. For this case we get α_B ("*flu*") = 3/5. It means that the concept "flu" can be characterized partially employing symptoms, Headache, Muscle-pain and Temperature. Taking only one symptom B = {Headache} we get $B_*(X) = \emptyset$, $B^*(X) = U$ and $\alpha_B(\text{"}flu\text{"}) = 0$, which means that the concept "flu" cannot be characterized in terms of attribute Headache only i.e., this attribute is not characteristic for flu whatsoever. However, taking the attribute B = {Temperature} we get $B_*(X) = \{p3, p6\}$, $B^*(X) = \{p1, p2, p3, p5, p6\}$ and $\alpha_B(X) = 2/5$, which means that the single symptom Temperature is less characteristic for flu, than the whole set of symptoms, but also characterizes flu partially.

4 Rough Membership Function

Rough sets can be also defined using a *rough membership function*, defined as

$$\mu_X^B(x) = \frac{card(B(x) \cap X)}{card(B(x))}.$$

Obviously

$$\mu_X^B(x) \in [0,1].$$

Value of the membership function $\mu_X^B(x)$ is kind of conditional probability, and can be interpreted as a degree of *certainty* that x can be classified as X, employing set of attributes B.

The rough membership function, can be used to define approximations and the boundary region of a set, as shown below:

$$B_*(X) = \{x \in U : \mu_X^B(x) = 1\},$$

$$B^*(X) = \{x \in U : \mu_X^B(x) > 0\},$$

$$BN_B(X) = \{x \in U : 0 < \mu_X^B(x) < 1\}.$$

The rough membership function can be generalized as follows [71]:

$$\mu(X,Y) = \frac{card(X \cap Y)}{card\,X},$$

where $X, Y \subseteq U, X \neq \emptyset$.

Function $\mu(X,Y)$ is an example of a *rough inclusion* [71] and expresses the degree to which X is included in Y. Obviously, if $\mu(X, Y) = 1$, then $X \subseteq Y$.

If X is included in a degree k we will write $X \subseteq_k Y$.

The rough inclusion function can be interpreted as a generalization of the mereological relation "part of", and reads as "part in a degree".

For example, $p1$ belongs to the concept "flu" (i.e. the set $\{p1, p2, p3, p6\}$) with degree 1, whereas $p2$ belongs to this set with degree 0,5.

5 Dependency of Attributes

Our main problem can be also formulated in another way. Instead of using approximations of sets we can use the concept of *dependency of attributes*.

Intuitively, a set of attributes D (called *decision attributes*) depends totally on a set of attributes C (called *condition attributes*), denoted $C \Rightarrow D$, if all values of attributes of D are uniquely determined by values of attributes of C. In other words, D depends totally on C, if there exists a functional dependency between values of D and C. In Table 1 there are not total dependencies whatsoever. If in Table 1, the value of the attribute Temperature for patient $p5$ were "no" instead of "high", there would be a total dependency {Temperature}$\Rightarrow$ {Flu}, because to each value of the attribute Temperature there would correspond unique value of the attribute Flu.

Formally dependency can be defined in the following way.

Let D and C be subsets of A. We say that D *depends totally* on C, if and only if $I(C) \subseteq I(D)$. That means that the partition generated by C is finer than the partition generated by D.

We would need also a more general concept of dependency of attributes, called a *partial dependency* of attributes. For example, in Table 1, the attribute Temperature determines uniquely only some values of the attribute Flu. That is, (Temperature, very high) implies (Flu, yes), similarly (Temperature, normal) implies (Flu, no), but (Temperature, high) does not imply always (Flu, yes). Thus the partial dependency means that only some values of D are determined by values of C.

Formally, the above idea can be formulated as follows.

Let D and C be subsets of A. We say that D *depends in degree k*, $0 \le k \le 1$, on C, denoted $C \Rightarrow_k D$, if

$$k = \gamma(C,D) = \frac{card(POS_C(D))}{card(U)} = \frac{\sum_{X \in U/D} card(C_*(X))}{card(U)},$$

where

$$POS_C(D) = \bigcup_{X \in U/I(D)} C_*(X).$$

The expression $POS_C(D)$, called a *positive region* of the partition U/D with respect to C, is the set of all elements of U that can be uniquely classified to blocks of the partition U/D, by means of C.

Notice that for $k = 1$ we get the previous definition of total dependency.

For dependency {Headache, Muscle-pain, Temperature}$\Rightarrow$ {Flu} we get $k = 4/6 = 2/3$, because four out of six patients can be uniquely classified as having flu or not, employing attributes Headache, Muscle-pain and Temperature.

If we were interested in how exactly patients can be diagnosed using only the attribute Temperature, that is – in the degree of the dependence {Temperature} $\Rightarrow$ {Flu}, we would get $k = 3/6 = 1/2$, since in this case only three patients $p3$, $p4$ and $p6$ out of six can be uniquely classified as having flu. In contrast to the previous case patient $p4$ cannot be classified now as having flu or not. Hence the single attribute Temperature offers worse classification than the whole set of attributes Headache, Muscle-pain and Temperature. It is interesting to observe that neither Headache nor Muscle-pain can be used to recognize flu, because for both dependencies {Headache}$\Rightarrow${Flu} and {Muscle-pain}$\Rightarrow${Flu} we have $k = 0$.

6 Reduction of Attributes

Another important issue in our approach is data reduction. For example, it is easily seen that if we drop in Table 1 either the attribute Headache or Muscle-pain we get the data set which is equivalent to the original one, in regard to approximations and dependencies. That is we get in this case the same accuracy of approximation and degree of dependencies as in the original table, however using smaller set of attributes.

This concept can be formulated more precisely as follows. Let $C \Rightarrow_k D$. A minimal subset C' of C, such that $\gamma(C, D) = \gamma(C', D)$ is called a *reduct* of C.

It is easily seen that in Table 1 we have two reducts, {Temperature, Muscle-pain} and {Temperature, Headache}.

Thus a reduct is a set of condition attributes that preserves the degree of dependency. It means that a reduct is a minimal subset of condition attributes that enables the same decisions as the whole set of condition attributes.

Obviously a set of condition attributes may have more then one reduct. Intersection of all reducts is called the *core*. The core in Table 1 is the attribute Temperature. Thus the core is the set of attributes that cannot be eliminated from the information table without changing its dependencies and approximations.

7 Decision Rules and Consistency Factor

It we distinguish in an information table two classes of attributes, *condition* and *decision* attributes, such tables are called *decision tables*. For example in Table 1 attributes Headache, Muscle-pain and Temperature are condition attributes, whereas the attribute Flu – is a decision attribute.

Each row of a decision table determines a *decision rule*, which specifies *decisions* (*actions*) that should be taken when conditions pointed out by condition attributes are satisfied. For example, in Table 1 the condition (Headache, no), (Muscle-pain, yes), (Temperature, high) determines uniquely the decision (Flu, yes). Decision rules 2) and 5) in Table 1 have the same conditions by different decisions. Such rules are called *inconsistent* (*nondeterministic, conflicting, possible*); otherwise the rules are referred to as *consistent* (*deterministic, non conflicting, sure*). Decision tables containing inconsistent decision rules are called *inconsistent*; otherwise the table is *consistent*.

Decision rules are often presented as implications and are called "*if..., then...*" rules. For example rule 1) in Table 1 can be presented as implication

if (Headache, no) and (Muscle-pain, yes) and (Temperature, high) then (Flu, yes).

To express this idea more precisely we need a formal language associated with any information table $S = (U, A)$. The language is defined in a standard way and we assume that the reader is familiar with the construction.

Given $x \in U$ and $B \subseteq A$ by $\Phi_x^B = \wedge_{a \in B}(a, v)$ we mean a formula such that $a(x) = v$ and $v \in V_a$.

Every dependency $C \Rightarrow_k D$ determines a set of *decision rules*

$$\{\Phi_x^C \rightarrow \Phi_x^D\}_{x \in U}.$$

We say that a decision rule $\Phi_x^C \rightarrow \Phi_x^D$ is ***true*** in S, if $|\Phi_x^C|_S \subseteq |\Phi_x^D|_S$, where $|\Phi_x^C|_S$ denotes the *meaning* of Φ_x^C in S, defined in a usual way.

Let $C_S(x) = |\Phi_x^C|_S$. Hence the decision rule $\Phi_x^C \rightarrow \Phi_x^D$ is true in S if $C_S(x) \subseteq D_S(x)$.

A decision rule $\Phi_x^C \rightarrow \Phi_x^D$ is ***true in a degree*** l in S, if $l = \mu(C_S(x), D_S(x)) > 0$, i.e., $C_S(x) \subseteq_l D_S(x)$.

Rough inclusion in this case boils down to the rough membership function. As a consequence rough membership can be interpreted as a generalized truth value.

The degree of truth of a decision rule can be also interpreted as a certainty factor of the rule.

Let us observe that the rough membership can be interpreted both as conditional probability and at the same time as partial truth value.

The above considerations lead to a inference rule, called the ***rough modus ponens***, defined as below:

$$\frac{\pi(\Phi_x^C);\ \mu(\Phi_x^C, \Psi_x^D)}{\pi(\Psi_x^C)},$$

where

$$\pi(\Phi_x^C) = \frac{card(|\Phi_x^C|_S)}{card(U)},$$

$$\mu(\Phi_x^C, \Psi_x^D) = \frac{card(|\Phi_x^C \wedge \Psi_x^D|_S)}{card\,|\Phi_x^C|_S}$$

and

$$\pi(\Psi_x^D) = \pi(\sim \Phi_x^C \wedge \Psi_x^D) + \pi(\Phi_x^C) \cdot \mu(\Phi_x^C, \Psi_x^D),$$

or

$$\pi(\Phi_D^x) = \sum_{y \in D(x)} (\pi(\Psi_y^C) \cdot \mu(\Psi_y^C,\ \Phi_y^D)).$$

The number $\pi(\Phi_x^C)$ can be interpreted as the probability, that x has the property Φ_x^C, and the number $\mu(\Phi_x^C,\ \Psi_x^D)$ – as *certainty factor* of the decision rule $\Phi_x^C \rightarrow \Psi_x^D$.

Hence the inference rule, the *rough modus ponens*, enables us to calculate the probability of conclusion Ψ_x^D as a function of the probability of the premise Φ_x^C and the certainty factor $\mu(\Phi_x^C, \Psi_x^D)$ of the decision rule $\Phi_x^C \rightarrow \Psi_x^D$.

8 Conclusions

Rough set theory attracted researchers and practitioners all over the world. They contributed essentially to its theoretical foundations as well as to wide range of non trivial applications of the theory. Besides, software based on rough set approach to data analysis has been developed in many countries.

The theory has many important advantages. Some of them are listed below.

- Provides efficient algorithms for finding hidden patterns in data.
- Finds minimal sets of data (data reduction).
- Evaluates significance of data.
- Generates minimal sets of decision rules from data.
- It is easy to understand.
- Offers straightforward interpretation of obtained results.

Despite many serious achievements in rough set theory further investigations are here still needed. Particularly its algebraic, logical and probabilistic aspects require more research.

Beside pure theoretical research many problems related closer to applications require due attention.

Despite of many valuable methods of efficient, optimal decision rule generation methods from data, developed in recent years based on rough set theory - more research here is needed, particularly, when quantitative attributes are involved. In this context also further discretization methods for quantitative attribute values are badly needed. Comparison to other similar methods still requires due attention, although important results have been obtained in this area. Particularly interesting seems to be a study of the relationship between neural network and rough set approach to feature extraction from data.

Rough control and rough databases seem very promising domains of research and applications in the years to come.

References

1. Albaraan, M.: Weak controllability in a parallel flow model of computation and its relationship with rough sets. In: P. P. Wang (ed.), Proceedings of the International Workshop on Rough Sets and Soft Computing at Second Annual Joint Conference on Information Sciences (JCIS'95), Wrightsville Beach, North Carolina, 28 September – 1 October (1995) 205–20
2. An, A., Chan, C., Shan, N., Cercone, N., Ziarko, W.: Applying knowledge discovery to predict water-supply consumption. IEEE Expert **12/4** (1997) 72–78

3. Baltzersen, J. K.: An attempt to predict stock market data: A rough sets approach. Master Thesis, supervisor J. Komorowski. Knowledge Systems Group, The Norwegian University of Science and Technology, Trondheim, Norway (1995)
4. Beaubouef, T., Petry, F. E., Buckles, B. P.: Extension of the relational database and its algebra with rough set techniques. In: W. Ziarko (ed.), Computational Intelligence: An International Journal **11/2** (1995) (special issue) 233–245
5. Cattaneo, G.: Mathematical foundations of roughness and fuzziness. In: S. Tsumoto at al, (eds.), The fourth International Workshop on Rough Sets, Fuzzy Sets and Machine Discovery, Proceedings, The University of Tokyo (1996) 241–247
6. Chakraborty, M. K., Banerjee, M.: In search of a common foundation for rough sets and fuzzy sets. In: Proceedings of the Fifth European Congress on Intelligent Techniques and Soft Computing (EUFIT'97), Aachen, Germany, Verlag Mainz (1997) 1 218–220
7. Chen, R., Lin, T.Y.: Supporting rough set theory in very large databases using Oracle RDBMS. In: Y.-Y. Chen, K. Hirota, and J.-Y. Yen (eds.), Proceedings of Asian Fuzzy Systems Symposium – Soft Computing in Intelligent Systems and Information Processing, December 11–14, Kenting, Taiwan, ROC. (1996) 332–337
8. Czogala, E., Mrozek, A., Pawlak, Z.: The idea of rough-fuzzy controller. International Journal of Fuzzy Sets and Systems **72** (1995) 61–63
9. Czyzewski, A.: New learning algorithms for the processing of old audio recordings. In: 99th Convention of the Audio Engineering Society, October 6–9, New York, USA, preprint 4078 (1995)
10. Czyzewski, A.: Speaker–independent recognition of digits – Experiments with neural networks, fuzzy logic and rough sets. In: T. Y. Lin (ed.), Journal of the Intelligent Automation and Soft Computing 2/2 (1996) 133–146
11. Czyzewski, A., Kostek, B.: Rough set-based filtration of sound applicable to hearing prostheses. In: Tsumoto, S. Kobayashi, T. Yokomori, H. Tanaka, and A. Nakamura (eds.), Proceedings of the Fourth International Workshop on Rough Sets, Fuzzy Sets, and Machine Discovery (RSFD'96). The University of Tokyo, November 6–8 (1996) 168–175
12. Czyzewski, A., Kostek, B.: Restoration of old records employing artificial intelligence methods. Proceedings of IASTED International Conference – Artificial Intelligence, Expert Systems and Neural Networks, August 19–21, Honolulu, Hawaii, USA (1996) 372–375
13. Deogun, J., Raghavan, V., Sarkar, A., Sever, H.: Data mining: Trends in research and development. In: T. Y. Lin, N. Cercone (eds.), Rough Sets and Data Mining. Analysis of Imprecise Data. Kluwer Academic Publishers, Boston, Dordrecht (1997) 9–45
14. Dubois, D., Parade, H.: Putting rough sets and fuzzy sets together. In: R. Slowinski (ed.), Intelligent Decision Support – Handbook of Advances and

Applications of the Rough Set Theory. Kluwer Academic Publishers, Dordrecht, Boston, London (1992) 203–232

15. Eiben, A. E., Euverman, T. J., Kowalczyk, W., Slisser, F.: Modelling customer retention with statistical techniques, rough data models, and genetic programming. In: S. K. Pal, A. Skowron (eds.), Fuzzy Sets, Rough Sets, and Decision Making Processes. Springer-Verlag, Singapore (in print)
16. Fernandes–Baizan, M. C., Menasalvas Ruiz, E., Pena, J. M., Santos, E.: Using RDMS to mine microbiological data. In: Nagib C. Callaos (ed.), Proceedings of the International Conference on Information Systems Analysis and Synthesis (ISAS'96), July 22–26, Orlando, USA (1996) 551–554
17. Frege, G.: Grundgezetze der Arithemtik: Begrieffschriftliche abgeleitet. Vol. 1. Jena (1893), Vol. 2, Jena (1903)
18. Garcia, A., Shasa, D.: Using rough sets to order questions leading to database queries. In: Nagib C. Callaos (ed.), Proceedings of the International Conference on Information Systems Analysis and Synthesis (ISAS'96), July 22–26, Orlando, USA (1996) 555–560
19. Golan, R., Ziarko, W.: A methodology for stock market analysis utilizing rough set theory. In: Proceedings of IEEE/IAFE Conference on Computational Intelligence for Financial Engineering, New York City (1995) 32–40
20. Greco, S., Matarazzo, B., Slowinski, R.: A new rough set approach to evaluation of bankruptcy risk. In: C. Zopounidis (ed.), New Operational Tools in the Management of Financial Risks, Kluwer Academic Publishers, Dordrecht (to appear)
21. Grzymala-Busse, J. W.: Knowledge acquisition under uncertainty – a rough set approach. Journal of Intelligent and Robotics Systems **1** (1988) 3–16
22. Grzymala-Busse, J. W., Goodwin, L. K.: Predicting preterm birth risk using machine learning from data with missing values. In: S. Tsumoto (ed.), Bulletin of International Rough Set Society **1/1** 17–21
23. Grzymala-Busse, J. W., Gunn, J. D.: Global temperature analysis based on the rule induction system LERS. In: Proceedings of the Fourth International Workshop on Intelligent Information Systems, Augustow, Poland, June 5–9, 1995, Institute of Computer Science, Polish Academy of Sciences, Warsaw (1995) 148–158
24. Grzymala-Busse, J. W., Sedelow, S. Y., Sedelow, W. A. Jr.: Machine learning & knowledge acquisition, rough sets, and the English semantic code. In: T. Y. Lin (ed.), Proceedings of the Workshop on Rough Sets and Data Mining at 23rd Annual Computer Science Conference. Nashville, Tennessee, March 2 (1995) 86–104; also in T. Y. Lin, N. Cercone (eds.), Rough Sets and Data Mining. Analysis of Imprecise Data. Kluwer Academic Publishers, Boston, Dordrecht (1997) 91–107
25. Gunn, J. D., Grzymala-Busse, J. W.: Global temperature stability by rule induction: An interdisciplinary bridge. Human Ecology **22** (1994) 59–81
26. Hadjimichael, M., Wasilewska, A.: Rough sets-based study of voter preference in 1988 USA presidential election. In: R. Slowinski (ed.), Intelligent

Decision Support–Handbook of Applications and Advances of the Rough Sets Theory. Kluwer Academic Publishers, Dordrecht (1992) 137–152

27. Ho, T. B., Funakoshi, K.: Information retrieval using rough sets (submitted to Journal of Japanese Society for Artificial Intelligence)
28. Jackson, A. G., Leclair, S. R., Ohmer, M. C., Ziarko, W., Al-Kamhawi, H.: Rough sets applied to material data. Acta Metallurgica et Materialia (1996) 44–75
29. Kostek, B., Szczerba, M.: Rough set–based analysis of musical databases. In: Proceedings of the Fourth European Congress on Intelligent Techniques and Soft Computing, (EUFIT'96), September 2–5, Aachen, Germany, Verlag Mainz (1996) **1** 144–148
30. Krysinski, J.: Application of the rough sets theory to the analysis of structure–activity relationships of antimicrobial pyridinium compounds. Die Pharmazie **50** (1995) 593–597
31. Krysinski, J.: Rough sets in the analysis of the structure–activity relationships of antifungal imidazolium compounds. Journal of Pharmaceutical Sciences **84/2** (1995) 243–247
32. Krusinska, E., Slowinski, R., Stefanowski, J.: Discriminant versus rough set approach to vague data analysis. Journal of Applied Statistics and Data Analysis 8 (1992) 43–56
33. Lin, T. Y.: Fuzzy reasoning and rough sets. In: W. Ziarko (ed.), Rough Sets, Fuzzy Sets and Knowledge Discovery (RSKD'93). Workshops in Computing, Springer-Verlag & British Computer Society, London, Berlin (1994) 343–348
34. T. Y. Lin (ed.): Proceedings of the Third International Workshop on Rough Sets and Soft Computing (RSSC'94). San Jose State University, San Jose, California, USA, November 10–12 (1994)
35. T. Y. Lin (ed.): Proceedings of the Workshop on Rough Sets and Data Mining at 23rd Annual Computer Science Conference. Nashville, Tennessee, March 2 (1995)
36. Lin, T. Y.: Rough-fuzzy controllers for complex systems. In: P. P. Wang (ed.), Proceedings of the International Workshop on Rough Sets and Soft Computing at Second Annual Joint Conference on Information Sciences (JCIS'95), Wrightsville Beach, North Carolina, 28 September – 1 October (1995) 18–21
37. Lin, T. Y.: Neighborhood systems – A qualitative theory for fuzzy and rough sets. In: P. P. Wang (ed.), Proceedings of the International Workshop on Rough Sets and Soft Computing at Second Annual Joint Conference on Information Sciences (JCIS'95), Wrightsville Beach, North Carolina, 28 September – 1 October (1995) 255–258
38. Lin, T. Y.: Fuzzy controllers: An integrated approach based on fuzzy logic, rough sets, and evolutionary computing. In: T. Y. Lin (ed.), Proc. of the Workshop on Rough Sets and Data Mining at 23-rd Annual Computer Science Conference, Nashville, Tennessee, 2 March (1995)

39. T. Y. Lin (ed.): CSC'95, 23rd Annual Computer Science Conference on Rough Sets and Database Mining, Conference Proceedings, March 2, San Jose State University, San Jose, California, USA (1995)
40. Lin, T. Y.: Fuzzy controllers: An integrated approach based on fuzzy logic, rough sets, and evolutionary computing. In: T. Y. Lin and N. Cecerone (eds.), Rough Sets and Data Mining. Analysis for Imprecise Data, Kluwer Academic Publishers, Dordrech (1997) 123–138
41. T. Y. Lin, N. Cercone (eds.): Rough Sets and Data Mining. Analysis of Imprecise Data. Kluwer Academic Publishers, Boston, Dordrecht (1997)
42. T. Y. Lin, A. M. Wilderberg (eds.): Soft Computing, Proceedings of the Third International Workshop on Rough Sets and Soft Computing (RSSC'94), November 10–12, San Jose State University, San Jose, California, USA (1994)
43. Lin, T. Y., Wildberger, M.: Algebra and geometry of rough logic controllers In: S. Tsumoto, S. Kobayashi, T. Yokomori, H. Tanaka and A. Nakamura (eds.), The fourth International Workshop on Rough Sets, Fuzzy Sets, and Machine Discovery, Proceedings (RS96FD), November 6–8, The University of Tokyo (1996) 111–117
44. Lingras, P.: Rough neural networks. In: Proceedings of the Sixth International Conference, Information Processing and Management of Uncertainty in Knowledge–Based Systems (IPMU'96), July 1–5, Granada, Spain (1996) 2 1445–1450
45. Lingras, P.: Learning using rough Kohonen neural networks classifiers. In: P. Borne, G. Dauphin-Tanguy, C. Sueur, and S. El Khattabi (eds.), Proceedings of IMACS Multiconference: Computational Engineering in Systems Applications (CESA'96) July 9–12, Lille, France, Gerf EC Lille – Cite Scientifique (1996) **3/4** 753–757
46. Mitra, S., Banerjee, M.: Knowledge-based neural net with rough sets. In: T. Yamakawa et al. (eds.), Methodologies for the Conception, Design, and Application of Intelligent Systems, Proceedings of the Fourth International Conference on Soft Computing (IIZUKA'96), Iizuka, Japan 1996, World Scientific (1996) 213–216
47. Moradi, H., Grzymala-Busse, J. W., Roberts, J.: Entropy of English text: Experiments with humans and machine learning system based on rough sets. In: P. P. Wang (ed.), Proceedings of the International Workshop on Rough Sets and Soft Computing at Second Annual Joint Conference on Information Sciences (JCIS'95), Wrightsville Beach, North Carolina, 28 September – 1 October (1995) 87–88
48. Mrozek, A.: Rough sets in computer implementation of rule-based control of industrial processes. In: R. Slowinski (ed.), Intelligent Decision Support – Handbook of Applications and Advances of the Rough Sets Theory. Kluwer Academic Publishers, Dordrecht (1992) 19–31
49. Munakata, T.: Rough control: A perspective. In: 23rd Annual Computer Science Conference on Rough Sets and Database Mining (CSC'95), Conference Proceedings, March 2, San Jose University, San Jose, California, USA (1995)

50. Munakata, T., Pawlak, Z.: Rough control application of rough set theory to control. Fourth European Congress on Intelligent Techniques and Soft Computing, Proceedings EUFIT'96), Volume I, September 2–5, Germany (1996) 209–218
51. Nakamura, A.: Fuzzy quantifiers and rough quantifiers. In: P. P. Wang (ed.), Advances in Fuzzy Theory and Technology II (1994) 111–131 Nguyen, H. Son, Szczuka, M., Slezak, D.: Neural network design: Rough set approach to real–valued data. In: J. Komorowski, J. Zytkow, (eds.), The First European Symposium on Principles of Data Mining and Knowledge Discovery (PKDD'97), June 25–27, Trondheim, Norway, Lecture Notes in Artificial Intelligence 1263, Springer-Verlag, Berlin (1997) 359–366
52. Nguyen, T., Swiniarski, R., Skowron, A., Bazan, J., Thagarajan, K.: Applications of rough sets, neural networks and maximum likelihood for texture classification based on singular value decomposition. In: T. Y. Lin (ed.), The Third International Workshop on Rough Sets and Soft Computing Proceedings (RSSC'94), November 10–12, San Jose State University, San Jose, California, USA, 332–339; see also in: T. Y. Lin and A. M. Wildberger (eds.), Soft Computing Councils, Inc., San Diego (1995) 157–160
53. Nowicki, R., Slowinski, R., Stefanowski, J.: Rough sets analysis of diagnostic capacity of vibroacoustic symptoms. Journal of Computers and Mathematics with Applications **24** (1992) 109–123
54. Nurmi, H., Kacprzyk, J., Fedrizzi, M.: Theory and methodology: Probabilistic, fuzzy and rough concepts in social choice. European Journal of Operational Research, Elsevier (1996) 264–277
55. E. Orlowska (ed.): Incomplete Information: Rough Set Analysis. Physica–Verlag, Heidelberg (1997)
56. Øhrn, A., Vinterbo, S., Szymanski, P., Komorowski, J.: Modelling cardiac patient set residuals using rough sets. In: Proceedings of AMIA Annual Fall Symposium (formerly SCAMC), Nashville, TN, USA, October 25–29 (1997) 203–207; see also: Technical Report, Knowledge Systems Group, Norwegian University of Science and Technology, Trondheim, Norway (1997) (extended version)
57. S. K. Pal, A. Skowron (eds.): Fuzzy Sets, Rough Sets and Decision Making Processes. Springer–Verlag, Singapore (in print)
58. Paszek, P., Wakulicz-Deja, A.: Optimization diagnose in progressive encephalopathy applying the rough set theory. In: Proceedings of the Fourth European Congress on Intelligent Techniques and Soft Computing (EUFIT'96), September 2–5, Aachen, Germany, Verlag Mainz (1996) **1** 192–196
59. Pawlak, Z.: Rough sets. International Journal of Computer and Information Sciences **11** (1982) 341–356
60. Pawlak, Z.: Rough sets and fuzzy sets. J. of Fuzzy Sets and Systems **17** (1985) 99–102

61. Pawlak, Z.: Rough sets and fuzzy sets. In: C. Jinshong (ed.), Proceedings of ACM, Computer Science Conference, February 28 – March 2, Nashville, Tennessee (1995) 262–264
62. Pawlak, Z.: Rough Sets, Theoretical Aspects of Reasoning above Data. Kluwer Academic Publishers, Dordrecht, Boston, London (1991)
63. Pawlak, Z., Skowron, A.: Rough membership functions. In: R. R. Yeager, M. Fedrizzi, J. Kacprzyk (eds.), Advances in the Dempster-Shafer Theory of Evidence, John Wiley and Sons, New York (1994) 251–271
64. Pawlak, Z., Slowinski, R.: Decision analysis using rough sets. International Transactions on Operational Research **1** (1994) 107–104
65. Pawlak, Z., Grzymala-Busse, J., Slowinski, R. Ziarko, W.: Rough sets. Communication of the ACM **38** (1995) 88–95
66. Peters III, J. F., Ramanna, S.: A rough set approach to assessing software quality: Concepts and rough Petri net models. In: S. K. Pal, A. Skowron (eds.), Fuzzy Sets, Rough Sets and Decision Making Processes. Springer–Verlag, Singapore (in preparation)
67. Peterson, G. I.: Rough classification of pneumonia patients using a clinical data–base. In: W. Ziarko (ed.), Rough Sets, Fuzzy Sets and Knowledge Discovery (RSKD'93). Workshops in Computing, Springer–Verlag & British Computer Society, London, Berlin (1994) 412–419
68. Plonka, L., Mrozek, A.: Rule-based stabilization of the inverted pendulum. Computational Intelligence: An International Journal 11 (1995) 348–356
69. Polkowski, L.: Mathematical morphology of rough sets. Bull. Polish Acad. Sci. Math. **41/3** (1993) 241–273
70. Polkowski, L, Skowron, A.: Rough mereology: A new paradigm for approximate reasoning. Journal of Approximate Reasoning **15/4** (1996) 333–365
71. Quafafou, M.: Towards a transition from the crisp rough set theory to a fuzzy one. In: Proceedings of the Poster Session of the Ninth International Symposium on Methodologies for Intelligent Systems (ISMIS'96), Zakopane, Poland, June 9–13, Oak Ridge Laboratory (1996) 67–80
72. Ruhe G.: Qualitative analysis of software engineering data using rough sets. In: S. Tsumoto, S. Kobayashi, T. Yokomori, H. Tanaka, and A. Nakamura (eds.), Proceedings of the Fourth International Workshop on Rough Sets, Fuzzy Sets, and Machine Discovery (RSFD'96). The University of Tokyo, November 6–8 (1996) 292–299
73. Shenoi, S.: Rough sets in fuzzy databases. In: P. P. Wang (ed.), Proceedings of the International Workshop on Rough Sets and Soft Computing at Second Annual Joint Conference on Information Sciences (JCIS'95), Wrightsville Beach, North Carolina, 28 September – 1 October (1995) 263–264
74. Skowron, A., Rauszer, C.: The discernibility matrices and functions in information systems. In: R. Slowinski (ed.), Intelligent Decision Support – Handbook of Advances and Applications of the Rough Set Theory. Kluwer Academic Publishers, Dordrecht, Boston, London (1992) 311–369

75. Skowron, A., Grzymala-Busse, J.: From rough set theory to evidence theory. In: R. R. Yeager, M. Fedrizzi, J. Kacprzyk (eds.) Advances in the Dempster-Shafer Theory of Evidence, John Wiley and Sons, New York (1994) 193–236

76. Slowinski, K., Sharif, E. S.: Rough sets approach to analysis of data of diagnostic peritoneal lavage applied for multiple injuries patients. In: W. Ziarko (ed.), Rough Sets, Fuzzy Sets and Knowledge Discovery (RSKD'93). Workshops in Computing, Springer–Verlag & British Computer Society, London, Berlin (1994) 420–425

77. Slowinski, K., Slowinski, R., Stefanowski, J.: Rough sets approach to analysis of data from peritoneal lavage in acute pancreatitis. Medical Informatics **13/3** (1988) 143–159

78. Slowinski, K., Stefanowski, J., Antczak, A., Kwas, Z.: Rough sets approach to the verification of indications for treatment of urinary stones by extracorporeal shock wave lithotripsy (ESWL). In: T.Y. Lin, A. M. Wildberger (eds.), Soft Computing: Rough Sets, Fuzzy Logic, Neural Networks, Uncertainty Management, Knowledge Discovery. Simulation Councils, Inc., San Diego, CA (1995) 93–96

79. R. Slowinski (ed.): Intelligent Decision Support – Handbook of Advances and Applications of the Rough Set Theory. Kluwer Academic Publishers, Dordrecht, Boston, London (1992)

80. Slowinski, R.: Rough set approach to decision analysis. AI Expert **10** (1995) 18–25

81. Slowinski, R., Zopounidis, C.: Applications of the rough set approach to evaluation of bankruptcy risk. Working Paper 93–08, Decision Support System Laboratory, Technical University of Crete, June (1993); see also: International J. Intelligent Systems in Accounting, Finance & Management **4/1** (1995) 27–41

82. Slowinski, R., Zopounidis, C.: Rough set sorting of firms according to bankruptcy risk. In: M. Paruccini (ed.), Applying Multiple Criteria Aid for Decision to Environmental Management, Kluwer, Dordrecht, Netherlands (1994) 339–357

83. Slowinski, R., Zopounidis, C., Dimitras, A.I.: Prediction of company acquisition in Greece by means of the rough set approach. European Journal of Operational Research **100** (1997) 1–15

84. Srinivasan, P.: The importance of rough approximations for information retrieval. Journal of Man–Machine Studies **34** (1991) 657–671

85. Swiniarski, R., Hunt, F., Chalvet, D., Pearson, D.: Feature selection using rough sets and hidden layer expansion for rupture prediction in a highly automated production system. In: Proceedings of the 12th International Conference on Systems Science, September 12–15, Wroclaw, Poland (1995); see also: Systems Science **23/1** (1997)

86. Swiniarski, R., Hunt, F., Chalvet, D., Pearson, D.: Intelligent data processing and dynamic process discovery using rough sets, statistical reasoning and neural networks in a highly automated production systems. In: Proceedings

of the First European Conference on Application of Neural Networks in Industry, August, Helsinki, Finland (1995)

87. Szczuka, M.: Rough set methods for constructing neural network. In: Proceedings of the Third Biennal Joint Conference On Engineering Systems Design and Analysis, Session on Expert Systems, Montpellier, France (1996) 9–14

88. Szladow, A., Ziarko, W.: Rough sets: Working with imperfect data. AI Expert **8** (1993) 36–41

89. Szladow, A., Ziarko W.: Adaptive process control using rough sets. Proceedings of the International Conference of Instrument Society of America, ISA/93, Chicago (1993) 1421–1430

90. Szladow, A., Ziarko W.: Application of rough sets theory to process control. Proceedings of Calgary 93 Symposium of Instrument Society of America, Calgary (1993)

91. Tanaka, H., Ishibuchi, H., Shigenaga, T.: Fuzzy inference system based on rough sets and its application to medical diagnostic. In: R. Slowinski (ed.), Intelligent Decision Support – Handbook of Applications and Advances of the Rough Sets Theory. Kluwer Academic Publishers, Dordrecht (1992) 111–117

92. Tanaka, H., Tsumoto, S.: Incremental learning of probabilistic rules from clinical databases based on rough set theory. In: P. P. Wang (ed.), Proceedings of the Fifth International Workshop on Rough Sets and Soft Computing (RSSC'97) at Third Annual Joint Conference on Information Sciences (JCIS'97). Duke University, Durham, NC, USA, Rough Set & Computer Science **3**, March 1–5 (1997) 387–390

93. Teghem, J., Benjelloun, M.: Some experiments to compare rough set theory and ordinal statistical methods. In: R. Slowinski (ed.), Intelligent Decision Support – Handbook of Applications and Advances of the Rough Sets Theory. Kluwer Academic Publishers, Dordrecht (1992) 267–286

94. Thiele, H.: Fuzzy rough sets versus rough fuzzy sets – An interpretation and a comparative study using concepts of modal logics. In: Proceedings of the Fifth European Congress on Intelligent Techniques and Soft Computing (EUFIT'97), September 9–11, Aachen, Germany, Verlag Mainz (1997) 159–167

95. Tseng, H. Ch., Lin, T. Y., Chi, C. W.: Adaptive aggregation of modular control. In: Y.-Y. Chen, K. Hirota, and J.-Y. Yen (eds.), Proceedings of 1996 ASIAN FUZZY SYSTEMS SYMPOSIUM – Soft Computing in Intelligent Systems and Information Processing, December 11–14, Kenting, Taiwan, ROC. (1996) 506–508

96. Tsumoto, S.: Domain experts' interpretation of rules induced from clinical databases. In: Proceedings of the Fifth European Congress on Intelligent Techniques and Soft Computing (EUFIT-97), Aachen, Germany, Verlag Mainz (1997) **1** 1639–1642

97. Tsumoto, S.: Extraction of expert's decision process from clinical databases using rough set model. In: J. Komorowski, J. Zytkow, (eds.), The First European Symposium on Principles of Data Mining and Knowledge Discovery

(PKDD'97), June 25–27, Trondheim, Norway, Lecture Notes in Artificial Intelligence **1263**, Springer–Verlag, Berlin (1997) 58–67

98. S. Tsumoto, S. Kobayashi, T. Yokomori, H. Tanaka, A. Nakamura (eds.): Proceedings of the Fourth International Workshop on Rough Sets, Fuzzy Sets, and Machine Discovery (RSFD'96). The University of Tokyo, November 6–8 (1996)
99. Tsumoto, S., Tanaka, H.: Automated discovery of functional components of proteins from amino-acid sequences based on rough sets and change of representation. In: U. M. Fayyad, R. Uthurusamy (eds.), Proceedings of the First International Conference on Knowledge Discovery and Data Mining (KDD'95), August 20–21, 1995, Montreal, AAAI Press, Menlo Park CA (1995) 318–324
100. Tsumoto, S., Ziarko, W.: The application of rough sets–based data mining technique to differential diagnosis of meningoencephalitis. In: Z. W. Ras, M. Michalewicz (eds.), Proceedings of the Ninth International Symposium on Methodologies for Intelligent Systems. Zakopane, Poland, June 9–13, Lecture Notes in Artificial Intelligence (ISMIS'96) **1079**, Springer–Verlag, Berlin (1996) 438–447
101. Wakulicz–Deja, A., Paszek, P.: Diagnose progressive encephalopathy applying the rough set theory. International Journal of Medical Informatics **46** (1997) 119–127
102. Wakulicz-Deja, A., Paszek, P., Marszal-Paszek, B., Emrich, E.: Applying rough sets to diagnosis in children's neurology. In: Proceedings of the Sixth International Conference, Information Processing and Management of Uncertainty in Knowledge–Based Systems (IPMU'96), July 1–5, Granada, Spain (1996) **3** 1463–1468
103. P. P. Wang (ed.): Proceedings of the International Workshop on Rough Sets and Soft Computing at Second Annual Joint Conference on Information Sciences (JCIS'-95), Wrightsville Beach, North Carolina, 28 September – 1 October (1995)
104. P. P. Wang (ed.): Proceedings of the Fifth International Workshop on Rough Sets and Soft Computing (RSSC'97) at Third Annual Joint Conference on Information Sciences (JCIS'97). Duke University, Durham, NC, USA, Rough Set & Computer Science **3**, March 1–5 (1997)
105. Woolery, L., Van Dyne, M., Grzymala-Busse, J. W., Tsatsoulis, C.: Machine learning for development of an expert system to support nurses' assessment of preterm birth risk. In: Nursing Informatics: An International Overview for Nursing in a Technological Era, Proceedings of the Fifth International Conference on Nursing Use of Computers and Information Sci., June 17–22, San Antonio, TX, Elsevier (1994) 357–361
106. Yao, Y. Y.: On combining rough and fuzzy sets. In: T. Y. Lin (ed.), Proceedings of the Workshop on Rough Sets and Data Mining at 23rd Annual Computer Science Conference. Nashville, Tennessee, March 2 (1995) 165–172

107. Yao, Y. Y.: Combination of rough and fuzzy sets based on alpha-level sets. In: T. Y. Lin, N. Cercone (eds.), Rough Sets and Data Mining. Analysis of Imprecise Data. Kluwer Academic Publishers, Boston, Dordrecht (1997) 301–321
108. Yao, Y. Y., Wong, S. K. M.: Generalization of rough sets using relationships between attribute values. In: Proceedings of the Second Annual Joint Conference on Information Sciences, Wrightsville Beach, N.C. USA, September 28 – October 1 (1995) 245–253
109. Yasdi, R.: Combining rough sets learning and neural learning method to deal with uncertain and imprecise information. Neurocomputing **7** (1995) 61–84
110. Zadeh, L.: Fuzzy graphs, rough sets and information granularity. In: Proc. Third Int. Workshop on Rough Sets and Soft Computing, November 10–12, San Jose (1994)
111. Zadeh, L.: Information granulation, fuzzy logic and rough sets. In: Tsumoto, S. Kobayashi, T. Yokomori, H. Tanaka, and A. Nakamura (eds.), Proceedings of the Fourth International Workshop on Rough Sets, Fuzzy Sets, and Machine Discovery (RSFD'96). The University of Tokyo, November 6–8 (1996)
112. Zhang, Q., Han, Z., Wen, F.: A new approach for fault diagnosis in power systems based on rough set theory. In: Proceedings of International Conference on Advances in Power System Control, Operation and Management (APSCOM'97), Hong Kong, China, November 11–14, (1997)
113. Ziarko, W.: Acquisition of control algorithms from operation data. In: R. Slowinski (ed.), Intelligent Decision Support, Handbook of Applications and Advances of the Rough Set Theory, Kluwer Academic Publishers, Boston, London, Dordrecht (1992) 61–75
114. Ziarko, W.: Generation of control algorithms for computerized controllers by operator supervised training. Proceedings of the Eleventh IASTED International Conference on Modeling, Identification and Control, Innsbruck, Austria (1992) 510–513
115. W. Ziarko (ed.): Rough Sets, Fuzzy Sets and Knowledge Discovery. Proceeding of the International Workshop on Rough Sets and Knowledge Discovery (RSKD'93), Banff, Alberta, Canada, Springer Verlag, Berlin, Heidelberg, New York, London, Paris, Tokyo, Hong Kong, Barcelona, Budapest (1993)
116. W. Ziarko (ed.): Rough Sets, Fuzzy Sets and Knowledge Discovery (RSKD'93). Workshops in Computing, Springer–Verlag & British Computer Society, London, Berlin (1994)
117. W. Ziarko (ed.): Computational Intelligence: An International Journal **11/2** (1995) (special issue)
118. Ziarko, W., Katzberg, J.: Control algorithms acquisition, analysis and reduction: machine learning approach. In: Knowledge-Based Systems Diagnosis, Supervision and Control, Plenum Press, Oxford (1989) 167–178

Generalizing the Explicit Concept of Rough Set on the Basis of Modal Logic*

Helmut Thiele

University of Dortmund, Department of Computer Science I
D-44221 Dortmund, Germany

Abstract. In usual publications on rough set theory, rough sets are very often defined (or are described) as ordered pairs of their lower and upper approximations with respect to a fixed equivalence relation on the universe considered.

In contrast to this approach we are of the opinion that a rough set is an unknown (or non-deterministic) set which generates a certain lower and upper approximation. Now, one is faced with the fact that different sets can generate the same lower and upper approximations (the fact of "non-determinism"). Following Z. PAWLAK and other authors this difficulty can be overcome by defining a rough set as the system of all sets which generate the same lower and the same upper approximation. For such systems of sets ("non-deterministic" sets) we define a partial order relation and operations like intersection and union as for usual crisp sets or fuzzy sets and investigate the obtained lattice.

Furthermore, we can state that the lower and the upper approximation can be interpreted by the modal box and diamond operator, respectively, where the reachability relation used is an equivalence relation on the universe considered. Now, we replace this equivalence relation by an arbitrary binary relation on the universe. Using this relation as the reachability relation in defining the box and diamond operator, we get a generalization of the lower and upper approximation. So, we obtain a generalization of the "classical" rough set theory in PAWLAK's sense. In particular, we can elaborate this approach using concepts of modal logic.

Keywords: Rough set theory. Lower and upper approximations. Modal logic. Box and diamond operator. Lattice theory.

1 Introduction

The intention of this paper is twofold.

Firstly, to develop an explicit concept of rough set such that one can operate with such rough sets as we are operating with crisp sets or fuzzy sets.

Secondly, to replace the equivalence relation used in "classical" rough set theory by an arbitrary binary relation and to develop this approach using concepts of modal logic by interpreting the lower and the upper approximation by the box and diamond operator, respectively.

With respect to the first aspect mentioned above in present publications on rough sets one can very often find approaches in which rough sets are defined as pairs

* This research was supported by the Deutsche Forschungsgemeinschaft as part of the Collaborative Research Center "Computational Intelligence" (531)

$[\underline{R}X, \overline{R}X]$ where $X \subseteq W$ is an unknown set and $\underline{R}X$ and $\overline{R}X$ are the lower and upper approximations of X, respectively, with respect to a fixed equivalence relation R on the given universe W.

This approach can already be found in Z. PAWLAK's seminal papers [30,33,32,31].

An introduction of lattice theoretic operations $\wedge$, $\vee$, and $\sim$ for such pairs is presented in [9]. Furthermore, in the paper [4] it is shown that the algebraic structure defined in [9] forms a STONE algebra. A realization of this approach on the basis of abstract completely distributive lattices is presented in [4] In an unpublished paper [8], L. ITURRIOZ added a further unary operation ∇. She could prove that the set of all pairs $[\underline{R}X, \overline{R}X]$ with $X \subseteq W$ is a three-valued ŁUKASIEWICZ algebra with respect to the operations $\wedge$, $\vee$, $\sim$, and ∇ (see also [13–20]).

Equivalence relations $\underset{\underline{R}}{\approx}$ and $\underset{\overline{R}}{\approx}$ on the power set $\mathfrak{P}W$ defined for $X, Y \subseteq W$ by

$$X \underset{\underline{R}}{\approx} Y =_{def} \underline{R}X = \underline{R}Y \text{ and } X \underset{\overline{R}}{\approx} Y =_{def} \overline{R}X = \overline{R}Y$$

are investigated in [27].

In the paper presented we do not hold the view described above because we are of the opinion that pairs of the form $[\underline{R}X, \overline{R}X]$ are not rough sets. Such pairs can only be considered as an approximation of an unknown set X. Furthermore, we are confronted with the fact that different sets X and Y can exist which have the same approximation, i. e. for which the equations $\underline{R}X = \underline{R}Y$ and $\overline{R}X = \overline{R}Y$ hold. So, one gets an equivalence relation $\underset{R}{\approx}$ on the power set $\mathfrak{P}W$ which for $X, Y \subseteq W$ is defined by

$$X \underset{R}{\approx} Y =_{def} \underline{R}X = \underline{R}Y \text{ and } \overline{R}X = \overline{R}Y,$$

and the equivalence classes from $\mathfrak{P}W/\underset{R}{\approx}$ can be considered as "rough sets" on W with respect to the equivalence relation R on W.

It is interesting to mention that the equivalence relation $\underset{R}{\approx}$ is already defined in [16–20]. This relation is applied in [8] to construct a three-valued ŁUKASIEWICZ algebra.

First ideas to define rough sets by applying such equivalence relations are due to PAWLAK [31].

The "philosophy" behind this approach is impressively expressed by D. DUBOIS and H. PRADE in [3] as follows: "a rough set is a collection of objects which cannot be precisely characterized in terms of the values of a set of attributes, while a lower and an upper approximation of the collection can be characterized in terms of these attributes".

Investigations of the equivalence relation $\underset{R}{\approx}$ in detail are contained in [28]. In the paper [37] the authors try to define an intersection and a union of rough sets, i. e. of elements from $\mathfrak{P}W/\underset{R}{\approx}$, as in the construction of factor structures of classical algebra.

The way was not successful because the equivalence relation $\underset{R}{\approx}$ is not stable with respect to the intersection and the union of sets $X, Y \subseteq W$, i. e. $\underset{R}{\approx}$ is not a congruence relation with respect to the operations mentioned (see also proposition 11 of this paper).

In the paper presented we introduce an intersection and a union for elements of $\mathfrak{P}W/_{\underset{R}{\approx}}$ in a natural way (see chapter 1.6). The basis for this are results from chapter 1.4 and chapter 1.5 where we shall show how the sets $\mathfrak{P}W/_{\underset{\underline{R}}{\approx}}$ and $\mathfrak{P}W/_{\underset{\overline{R}}{\approx}}$ can be considered as lattices.

The second intention of this paper consists of the observation that many results of the "classical" rough set theory remain true if the equivalence relation used is replaced by a more general binary relation, for instance, if this relation is only reflexive on the universe and transitive (see theorems 4, 6, and 11). Furthermore, it is well-known that the lower approximation $\underline{R}X$ and the upper approximation $\overline{R}X$ can be expressed by the box operator and the diamond operator, respectively, if the reachability relation used in defining these operators is an equivalence relation on the universe considered. So, a generalized rough set theory can be developed using concepts of modal logic.

2 Some Concepts and Results from Lattice Theory and Modal Logic

In this chapter for definiteness we recall some well-known concepts, denotations and results from lattice theory and modal logic.

We fix a non-empty set W called universe or set of possible worlds. In the following we shall use the usual denotations of crisp set theory. For arbitrary subsets $X, Y \subseteq W$ we denote the intersection and the union of X and Y by $X \cap Y$ and $X \cup Y$, respectively. $\overline{X}$ is the complement of X with respect to W, i. e. $\overline{X} = W \setminus X$ where $W \setminus X$ denotes the set-theoretical difference of W and X. The empty set is denoted by $\varnothing$. $\mathfrak{P}W$ is the power set of W, i. e. the set of all subsets $X \subseteq W$. For a system $\mathfrak{X}$ of subsets $X \subseteq W$, i. e. $\mathfrak{X} \subseteq \mathfrak{P}W$, we denote by $\bigcap \mathfrak{X}$ and $\bigcup \mathfrak{X}$ the intersection and the union of all sets of $\mathfrak{X}$, respectively. Note that for the empty system $\emptyset \subseteq \mathfrak{P}W$ we have $\bigcap \emptyset = W$ and $\bigcup \emptyset = \varnothing$. For arbitrary sets X and Y the Cartesian product $X \times Y$ is the set of all ordered pairs $[x, y]$ where $x \in X$ and $y \in Y$. A binary relation R on W is a subset of $W \times W$. We denote the fact that $[x, y] \in R$ also by xRy.

Let R be a binary relation on W.

Definition 1. *1. R is said to be reflexive on W*
$=_{def} \forall x(x \in W \rightarrow xRx)$

2. *R is said to be symmetric*
$=_{def} \forall x \forall y(xRy \rightarrow yRx)$

3. *R is said to be antisymmetric*
   $=_{def} \forall x \forall y(xRy \wedge yRx \rightarrow x = y)$
4. *R is said to be transitive*
   $=_{def} \forall x \forall y \forall z(xRy \wedge yRz \rightarrow xRz)$
5. *R is said to be a tolerance relation on W*
   $=_{def}$ *R is reflexive on W and R is symmetric*
6. *R is said to be an S_4-relation on W*
   $=_{def}$ *R is reflexive on W and R is transitive*
7. *R is said to be an equivalence relation on W*
   $=_{def}$ *R is reflexive on W and R is transitive and symmetric*
8. *R is said to be a partial order relation on W*
   $=_{def}$ *R is reflexive on W and R is transitive and antisymmetric.*

Now let's recall some well-known concepts and results of lattice theory.

Assume that R is a partial order relation on W. For better understanding we denote R by $\leq$ and for $[x, y] \in R$ we write $x \leq y$. Put $\Pi =_{def} [W, \leq]$ and call Π a partially ordered set. Assume $l, u, i, s \in W$ and $S \subseteq W$.

Definition 2. *1. l is said to be a lower bound of S in* Π
   $=_{def} \forall x(x \in S \rightarrow l \leq x)$
2. *u is said to be an upper bound of S in* Π
   $=_{def} \forall x(x \in S \rightarrow x \leq u)$
3. *i is said to be an infimum of S in* Π
   $=_{def}$ *i is a lower bound of S in* Π *and* $\forall x$(*x is a lower bound of S in* $\Pi \rightarrow x \leq i$)
4. *s is said to be a supremum of S in* Π
   $=_{def}$ *i is an upper bound of S in* Π *and*
   $\forall x$(*x is an upper bound of S in* $\Pi \rightarrow s \leq x$)

Proposition 1. *1.* $\forall i \forall j$(*i and j are infima of S in* $\Pi \rightarrow i = j$)
2. $\forall s \forall t$(*s and t are suprema of S in* $\Pi \rightarrow s = t$)

Definition 3. *1.* Π *is said to be a semilattice with respect to its infimum (supremum, respectively)*
   $=_{def} \forall x \forall y(x, y \in W \rightarrow$
   the infimum (the supremum, respectively) of $\{x, y\}$ *in* Π *exists*)
2. Π *is said to be a complete semilattice with respect to its infimum (supremum, respectively)*
   $=_{def} \forall S(S \subseteq W \rightarrow$ *the infimum (the supremum, respectively) of S in* Π *exists*)
3. Π *is said to be a lattice*
   $=_{def} \Pi$ *is a semilattice with respect to its infimum and supremum*
4. Π *is said to be a complete lattice*
   $=_{def} \Pi$ *is a complete semilattice with respect to its infimum and supremum.*

Proposition 2. *If* Π *is a complete semilattice with respect to its infimum or with respect to its supremum then* Π *is a complete lattice.*

Let $\Pi = [W, \leq]$ and $\Pi' = [W', \leq']$ be partially ordered sets.

Definition 4. *1.* φ *is said to be an order isomorphism from* Π *onto* Π'
$=_{def}$ *1.* $\varphi: W \to W'$ *is a bijection.*
2. $\forall x \forall y(x \leq y \leftrightarrow \varphi(x) \leq \varphi(y))$

2. φ *is said to be a dual order isomorphism from* Π *onto* Π'
$=_{def}$ *1.* $\varphi: W \to W'$ *is a bijection.*
2. $\forall x \forall y(x \leq y \leftrightarrow \varphi(y) \leq \varphi(x))$

Proposition 3. *If* φ *is an order isomorphism from* Π *onto* Π' *then*

1. Π *is a semilattice with respect to its infimum (supremum, respectively) if and only if* Π' *has the same properties.*
2. Π *is a complete semilattice with respect to its infimum (supremum, respectively) if and only if* Π' *has the same properties.*

Proposition 4. *If* φ *is a dual order isomorphism from* Π *onto* Π' *then*

1. Π *is a semilattice with respect to its infimum (supremum, respectively) if and only if* Π' *is a semilattice with respect to its supremum (infimum, respectively).*
2. Π *is a complete semilattice with respect to its infimum (supremum, respectively) if and only if* Π' *is a complete semilattice with respect to its supremum (infimum, respectively).*

Let $\Pi_1 = [W_1, \leq_1]$ and $\Pi_2 = [W_2, \leq_2]$ be partially ordered sets. We define the direct product $\Pi_1 \times \Pi_2 = [W, \leq]$ as follows where $x_1, y_1 \in W_1$ and $x_2, y_2 \in W_2$.

Definition 5. *1.* $W =_{def} W_1 \times W_2$
2. $[x_1, x_2] \leq [y_1, y_2] =_{def} x_1 \leq y_1 \wedge x_2 \leq y_2$

Proposition 5. *1.* $\Pi_1 \times \Pi_2$ *is a partially ordered set.*
2. *If* Π_1 *and* Π_2 *are lattices then* $\Pi_1 \times \Pi_2$ *is a lattice.*
3. *If* Π_1 *and* Π_2 *are complete lattices then* $\Pi_1 \times \Pi_2$ *is a complete lattice.*
4. *If* Π_1 *and* Π_2 *are distributive lattices then* $\Pi_1 \times \Pi_2$ *is a distributive lattice.*

Now, we turn over to modal logic.

Assume R is an arbitrary binary relation on W. From modal logic we adopt the definition of the box operator $[R]$ and the diamond operator $\langle R \rangle$ generated as follows where $X \subseteq W$.

Definition 6. *1.* $[R]X = \{x | \forall y(xRy \to y \in X)\}$
2. $\langle R \rangle X = \{x | \exists y(xRy \wedge y \in X)\}$

Proposition 6. *1.* $\forall X \forall Y(X, Y \subseteq W \to$
$$[R](X \cap Y) = [R]X \cap [R]Y \wedge \langle R \rangle (X \cap Y) \subseteq \langle R \rangle X \cap \langle R \rangle Y)$$
2. $\forall \mathfrak{X}(\mathfrak{X} \subseteq \mathfrak{P}W \to$
$$[R]\left(\bigcap \mathfrak{X}\right) = \bigcap \{[R]X | X \in \mathfrak{X}\} \wedge \langle R \rangle \left(\bigcap \mathfrak{X}\right) \subseteq \bigcap \{\langle R \rangle X | X \in \mathfrak{X}\})$$

Proposition 7. *1.* $\forall X \forall Y(X, Y \subseteq W \to$
$$\langle R \rangle (X \cup Y) = \langle R \rangle X \cup \langle R \rangle Y \wedge [R](X \cup Y) \supseteq [R]X \cup [R]Y)$$
2. $\forall \mathfrak{X}(\mathfrak{X} \subseteq \mathfrak{P}W \to$
$$\langle R \rangle \left(\bigcup \mathfrak{X}\right) = \bigcup \{\langle R \rangle X | X \in \mathfrak{X}\} \wedge [R]\left(\bigcup \mathfrak{X}\right) \supseteq \bigcup \{[R]X | X \in \mathfrak{X}\})$$

Proposition 8. *1.* $[R]\overline{X} = \overline{\langle R \rangle X}$
2. $\langle R \rangle \overline{X} = \overline{[R]X}$

3 Lower Rough Sets, Upper Rough Sets, and Rough Sets

Assume R is an equivalence relation on W. Denote by $W/_R$ the partition of W generated by R. For $X \subseteq W$ PAWLAK defined the R-lower approximation $\underline{R}X$ of X and the R-upper approximation $\overline{R}X$ of X as follows.

Definition 7. *1.* $\underline{R}X = \bigcup\left\{P \middle| P \in W/_R \wedge P \subseteq X\right\}$

2. $\overline{R}X = \bigcup\left\{P \middle| P \in W/_R \wedge P \cap X \neq \varnothing\right\}$

Trivially follows

Proposition 9. *If R is an equivalence relation then*

1. $\underline{R}X = [R]X$
2. $\overline{R} = \langle R\rangle X$

This proposition means that the approximation concepts can be expressed by means of modal logic.

Now, we are going to make precise the "philosophy" of DUBOIS and PRADE mentioned in chapter 1.1 of this paper (see [3], see also [8,18,31,37]).

For this purpose we define three binary relations $\underset{[R]}{\approx}$, $\underset{\langle R\rangle}{\approx}$, and $\underset{R}{\approx}$ on $\mathfrak{P}W$ where R is an arbitrary fixed binary relation on W. Assume $X, Y \subseteq W$.

Definition 8. *1.* $X \underset{[R]}{\approx} Y =_{def} [R]X = [R]Y$

2. $X \underset{\langle R\rangle}{\approx} Y =_{def} \langle R\rangle X = \langle R\rangle Y$
3. $X \underset{R}{\approx} Y =_{def} X \underset{[R]}{\approx} Y \wedge X \underset{\langle R\rangle}{\approx} Y$

Proposition 10. *The relations* $\underset{[R]}{\approx}$, $\underset{\langle R\rangle}{\approx}$, *and* $\underset{R}{\approx}$ *are equivalence relations on* $\mathfrak{P}W$.

Proof. Trivial.

Now, we factorize the power set $\mathfrak{P}W$ by the equivalence relations defined.

The equivalence class generated by a set $X \subseteq W$ with respect to $\underset{[R]}{\approx}$, $\underset{\langle R\rangle}{\approx}$, and $\underset{R}{\approx}$ we denote by $\mathcal{C}\ell(X,[R])$, $\mathcal{C}\ell(X,\langle R\rangle)$, and $\mathcal{C}\ell(X,R)$, respectively, i. e. we define

Definition 9. *1.* $\mathcal{C}\ell(X,[R]) =_{def} \left\{Y \middle| Y \subseteq W \wedge Y \underset{[R]}{\approx} X\right\}$

2. $\mathcal{C}\ell(X,\langle R\rangle) =_{def} \left\{Y \middle| Y \subseteq W \wedge Y \underset{\langle R\rangle}{\approx} X\right\}$
3. $\mathcal{C}\ell(X,R) =_{def} \left\{Y \middle| Y \subseteq W \wedge Y \underset{R}{\approx} X\right\}$

Furthermore, we define

Definition 10. *1.* $\mathrm{LRS}(W,R) =_{def} \mathfrak{P}W/\underset{[R]}{\approx}$

2. $\mathrm{URS}(W,R) =_{def} \mathfrak{P}W/\underset{\langle R\rangle}{\approx}$

3. $\mathrm{RS}(W,R) =_{def} \mathfrak{P}W/\underset{R}{\approx}$

The elements $L \in \mathrm{LRS}(W,R)$ are called lower rough sets of W with respect to R. Analogously, we call the elements $U \in \mathrm{URS}(W,R)$ and $C \in \mathrm{RS}(W,R)$ upper rough sets and rough sets of W with respect to R, respectively.

For the considerations in the next chapters it is important to state the following facts of stability and unstability, respectively, of the equivalence relations defined.

Proposition 11. *1.* $\forall X \forall X' \forall Y \left(X, X', Y \subseteq W \wedge X \underset{[R]}{\approx} X' \rightarrow X \cap Y \underset{[R]}{\approx} X' \cap Y \right)$

2. $\forall X \forall X' \forall Y \left(X, X', Y \subseteq W \wedge X \underset{\langle R\rangle}{\approx} X' \rightarrow X \cup Y \underset{\langle R\rangle}{\approx} X' \cup Y \right)$

3. $\forall X \forall Y \left(X, Y \subseteq W \wedge X \underset{[R]}{\approx} Y \rightarrow \overline{X} \underset{\langle R\rangle}{\approx} \overline{Y} \right)$

4. $\forall X \forall Y \left(X, Y \subseteq W \wedge X \underset{\langle R\rangle}{\approx} Y \rightarrow \overline{X} \underset{[R]}{\approx} \overline{Y} \right)$

5. $\forall X \forall Y \left(X, Y \subseteq W \wedge X \underset{R}{\approx} Y \rightarrow \overline{X} \underset{R}{\approx} \overline{Y} \right)$

Proof. By proposition 6, 7, and 8.

Note that the following statements 6 and 7 do not hold, in general.

6. $\forall X \forall X' \forall Y \left(X, X', Y \subseteq W \wedge X \underset{R}{\approx} X' \rightarrow X \cap Y \underset{R}{\approx} X' \cap Y \right)$

7. $\forall X \forall X' \forall Y \left(X, X', Y \subseteq W \wedge X \underset{R}{\approx} X' \rightarrow X \cup Y \underset{R}{\approx} X' \cup Y \right)$

Furthermore, it is important to state that lower rough sets and upper rough sets satisfy the following closedness conditions.

Proposition 12. *If $L \in \mathrm{LRS}(W,R)$ then*

1. $\forall X \forall Y (X, Y \in L \rightarrow X \cap Y \in L)$
2. $\forall \mathfrak{X} \left(\mathfrak{X} \subseteq L \rightarrow \bigcap \mathfrak{X} \in L \right)$

Proof. Proposition 6.

Proposition 13. *If $U \in \mathrm{URS}(W,R)$ then*

1. $\forall X \forall Y (X, Y \in U \rightarrow X \cup Y \in U)$
2. $\forall \mathfrak{X} \left(\mathfrak{X} \subseteq U \rightarrow \bigcup \mathfrak{X} \in U \right)$

Proof. Proposition 7.

Remarks

1. Proposition 12 means that every lower rough set $L \in \mathrm{LRS}(W, R)$ is a closure system in the sense of universal algebra. It is well-known that there exists a bijection between all closure systems of a set W and all closure operators on W. In a forthcoming paper this bijection is to be investigated in more detail, in particular, if the closure systems considered are generated as lower rough sets. For instance, we shall ask which relations exist between closure operators on W with special properties (compactness, topological properties) and binary relations R on W which generate these closure operators by special closure systems, i. e. by lower rough sets.
2. Proposition 13 describes the "dual" properties of upper rough sets. In particular, this proposition gives the possibility to generate "dual" closure operators and to study respective "dual" properties.
3. Rough sets do not satisfy proposition 12 or proposition 13, in general.

The following proposition is very important in chapter 1.6 where we shall define algebraic operations with rough sets.

Proposition 14. *1.* $\forall A(A \in \mathrm{RS}(W, R) \rightarrow$
$$\exists L \exists U(L \in \mathrm{LRS}(W, R) \wedge U \in \mathrm{URS}(W, R) \wedge A = L \cap U))$$
2. $\forall L \forall M \forall U \forall V$
$$(L, M \in \mathrm{LRS}(W, R) \wedge U, V \in \mathrm{URS}(W, R) \wedge L \cap U = M \cap V \wedge L \cap U \neq \varnothing \rightarrow L = M \wedge U = V)$$

Proof. **ad 1.** Trivial by definition of $\mathrm{RS}(W, R)$.
ad 2. From $L \cap U \neq \varnothing$ we get that there is an $X \subseteq W$ such that $X \in L$ and $X \in U$, hence by $L \cap U = M \cap V$, $X \in M$ and $X \in V$. Because L, M are equivalence classes of $\underset{[R]}{\approx}$ we get $L = M$, and because U, V are equivalence classes of $\underset{\langle R \rangle}{\approx}$ we obtain $U = V$.

4 The Lattice of Lower Rough Sets

The starting point of this chapter is the following definition of an inclusion relation $\underset{[R]}{\leq}$ for lower rough sets $L, M \in \mathrm{LRS}(W, R)$.

Definition 11. $L \underset{[R]}{\leq} M =_{def} \exists X \exists Y(X \in L \wedge Y \in M \wedge [R]X \subseteq [R]Y)$

The following proposition shows that this definition is independent of the choice of the representatives $X \in L$ and $Y \in M$.

Proposition 15. $L \underset{[R]}{\leq} M \leftrightarrow \forall X' \forall Y'(X' \in L \wedge Y' \in M \rightarrow [R]X' \subseteq [R]Y')$

Proof. I. (→)
Assume

$$L \underset{[R]}{\leq} M, \tag{1.1}$$

hence by definition of $\underset{[R]}{\leq}$,

$$\exists X \exists Y (X \in L \wedge Y \in M \wedge [R]X \subseteq [R]Y). \tag{1.2}$$

Furthermore assume

$$X' \in L \wedge Y' \in M, \tag{1.3}$$

hence from (1.2),

$$[R]X = [R]X' \wedge [R]Y = [R]Y', \tag{1.4}$$

hence again from (1.2),

$$[R]X' \subseteq [R]Y'. \tag{1.5}$$

II. (←)
Assume

$$\forall X' \forall Y' (X' \in L \wedge Y' \in M \rightarrow [R]X' \subseteq [R]Y'). \tag{1.6}$$

Because $\underset{[R]}{\approx}$ is an equivalence relation on $\mathfrak{P}W$ we have

$$L \neq \emptyset \wedge M \neq \emptyset, \tag{1.7}$$

i. e.

$$\exists X (X \in L) \wedge \exists Y (Y \in M), \tag{1.8}$$

hence by (1.6),

$$[R]X \subseteq [R]Y, \tag{1.9}$$

i. e.

$$L \underset{[R]}{\leq} M. \tag{1.10}$$

Proposition 16. *The relation* $\underset{[R]}{\leq}$ *is a partial ordering on* LRS(W, R).

Proof. We have to show that $\underset{[R]}{\leq}$ is reflexive on LRS(W, R) and, furthermore, it is transitive and antisymmetric.

ad 1. Reflexivity

We have to show

$$\forall L\left(L \in \mathrm{LRS}(W, R) \rightarrow L \underset{[R]}{\leq} L\right). \tag{1.1}$$

Assume

$$L \in \mathrm{LRS}(W, R), \tag{1.2}$$

hence

$$L \neq \emptyset, \text{ i. e. } \exists X(X \in L), \tag{1.3}$$

thus

$$[R]X \subseteq [R]X, \tag{1.4}$$

i. e. (1.1) holds.

ad 2. Transitivity

We have to show

$$\forall L \forall M \forall N\left(L \underset{[R]}{\leq} M \wedge M \underset{[R]}{\leq} N \rightarrow L \underset{[R]}{\leq} N\right). \tag{1.5}$$

From $L \underset{[R]}{\leq} M$ we get that there are $X \in L$ and $Y \in M$ such that

$$[R]X \subseteq [R]Y. \tag{1.6}$$

Furthermore, from $M \underset{[R]}{\leq} N$ we get that there are $Y' \in M$ and $Z' \in N$ such that

$$[R]Y' \subseteq [R]Z'. \tag{1.7}$$

From $Y \in M$ and $Y' \in M$ we obtain

$$[R]Y = [R]Y', \tag{1.8}$$

hence from (1.6), (1.7), and (1.8)

$$[R]X \subseteq [R]Z', \text{ i. e. } L \underset{[R]}{\leq} N. \tag{1.9}$$

ad 3. Antisymmetry

We have to show

$$\forall L \forall M\left(L \underset{[R]}{\leq} M \wedge M \underset{[R]}{\leq} L \rightarrow L = M\right). \tag{1.10}$$

From $L \underset{[R]}{\leq} M$ we get that there are $X \in L$ and $Y \in M$ such that

$$[R]X \subseteq [R]Y. \tag{1.11}$$

Furthermore, from $M \underset{[R]}{\leq} L$ we obtain that there are $Y' \in M$ and $X' \in L$ such that

$$[R]Y' \subseteq [R]X'. \tag{1.12}$$

Because of $X, X' \in L$ and $Y, Y' \in M$ we have

$$[R]X = [R]X' \text{ and } [R]Y = [R]Y', \tag{1.13}$$

hence by (1.12)

$$[R]Y \subseteq [R]X, \tag{1.14}$$

thus by (1.11)

$$[R]X = [R]Y, \tag{1.15}$$

so $L = M$.

Now, we are going to prove that the structure $\left[\mathrm{LRS}(W, R), \underset{[R]}{\leq}\right]$ is a complete semilattice with respect to its infimum.

First, we shall show that for every lower rough set $L, M \in \mathrm{LRS}(W, R)$ the infimum with respect to $\underset{[R]}{\leq}$ of the set $\{L, M\}$ exists.

As a mean for constructing this infimum we consider the lower rough set $\mathcal{C}\ell(X \cap Y, [R])$, where $X, Y \subseteq W$.

Very important is the following

Lemma 1. $\forall X \forall X' \forall Y \forall Y'$
$$\left(X, X', Y, Y' \subseteq W \wedge X \underset{[R]}{\approx} X' \wedge Y \underset{[R]}{\approx} Y' \to \mathcal{C}\ell(X \cap Y, [R]) = \mathcal{C}\ell(X' \cap Y', [R])\right)$$

Proof. Assume for $X, X', Y, Y' \subseteq W$

$$X \underset{[R]}{\approx} X' \text{ and } Y \underset{[R]}{\approx} Y', \tag{1.1}$$

hence by definition of $\underset{[R]}{\approx}$

$$[R]X = [R]X' \text{ and } [R]Y = [R]Y'. \tag{1.2}$$

It is sufficient to show

$$\forall Z(Z \in \mathcal{C}\ell(X \cap Y, [R]) \leftrightarrow Z \in \mathcal{C}\ell(X' \cap Y', [R])). \tag{1.3}$$

By definition of the equivalence classes $\mathfrak{P}W/_{\underset{[R]}{\approx}}$ it is sufficient to prove

$$[R](X \cap Y) = [R](X' \cap Y'). \tag{1.4}$$

But (1.4) holds because of proposition 6 and (1.2).

Lemma 2. *If $L, M \in \mathrm{LRS}(W,R)$ and $X \in L$, $Y \in M$ then $\mathcal{C}\ell(X \cap Y, [R])$ is a lower bound of $\{L, M\}$ with respect to $\underset{[R]}{\leq}$.*

Proof. Without loss of generality we only show

$$\mathcal{C}\ell(X \cap Y, [R]) \underset{[R]}{\leq} L. \tag{1.1}$$

By definition of $\underset{[R]}{\leq}$ it is sufficient to show

$$\exists Z \exists Z' (Z \in \mathcal{C}\ell(X \cap Y, [R]) \wedge Z' \in L \wedge [R]Z \subseteq [R]Z'). \tag{1.2}$$

Put

$$Z =_{def} X \cap Y \text{ and } Z' =_{def} X. \tag{1.3}$$

Then we get

$$Z \subseteq Z', \tag{1.4}$$

hence by monotonicity of $[R]$

$$[R]Z \subseteq [R]Z', \tag{1.5}$$

so (1.1) holds.

Lemma 3. *If $L, M \in \mathrm{LRS}(W,R)$ and $X \in L$, $Y \in M$ then $\mathcal{C}\ell(X \cap Y, [R])$ is the greatest lower bound of $\{L, M\}$ with respect to $\underset{[R]}{\leq}$.*

Proof. We have to prove

$$\forall K \left(K \in \mathrm{LRS}(W,R) \wedge K \underset{[R]}{\leq} L \wedge K \underset{[R]}{\leq} M \rightarrow K \underset{[R]}{\leq} \mathcal{C}\ell(X \cap Y, [R]) \right). \tag{1.1}$$

For $K \in \mathrm{LRS}(W,R)$ assume

$$K \underset{[R]}{\leq} L \text{ and } K \underset{[R]}{\leq} M, \tag{1.2}$$

hence by $X \in L$, $Y \in M$, and Lemma 1 there exists a $Z \in K$ such that

$$[R]Z \subseteq [R]X \text{ and } [R]Z \subseteq [R]Y, \tag{1.3}$$

thus

$$[R]Z \subseteq [R]X \cap [R]Y, \tag{1.4}$$

so by proposition 6

$$[R]Z \subseteq [R](X \cap Y). \tag{1.5}$$

Because of $Z \in K$ and $X \cap Y \in \mathcal{C}\ell(X \cap Y, [R])$ we obtain $K \underset{[R]}{\leq} \mathcal{C}\ell(X \cap Y, [R])$.

Theorem 1. *The structure $\left[\mathrm{LRS}(W,R), \underset{[R]}{\leq}\right]$ is a semilattice with respect to its infimum.*

Proof. Lemma 2 and 3.

Remark As usual in lattice theory for $L, M \in \mathrm{LRS}(W, R)$ we denote the infimum of $\{L, M\}$ in the semilattice above by $L \underset{[R]}{\wedge} M$. Obviously, we have the equation

$$L \underset{[R]}{\wedge} M = \mathcal{C}\ell(X \cap Y, [R])$$

for every $X \in L$ and $Y \in M$.

Now, we shall show that this semilattice is complete, i. e. that for every $\mathcal{L} \subseteq \mathrm{LRS}(W, R)$ the infimum of $\mathcal{L}$ with respect to $\underset{[R]}{\leq}$ exists.

First, we prove the following generalization of lemma 1 (see lemma 4).

Assume $\mathcal{L} \subseteq \mathrm{LRS}(W, R)$. In order to formulate lemma 4 we use the well-known notion of choice function α of $\mathcal{L}$, i. e.

$$\alpha : \mathcal{L} \to \bigcup \mathcal{L}$$

and

$$\forall L (L \in \mathcal{L} \to \alpha(\mathcal{L}) \in L).$$

Lemma 4. *If α and β are choice functions of $\mathcal{L}$ then*

$$\mathcal{C}\ell\left(\bigcap \{\alpha(L) | L \in \mathcal{L}\}, [R]\right) = \mathcal{C}\ell\left(\bigcap \{\beta(L) | L \in \mathcal{L}\}, [R]\right).$$

Proof. Because α and β are choice functions of $\mathcal{L}$ we get

$$\forall L \left(L \in \mathcal{L} \to [R]\alpha(L) = [R]\beta(L)\right), \tag{1.1}$$

hence

$$\bigcap \{[R]\alpha(L) | L \in \mathcal{L}\} = \bigcap \{[R]\beta(L) | L \in \mathcal{L}\}, \tag{1.2}$$

thus by proposition 6

$$[R]\left(\bigcap \{\alpha(L) | L \in \mathcal{L}\}\right) = [R]\left(\bigcap \{\beta(L) | L \in \mathcal{L}\}\right), \tag{1.3}$$

so by definition of $\mathcal{C}\ell$

$$\mathcal{C}\ell\left(\bigcap \{\alpha(L) | L \in \mathcal{L}\}, [R]\right) = \mathcal{C}\ell\left(\bigcap \{\beta(L) | L \in \mathcal{L}\}, [R]\right). \tag{1.4}$$

The following lemma is a generalization of lemma 2.

Lemma 5. *If $\mathcal{L} \subseteq \mathrm{LRS}(W, R)$ and α is a choice function of $\mathcal{L}$ then $\mathcal{C}\ell\left(\bigcap \{\alpha(L) | L \in \mathcal{L}\}, [R]\right)$ is a lower bound of $\mathcal{L}$ with respect to $\underset{[R]}{\leq}$.*

Proof. By definition of lower bound we have to show

$$\forall L \left(L \in \mathcal{L} \to \mathcal{C}\ell\left(\bigcap \{\alpha(L') | L' \in \mathcal{L}\}, [R]\right) \underset{[R]}{\leq} L\right). \tag{1.1}$$

Assume $L \in \mathcal{L}$. We have to show

$$\exists Z \exists Z' \left(Z \in \mathcal{C}\ell\left(\bigcap\{\alpha(L') | L' \in \mathcal{L}\}, [R]\right) \wedge Z' \in L \wedge [R]Z \subseteq [R]Z'\right). \tag{1.2}$$

Define

$$\begin{aligned} Z &=_{def} \bigcap\{\alpha(L') | L' \in \mathcal{L}\} \\ Z' &=_{def} \alpha(L) \end{aligned} \tag{1.3}$$

Then we get

$$Z \in \mathcal{C}\ell\left(\bigcap\{\alpha(L') | L' \in \mathcal{L}\}, [R]\right), \tag{1.4}$$

$$Z' \in L \quad \text{and}$$

$$Z \subseteq Z', \tag{1.5}$$

hence from (1.5) by monotonicity of $[R]$

$$[R]Z \subseteq [R]Z'. \tag{1.6}$$

From (1.4) and (1.6) we obtain (1.1).

The following lemma is a generalization of lemma 3.

Lemma 6. *If* $\mathcal{L} \subseteq \mathrm{LRS}(W, R)$ *and* α *is a choice function of* $\mathcal{L}$ *then* $\mathcal{C}\ell\left(\bigcap\{\alpha(L') | L' \in \mathcal{L}\}, [R]\right)$ *is the greatest lower bound of* $\mathcal{L}$ *with respect to* $\underset{[R]}{\leq}$.

Proof. We have to show

$$\forall K\left(K \in \mathrm{LRS}(W, R) \wedge \forall L\left(L \in \mathcal{L} \rightarrow L \underset{[R]}{\leq} L\right) \rightarrow K \underset{[R]}{\leq} \mathcal{C}\ell\left(\bigcap\{\alpha(L') | L' \in \mathcal{L}\}, [R]\right)\right). \tag{1.1}$$

Assume

$$K \in \mathrm{LRS}(W, R) \text{ and } X \in K. \tag{1.2}$$

Furthermore assume

$$\forall L\left(L \in \mathcal{L} \rightarrow K \underset{[R]}{\leq} L\right). \tag{1.3}$$

Hence by definition of $\underset{[R]}{\leq}$ and because α is a choice function of $\mathcal{L}$, we obtain

$$\forall L(L \in \mathcal{L} \rightarrow [R]X \subseteq [R]\alpha(L)), \tag{1.4}$$

consequently

$$[R]X \subseteq \bigcap\{[R]\alpha(L) | L \in \mathcal{L}\}. \tag{1.5}$$

By proposition 6 we have

$$\bigcap\{[R]\alpha(L)|L\in \mathcal{L}\}=[R]\left(\bigcap\{\alpha(L)|L\in \mathcal{L}\}\right), \tag{1.6}$$

hence by (1.5)

$$[R]X\subseteq [R]\left(\bigcap\{\alpha(L)|L\in \mathcal{L}\}\right). \tag{1.7}$$

Because of $X\in K$ and $\bigcap\{\alpha(L)|L\in \mathcal{L}\}\in \mathcal{C}\ell\left(\bigcap\{\alpha(L)|L\in \mathcal{L}\},[R]\right)$ from (1.7) we obtain

$$K\underset{[R]}{\leq}\mathcal{C}\ell\left(\bigcap\{\alpha(L)|L\in \mathcal{L}\},[R]\right). \tag{1.8}$$

Theorem 2. *The structure* $\left[\mathrm{LRS}(W,R),\underset{[R]}{\leq}\right]$ *is a complete semilattice with respect to its infimum.*

Proof. Lemma 5 and 6.

Remark The infimum of the set $\mathcal{L}$ in the complete semilattice is denoted by $\bigwedge\limits_{[R]}\mathcal{L}$. Obviously, for every choice function α of $\mathcal{L}$ we have the equation

$$\bigwedge_{[R]}\mathcal{L}=\mathcal{C}\ell\left(\bigcap\{\alpha(L)|L\in \mathcal{L}\},[R]\right).$$

Now, for $\mathcal{L}\subseteq \mathrm{LRS}(W,R)$ and $L,M\in \mathrm{LRS}(W,R)$ we define

Definition 12. *1.* $\overset{[R]}{\bigvee}\mathcal{L}=_{def}\bigwedge\limits_{[R]}\left\{M\,\middle|\,M\in \mathrm{LRS}(W,R)\wedge\forall L\left(L\in\mathcal{L}\rightarrow L\underset{[R]}{\leq}M\right)\right\}$

2. $L\overset{[R]}{\vee}M=_{def}\overset{[R]}{\bigvee}\{L,M\}$

Lemma 7. *The lower rough set* $\overset{[R]}{\bigvee}\mathcal{L}$ *is the supremum of* $\mathcal{L}$ *with respect to* $\underset{[R]}{\leq}$.

Proof. This lemma is a well-known structure theorem of lattice theory.

Theorem 3. *The structure* $\left[\mathrm{LRS}(W,R),\underset{[R]}{\leq}\right]$ *is a complete lattice.*

Proof. Theorem 2 and lemma 7.

Remarks Obviously, further interesting properties of the lattice $\left[\mathrm{LRS}(W,R),\underset{[R]}{\leq}\right]$, for instance, whether this lattice is modular, distributive, complementar, atomar, a BOOLEan algebra etc., depend on the binary relation $R\subseteq W\times W$.

In a forthcoming paper we shall systematically investigate this problem.

As an example we discuss this problem if the relation R is reflexive on W and transitive. Obviously, this case characterizes the modal S_4-system. Furthermore, the "classical" rough set where R is an equivalence relation on W is covered.

Lemma 8. *If R is reflexive on W and transitive then for every $L, M \in \mathrm{LRS}(W, R)$ and $X \in L$, $Y \in M$ the equation*

$$\overset{[R]}{\bigvee}\{L, M\} = \mathcal{C}\ell([R]X \cup [R]Y, [R])$$

holds.

Proof. In order to prove the equation above it is sufficient to show

I. $\mathcal{C}\ell([R]X \cup [R]Y, [R])$ is an upper bound of $\{L, M\}$ with respect to $\underset{[R]}{\leq}$.
II. $\mathcal{C}\ell([R]X \cup [R]Y, [R])$ is the smallest upper bound of $\{L, M\}$ with respect to $\underset{[R]}{\leq}$.

First of all, from modal logic we know that for every $X \subseteq W$

$$\text{If } R \text{ is reflexive on } W \text{ then } [R]X \subseteq X. \tag{1.1}$$

$$\text{If } R \text{ is transitive then } [R]X \subseteq [R][R]X. \tag{1.2}$$

$$\text{If } R \text{ is reflexive on } W \text{ and transitive then } [R]X = [R][R]X. \tag{1.3}$$

ad I. Without loss of generality we only show

$$L \underset{[R]}{\leq} \mathcal{C}\ell([R]X \cup [R]Y, [R]). \tag{1.4}$$

Obviously, it is sufficient to prove

$$[R]X \subseteq [R]([R]X \cup [R]Y). \tag{1.5}$$

We have

$$[R]X \subseteq [R]X \cup [R]Y, \tag{1.6}$$

hence by monotonicity of $[R]$

$$[R][R]X \subseteq [R]([R]X \cup [R]Y), \tag{1.7}$$

hence by (1.2), (1.5) holds.
ad II. We have to show

$$\forall K \left(K \in \mathrm{LRS}(W, R) \wedge L \underset{[R]}{\leq} K \wedge M \underset{[R]}{\leq} K \rightarrow \mathcal{C}\ell([R]X \cup [R]Y, [R]) \underset{[R]}{\leq} K \right). \tag{1.8}$$

Assume $X \in K$, $Y \in L$, and $Z \in M$. Then from $L \underset{[R]}{\leq} K$ and $M \underset{[R]}{\leq} K$ we obtain

$$[R]X \subseteq [R]Z \text{ and } [R]Y \subseteq [R]Z, \tag{1.9}$$

hence

$$[R]X \cup [R]Y \subseteq [R]Z, \tag{1.10}$$

thus by monotonicity of $[R]$

$$[R]([R]X \cup [R]Y) \subseteq [R][R]Z, \tag{1.11}$$

so by (1.1)

$$[R]([R]X \cup [R]Y) \subseteq [R]Z. \tag{1.12}$$

Because $[R]X \cup [R]Y \in \mathcal{C}\ell([R]X \cup [R]Y, [R])$ and $Z \in K$ we obtain $\mathcal{C}\ell([R]X \cup [R]Y, [R]) \underset{[R]}{\leq} K$.

Using lemma 8 we can prove

Theorem 4. *If R is reflexive on W and transitive then the lattice* $\left[\mathrm{LRS}(W,R), \underset{[R]}{\leq}\right]$ *is distributive.*

Proof. From lattice theory it is well-known that it is sufficient for every $K, L, M \in \mathrm{LRS}(W,R)$ to prove the equation

$$K \underset{[R]}{\wedge} \left(L \overset{[R]}{\vee} M \right) = \left(K \underset{[R]}{\wedge} L \right) \overset{[R]}{\vee} \left(K \underset{[R]}{\wedge} M \right). \tag{1.1}$$

Assume $X \in K$, $Y \in L$, and $Z \in M$. Then we have

$$K \underset{[R]}{\wedge} \left(L \overset{[R]}{\vee} M \right) = \mathcal{C}\ell(X \cap ([R]Y \cup [R]Z), [R]). \tag{1.2}$$

Furthermore, we have

$$\left(K \underset{[R]}{\wedge} L \right) \overset{[R]}{\vee} \left(K \underset{[R]}{\wedge} M \right) = \mathcal{C}\ell([R](X \cap Y) \cup [R](X \cap Z), [R]). \tag{1.3}$$

Obviously, (1.1) holds if we have

$$[R](X \cap ([R]Y \cup [R]Z)) = [R]([R](X \cap Y) \cup [R](X \cap Z)). \tag{1.4}$$

By proposition 6 we obtain

$$[R](X \cap Y) \cup [R](X \cap Z) = ([R]X \cap [R]Y) \cup ([R]X \cap [R]Z) = [R]X \cap ([R]Y \cup [R]Z). \tag{1.5}$$

Hence in order to prove (1.4) it is sufficient to show

$$[R](X \cap ([R]Y \cup [R]Z)) = [R]([R]X \cap ([R]Y \cup [R]Z)). \tag{1.6}$$

But (1.6) holds because for every $V \subseteq W$ we have

$$[R](X \cap V) = [R]([R]X \cap V) \tag{1.7}$$

which follows from $[R]X = [R][R]X$ and proposition 6.

5 The Lattice of Upper Rough Sets

Analogously to definition 11 we define for upper rough sets $U, V \in \mathrm{URS}(W, R)$.

Definition 13. $U \underset{\langle R\rangle}{\leq} V =_{def} \exists X \exists Y \left(X \in U \wedge Y \in V \wedge \langle R\rangle X \subseteq \langle R\rangle Y\right)$

As for $\underset{[R]}{\leq}$ we can also show that the definition of $\underset{\langle R\rangle}{\leq}$ is independent of the representatives $X \in U$ and $Y \in V$, i. e. we have

Proposition 17. $U \underset{\langle R\rangle}{\leq} V \leftrightarrow \forall X' \forall Y' \left(X' \in U \wedge Y' \in V \rightarrow \langle R\rangle X' \subseteq \langle R\rangle Y'\right)$

Proof. Like proof of proposition 15.

Proposition 18. *The relation* $\underset{\langle R\rangle}{\leq}$ *is a partial ordering on* $\mathrm{URS}(W, R)$.

Proof. Like proof of proposition 16.

Now, we shall state that between the partially ordered sets $\left[\mathrm{LRS}(W, R), \underset{[R]}{\leq}\right]$ and $\left[\mathrm{URS}(W, R), \underset{\langle R\rangle}{\leq}\right]$ there exists a dual order isomorphism. Therefore for every lower rough set $L \in \mathrm{LRS}(W, R)$ and every upper rough set $U \in \mathrm{URS}(W, R)$ (with respect to the same binary relation R) we introduce its upper dual $\mathrm{UDUAL}(L)$ and its lower dual $\mathrm{LDUAL}(U)$, respectively, as follows. Assume $X \in L$ and $Y \in U$.

Definition 14. *1.* $\mathrm{UDUAL}(L) =_{def} \mathcal{C}\ell\left(\overline{X}, \langle R\rangle\right)$
2. $\mathrm{LDUAL}(U) =_{def} \mathcal{C}\ell\left(\overline{Y}, [R]\right)$

Lemma 9. *The defined operators do not depend on the choice of the representatives* $X \in L$ *and* $Y \in U$, *i. e. it holds*

1. $X \underset{[R]}{\approx} X' \rightarrow \mathcal{C}\ell\left(\overline{X}, \langle R\rangle\right) = \mathcal{C}\ell\left(\overline{X'}, \langle R\rangle\right)$
2. $Y \underset{\langle R\rangle}{\approx} Y' \rightarrow \mathcal{C}\ell\left(\overline{Y}, [R]\right) = \mathcal{C}\ell\left(\overline{Y'}, [R]\right)$

Proof. **ad 1.** We have

$$X \underset{[R]}{\approx} Y, \tag{1.1}$$

i. e.

$$[R]X = [R]Y, \tag{1.2}$$

hence

$$\overline{[R]X} = \overline{[R]Y} \tag{1.3}$$

thus

$$\langle R\rangle\overline{X} = \langle R\rangle\overline{Y}, \tag{1.4}$$

so by definition of $\mathcal{C}\ell(Z, \langle R\rangle)$

$$\mathcal{C}\ell(\overline{X}, \langle R\rangle) = \mathcal{C}\ell(\overline{Y}, \langle R\rangle). \tag{1.5}$$

ad 2. Analogously.

Proposition 19. *1.* $\forall L(L \in \mathrm{LRS}(W,R) \to \mathrm{LDUAL}(\mathrm{UDUAL}(L)) = L)$
 2. $\forall U(U \in \mathrm{URS}(W,R) \to \mathrm{UDUAL}(\mathrm{LDUAL}(U)) = U)$
 3. UDUAL *is a bijection from* LRS(W, R) *onto* URS(W, R).
 4. LDUAL *is a bijection from* URS(W, R) *onto* LRS(W, R).

Proof. **ad 1.** We have to prove

$$\forall X(X \in \mathrm{LDUAL}(\mathrm{UDUAL}(L)) \leftrightarrow X \in L). \tag{1.1}$$

By definition LDUAL we have

$$X \in \mathrm{LDUAL}(\mathrm{UDUAL}(L)) \leftrightarrow \exists Y\left(Y \in \mathrm{UDUAL}(L) \wedge [R]X = [R]\overline{Y}\right). \tag{1.2}$$

Furthermore, by the definition of UDUAL we have

$$Y \in \mathrm{UDUAL}(L) \leftrightarrow \exists Z\left(Z \in L \wedge \langle R\rangle Y = \langle R\rangle\overline{Z}\right), \tag{1.3}$$

hence by (1.2) and (1.3),

$$X \in \mathrm{LDUAL}(\mathrm{UDUAL}(L)) \leftrightarrow \\ \exists Y \exists Z\left(Y \subseteq W \wedge Z \in L \wedge [R]X = [R]\overline{Y} \wedge \langle R\rangle Y = \langle R\rangle\overline{Z}\right). \tag{1.4}$$

From $[R]X = [R]\overline{Y}$ and $\langle R\rangle Y = \langle R\rangle\overline{Z}$ we obtain

$$[R]X = [R]\overline{Y} = \overline{\langle R\rangle Y} = \overline{\langle R\rangle\overline{Z}} = [R]Z, \tag{1.5}$$

hence

$$X \in \mathrm{LDUAL}(\mathrm{UDUAL}(L)) \leftrightarrow \exists Z(Z \in L \wedge [R]X = [R]Z). \tag{1.6}$$

By definition of lower rough sets we have

$$\exists Z(Z \in L \wedge [R]X = [R]Z) \leftrightarrow X \in L, \tag{1.7}$$

hence by (1.6) we have (1.1)
ad 2. Like assertion 1.
ad 3.

$$\text{UDUAL is a mapping from } \mathrm{LRS}(W,R) \text{ into } \mathrm{URS}(W,R). \tag{1.8}$$

This assertion trivially holds by construction of UDUAL.

UDUAL is an injection, i. e.

$$\forall L\forall M(L, M \in LRS(W,R) \wedge \text{UDUAL}(L) = \text{UDUAL}(M) \to L = M). \quad (1.9)$$

From UDUAL(L) = UDUAL(M) we get

$$\text{LDUAL}(\text{UDUAL}(L)) = \text{LDUAL}(\text{UDUAL}(M)),$$

hence by assertion 1,

$$L = M,$$

i. e. (1.9) holds.

UDUAL is a surjection, i. e.

$$\forall U(U \in \text{URS}(W,R) \to \exists L(L \in \text{LRS}(W,R) \wedge \text{UDUAL}(L) = U)). \quad (1.10)$$

Assume $U \in \text{URS}(W,R)$. Put

$$L =_{def} \text{LDUAL}(U). \quad (1.11)$$

From (1.11) by assertion 2,

$$\text{UDUAL}(L) = \text{UDUAL}(\text{LDUAL}(U)) = U,$$

hence (1.10) holds.

ad 4. Like assertion 3.

Theorem 5. *1.* UDUAL *is a dual order isomorphismus from* $\left[\text{LRS}(W,R), \underset{[R]}{\leq}\right]$ *onto* $\left[\text{URS}(W,R), \underset{\langle R\rangle}{\leq}\right]$.

2. LDUAL *is a dual order isomorphismus from* $\left[\text{URS}(W,R), \underset{\langle R\rangle}{\leq}\right]$ *onto* $\left[\text{LRS}(W,R), \underset{[R]}{\leq}\right]$.

Proof. Because of proposition 19 it remains to show

$$\forall L\forall M\left(L, M \in \text{LRS}(W,R) \wedge L \underset{[R]}{\leq} M \to \text{UDUAL}(M) \underset{[R]}{\leq} \text{UDUAL}(L)\right). \quad (1.1)$$

Assume $L \underset{[R]}{\leq} M$, hence by definition of $\underset{[R]}{\leq}$

$$\exists X\exists Y(X \in L \wedge Y \in M \wedge [R]X \subseteq [R]Y). \quad (1.2)$$

By definition of UDUAL it is sufficient to show

$$\mathcal{C}\ell\left(\overline{Y}, \langle R\rangle\right) \underset{\langle R\rangle}{\leq} \mathcal{C}\ell\left(\overline{X}, \langle R\rangle\right) \quad (1.3)$$

In order to prove (1.3) it is sufficient to show

$$\exists U \exists V \left(U \in \mathcal{C}\ell\left(\overline{Y}, \langle R \rangle\right) \wedge V \in \mathcal{C}\ell\left(\overline{X}, \langle R \rangle\right) \wedge \langle R \rangle U \subseteq \langle R \rangle V\right). \tag{1.4}$$

Put

$$U =_{def} \overline{Y} \text{ and } V =_{def} \overline{X}. \tag{1.5}$$

Then we have trivially

$$U \in \mathcal{C}\ell\left(\overline{Y}, \langle R \rangle\right) \text{ and } V \in \mathcal{C}\ell\left(\overline{X}, \langle R \rangle\right).$$

From (1.2) we have

$$[R]X \subseteq [R]Y,$$

hence

$$\overline{[R]Y} \subseteq \overline{[R]X},$$

thus

$$\langle R \rangle \overline{Y} \subseteq \langle R \rangle \overline{X},$$

i. e. (1.4) holds.

Corollary 1. *The partially ordered set* $\left[\mathrm{URS}(W, R), \underset{\langle R \rangle}{\leq}\right]$ *is a lattice.*

Proof. By theorem 5 and proposition 4.

Corollary 2. *For every* $U, V \in \mathrm{URS}(W, R)$ *and* $X \in U$, $Y \in V$ *the rough set* $\mathcal{C}\ell(X \cup Y, \langle R \rangle)$ *is the supremum of the set* $\{U, V\}$ *with respect to* $\underset{\langle R \rangle}{\leq}$, *i. e. the equation*

$$U \overset{\langle R \rangle}{\vee} V = \mathcal{C}\ell(X \cup Y, \langle R \rangle)$$

holds.

Proof. Lemma 3, theorem 1, and theorem 5.

Corollary 3. *The lattices* $\left[\mathrm{LRS}(W, R), \underset{[R]}{\leq}\right]$ *and* $\left[\mathrm{URS}(W, R), \underset{\langle R \rangle}{\leq}\right]$ *are dually isomorphic.*

Proof. Theorem 5 and corollary 1.

Corollary 4. *The partially ordered set* $\left[\mathrm{URS}(W, R), \underset{\langle R \rangle}{\leq}\right]$ *is a complete lattice.*

Proof. By theorem 5 and proposition 4.

Corollary 5. *The complete lattices* $\left[\mathrm{LRS}(W,R), \underset{[R]}{\leq}\right]$ *and* $\left[\mathrm{URS}(W,R), \underset{\langle R\rangle}{\leq}\right]$ *are dually isomorphic.*

Proof. By theorem 5 and corollary 3.

Finally, we assume that the binary relation R considered is reflexive on W and transitive. Analogously to chapter 1.4 we can show that the lattice $\left[\mathrm{URS}(W,R), \underset{\langle R\rangle}{\leq}\right]$ is distributive.

First, we show

Lemma 10. *If R is reflexive on W and transitive then for every $U, V \in \mathrm{URS}(W,R)$ and $X \in U$, $Y \in V$, the rough set $\mathcal{C}\ell(\langle R\rangle X \cap \langle R\rangle Y, \langle R\rangle)$ is the infimum of the set $\{U, V\}$ with respect to $\underset{\langle R\rangle}{\leq}$.*

Proof. We have to show

I. $\mathcal{C}\ell(\langle R\rangle X \cap \langle R\rangle Y, \langle R\rangle)$ is a lower bound of $\{U, V\}$ with respect to $\underset{\langle R\rangle}{\leq}$.

II. $\mathcal{C}\ell(\langle R\rangle X \cap \langle R\rangle Y, \langle R\rangle)$ is the greatest lower bound of $\{U, V\}$ with respect to $\underset{\langle R\rangle}{\leq}$.

First of all, from modal logic we recall that for every $X \subseteq W$ we have

If R is reflexive on W then $X \subseteq \langle R\rangle X$. (1.1)

If R is transitive then $\langle R\rangle\langle R\rangle X \subseteq \langle R\rangle X$. (1.2)

If R is reflexive on W and transitive then $\langle R\rangle X = \langle R\rangle\langle R\rangle X$. (1.3)

ad I. Without loss of generality we only show

$$\mathcal{C}\ell(\langle R\rangle X \cap \langle R\rangle Y, \langle R\rangle) \underset{\langle R\rangle}{\leq} U. \tag{1.4}$$

By definition of $\underset{\langle R\rangle}{\leq}$ it is sufficient to prove

$$\langle R\rangle(\langle R\rangle X \cap \langle R\rangle Y) \subseteq \langle R\rangle X. \tag{1.5}$$

We have

$$\langle R\rangle X \cap \langle R\rangle Y \subseteq \langle R\rangle X, \tag{1.6}$$

hence by monotonicity of $\langle R\rangle$,

$$\langle R\rangle(\langle R\rangle X \cap \langle R\rangle Y) \subseteq \langle R\rangle\langle R\rangle X, \tag{1.7}$$

so by (1.2), (1.5) holds.

ad II. We have to show

$$\forall T\left(T \in \mathrm{URS}(W,R) \wedge T \underset{\langle R\rangle}{\leq} U \wedge T \underset{\langle R\rangle}{\leq} V \rightarrow T \underset{\langle R\rangle}{\leq} \mathcal{C}\ell(\langle R\rangle X \cap \langle R\rangle Y, \langle R\rangle)\right). \tag{1.8}$$

Assume $X \in T, Y \in U, Z \in V$. Then from $T \underset{\langle R\rangle}{\leq} U$ and $T \underset{\langle R\rangle}{\leq} V$ we obtain

$$\langle R\rangle X \subseteq \langle R\rangle Y \text{ and } \langle R\rangle X \subseteq \langle R\rangle Z, \tag{1.9}$$

hence

$$\langle R\rangle X \subseteq \langle R\rangle Y \cap \langle R\rangle Z, \tag{1.10}$$

thus by monotonicity of $\langle R\rangle$,

$$\langle R\rangle\langle R\rangle X \subseteq \langle R\rangle(\langle R\rangle Y \cap \langle R\rangle Z), \tag{1.11}$$

so by (1.1),

$$\langle R\rangle X \subseteq \langle R\rangle(\langle R\rangle Y \cap \langle R\rangle Z). \tag{1.12}$$

Because of $X \in T$ and $\langle R\rangle Y \cap \langle R\rangle Z \in \mathcal{C}\ell(\langle R\rangle Y \cap \langle R\rangle Z, \langle R\rangle)$ we obtain $T \underset{\langle R\rangle}{\leq} \mathcal{C}\ell(\langle R\rangle Y \cap \langle R\rangle Z, \langle R\rangle)$.

Using lemma 10 we can prove

Theorem 6. *If R is reflexive on W and transitive then the lattice* $\left[\mathrm{URS}(W,R), \underset{\langle R\rangle}{\leq}\right]$ *is distributive.*

Proof. From lattice theory it is well-known that it is sufficient for every $T,U,V \in \mathrm{URS}(W,R)$ to prove the equation

$$T \overset{\langle R\rangle}{\vee} \left(U \underset{\langle R\rangle}{\wedge} V\right) = \left(T \overset{\langle R\rangle}{\vee} U\right) \underset{\langle R\rangle}{\wedge} \left(T \overset{\langle R\rangle}{\vee} V\right). \tag{1.1}$$

Assume $X \in T, Y \in U$, and $Z \in V$. Then we get

$$T \overset{\langle R\rangle}{\vee} \left(U \underset{\langle R\rangle}{\wedge} V\right) = \mathcal{C}\ell(X \cup (\langle R\rangle Y \cap \langle R\rangle Z), \langle R\rangle). \tag{1.2}$$

Furthermore, we have

$$\left(T \overset{\langle R\rangle}{\vee} U\right) \underset{\langle R\rangle}{\wedge} \left(T \overset{\langle R\rangle}{\vee} V\right) = \mathcal{C}\ell(\langle R\rangle(X \cup Y) \cap \langle R\rangle(X \cup Z), \langle R\rangle). \tag{1.3}$$

Obviously, (1.1) holds if we have

$$\langle R\rangle(X\cup(\langle R\rangle Y\cap\langle R\rangle Z))=\langle R\rangle(\langle R\rangle(X\cup Y)\cap\langle R\rangle(X\cup Z)). \tag{1.4}$$

By proposition 7 we obtain

$$\begin{aligned}&\langle R\rangle(X\cup Y)\cap\langle R\rangle(X\cup Z)=\\&\qquad(\langle R\rangle X\cup\langle R\rangle Y)\cap(\langle R\rangle X\cup\langle R\rangle Z)=\langle R\rangle X\cup(\langle R\rangle Y\cap\langle R\rangle Z),\end{aligned} \tag{1.5}$$

hence in order to prove (1.4) it is sufficient to show

$$\langle R\rangle(X\cup(\langle R\rangle Y\cap\langle R\rangle Z))=\langle R\rangle(\langle R\rangle X\cup(\langle R\rangle Y\cap\langle R\rangle Z)). \tag{1.6}$$

But (1.6) holds because for every $V\subseteq W$ we have

$$\langle R\rangle(X\cup V)=\langle R\rangle(\langle R\rangle X\cup V) \tag{1.7}$$

which follows from $\langle R\rangle X=\langle R\rangle\langle R\rangle X$ and proposition 7.

Remark A second proof of theorem 6 we get by application of theorem 4, theorem 5, and a corresponding generalization of proposition 4.

6 The Lattice of Rough Sets

We recall that rough sets on W with respect to R are the elements of the partition $\mathfrak{P}W/_{\underset{R}{\approx}}$ where $\underset{R}{\approx}$ is the equivalence relation on $\mathfrak{P}W$ defined by

$$X\underset{R}{\approx}Y=_{def}[R]X=[R]Y\wedge\langle R\rangle X=\langle R\rangle Y$$

where $X,Y\subseteq W$.

We denoted $\mathfrak{P}W/_{\underset{R}{\approx}}$ also by RS(W,R). Then we recall

$$\mathrm{RS}(W,R)=\{L\cap U\mid L\in\mathrm{LRS}(W,R)\wedge U\in\mathrm{URS}(W,R)\wedge L\cap U\neq\varnothing\}.$$

Furthermore, we recall proposition 14, i. e. that for every rough set $A\in\mathrm{RS}(W,R)$ there exists a uniquely determined ordered pair $[L,U]$ where L is a lower rough set from LRS(W,R) and U is an upper rough set from URS(W,R) such that

$$A=L\cap U.$$

Using these facts we define for arbitrary rough sets $A=L\cap U$ and $B=M\cap V$ of RS(W,R) where $L,M\in\mathrm{LRS}(W,R)$ and $U,V\in\mathrm{URS}(W,R)$ a binary relation $\underset{R}{\leq}$ as follows.

Definition 15. $A\underset{R}{\leq}B=_{def}L\underset{[R]}{\leq}M$ *and* $U\underset{\langle R\rangle}{\leq}V$

Theorem 7. $\Pi = \left[\mathrm{RS}(W,R), \underset{R}{\leq}\right]$ *is a partially ordered set.*

Proof. Trivial by proposition 14, proposition 16, proposition 18, and definition 15.

Now, starting with the partially ordered sets $\Pi_1 = \left[\mathrm{LRS}(W,R), \underset{[R]}{\leq}\right]$ and $\Pi_2 = \left[\mathrm{URS}(W,R), \underset{\langle R\rangle}{\leq}\right]$ and following definition 5 we construct the direct product Π^* of Π_1 and Π_2, i. e.

$$\Pi^* = \left[\mathrm{LRS}(W,R)\times\mathrm{URS}(W,R), \underset{R}{\leq^*}\right]$$

where for $L, M \in \mathrm{LRS}(W,R)$ and $U, V \in \mathrm{URS}(W,R)$

$$[L,U] \underset{R}{\leq^*} [M,V] =_{def} L \underset{[R]}{\leq} M \text{ and } U \underset{\langle R\rangle}{\leq} V.$$

Theorem 8. Π^* *is a complete lattice.*

Proof. Theorem 3, corollary 4, and proposition 5.

Define the set PERPAIRS(W,R) of all "permissible" pairs $[L,U]$ from $\mathrm{LRS}(W,R)\times\mathrm{URS}(W,R)$ with respect to W and R, furthermore the binary relation $\leq^*$ and the structure Π^* as follows.

Definition 16. *1.* $\mathrm{PERPAIRS}(W,R) =_{def}$
$$\{[L,U] \mid L \in \mathrm{LRS}(W,R) \wedge U \in \mathrm{URS}(W,R) \wedge L \cap U \neq \varnothing\}$$
2. $\underset{R}{\leq}' =_{def}$ *The restriction of* $\underset{R}{\leq^*}$ *to* PERPAIRS(W,R)
3. $\Pi' =_{def} \left[\mathrm{PERPAIRS}(W,R), \underset{R}{\leq}'\right]$

Theorem 9. *1.* Π' *is a complete lattice*
2. Π' *is a sublattice of* Π^*

Assume $L \in \mathrm{LRS}(W,R)$, $U \in \mathrm{URS}(W,R)$, and $L \cap U \neq \varnothing$.

Definition 17. $\Phi([L,U]) =_{def} L \cap U$

Proposition 20. Φ *is an order isomorphism from* Π' *on* Π.

Proof. Definition 17, proposition 14, theorem 7, and theorem 9.

Theorem 10. Π *is a complete lattice.*

Proof. Theorem 9, proposition 20, and proposition 3.

Theorem 11. *If* R *is reflexive on* W *and* R *is transitive, then* Π *is a distributive lattice.*

Proof. Theorem 4, theorem 6, and proposition 5.

7 Concluding Remarks

In forthcoming papers we shall investigate the lattices $\left[\mathrm{LRS}(W,R), \underset{[R]}{\leq}\right]$, $\left[\mathrm{URS}(W,R), \underset{\langle R\rangle}{\leq}\right]$, and $\left[\mathrm{RS}(W,R), \underset{R}{\leq}\right]$ in detail, in particular, which properties of R imply certain properties of the lattices above and vice versa.

Acknowledgement

The author wishes to thank ULRICH FIESELER for his help in preparing the manuscript.

References

1. LUDWIK BORKOWSKI (editor). *Selected works of* J. ŁUKASIEWICZ. North-Holland, Amsterdam, 1970.
2. C. DAVIS. *Modal operators, equivalence relations, and projective algebras*. American Journal of Mathematics **76**, 747–762, 1954.
3. DIDIER DUBOIS and HENRI PRADE. *Twofold fuzzy sets and rough sets, some issues in knowledge representation*. Fuzzy Sets and Systems pages 3–18, 1987.
4. MAI GEHRKE and ELBERT WALKER. *On the Structure of Rough Sets*. Bull. Polish Acad. Sci., Math. **40**, 235–245, 1992.
5. P. R. HALMOS. *Algebraic Logic, I. Monadic* BOOLE*an algebras*. Compositio Mathematica **12**, 217–249, 1955.
6. P. R. HALMOS. *Algebraic Logic*. Chelsea, New York, 1962.
7. *Proceedings of the Sixth International Conference on Information Processing and Management of Uncertainty in Knowledge-Based Systems*, Granada, Spain, July 1–5, 1996.
8. LUISA ITURRIOZ. *Rough sets and three-valued structures*. Unpublished paper. Personal communication.
9. TADEUSZ B. IWIŃSKI. *Algebraic Approach to Rough Sets*. Bull. Polish Acad. Sci., Math. **35**, 673–682, 1987.
10. E. E. KERRE. *A First View on the Alternatives of Fuzzy Set Theory*. In: *This volume*.
11. T. Y. LIN. *Neighborhood Systems and Approximation in Relational Databases and Knowledge Bases*. In: *Methodologies for Intelligent Systems*, volume 4, October 12–14, 1989. Poster session.
12. T. Y. LIN, K. J. HUANG, Q. LIU and W. CHEN. *Rough Sets, Neighborhood Systems and Approximation*. In: *Methodologies for Intelligent Systems*, volume 5, October 25–27, 1990. Selected paper.
13. GR. C. MOISIL. *Recherches sur les logiques non-chrysipiennes*. Annales Scientifiques de l'Université de Jassy **26**, 431–466, 1940. reproduced in [15].
14. GR. C. MOISIL. *Les logiques non-Chrysipiennes et leurs Applications*. Acta Philosophica Fennica **16**, 137–152, 1963.
15. GR. C. MOISIL. *Essais sur les logiques non chrysipiennes*. Académie R. S. de Roumanie, Bucarest, 1972.

16. A. MONTEIRO. *Algebras Monádicas*. In: *Actas do Segundo Colóquio Brasileiro de Matemática*, pages 33–52, São Paulo, 1960. A French translation is published as Notas de Lógica Matemática n° 7, Instituto de Matemática, Universidad Nacional del Sur, Bahía Blanca, Argentina, 1974.
17. A. MONTEIRO. *Sur la définition des algèbres de* ŁUKASIEWICZ *trivalentes*. Bulletin Mathématique de la Société des Sciences Mathématique et Physiques de la R. P. Roumaine **7**, 3–12, 1963. A preprint is published as Notas de Lógica Matemática n° 21, Instituto de Matemática, Universidad Nacional del Sur, Bahía Blanca, Argentina, 1974, 1–20.
18. A. MONTEIRO. *Construction des algèbres de* ŁUKASIEWICZ *trivalentes dans les algèbres de* BOOLE *monadiques—I*. Mathematica Japonicae **12**, 1–23, 1967.
19. A. MONTEIRO. *Sur les algèbres de* HEYTING *symétriques*. Portugaliae Mathematica **39**, 1–237, 1980. (Prix Gulbenkian de Science et Technologie).
20. L. MONTEIRO and C. L. GONZALEZ. *Sur une construction des Algèbres de* ŁUKASIEWICZ *Trivalentes*. Portugaliae Mathematica **23**, 157–167, 1964. A preprint is published as Notas de Lógica Matemática n° 17, Instituto de Matemática, Universidad Nacional del Sur, Bahía Blanca, Argentina, 1964, 17 pages.
21. TETSUYA MURAI, H. KANEMITSU and MASARU SHIMBO. *Standard possible-worlds semantics for rough set theory*. In: IPMU '96 [7], pages 365–370.
22. A. NAKAMURA. *A logic of imprecise monadic predicates and its relation to the S5-modal fuzzy logic*. In: *European Conference on Symbolic and Quantitative Approaches to Uncertainty*, volume 548 of *Lecture Notes in Computer Science*, pages 254–261, Marseille, October 1991.
23. J. NIEMINEN. *Rough Tolerance Equality and Tolerance Black Boxes*. Fundamenta Informaticae **11**, 289–296, 1988.
24. J. NIEMINEN. *Rough Sets, Screens, Roundings and Relations*. Bull. Polish Acad. Sci., Tech. **37**, 351–358, 1990.
25. M. NOVOTNÝ and Z. PAWLAK. *On Representation of Rough Sets by Means of Information Systems*. Fundamenta mathematice **6**, 289–296, 1983.
26. M. NOVOTNÝ and Z. PAWLAK. *Black Box Analysis and Rough Top Equality*. Bull. Polish Acad. Sci., Math. **33**, 105–113, 1985.
27. M. NOVOTNÝ and Z. PAWLAK. *Characterization of Rough Top Equalities and Rough Bottom Equalities*. Bull. Polish Acad. Sci., Math. **33**, 91–97, 1985.
28. M. NOVOTNÝ and Z. PAWLAK. *On Rough Equalities*. Bull. Polish Acad. Sci., Math. **33**, 99–104, 1985.
29. ADAM OBTUŁOWICZ. *Rough Sets and* HEYTING *Algebra Valued Sets*. Bull. Polish Acad. Sci., Math. **35**, 667–671, 1987.
30. Z. PAWLAK. *Rough Sets, Basic Notions*. ICS PAS Report 436, 1981.
31. Z. PAWLAK. *Rough Sets*. International Journal of Information and Computer Science **11**, 341–356, 1982.
32. Z. PAWLAK. *Rough Sets, Algebraic and Topological Approach*. ICS PAS Report 482, 1982.
33. Z. PAWLAK. *Rough Sets, Power Set Hierarchy*. ICS PAS Report 470, 1982.
34. Z. PAWLAK. *Rough sets and fuzzy sets*. Fuzzy Sets and Systems **17**, 99–102, 1985.
35. Z. PAWLAK. *Indiscernibility, Partitions and Rough Sets*. In: R. NARASIMHAN (editor), *Commemorative Volume on Theoretical Computer Science—in Honor of Prof. Siromony*. World Scientific Publishing Comp., Co., Singapore, 1989.
36. Z. PAWLAK. *Rough sets, Theoretical Aspects of Reasoning about Data*. Kluwer Acad. Publ., Dordrecht, 1991.

37. JACEK POMYKAŁA and JANUSZ A. POMYKAŁA. *The* STONE *Algrebra of Rough Sets*. Bull. Polish Acad. Sci., Math. **36**, 495–508, 1988.
38. JANUSZ A. POMYKAŁA. *Approximations in Approximation Space*. Bull. Polish Acad. Sci., Math. **35**, 653–662, 1987.
39. J. STEPANIUK. *Rough sets, first order logic and attribute construction*. In: IPMU '96 [7], pages 887–890.
40. HELMUT THIELE. *On the Definitions of Modal Operators in Fuzzy-Logic*. In: *23rd International Symposium on Multiple-Valued Logic — Conference Proceedings*, pages 62–67, Sacramento, California, May 24–27, 1993.
41. HELMUT THIELE. *On Soft Dynamic Logic*. In: *International Conference on Information Processing and Management of Uncertainty in Knowledge-Based Systems — Conference Proceedings*, volume II, pages 1159–1164, Paris, France, July 4–8, 1994.
42. HELMUT THIELE. *Fuzzy Rough Sets versus Rough Fuzzy Sets — An Interpretation and a Comparative Study using Concepts of Modal Logics*. In: *5th European Congress on Intelligent Techniques and Soft Computing (EUFIT '97) — Proceedings*, volume 1, pages 159–167, Aachen, Germany, September 8–11, 1997. Extended Version in [43].
43. HELMUT THIELE. *Fuzzy Rough Sets versus Rough Fuzzy Sets — An Interpretation and a Comparative Study using Concepts of Modal Logics*. Technical Report CI-30/98, University of Dortmund, Collaborative Research Center 531 (Computational Intelligence), April 1998. Extended Version of [42].
44. ANTONI WIWEGER. *On Topological Rough Sets*. Bull. Polish Acad. Sci., Math. **37**, 89–93, 1989.
45. S. K. M. WONG and W. ZIARKO. *Comparison of the probabilistic approximate classification and the fuzzy set model*. Fuzzy Sets and Systems **21**, 357–362, 1987.
46. URSZULA WYBRANIEC-SKARDOWSKA. *On a Generalization of Approximation Space*. Bull. Polish Acad. Sci., Math. **37**, 51–62, 1989.
47. Y. Y. YAO, S. K. M. WONG and LINGRAS PAWAN. *A Decision-Theoretic Rough Set Model*. In: Z. W. RAS, M. ZEMANKOVA and M. L. EMRICH (editors), *Methodologies for Intelligent Systems*, volume 5, pages 17–24. Elsevier Science Publishing Co., Inc., 1990.

Probalistic Networks and Fuzzy Clustering as Generalizations of Naive Bayes Classifiers

Christian Borgelt, Heiko Timm and Rudolf Kruse

Dept. of Kowledge Processing and Language Engineering
Otto-von-Guericke-University of Magdeburg
Universitätsplatz 2, D-39106 Magdeburg, Germany
{borgelt, htimm, kruse}@iws.cs.uni-magdeburg.de

Abstract. Although at first sight probabilistic networks and fuzzy clustering seem to be disparate areas of research, a closer look reveals that they can both be seen as generalizations of naive Bayes classifiers. If all attributes are numeric (except the class attribute, of course), naive Bayes classifiers often assume an axis-parallel multidimensional normal distribution for each class as the underlying model. Probabilistic networks remove the requirement that the distributions must be axis-parallel by taking the covariance of the attributes into account, where this is necessary. Fuzzy clustering is an unsupervised method that tries to find general or axis-parallel distributions to cluster the data. Although it does not take into account the class information, it can be used to improve the result of naive Bayes classifiers and probabilistic networks by removing the restriction that there can be only one distribution per class.

1 Introduction

Probabilistic networks are a method to decompose a multivariate probability distribution in order to make reasoning in multi-dimensional domains feasible. Fuzzy clustering is a method to find groups of similar objects or cases, which compared to classical (crisp) clustering has the advantage that an object or a case can belong (with a degree between 0 and 1) to more than one cluster. Thus, at first sight, there seems to be little connection between these two methods. Nevertheless, in this paper we venture to discuss them together, since they can both be seen as generalizations of naive Bayes classifiers.

Our rationale is that the three techniques mentioned above—naive Bayes classifiers, probabilistic networks, and fuzzy clustering—share the idea that underlying the dataset to process there is a model consisting of a set of probability distributions/density functions that generated the data. They differ w.r.t. the assumptions they make about the distributions/density functions and whether they take into account the value of a distinguished class attribute (supervised methods: naive Bayes classifiers, probabilistic networks) or not (unsupervised methods: fuzzy clustering). Of course, there are still other methods, for example, radial basis function neural networks [19], that can be interpreted in much the same fashion. However, a complete list of such methods and a discussion of their similarities and differences is beyond the scope of this paper. We selected the three methods mentioned above as examples, because the first two (naive Bayes classifiers, probabilistic networks) show very clearly the properties we are interested in and because the connection to fuzzy clustering points out interesting directions to improve these techniques.

To simplify the explanation of the ideas this paper tries to convey, we confine ourselves to numeric attributes (with the exception of the class attribute, of course). That is, we consider only those attributes used to characterize an object or case under consideration that can be described by real numbers. With this restriction a common assumption, that is made with all three methods we are going to discuss, is that the data to process was generated by a set of multidimensional normal distributions (also called *Gaussians*). The three methods differ in the constraints they place on this set of distributions. Naive Bayes classifiers and probabilistic networks (if the latter are used for classification tasks) restrict the number of distributions to the number of classes, since they assume exactly one distribution per class. Naive Bayes classifiers, in addition, assume that for each multivariate normal distribution, i.e., for each class, the attributes are independent, thus requiring the distributions to be axis-parallel. Of fuzzy clustering algorithms, there are also general and axis-parallel variants. In fuzzy clustering, however, the number of multivariate normal distributions is not restricted to the number of classes (it is an unsupervised method and does not take the class information into account), but can be chosen freely. This often leads to a better fit to the data and may be exploited to improve the two other methods.

The brief overview just given already fixes the order in which we discuss the methods. In section 2 we examine naive Bayes classifiers. In section 3 we turn to probabilistic networks and show how a naive Bayes classifier can be seen as a special Bayesian network and how general Bayesian networks remove the strong independence assumptions underlying naive Bayes classifiers. In section 4 we study fuzzy clustering algorithms from the specific point of view indicated above (as estimators of an underlying set of probability distributions/density functions) and show how they can improve the aforementioned methods by removing the restriction of one distribution per class. Finally, in section 5, we draw conclusions from our discussion.

2 Naive Bayes Classifiers

Naive Bayes classifiers [11, 6, 16, 17] are an old and well-known type of classifiers, i.e., of programs that assign a class from a predefined set to an object or case under consideration based on the values of attributes used to describe this object or case. They do so using a probabilistic approach, i.e., they try to compute conditional class probabilities and then predict the most probable class. To be more precise, let C denote a class attribute with a finite domain of m classes, i.e., $\text{dom}(C) = \{c_1, \ldots, c_m\}$, and let $A_1, \ldots, A_n$ be a set of other attributes used to describe a case or an object of the domain under consideration. These other attributes may be symbolic, i.e., $\mathrm{dom}(A_j) = \{a_1^{(j)}, \ldots, a_{m_j}^{(j)}\}$, or numeric, i.e., $\mathrm{dom}(A_j) = \mathbb{R}$. For simplicity, we always use the notation $a_{i_j}^{(j)}$ for a value of an attribute A_k, independent of whether it is a symbolic or a numeric one.[1] With this notation, a case or an object can be described by an instantiation $\omega = (a_{i_1}^{(1)}, \ldots, a_{i_n}^{(n)})$ of the attributes $A_1, \ldots, A_n$ and thus the universe of discourse is $\Omega = \mathrm{dom}(A_1) \times \ldots \times \mathrm{dom}(A_n)$.

For a given instantiation ω, a naive Bayes classifier tries to compute the conditional probability

$$P(C = c_i \mid \omega) = P(C = c_i \mid A_1 = a_{i_1}^{(1)}, \ldots, A_n = a_{i_n}^{(n)})$$

for all c_i and then predicts the class c_i for which this probability is highest. Of course, it is usually impossible to store all of these conditional probabilities explicitly, so that a simple lookup would be all that is needed to find the most probable class. If there are numeric attributes, this is obvious (we need some parameterized function then). But even if all attributes are symbolic, such an approach most often is infeasible: We would have to store a class (or a class probability distribution) for each point of the Cartesian product of the attribute domains, whose size grows exponentially with the number of attributes. To circumvent this problem, naive Bayes classifiers exploit—as their name already indicates—Bayes rule and a set of conditional independence assumptions. With Bayes rule

$$P(Y \mid X) = \frac{P(X \mid Y) \cdot P(Y)}{P(X)},$$

where X and Y are events, the conditional probabilities are inverted. That is, naive Bayes classifiers consider[2]

$$\begin{aligned} &P(C = c_i \mid A_1 = a_{i_1}^{(1)}, \ldots, A_n = a_{i_n}^{(n)}) \\ &= \frac{f(A_1 = a_{i_1}^{(1)}, \ldots, A_n = a_{i_n}^{(n)} \mid C = c_i) \cdot P(C = c_i)}{f(A_1 = a_{i_1}^{(1)}, \ldots, A_n = a_{i_n}^{(n)})}. \end{aligned}$$

Of course, for this inversion to be always possible, the probability density function $f(A_1 = a_{i_1}^{(1)}, \ldots, A_n = a_{i_n}^{(n)})$ must be strictly positive.

There are two observations to be made about the inversion carried out above. In the first place, we can neglect the denominator of the fraction on the right, since for a given case or object to be classified, it is fixed and therefore does not have any influence on the class ranking (which is all we are interested in). In

[1] To be able to use this notation for numeric attributes, we simply have to choose an appropriate uncountably infinite index set $\mathcal{I}_j$, from which the index i_j is to be taken.

[2] For simplicity, we always use a probability density function f, although this is strictly correct only, if there is at least one numeric attribute. If all attributes are symbolic, this should be a probability P. The only exception is the class attribute, since it necessarily has a finite domain.

addition, its influence can always be restored by normalizing the distribution on the classes, i.e., we can exploit

$$\begin{aligned} &f(A_1 = a_{i_1}^{(1)}, \ldots, A_n = a_{i_n}^{(n)}) \\ &= \sum_{j=1}^{m} f(A_1 = a_{i_1}^{(1)}, \ldots, A_n = a_{i_n}^{(n)} \mid C = c_j) \cdot P(C = c_j). \end{aligned}$$

It follows that we only need to consider

$$\begin{aligned} &P(C = c_i \mid A_1 = a_{i_1}^{(1)}, \ldots, A_n = a_{i_n}^{(n)}) \\ &= \frac{1}{S} \cdot f(A_1 = a_{i_1}^{(1)}, \ldots, A_n = a_{i_n}^{(n)} \mid C = c_i) \cdot P(C = c_i), \end{aligned}$$

where S is a normalization constant.[3]

Secondly, we can see that just inverting the probabilities does not buy us anything, since the probability space is just as large as it was before the inversion. However, here the second ingredient of naive Bayes classifiers, which is responsible for the "naive" in their name, comes in, namely the conditional independence assumptions. To exploit them, we first apply the chain rule of probability:[4]

$$\begin{aligned} &P(C = c_i \mid A_1 = a_{i_1}^{(1)}, \ldots, A_n = a_{i_n}^{(n)}) \\ &= \frac{1}{S} \cdot f(A_n = a_{i_n}^{(n)} \mid A_{n-1} = a_{i_{n-1}}^{(n-1)}, \ldots, A_1 = a_{i_1}^{(1)}, C = c_i) \\ &\qquad \ldots \\ &\qquad \cdot f(A_2 = a_{i_2}^{(2)} \mid A_1 = a_{i_1}^{(1)}, C = c_i) \\ &\qquad \cdot f(A_1 = a_{i_1}^{(1)} \mid C = c_i) \\ &\qquad \cdot P(C = c_i). \end{aligned}$$

Now we make the crucial assumption that given the value of the class attribute, any attribute A_j is independent of any other. That is, we assume that knowing the class is enough to determine the probability (density) for a value $a_{i_j}^{(j)}$, i.e., that we need not know the values of any other attributes. Of course, this is a pretty strong assumption, which is very likely to fail. It is truly "naive" to make it nevertheless. However, it considerably simplifies the formula stated above, since with it we can cancel all attributes A_j appearing in the conditions:

$$P(C = c_i \mid A_1 = a_{i_1}^{(1)}, \ldots, A_n = a_{i_n}^{(n)}) = \frac{1}{S} \cdot P(C = c_i) \cdot \prod_{j=1}^{n} f(A_j = a_{i_j}^{(j)} \mid C = c_i)$$

---

[3] Strictly speaking, the constant S depends on the instantiation $(a_{i_1}^{(1)}, \ldots, a_{i_n}^{(n)})$. However, as already said above, when classifying a given case or object, this instantiation is fixed and hence we need to consider only one value S.

[4] Again we always use a probability density function f, although this is strictly correct only, if the conditioned attribute is numeric.

This is the fundamental formula underlying naive Bayes classifiers. For a symbolic attribute A_j the conditional probabilities $P(A_j = a_{i_j}^{(j)} \mid C = c_i)$ are stored as a simple conditional probability table. This is feasible now, since there is only one condition and hence only $m \cdot m_j$ probabilities have to be stored.[5] For numeric attributes it is usually assumed that the probability density is a Gaussian function (a normal distribution) and hence only the expected values $\mu_j(c_i)$ and the variances $\sigma_j^2(c_i)$ need to be stored in this case. Alternatively, numeric attributes may be discretized [5] and then treated like symbolic attributes. In this paper, however, we make the normal distribution assumption, since we need it for the connection to fuzzy clustering.

Naive Bayes classifiers can easily be induced from a dataset of preclassified sample cases. All we have to do is to estimate the conditional probabilities/probability densities $f(A_j = a_{i_j}^{(j)} \mid C = c_i)$ using, for instance, maximum likelihood estimation. For symbolic attributes, this yields

$$\hat{P}(A_j = a_{i_j}^{(j)} \mid C = c_i) = \frac{\#(A_j = a_{i_j}^{(j)}, C = c_i)}{\#(C = c_i)},$$

where $\#(C = c_i)$ is the number of sample cases that belong to the class c_i and $\#(A_j = a_{i_j}^{(j)}, C = c_i)$ is the number of sample cases that belong to class c_i and have the value $a_{i_j}^{(j)}$ for the attribute A_j. To ensure that the probability is strictly positive (see above), it is assumed that there is at least one example for each class in the dataset. Otherwise the class is simply removed from the domain of the class attribute. If an attribute value does not occur given some class, its probability is either set to $\frac{1}{2N}$, where N is the number of sample cases, or a uniform prior of $\frac{1}{N}$ is added to the estimated distribution, which is then renormalized (Laplace correction). For a numeric attribute A_j the standard maximum likelihood estimation functions

$$\hat{\mu}_j(c_i) = \frac{1}{\#(C = c_i)} \sum_{k=1}^{\#(C=c_i)} a_{i_j(k)}^{(j)}$$

for the expected value, where $a_{i_j(k)}^{(j)}$ is the value of the attribute A_j in the k-th sample case belonging to class c_i, and

$$\hat{\sigma}_j^2(c_i) = \frac{1}{\#(C = c_i)} \sum_{k=1}^{\#(C=c_i)} \left(a_{i_j(k)}^{(j)} - \hat{\mu}_j(c_i)\right)^2$$

for the variance can be used.

[5] Actually only $m \cdot (m_j - 1)$ probabilities are really necessary. Since the probabilities have to add up to one, one value can be discarded from each conditional distribution. However, in implementations it is usually much easier to store all probabilities.

3 Probabilistic Networks

Probabilistic inference networks—especially Bayesian networks [20], but also Markov networks [18]—are well-known tools for reasoning under uncertainty in multidimensional domains. The idea underlying them is to exploit independence relations between the attributes used to describe a domain in order to decompose a multivariate probability distribution into a set of (conditional or marginal) distributions on lower-dimensional subspaces. Early efficient implementations include HUGIN [1] and PATHFINDER [12].

Dependence and independence relations have been studied extensively in the field of graphical modeling [14, 24] and though using them to facilitate reasoning in multidimensional domains has originated in the probabilistic setting, this approach has been generalized to be usable with other uncertainty calculi [22], for instance, in the so-called valuation-based networks [23] and has been implemented, for example, in PULCINELLA [21]. Due to their connection to fuzzy systems, which in the past have successfully been applied to solve control problems, and due to their ability to deal not only with uncertainty but also with imprecision, recently possibilistic networks also gained some attention. They can be based on the context-model interpretation of a degree of possibility, which focuses on imprecision [9], and have been implemented, for example, in POSSINFER [10, 15]. In this paper, however, we focus on Bayesian networks, since they are closest to naive Bayes classifiers and thus to fuzzy clustering.

A Bayesian network is a directed acyclic graph in which each node represents an attribute (interpreted as a random variable), that is used to describe some domain of interest, and each edge represents a direct dependence between two attributes. The structure of the directed graph encodes a set of conditional independence statements that can be read from the graph using a graph theoretic criterion called ***d-separation*** [20]. In addition, the graph represents a particular joint probability distribution, which is specified by assigning to each node in the network a (conditional) probability distribution for the values of the corresponding attribute given its parent attributes in the network (if any).

Formally, a Bayesian network describes a factorization of a multivariate probability distribution/density function. This factorization results from applying first the chain rule of probability to the joint distribution/density function. Then the factors are simplified by exploiting ***conditional independence statements*** of the form $\forall \omega \in \Omega$:

$$P(\omega_{X \cup Y} \mid \omega_Z) = P(\omega_X \mid \omega_Z) \cdot P(\omega_Y \mid \omega_Z)$$

whenever $P(\omega_Z) > 0$, where X, Y, and Z are three disjoint sets of attributes and $\omega_X = \text{proj}_X(\omega)$ is the projection of an instantiation $\omega = (A_1 = a_{i_1}^{(1)}, \ldots, A_n = a_{i_n}^{(n)})$ to the attributes in X. As one can easily verify, these statements are equivalent to statements of the form $\forall \omega \in \Omega$:

$$P(\omega_X \mid \omega_{Y \cup Z}) = P(\omega_X \mid \omega_Z).$$

From the description given up to now one can already guess the connection to naive Bayes classifiers. To be more precise, consider a probability distribution/density function f on the joint domain of a set of attributes $A_1, \dots A_n$. We first apply the chain rule of probability to obtain (we use the same notation as in the preceding section):

$$\begin{aligned}
& f(A_1 = a^{(1)}_{i_1}, \dots, A_n = a^{(n)}_{i_n}) \\
&= f(A_n = a^{(n)}_{i_n} \mid A_{n-1} = a^{(n-1)}_{i_{n-1}}, \dots, A_1 = a^{(1)}_{i_1}) \\
&\cdot\ f(A_{n-1} = a^{(n-1)}_{i_{n-1}} \mid A_{n-2} = a^{(n-2)}_{i_{n-2}}, \dots, A_1 = a^{(1)}_{i_1}) \\
&\quad \dots \\
&\cdot\ f(A_2 = a^{(2)}_{i_2} \mid A_1 = a^{(1)}_{i_1}) \\
&\cdot\ f(A_1 = a^{(1)}_{i_1}).
\end{aligned}$$

Then we exploit conditional independence statements to simplify the conditions by removing those attributes of which the conditioned attribute is independent given the values of the remaining attributes. Thus the joint distribution/density function can be computed from $\forall i_1, \dots, i_n$:

$$f(\omega) = f(A_1 = a^{(1)}_{i_1}, \dots, A_n = a^{(n)}_{i_n}) = \prod_{i=1}^{n} P(A_j = a^{(j)}_{i_j} \mid \omega_{\text{parents}(A_i)}),$$

where parents(A_j) is the set of attributes of which to know the instantiations is sufficient to determine the probability (density) of the values of attribute A_j. The name "parents(A_j)" stems from the fact that in a Bayesian network the conditioning attributes are connected by directed edges to the conditioned attributes and hence are the parents of this attribute in the graph. This makes it very simple to read the factorization formula from a Bayesian network: For each attribute (node) there is exactly one factor in which it is the conditioned attribute, and the conditions of this factor are the attributes corresponding to the attribute's parent nodes in the graph. An example is shown on the left in figure 1, which represents the factorization $\forall i_1, \dots, i_7$:

$$\begin{aligned}
& f(A_1 = a^{(1)}_{i_1}, \dots, A_7 = a^{(7)}_{i_7}) \\
&= f(A_1 = a^{(1)}_{i_1}) \cdot f(A_2 = a^{(2)}_{i_2} \mid A_1 = a^{(1)}_{i_1}) \cdot f(A_3 = a^{(3)}_{i_3}) \\
&\cdot\ f(A_4 = a^{(4)}_{i_4} \mid A_1 = a^{(1)}_{i_1}, A_2 = a^{(2)}_{i_2}) \cdot f(A_5 = a^{(5)}_{i_5} \mid A_2 = a^{(2)}_{i_2}, A_3 = a^{(3)}_{i_3}) \\
&\cdot\ f(A_6 = a^{(6)}_{i_6} \mid A_4 = a^{(4)}_{i_4}, A_5 = a^{(5)}_{i_5}) \cdot f(A_7 = a^{(7)}_{i_7} \mid A_5 = a^{(5)}_{i_5})
\end{aligned}$$

It is obvious that a sparse graph is desirable to obtain a factorization with "small" factors. Whether a sparse graph can be found sometimes depends on the order of the attributes, but it cannot be guaranteed that a sparse graph exists for a given domain. In such cases usually an approximation is accepted.

Bayesian networks can be used for probabilistic reasoning by fixing the values of some (observed) attributes and then propagating this information in the

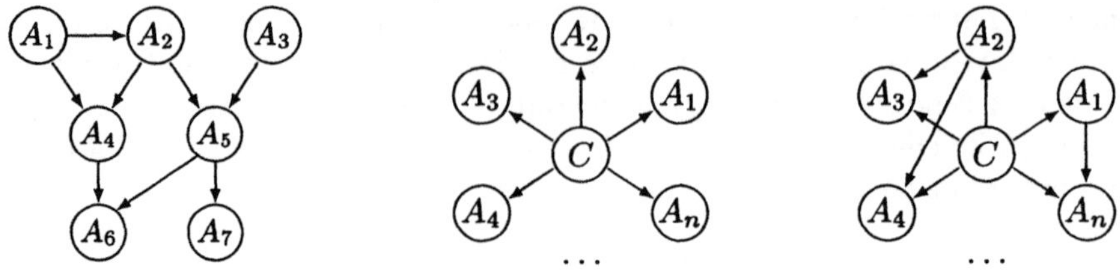

Fig. 1. A simple Bayesian network on a domain consisting of seven attributes (left). A naive Bayes classifier is a Bayesian network with a star-like structure (middle). It can easily be extended by adding edges between attributes that are still dependent given the class (right).

network to obtain the probabilities/densities for values of other (unobserved) attributes. This process, which is usually called evidence propagation, basically consists in replacing the prior probability distribution/density function with the posterior one, that is, the one conditioned on the values of the observed attributes. To make it efficient, a Bayesian network is often transformed into a clique tree for which a simple propagation scheme exists. The evidence is propagated along the edges of this clique tree using the marginal probability distributions/density functions associated with the nodes that represent the cliques. For details on clique tree construction and the clique tree propagation (CTP) algorithm, see e.g. [18].

It is easy to see that Bayesian networks are directly related to naive Bayes classifiers. In fact, a naive Bayes classifier is just a special Bayesian network with a star-like structure as shown in the middle of figure 1. That is, there is a distinguished attribute, namely the class attribute. It is the only unconditioned attribute (the only one without parents). All other attributes are conditioned on the class attribute and on the class attribute only. Reasoning consists in propagating the evidence about the values of the attributes $A_1, \ldots, A_n$ along the edges to obtain information about the class. This information is then accumulated.

The main drawback of naive Bayes classifiers are the very strong conditional independence assumptions underlying them (see above). Although these assumptions necessarily lead to sparse graph, a lot of information can get lost. Fortunately, exploiting the more general approach underlying Bayesian networks, this severe constraint can be relaxed. That is, we may add edges between those of the attributes $A_1, \ldots, A_j$ which are still dependent given the class (see figure 1 on the right). This can lead to improved classification results, since the extended conditional probability distributions are better suited to capture the dependence structure of the domain. To keep the resulting graph sparse, one may introduce the restriction that no attribute may have more than a fixed number of parents. Probabilistic networks of this type have been successfully applied in telecommunication [7].

As an illustrative example, let us take a look at the well-known iris data. The classification problem here is to predict the iris type (iris setosa, iris versicolor,

iris type	iris setosa	iris versicolor	iris virginica
prior probability	0.333	0.333	0.333
petal length	1.46 ± 0.17	4.26 ± 0.46	5.55 ± 0.55
petal width	0.24 ± 0.11	1.33 ± 0.20	2.03 ± 0.27

Table 1. A naive Bayes classifier for the iris data. The normal distributions are described by stating $\hat{\mu} \pm \hat{\sigma}$. It is easy to see from this table how different petal lengths and widths provide evidence for the different types of iris flowers.

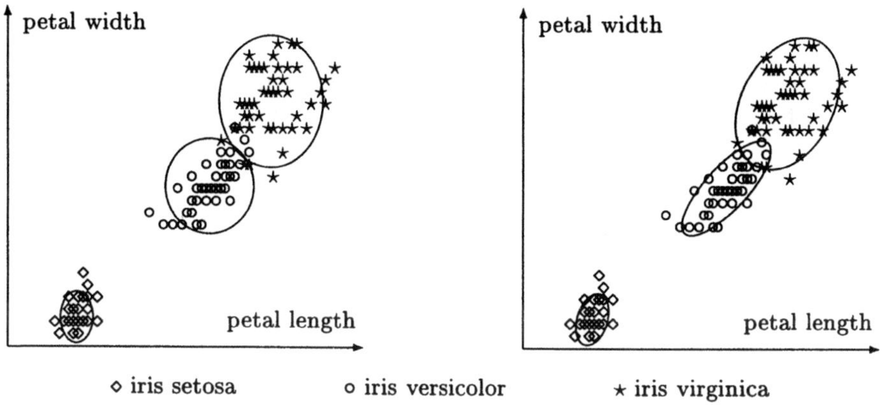

Fig. 2. Naive Bayes density functions for the iris data (axis-parallel ellipses, left) and density functions that take into account the covariance of the two measures (general ellipses, right). The ellipses are the 2σ-boundaries of the probability density functions.

or iris virginica) from measurements of the sepal length and width and the petal length and width. Due to the limited number of dimensions of a sheet of paper we confine ourselves to the latter two measures. The naive Bayes classifier induced from these two measures and all 150 cases is shown in table 1. The conditional probability density functions used by this classifier to predict the iris type are shown graphically in figure 2 on the left. The ellipses are the 2σ-boundaries of the (bivariate) normal distribution. These ellipses are axis-parallel, which is a consequence of the strong conditional independence assumptions made by a naive Bayes classifier: The normal distributions are estimated separately for each dimension and no covariance is taken into account. However, even a superficial glance at the data points reveals that the two measures are far from independent given the iris type. Especially for iris versicolor the density function is a rather bad estimate. However, if we allow for an additional edge between the petal length and the petal width, which, in this case, is most easily implemented by estimating the covariance matrix of the two measures, a much better fit to the data can be achieved (see figure 2 on the right, again the ellipses are the 2σ-boundaries of the probability density function). As a consequence the number of misclassifications drops from six to four (which can easily be made out in figure 2).

To summarize, probabilistic networks generalize naive Bayes classifiers in two ways. In the first place, by additional edges, the restriction to axis-parallel density functions can be removed and thus conditional dependences between the attributes can be taken into account. Secondly, in probabilistic networks there is usually no distinguished class attribute. Any attribute (or any set of attributes) can be made the focus of inferences. Thus several, quite different reasoning tasks can be solved with the same probabilistic network.

However, there is still the restriction that only one density function is estimated for each class. This is not always appropriate, especially under the normal distribution assumption. A better fit can often be achieved, if more than one "normal distribution cluster" per class is assumed. Such a generalization may be achieved by exploiting ideas from fuzzy clustering, which we study in the next section.

4 Fuzzy Clustering

The terms "classification" and "to classify" are ambiguous. In the preceding sections they are used to describe the process of assigning a class from a *predefined* set to an object or case under consideration. In classical statistics, however, these terms usually have a different meaning: They are used to describe the process of dividing a dataset of sample cases into groups of similar cases, with the groups *not* predefined, but to be found by the classification algorithm. This process is also called classification, because the groups to be found are usually (and confusingly) called *classes*. To avoid the confusion that may result from this ambiguity, the latter process, i.e., dividing a dataset into groups of similar cases, is often called *clustering* or *cluster analysis*, thus replacing the ambiguous term *class* with the less ambiguous *cluster*. Nevertheless a reader should keep in mind that in this section "to classify" has a different meaning than in the preceding ones (except where explicitly indicated otherwise).

Cluster analysis is, as already mentioned, a technique to classify data, i.e., to divide a given dataset of sample cases into a set of classes or *clusters*. The goal is to divide the dataset in such a way that two cases from the same cluster are as similar as possible and two cases from different clusters are as dissimilar as possible. Thus one tries to model the human ability to group similar objects or cases into classes and categories.

In classical cluster analysis [2] each case or object is assigned to exactly one cluster. That is, classical cluster analysis yields a crisp partitioning of a dataset with "sharp" boundaries between the clusters. It is therefore also called *crisp cluster analysis*. A crisp partitioning of the dataset, however, though often undisputedly successful, is not always appropriate. If the "clouds" formed by the data points corresponding to the cases or objects under consideration are not clearly separated by regions bare of any data points, but if, in contrast, in the joint domain of the attributes there are only regions of higher and lesser data point density, then the boundaries between the clusters can only be drawn with a certain amount of arbitrariness. Due to this arbitrariness it may be doubted, at least for data points close to the boundaries, whether a definite assignment to one class is justified.

An intuitive approach to deal with such situations is to make it possible that a data point belongs in part to one cluster, in part to a second etc. ***Fuzzy cluster analysis*** does just this: It relaxes the requirement that a data point must be assigned to exactly one cluster by allowing gradual memberships, thus offering the opportunity to deal with data points that do not belong definitely to one cluster [3, 4]. In general the performance of fuzzy clustering algorithms is superior to that of the corresponding crisp clustering algorithms [3].

Most fuzzy clustering algorithms are objective function based: They determine an optimal classification by minimizing an objective function. In objective function based clustering usually each cluster is represented by a ***cluster prototype***. This prototype consists of a ***cluster center*** (whose name already indicates its meaning) and maybe some additional information about the size and the shape of the cluster. The cluster center is an instantiation of the attributes used to describe the domain, just as the data points in the dataset to divide. However, the cluster center is computed by the clustering algorithm and may or may not appear in the dataset. The size and shape parameters determine the extension of the cluster in different directions of the underlying domain.

The degrees of membership to which a given data point belongs to the different clusters are computed from the distances of the data point to the cluster centers w.r.t. the size and the shape of the cluster as stated by the additional prototype information. The closer a data point lies to the center of a cluster (w.r.t. size and shape), the higher is its degree of membership to this cluster. Hence the problem to divide a dataset $X = \{\boldsymbol{x}_1, \ldots, \boldsymbol{x}_r\} \subseteq \mathbb{R}^n$ into m clusters can be stated as the task to minimize the distances of the data points to the cluster centers, since, of course, we want to maximize the degrees of membership.

Several fuzzy clustering algorithms can be distinguished depending on the additional size and shape information contained in the cluster prototypes, the way in which the distances are determined, and the restrictions that are placed on the membership degrees. We confine ourselves to a subset of all possible algorithms that is best suited to demonstrate the ideas we are interested in. To be more precise, we consider the task to minimize the objective function

$$J(\mathbf{X}, \mathbf{U}, \mathbf{B}) = \sum_{i=1}^{m} \sum_{j=1}^{r} u_{ij}^{\alpha} d^2(\boldsymbol{\beta}_i, \boldsymbol{x}_j) \tag{1}$$

subject to

$$\sum_{j=1}^{r} u_{ij} > 0, \quad \text{for all } i \in \{1, \ldots, m\}, \tag{2}$$

$$\sum_{i=1}^{m} u_{ij} = 1, \quad \text{for all } j \in \{1, \ldots, r\}, \tag{3}$$

where $u_{ij} \in [0,1]$ is the membership degree of datum $\boldsymbol{x}_j$ to cluster c_i, $\boldsymbol{\beta}_i$ is the prototype of cluster c_i, and $d(\boldsymbol{\beta}_i, \boldsymbol{x}_j)$ is the distance between datum $\boldsymbol{x}_j$ and prototype $\boldsymbol{\beta}_i$. $\mathbf{B}$ is the set of all m cluster prototypes $\boldsymbol{\beta}_1, \ldots, \boldsymbol{\beta}_m$. The $m \times r$ matrix $\mathbf{U} = [u_{ij}]$ is called the fuzzy partition matrix and the parameter α is called the fuzzifier. This parameter determines the "fuzziness" of the classification. With higher values for α the boundaries between the clusters become softer, with lower values they get harder. Usually $\alpha = 2$ is chosen.

Constraint (2) guarantees that no cluster is empty and constraint (3) ensures that the sum of the membership degrees for each datum equals 1. Fuzzy clustering algorithms which minimize the objective function J subject to these constraints are usually called *probabilistic clustering algorithms*, since the membership degrees for a given datum formally resemble the probabilities of its being a member of the corresponding cluster.

The objective function $J(\mathbf{X}, \mathbf{U}, \mathbf{B})$ is usually minimized by updating the membership degrees u_{ij} and the prototypes $\boldsymbol{\beta}_i$ in an alternating fashion, until the change $\Delta\mathbf{U}$ of the membership degrees is less than a given tolerance ε. This approach is also known as the *alternating optimization method.*

Skeleton of a Fuzzy Clustering Algorithm

Fix the number of clusters m
Fix α, $\alpha \in (1, \infty)$
Initialize the fuzzy m*-partition* $\mathbf{U}$
REPEAT
  Update the parameters of each clusters prototype
  Update the fuzzy m*-partition* $\mathbf{U}$ *using equation (4) (see below)*
UNTIL $|\Delta\mathbf{U}| < \varepsilon$

To minimize the objective function J, the membership degrees are updated using equation (4) below. This equation can be derived by differentiating the objective function J.

$$u_{ij} = \begin{cases} \dfrac{1}{\sum_{k=1}^{m} \left(\dfrac{d^2(\boldsymbol{x}_j, \boldsymbol{\beta}_i)}{d^2(\boldsymbol{x}_j, \boldsymbol{\beta}_k)} \right)^{\frac{1}{\alpha-1}}}, & \text{if } I_j = \emptyset, \\ 0, & \text{if } I_j \neq \emptyset \text{ and } i \notin I_j, \\ x, x \in [0,1] \text{ such that } \sum_{i \in I_j} u_{ij} = 1, & \text{if } I_j \neq \emptyset \text{ and } i \in I_j, \end{cases} \tag{4}$$

where $I_j = \{i | 1 \leq i \leq m, d^2(\boldsymbol{x}_j, \boldsymbol{\beta}_i) = 0\}$, i.e., I_j represents (by their indices) the set of all clusters, to whose centers the datum $\boldsymbol{x}_i$ is identical.

Equation 4 is used to update the membership degrees in all probabilistic clustering algorithms. In contrast to this, the formulae for computing the prototypes vary depending on what additional information is included in the prototypes (size and shape parameters) and how the distances are determined. Each choice leads to a different algorithm.

The simplest choice, of course, is to include in the cluster prototypes only the cluster centers and to use a Euclidean distance function (thus implicitely fixing that the clusters are spheres of equal size). The result is the well-known fuzzy C means algorithm, which was developed by Bezdek [3]. This algorithm, however, is very inflexible and thus often leads to an insufficient fit to the data. In addition, it cannot easily be interpreted probabilistically, which is important for our considerations. Therefore, in the following, we discuss a more flexible algorithm that is explicitely based on a probabilistic model.

In [8] Gath and Geva suggested a fuzzy clustering algorithm (the *FMLE*—Fuzzy Maximum Likelihood Estimation) which is based on the assumption that the dataset to be classified was generated by m n-dimensional normal distributions, where m is the number of clusters. To represent the necessary parameters, each cluster prototype is a triple $\boldsymbol{\beta}_i = (\boldsymbol{\mu}_i, \boldsymbol{\Sigma}_i, p_i)$, where $\boldsymbol{\mu}_i$ is the expected value of the multivariate normal distribution, $\boldsymbol{\Sigma}_i$ is the $n \times n$ covariance matrix, and p_i is the probability of the cluster c_i, such that $\sum_{i=1}^{m} p_i = 1$. Intuitively, $\boldsymbol{\mu}_i$ is the cluster center, $\boldsymbol{\Sigma}_i$ describes the size and shape of the cluster (the determinant of $\boldsymbol{\Sigma}_i$, for example, is a measure of the cluster size), and p_i determines the relative frequency of data points that are generated by the cluster c_i. The set of all cluster prototypes defines a complex probability density function on the n-dimensional domain under consideration, from which the probability densities at the data points in the dataset X can be determined.

The fuzzy maximum likelihood estimation algorithm classifies the data using a maximum likelihood approach. That is, it tries to determine the parameters of the cluster prototypes in such a way that the probability of the dataset (or, to be more precise, the sum of the probability densities at the data points in the dataset) is maximized. The rationale underlying this is that before observing the data all sets of prototypes are equally likely. With this assumption, the posterior probability of the dataset given the prototypes is a direct measure of the probability of the prototypes given the dataset (simply apply Bayes rule).

To maximize the likelihood of the data, the distance measure used in the fuzzy maximum likelihood estimation algorithm is inversely proportional to the probability density as defined by a cluster prototype. To be more precise, the distance is computed as

$$d(\boldsymbol{x}_j, \boldsymbol{\beta}_i) = \text{const.} \cdot \left(\frac{p_i}{\sqrt{|\boldsymbol{\Sigma}_i|(2\pi)^n}} \ \exp\left(-\frac{1}{2} (\boldsymbol{x}_j - \boldsymbol{\mu}_i)^T \boldsymbol{\Sigma}_i^{-1} (\boldsymbol{x}_j - \boldsymbol{\mu}_i) \right) \right)^{-1}.$$

Based on this distance measure the membership degrees are computed using equation (4).

However, if the fuzzy maximum likelihood estimation algorithm is applied exactly in the way outlined above, it tends to be unstable, mainly because of the large number of degrees of freedom. To make it more stable, it is advisable to introduce some restrictions. A serious problem that occurred frequently during our experiments was that one of the clusters became very small, with the shape either a sphere or a very thin and long ellipsoid. Therefore, in some experiments, we restricted the relative size of the clusters by introducing a constraint on the relative values of the determinants: If they deviate more than by a factor of three from the average, they are forced back into the range defined by the average and this factor. This lead to a much more stable behaviour and better results.

Let us now compare the fuzzy maximum likelihood estimation algorithm to a naive Bayes classifier. If we assume that the attributes are independent of each other given the clusters, just as we did for the naive Bayes classifier, then the clusters are defined by their probability, their centers, and the variances for each dimension (or, in other words, in the covariance matrix all elements but the diagonal elements are zero). Intuitively, with this assumption, the clusters are axis-parallel (see above). In this case the degree of membership of a datum to a clusters is computed in much the same way as a naive Bayes classifier computes the conditional class probabilities. Thus, an axis-parallel variant of the fuzzy maximum likelihood estimation algorithm [13] can be seen as a direct analogon of a naive Bayes classifier. The only difference, of course, is that a naive Bayes classifier already knows the classes the cases in the dataset belong to, whereas the clustering algorithm tries to find a good partitioning into classes. Nevertheless, if there is class information, and if the attributes convey information about the class, the class information can often be used to assess the quality of a clustering result.

As an illustrative example we turn again to the iris data we already used above. Figure 3 shows the result of the axis-parallel variant of the fuzzy maximum likelihood estimation algorithm on the iris data, if all four attributes are used (although—for technical reasons—only three dimensions are shown). On the left the data points are connected to the centers of the clusters for which their degree of membership is highest. The ellipsoids on the right indicate the 3σ-boundaries of the multivariate normal distributions.[6] It is easy to see that the result closely resembles the result of the naive Bayes classifier.

If the assumption that the attributes are independent given the class does not hold, the normal version of the fuzzy maximum likelihood estimation algorithm can be applied. Since it uses a full covariance matrix, dependencies between the attributes can be taken into account. Again we illustrate this with the help of the iris data. Figure 4 shows the result of the normal version of the fuzzy maximum likelihood estimation algorithm, if all four attributes are used (although only three dimensions are shown). On the left the data points are connected to the center of the cluster for which their degree of membership is highest. The ellipsoids on the right indicate the 3σ-boundaries of the multivariate normal distributions. Although this figure, especially the ellipsoids on the right, are a little harder to visualize in three dimensions, it is fairly obvious that the fit to the data is better than in figure 3.

As indicated, the results shown in figure 3 and 4 are computed using all attributes of the iris data set. However, usually the iris data set is classified based on the petal length and width only, since these are the two most informative attributes. In addition, comparing the results to the results of the preceding sections is easier, if we confine ourselves to these two dimensions. Of course,

---

[6] The fuzzy data analysis program `fcluster` which was used to create these screen shots can be obtained free of charge from our WWW-site: `http://fuzzy.cs.uni-magdeburg.de`.

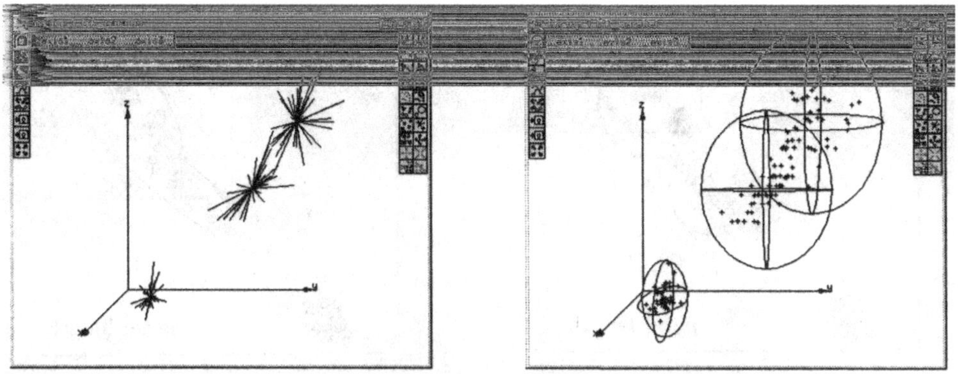

Fig. 3. The iris dataset classified with the axis-parallel variant of the fuzzy maximum likelihood algorithm, all attributes used. The vertical axis is the petal width, the horizontal the petal length and the depth is the sepal width. On the left each data point is connected to the center of that cluster to which it has the highest degree of membership. The ellipsoids on the right indicate the 3σ-boundaries of the multivariate normal distribution.

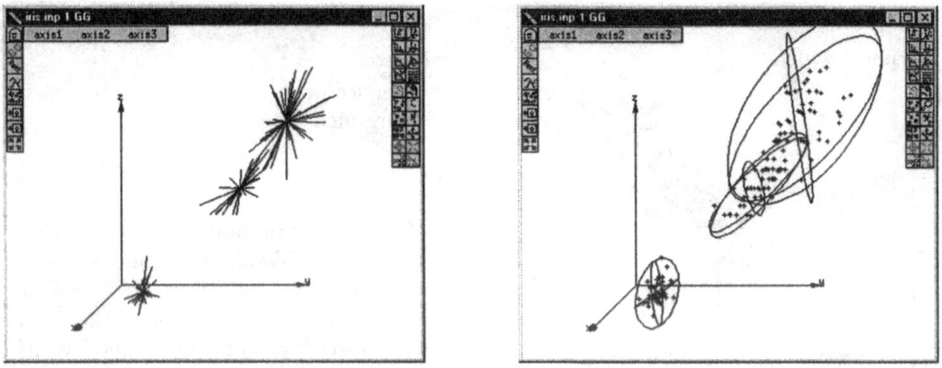

Fig. 4. The iris dataset classified with the normal fuzzy maximum likelihood algorithm, all attributes used. The vertical axis is the petal width, the horizontal the petal length and the depth is the sepal width. On the left each data point is connected to the center of that cluster to which it has the highest degree of membership. The ellipsoids on the right indicate the 3σ-boundaries of the multivariate normal distribution.

this changes the results of the clustering algorithms, since the distance functions change. Figure 5 shows the result of the axis-parallel variant of the fuzzy maximum likelihood estimation algorithm on the iris data, if only the petal length and width are used. The clusters found are hardly distinguishable from the naive Bayes clusters shown on the left in figure 2. If the three iris types are assigned to the clusters and the dataset is classified (in the sense of predicting the iris type), the number of errors is the same as for a naive Bayes classifier.

The result of the fuzzy maximum likelihood estimation algorithm, shown on the right in figure 5, however, does not resemble the one obtained by a proba-

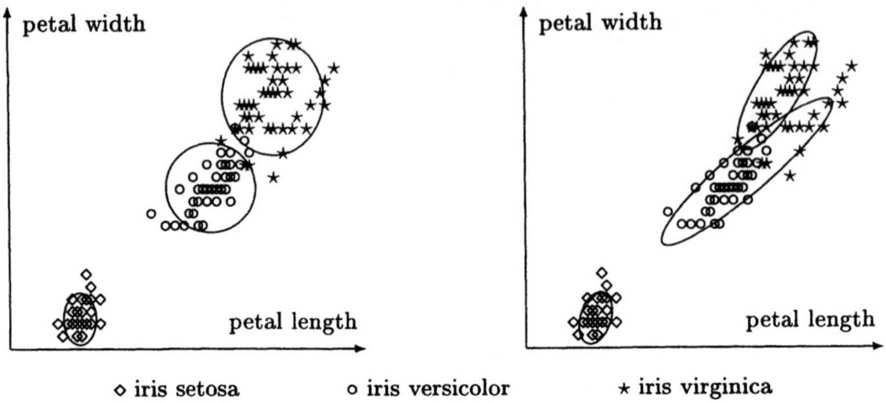

Fig. 5. Density functions generated by the fuzzy maximum likelihood estimation algorithm for the iris data, three clusters, axis-parallel version (left) and normal version (right). The ellipses are the 2σ-boundaries of the probability density functions. Petal width and petal length used only.

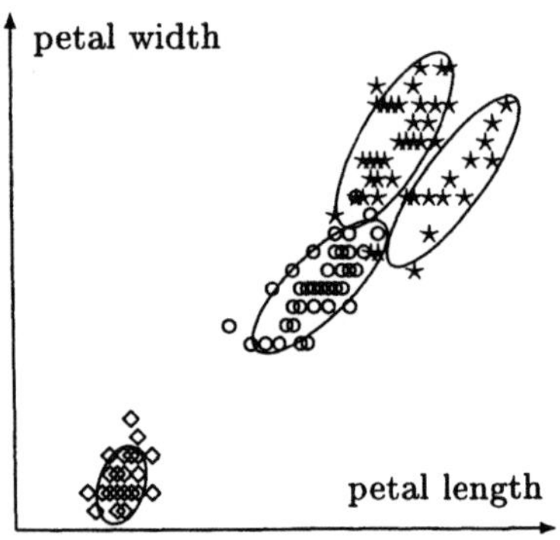

◇ iris setosa
○ iris versicolor
⋆ iris virginica

Fig. 6. Density functions generated by the fuzzy maximum likelihood estimation algorithm for the iris data, four clusters. The ellipses are the 2σ-boundaries of the probability density functions. Only petal width and length used.

bilistic network that takes into account the covariance of the two measures. Obviously the problem is that the fuzzy maximum likelihood estimation algorithm does not use any class information: Without such information the partitioning found is much more likely than the the probabilistic network clusters.

Fortunately, we can exploit the fact that in fuzzy clustering, since no class information is taken into account, we are not bound to using just one cluster per class (as already mentioned above). We may choose freely, and if we take a closer look at the iris data, a choice of four clusters suggests itself. Indeed, with this number of clusters the algorithm yields a model that excellently fits the data as shown in figure 6. The iris virginica cases have been divided into two clusters, which, indeed, is what a human would do under these circumstances. It has to be admitted though that even with the constraint on the cluster sizes introduced above, the fuzzy maximum likelihood estimation algorithm is not completely stable and that this is not the only classification we obtained. Fortunately, the different results can easily be ranked by simply computing the value of the objective function. Since this function has to be minimized, a smaller value indicates a better solution. The value of the objective function for the result shown in figure 6 is only half as large as the value for any other result we obtained and thus this solution can clearly be regarded as the one to be chosen.

This example indicates how naive Bayes classifiers and maybe also probabilistic networks can profit from fuzzy clustering. Using more than one cluster per class can often improve the fit to the data and thus in the future we plan to investigate combinations of the discussed methods.

5 Conclusions

In this paper we discussed the relationship between naive Bayes classifiers, probabilistic networks, and fuzzy cluster analysis. As we hope to have made clear, both probabilistic networks and the fuzzy maximum likelihood estimation algorithm can be seen as generalizations of naive Bayes classifiers. However, they generalize them to different degrees. Whereas probabilistic networks only remove the requirement that the multivariate normal distributions have to be axis-parallel (by taking covariances into account), fuzzy clustering does not only this, but also lets us use more than one cluster per class. Since the normal distribution assumption, even if covariances are taken into account, is not always appropriate, this opens up a route to enhance the capabilities of the former methods. The idea is simply to split one or more classes into pseudo-subclasses, each with a multivariate normal distribution of its own. To find a good split into subclasses, fuzzy clustering methods may be used, as the example shown clearly indicates.

References

1. S.K. Andersen, K.G. Olesen, F.V. Jensen, and F. Jensen. HUGIN — A Shell for Building Bayesian Belief Universes for Expert Systems. *Proc. 11th Int. J. Conf. on Artificial Intelligence (IJCAI'89, Detroit, MI, USA)*, 1080–1085. Morgan Kaufman, San Mateo, CA, USA 1989
2. M.J.A. Berry and G. Linoff. *Data Mining Techniques — For Marketing, Sales and Customer Support.* J. Wiley & Sons, Chichester, England 1997
3. J.C. Bezdek. *Pattern Recognition with Fuzzy Objective Function Algorithms.* Plenum Press, New York, NY, USA 1981
4. J.C. Bezdek and S.K. Pal. *Fuzzy Models for Pattern Recognition — Methods that Search for Structures in Data.* IEEE Press, Piscataway, NJ, USA 1992
5. J. Dougherty, R. Kohavi, and M. Sahami. Supervised and Unsupervised Discretization of Continuous Features. *Proc. 12th Int. Conf. on Machine Learning (ICML'95, Lake Tahoe, CA, USA)*, 194–202. Morgan Kaufman, San Mateo, CA, USA 1995
6. R.O. Duda and P.E. Hart. *Pattern Classification and Scene Analysis.* J. Wiley & Sons, New York, NY, USA 1973
7. K.J. Ezawa and S.W. Norton. Knowledge Discovery in Telecommunication Services Data Using Bayesian Network Models. *Proc. 1st Int. Conf. on Knowledge Discovery*

and Data Mining (KDD'95, Montreal, Canada), 100–105. AAAI Press, Menlo Park, CA, USA 1995

8. I. Gath and A.B. Geva. Unsupervised Optimal Fuzzy Clustering. *IEEE Trans. Pattern Anal. Mach. Intelligence* 11:773–781. IEEE Press, Piscataway, NJ, USA, 1989
9. J. Gebhardt and R. Kruse. The Context Model — An Integrating View of Vagueness and Uncertainty *Int. Journal of Approximate Reasoning* 9:283–314. North-Holland, Amsterdam, Netherlands 1993
10. J. Gebhardt and R. Kruse. POSSINFER — A Software Tool for Possibilistic Inference. In: D. Dubois, H. Prade, and R. Yager, eds. *Fuzzy Set Methods in Information Engineering: A Guided Tour of Applications*, 407–418. J. Wiley & Sons, New York, NY, USA 1996
11. I.J. Good. *The Estimation of Probabilities: An Essay on Modern Bayesian Methods.* MIT Press, Cambridge, MA, USA 1965
12. D. Heckerman. *Probabilistic Similarity Networks.* MIT Press, Cambridge, MA, USA 1991
13. F. Höppner, F. Klawonn, R. Kruse, and T. Runkler. *Fuzzy Cluster Analysis.* J. Wiley & Sons, Chichester, England 1999
14. R. Kruse, E. Schwecke, and J. Heinsohn. *Uncertainty and Vagueness in Knowledge-based Systems: Numerical Methods (Series Artificial Intelligence).* Springer, Berlin, Germany 1991
15. R. Kruse, J. Gebhardt, and F. Klawonn. *Foundations of Fuzzy Systems.* J. Wiley & Sons, Chichester, England 1994
16. P. Langley, W. Iba, and K. Thompson. An Analysis of Bayesian Classifiers. *Proc. 10th Nat. Conf. on Artificial Intelligence (AAAI'92, San Jose, CA, USA)*, 223–228. AAAI Press and MIT Press, Menlo Park and Cambridge, CA, USA 1992
17. P. Langley and S. Sage. Induction of Selective Bayesian Classifiers. *Proc. 10th Conf. on Uncertainty in Artificial Intelligence (UAI'94, Seattle, WA, USA)*, 399–406. Morgan Kaufman, San Mateo, CA, USA 1994
18. S.L. Lauritzen and D.J. Spiegelhalter. Local Computations with Probabilities on Graphical Structures and Their Application to Expert Systems. *Journal of the Royal Statistical Society, Series B*, 2(50):157–224. Blackwell, Oxford, United Kingdom 1988
19. D. Nauck, F. Klawonn, and R. Kruse. *Foundations of Neuro-Fuzzy Systems.* J. Wiley & Sons, Chichester, England 1997
20. J. Pearl. *Probabilistic Reasoning in Intelligent Systems: Networks of Plausible Inference (2nd edition).* Morgan Kaufman, San Mateo, CA, USA 1992
21. A. Saffiotti and E. Umkehrer. PULCINELLA: A General Tool for Propagating Uncertainty in Valuation Networks. *Proc. 7th Conf. on Uncertainty in Artificial Intelligence (UAI'91, Los Angeles, CA, USA)*, 323–331. Morgan Kaufman, San Mateo, CA, USA 1991
22. G. Shafer and P.P. Shenoy. *Local Computations in Hypertrees (Working Paper 201).* School of Business, University of Kansas, Lawrence, KS, USA 1988
23. P.P. Shenoy. *Valuation-based Systems: A Framework for Managing Uncertainty in Expert Systems (Working Paper 226).* School of Business, University of Kansas, Lawrence, KS, USA 1991
24. J. Whittaker. *Graphical Models in Applied Multivariate Statistics.* J. Wiley & Sons, Chichester, England 1990

Granular Computing in Fuzzy Modeling and Data Mining

Witold Pedrycz

Department of Electrical and Computer Engineering
University of Alberta
Edmonton T6R 2G7, Canada
pedrycz@ee.ualberta.ca
and
Systems Research Institute, Polish Academy of Sciences
Warsaw, Poland

Abstract This study is concerned with the concept of information granularity, its representation and use along with a discussion on selected application areas. We discuss several key methodologies involved therein with a particular focus on fuzzy set technology. The agenda of the paper embraces two key issues: (i) underlying fundamentals of information granularity and various ways of processing of information granules and (ii) the use of the methodology of granular computing to a broad range of problems of system modeling, control, and classification. Activities carried out under the auspices of fuzzy sets (fuzzy modeling) as well as data mining and neural networks exploit the ideas of granular computing. We discuss them in more detail highlighting their advantages and design practices.

Keywords Granular computing, data mining, fuzzy sets, unsupervised learning, context-sensitive fuzzy clustering, information granules, linguistic labels

1. Introduction

Data mining is aimed at searching for stable, meaningful, easily interpretable patterns in databases. The area, arising in the late eighties, comes as a direct response to the problems with an interpretation, revealing, and understanding main associations stored in large databases. Data mining is an immensely heterogeneous research area embracing techniques and ideas stemming from statistics, neurocomputing, rough sets, fuzzy sets, data visualization, databases, etc. In spite of such profound diversity, the focal point of all data mining pursuits is the same: revealing patterns that are not only meaningful but easily comprehensible. This calls for representing and processing that are carried out at a certain level of information granularity rather than being confined exclusively to tedious number crunching activities. Information granules, and granular computing tend to dominate all data mining pursuits. They are easily understood by the user, carry enough conceptual substance, and help understand interesting relationships determined within the data. Information granularity is accomplished in many possible ways including set theory, fuzzy sets, random sets, probabilities, and rough sets. In this study, we concentrate on the technology of fuzzy sets as being highly intuitive and appealing to the end user through the concept of partial membership explicitly captured by fuzzy sets. Furthermore we revisit the ideas of unsupervised learning enriched by domain knowledge being conveyed in terms of linguistic contexts and viewed as fuzzy sets or fuzzy relations. Owing to the elements of domain knowledge that are represented via linguistic contexts, the resulting context-based clustering becomes a useful data mining tool. The introduced contexts imply a certain modularization effect that enhances a computational efficiency of the method. The study is illustrated by a series of carefully selected experimental studies.

2. Data mining: making sense of data

Every day business and industry are faced with a flood of data. As a matter of fact, this abundance of data becomes the most evident sign of the ongoing information revolution. Information is an important commodity. It comes with a genuine challenge. Just to name a few of evident problems one has to tackle with, let us refer to some evident facts:
- Wal-mart completes around 20 million transactions per day,
-the planned NASA earth observing system to be launched around 1999 will generate 50Gb of image data per hour,
- the rapidly expanding information highway will require advanced tools of mining through data; currently these are also referred to as intelligent agents.
Indisputably, we live in a society that is data *rich* and knowledge *poor*. Having said that, any meaningful effort to distill and interpret revealing relationships becomes a must. Quite descriptively, a key mission of knowledge discovery is to make sense of data. The term of knowledge discovery commonly defined in the literature, " *knowledge discovery in databases is concerned with identifying interesting patterns and describing them in a concise and meaningful manner* " (Fayyad et al., 1996a; Fayyad et al, 1996b; Frawley et al., 1991). If we are primarily concerned with the process of revealing patterns not concentrating on the underlying mechanisms of interaction with databases (and the ensuing optimization machinery including specialized query language), then we refer to this process as data mining (DM) activities. The panoply of currently investigated discussed methodologies of knowledge discovery, especially those emerging at the level of data mining, is impressive. It ranges from various techniques of data visualization to more profound approaches hinging on statistics, neurocomputing, set theory, machine learning, and rough sets. For the recent overview of the area of knowledge discovery the reader may refer to Fayyad et al. (1996) as well as a special issue of Int. J. Intelligent Systems (1992) and the Communications of the ACM (1996).

As already underlined, data mining is aimed at sifting data in order to reveal useful information required by a user while compressing huge records of data. In the sequel, it means that the required methodology and tools should exhibit

some particular features to support the process of data mining. It is worth to elaborate on the notion of interestingness as being the central feature on an agenda of any data mining endeavor. It entails several essential constituents :
validity This property pertains to significance of knowledge that has been discovered
novelty describes how much the discovered patterns deviate from prior knowledge that has already been gained
usefulness relates the finding of the knowledge discovery activities to the goals of the user especially an impact these findings may have on decisions to be made
simplicity is primarily concerned with the aspects of syntactic complexity of the presentation of a finding; higher simplicity promotes significant easiness of its interpretation
generality entails a fraction of the population a particular finding refers to.
An important observation about all data mining pursuits deals with their highly user-oriented character. In spite of some level of automation, this is a user who decides on the character of the resulting mining, its depth, main directions to be taken, refinement of already produced outcomes, etc. It is also a striking phenomenon that what becomes presented as final results of data mining needs to be easily interpreted. Evidently, the compactness of the results as well as their ease of interpretation call for the mechanisms of granular computing rather than pure number crunching attempts.

3. Granular computing

All pursuits of granular computing are geared toward representing and processing basic entities - information granules. Generally speaking, we can regard information granules as generic components that help organize, conceptualize, and utilize or reveal knowledge about the problem at hand in an efficient and user-transparent fashion. The suitable granulation helps us defend against a siege of numeric data. As an important goal, it is also in concert with the main agenda of data mining. Subsequently, any process of forming information granules is usually referred to as information granulation. By information granules we mean a collection of objects (entities) bundled together where this activity is implied by a similarity (commonalities) between the individual elements arising either at a functional or descriptive (e.g., spatial or temporal) level.
As a matter of fact, the rationale behind granular computing is twofold:
- *conceptual* In this case information granulation helps describe data and reveal relationships at a suitable level of specificity supporting more organized and highly focused insight into a system under consideration.
- *computational* By operating at the level of information granules rather than individual numeric quantities we substantially reduce a computational overhead associated with processing in databases.

Interestingly, the concept of information granulation has been around for a long time even though it has manifested in some specific and somewhat limited way.

For instance, an effect of *temporal* granulation occurs in any analog-to-digital (A/D) conversion equipped with an averaging window: one uniformly granulates an incoming signal over uniform time slices. An effect of *spatial* granulation occurs quite evidently in image processing, especially when we are concerned with any facet of image compression.

There are a number of conceptual vehicles that construct, manage, and process information granules:
- *set theory* With its basic conceptual skeleton of sets and relations, this theory is the generic vehicle aimed at encapsulating individual elements. As a matter of fact, sets gave rise to interval analysis (Moore, 1966) that plays a dominant role in computing with numerical hypercubes and numerical intervals, in particular. Set-theoretic approaches have been encountered in many optimization problems
- *fuzzy sets* (Zadeh, 1965) arise as an interesting augmentation of set theory that help resolve dilemmas inherently associated with a dichotomization (yes - no) problem associated with the use of sets. By admitting continuous rather than abrupt boundaries between complete belongingness and complete exclusion, fuzzy sets capture a notion of a partial membership - a concept permeating most of advanced descriptors encountered in real-world problems ranging from commonsense notions (tall individual, low inflation, steady income) to very specific technical terms (ill-defined matrix, small negative error in a control loop, medium power dissipation, etc.).
rough sets (Pawlak, 1982) have been proposed in order to deal with a lack of complete discrimination between classes. Most of their current applications occur in information systems and data mining.
random sets formed a cornerstone of mathematical morphology and have been frequently exploited in image processing
- *probability* probability density functions (pdf) are other interesting examples of information granules that embrace elements of some specific characteristics. For instance, in classification problems, a conditional pdf (with the condition being formed by a given class) is an information granule specific to the given class of patterns.

Each of the above methodologies of information granules has its own research agenda, application targets and open questions. In many cases they interact and cooperate rather than compete. In the reminder of this study we select a single methodology of fuzzy sets and discuss its further pursuits in the setting of data mining.

3.1. Fuzzy sets as linguistic granules

A fuzzy set can be regarded as an elastic constraint imposed on the elements of a universe (Zadeh, 1965; Klir and Folger, 1988; Pedrycz, 1995, 1997). By admitting a certain form of elasticity when defining concepts and introducing various mechanisms of Conceptually, fuzzy sets help alleviate problems with the classification of elements of boundary nature by allowing for a notion of a partial membership to a category. Algorithmically, fuzzy sets make the problems continuous. Let us underline an important enhancement that is inherently associated with fuzzy sets. By their very nature, sets are nondifferentiable constructs that practically eliminate gradient-based optimization methods and force us to resort to some other types of optimization instruments such as random search or genetically-guided methods. Fuzzy sets deliver a highly welcome continuity aspect to the discussed problem. On the operational side of the technology of fuzzy sets, we are provided with a vast arsenal of methods supporting all facets of computing with fuzzy sets. Operations on fuzzy sets, linguistic modifiers, linguistic approximation, fuzzy arithmetic are just a few among all basic computational vehicles available in the area.

The success of fuzzy sets viewed as a backbone of many real-world approaches and is evident. The industrial facet of the technology is apparently visible and a number of successful systems is well documented (Hirota, 1993). Hirota (1995) provides a comprehensive overview of the worldwide advancements in the theory and applications of fuzzy sets.

In the following discussion we underline two points that are predominant in many applications. We elaborate on the aspect of information granularity conveyed by fuzzy sets and a concept of a frame of cognition.

3.1.1. Information granularity of fuzzy sets

The first issue helps answer questions about information content residing within the given linguistic information granules. The terms of specificity and cardinality of fuzzy sets are the most relevant with this regard. An introduction of such measures is motivated by the need of quantifying a level of difficulty (or hesitation) when picking up a single element in the universe of discourse that is regarded as a reasonable representative of the fuzzy set. Two limit cases are intuitively easy to handle:

-if the fuzzy set is of a degenerated form, namely it is already a single element, $A=\{x_0\}$, there is no hesitation in the selection of x_0 as an excellent (and the only one) representative of A,

-if A covers almost the entire universe of discourse and embraces a lot of elements with membership equal 1, then the choice of only one element causes a lot of hesitation.

In the first instance, the fuzzy set is very specific whereas the specificity of the fuzzy set occurring in the second situation is zero. The specificity measure (Yager, 1982, 1983) of fuzzy set A defined in **X**, Sp(A), assigns to a fuzzy set A a nonnegative number such that

- Sp(A) =1 if and only if there exists only one element of **X** for which A assumes 1 while the remaining membership values are equal zero

-if A(x)=0 for all elements of **X** then Sp(A) =0

- if $A_1 \supset A_2$ then $Sp(A_1) \leq Sp(A_2)$

In Yager (1982) the specificity measure is defined as the integral

$$Sp(A) = \int_0^{\alpha_{max}} \frac{1}{card(A_\alpha)} d\alpha$$

where α_{max} is the maximal value of the membership function A. If we confine ourselves to normal fuzzy sets (namely, fuzzy sets whose maximal membership values attain 1), then a standard σ-count

$$\sigma(A) = \int_X A(x)dx$$

could serve as a plausible measure of granularity. In this setting this denotes a summation of the elements embraced (at least partially) by the given fuzzy set. The original definition of specificity exhibits some computational drawbacks (particularly it may be indefinite for continuous membership functions); to alleviate them we propose its modified version assuming the form

$$Sp(A) = \int_0^{\alpha_{max}} \frac{1}{1 + \exp(-\frac{1}{card(A_\alpha} - 0.5)} d\alpha$$

3.1.2. The frame of cognition

So far we have discussed a single fuzzy set and proposed scalar characterizations. What really matters in most applications of fuzzy sets technology are the families of fuzzy sets. We usually refer to them as a frame of cognition. This notion emerges in the fuzzy modelling, fuzzy controllers, classifiers, etc. Primarily, any use of fuzzy sets call for some form of interfacing with any real world process. Generally speaking, the frame consists of several normal fuzzy sets called also linguistic *labels* that are used as basic reference points for fuzzy information processing. Sometimes in order to emphasize their focal role in this processing they are referred to as linguistic landmarks. When the aspects of fuzzy information processing need to be emphasized, we may refer to these fuzzy sets as a fuzzy codebook - a concept widely exploited in information coding and its transmission. By adjusting the granularity of the labels one can easily implement the principle of incompatibility. In particular, this allows to cover a broad spectrum of information granularity spreading between that of a qualitative form (symbols) up to that of the numerical character with the highest granularity possible.

Let us now get into a more formal definition. A frame of cognition (Pedrycz, 1990; 1992)

$$\mathcal{A} = \{A_1, A_2, \ldots, A_n\}$$

is a collection of the fuzzy sets above is defined in the same universe of discourse **X** and satisfying the following conditions:
(i) coverage: $\mathcal{A}$ *covers* **X**, that is any element of $x \in \mathbf{X}$ belongs to at least one label of $\mathcal{A}$. More precisely, this requirement can be written down in the form

$$\forall_{x \in \mathbf{X}} \ \exists_{i=1,2,\ldots,c} \ A_i(x) > 0$$

The notion of coverage emphasizes the universe of discourse **X** becomes represented by the collection of the linguistic terms. Being more stringent, we may demand an ε-level of coverage of **X**, that formalizes in the following form,

$$\forall_{x \in \mathbf{X}} \ \exists_{i=1,2,\ldots,c} \ A_i(x) > \varepsilon$$

where $\varepsilon \in [0, 1]$ stands for the assumed coverage level. This simply means that any element of **X** belongs to at least one label to a degree not less than ε. Otherwise, we can regard this label as a representative of this element to a nonzero extent. The condition of coverage assures us that each element of **X** is sufficiently represented by $\mathcal{A}$. Moreover, if the membership functions of sum up to 1 over **X**

$$\forall_{x \in \mathbf{X}} \sum_{i=1}^{c} A_i(x) = 1$$

then the frame of cognition is referred to as a fuzzy partition.

(ii) semantic soundness of $\mathcal{A}$: this condition translates into a general requirement of a linguistic "interpretability" of its elements. Especially, we may pose a few more detailed conditions characterizing this notion in more detail; see also Pedrycz and Oliveira(1993):

- A_i s are unimodal and normal fuzzy sets; in this way they identify the regions of **X** that are semantically equivalent with the linguistic terms,
- A_i are sufficiently disjoint; this requirement assures that the terms are sufficiently distinct and therefore become linguistically meaningful.
- The number of the elements of $\mathcal{A}$ is usually quite reduced; some psychological findings suggest 7 ± 2 linguistic terms to constitute an upper limit for the cardinality of the frame of cognition when being perceived in the sense of a basic vocabulary of the linguistic terms.

The above features are given in a rather descriptive than formal format and should be then treated as a collection of useful guidelines rather than completely strict definitions. Especially, some threshold levels (like ε need to be specified numerically).

Data mining calls for a multitude of activities depending upon the category of potential users. For instance, a corporative report usually requires pieces of knowledge about associations between various factors (variables) collected at a highly general level. They help gain a global look at the problem, identify the most crucial relationships and undertake some strategic decisions. On the other end of the spectrum arise far more specific situations in which we require specific, yet very *local* information. What is common to these two decision scenarios (and many others) is a concept of information granularity. In a nutshell, information granularity concerns an issue of information summarization (compression). Fuzzy sets, as well as set theory to same extent, support this essential feature. They can be regarded as conceptual " filters" (or data mining *anchors*) that help us focus on some specific level of details to be searched and eventually discovered throughout a database.

Consider a few examples of fuzzy sets as shown in Figure 1. They directly allude to the notion of information granularity. For instance, the fuzzy set in the upper part of the same figure is far more specific (detailed) than the one displayed at the bottom where we are not concerned about details (and, in fact, they become *hidden* in the description of interest).

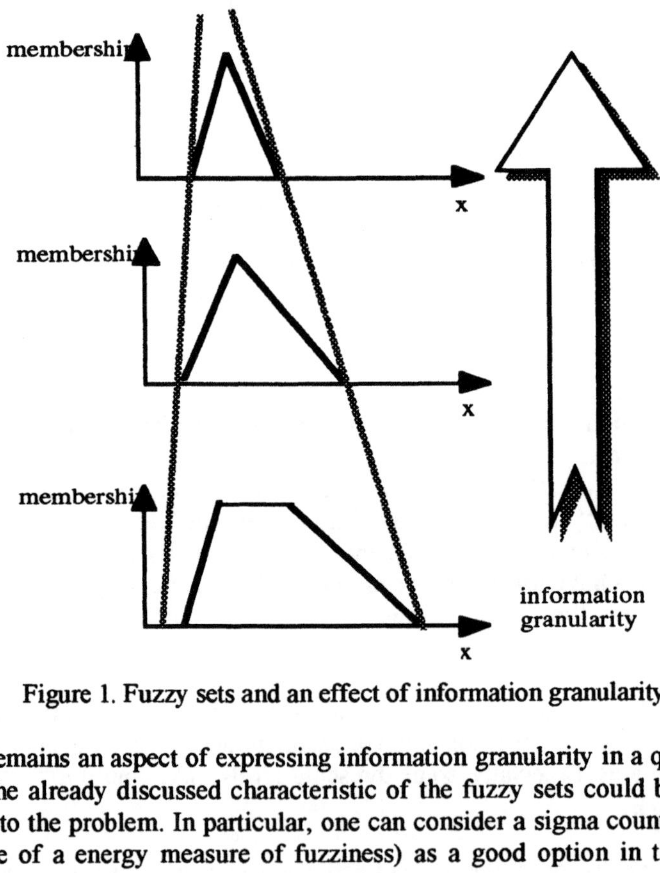

Figure 1. Fuzzy sets and an effect of information granularity

There remains an aspect of expressing information granularity in a quantitative way. The already discussed characteristic of the fuzzy sets could be a viable answer to the problem. In particular, one can consider a sigma count (being an example of a energy measure of fuzziness) as a good option in the case of normal fuzzy sets. More generally, for subnormal fuzzy sets one can deal with the specificity measure. Following the semantics of fuzzy sets, one can easily construct hierarchies of concepts starting off with very specific and detailed description and ending up with general ones. In the first instance, we use a standard OR operation that leads to the expression,

$$A_2 \text{ or } A_3 \text{ or } A_4$$

In the second method, we apply iteratively a linguistic modifier of fuzzification (*more or less*), ending up effectively with a sequence of statements

A_3
more or less A_3
more or less (*more or less* A_3)
etc.

The contrast intensification operation has an opposite effect on the original fuzzy set leading to its specification (refinement), say

A_3
very A_3
very (*very* A_3)

A similar effect of increasing information granularity can be achieved by applying the AND operation while starting from a union of several fuzzy sets. Note that the AND operation produces a subnormal fuzzy set.

4. Fuzzy clustering in data mining

In this section we discuss a role of unsupervised learning (clustering) in the problem of data mining. A highly enlightening and appealing characterization of the clustering approach (grouping), can be found in the existing literature (Kaufman, Rousseeuw, 1990):

... cluster analysis is the art of finding groups in data.

This emphasizes the primary thrust of clustering is to arrange a collection of data into a small number of groups (clusters) so that the elements that are similar become allocated to the same group. The elements (patterns) that are quite distant should be placed into separate categories. The literature on this subject is enormously rich; the reader may refer to some classical references such as Anderberg (1973), Everitt(1974), Jain and Dubes (1988), Hartigan (1975). One among the latest publications concentrate on knowledge-based approaches (Backer, 1995).

It is of primordial importance to position the clustering techniques as a viable methodology of data mining. Does clustering live up to expectations raised in the setting of data mining? In order to answer this crucial question, one should reiterate the main postulates of data mining:

a proactive role of a potential user in the process of data mining. While autonomous to a high extent, the overall procedure is generally guided by a user interested in different ways in which the data can be looked at. There are several detailed conceptual and operational facets including:

information granularity at which all mechanisms of DM become activated. This granularity could be (and usually is) highly diversified in terms of the level of granularity. In regions of particular interest one may pay attention to minute details which dictates a high information granularity (eventually at a numeric level). Otherwise, the regions of low interest call for an allocation of relatively coarse (linguistic) information granules. The variable level of information granularity supports the idea of interestingness (see Section 2) and leads to its efficient implementation.

transparency of generated summary of main associations revealed through data mining. Here the transparency is viewed in terms of ease of understandability of the summary as well as their relevancy. Again, the role of information granulation become apparent.

These two considerations suggest that clustering algorithms are to be embedded in the auxiliary framework that implants these data mining requirements. In the following discussion we elaborate on context-oriented fuzzy clustering. The choice is primarily dictated by their conceptual simplicity along with an algorithmic efficiency.

5. Context-oriented fuzzy clustering

To illustrate the very idea in which clustering, and fuzzy clustering, in particular, plays in data mining, let us consider a relational table (array) $\mathfrak{X}$ comprising objects regarded as vectors of real numbers. We are interested in revealing (discovering) a structure and eventually quantify functional dependences manifesting throughout this table. The focal nature of data mining is achieved by specifying linguistic term(s) prior to launching any detailed analysis and running computationally intensive algorithms. While there is a great diversity of data mining processes, we highlight only a few most representative and interesting scenarios:

(a) Let us consider one of the attributes of interest as a context variable and define therein a fuzzy set (linguistic term of focus) such that

$$A : \mathbf{Y} \rightarrow [0, 1]$$

where **Y** stands for a universe of discourse of this attribute (variable). The problem transforms as follows

$$\text{reveal structure in } \mathcal{X} \text{ in context } \mathcal{A}$$

where the context of data mining is established as

$$\mathcal{A} = \{ \text{A}: \mathbf{X} \rightarrow [0,1]\}$$

The essence of such clustering is shown in Figure 2. If we confine ourselves to one of the variables as a context variable (say, pressure) over which one defines a collection of the linguistic terms (information granules), this particular choice sheds light on some sections of the entire data set that becomes of interest in light of the assumed context.

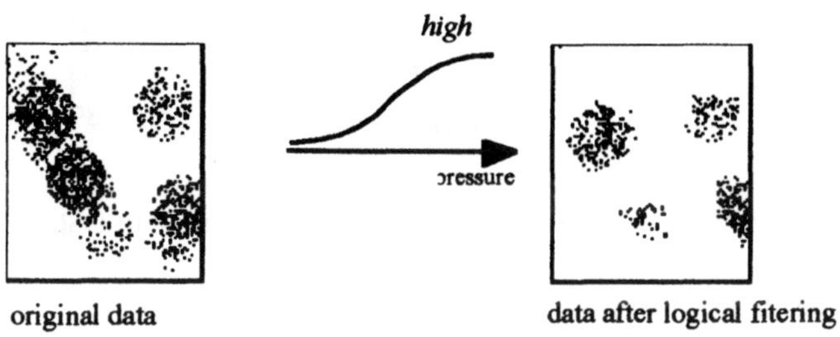

Figure 2. The use of linguistic context (high pressure) in zooming in at some regions of the data space

Note that the selected information granule (context) directly impact the resulting data to be looked into. As a matter of fact, the context can be regarded as a window (or a focal point) of data mining.

The problem of data mining reads as follows

$$\text{reveal structure in } \mathcal{X} \text{ in context } \{\text{pressure} = \textit{high}\}$$

Similarly, if we may be interested in the characterization of customers of medium or high disposable income, the resulting clustering task would then read as follows:

> reveal structure in market database in context {disposable income = *medium* or *high*}

(b) Several attributes can form the composite context. For instance, let A and B be two fuzzy sets defined in **Y** and **Z**, respectively. Then any composite context $\mathcal{A}$ is formed as a Cartesian product of A and B

$$\mathcal{A} = \{ A \times B: \mathbf{Y} \times \mathbf{Z} \rightarrow [0,1]\}$$

Similarly, we may arrive at the problem formulated as

reveal structure in $\mathcal{X}$ in context {pressure = *small* and temperature = *medium*}

In addition to the two basic forms of the linguistic contexts, there are a number of interesting extensions, see Figure 3.

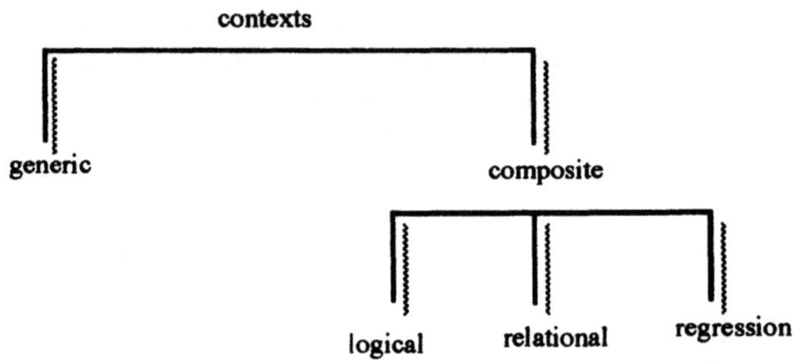

Figure 3. A taxonomy of linguistic contexts exploited in Data Mining

The examples below illustrate each of these contexts:

- composite logical context: (pressure is *small* and temperature is *low*) or humidity is *medium*
- composite relational context: prices of product "a" and discount prices of product "b" are *similar*
- composite regression context: error of linear regression model $x_i = f(x_j, a)$ is negative *small*

It is instructive to recall that the clustering problem of the form

reveal structure in $\mathcal{X}$

is context - free and comes exactly in the same format as commonly studied in the standard domain of data clustering.

5.1. The algorithm

The conditioning aspect (context sensitivity) of the clustering mechanism is introduced into the algorithm by taking into consideration the conditioning variable (context) assuming the values $f_1, f_2, \ldots, f_N$ on the corresponding patterns. More specifically, f_k describes a level of involvement of x_k in the assumed context, $f_k = \mathcal{A}(k)$. In other words, $\mathcal{A}$ acts as a data mining filter (or a focal element or a data window) by focusing attention on some specific subsets of data. The way in which f_k can be associated with or allocated among the computed membership

values of x_k, say $u_{1k}, u_{2k}, \ldots, u_{ck}$, is not unique. Two possibilities are worth exploring:
• we admit f_k to be distributed additively across the entries of the k-th column of the partition matrix meaning that

$$\sum_{i=1}^{c} u_{ik} = f_k$$

k=1, 2, ..., N
• we may request that the maximum of the membership values within the corresponding column equals f_k,

$$\max_{i=1}^{c} u_{ik} = f_k$$

k=1, 2, ..., N.
We confine ourselves to the first way of distribution of the conditioning variable. Bearing this in mind, we modify the requirements for the partition matrices and define the family

$$\mathcal{U}(\mathbf{f}) = \{\, u_{ik} \in [0, 1] \mid \sum_{i=1}^{c} u_{ik} = f_k \ \forall_k \text{ and } 0 < \sum_{k=1}^{N} u_{ik} < N \ \forall_i \}$$

Thus the standard normalization condition where the membership values sum up to 1 is replaced by the involvement (conditioning) constraint. The optimization problem is now reformulated accordingly (Pedrycz, 1996, 1997)

$$\min_{U, \mathbf{v}_1, \mathbf{v}_2, \ldots, \mathbf{v}_c} Q$$

subject to

$$U \in \mathcal{U}(\mathbf{f})$$

Let us proceed with deriving a complete solution to this optimization problem. Essentially, it can be divided into two separate subproblems:
- optimization of the partition matrix U
- optimization of the prototypes

As these tasks can be handled independently of each other, we start with the partition matrix. Moreover, we notice that each column of U can be optimized independently, so let us fix the index of the data point (k) and reformulate the resulting problem:

$$\min_U \sum_{i=1}^{c} u_{ik}^m d_{ik}^2$$

subject to

$$\sum_{i=1}^{c} u_{ik} = f_k$$

(in other words, having the fixed data index, we have to solve "N" independent optimization problems). To make the notation more concise, we have introduced the notation d_{ik} to describe the distance between the pattern and the prototype, namely $d_{ik}^2 = ||\mathbf{x}_k - \mathbf{v}_i||^2$

As the above is an example of optimization with constraints, we can easily convert this into unconstrained optimization by using the technique of Lagrange multipliers. The overall algorithm is summarized as a sequence of steps

Given: The number of clusters (c). Select the distance function ||.||, termination criterion e (>0) and initialize partition matrix $U \in \mathcal{U}$
1. Calculate centers (prototypes) of the clusters

$$\mathbf{v}_i = \frac{\sum_{k=1}^{N} u_{ik}^2 \mathbf{x}_k}{\sum_{k=1}^{N} u_{ik}^2}$$

i=1, 2, ..., c
2. Update partition matrix

$$u_{ik} = \frac{f_k}{\sum_{j=1}^{c} \left(\frac{||\mathbf{x}_k - \mathbf{v}_i||}{||\mathbf{x}_k - \mathbf{v}_j||} \right)^2}$$

i=1, 2, ..., c, j=1, 2, ..., N

3. Compare U' to U, if termination criterion ||U' - U|| <e then stop, else go to 1 with U = U'
Result: partition matrix and prototypes

There are two important design components of the clustering method, namely the distance function ||.|| being a primordial component of the minimized objective function and the fuzzification parameter (m). The distance function articulates a notion of similarity (or dissimilarity) between two elements in the data space. The popular and commonly used variants concern Euclidean, Hamming, and Tschebyschev distance functions. The Euclidean one is eventually the most commonly used. The Hamming distance promotes some important robustness features. The values of the fuzzification factor become reflected in the form of the clusters being produced (or, equivalently, the form of membership function). With the increasing values of "m" there is a profound rippling effect where the membership functions tend to show up more local minima. For lower values of the fuzzification factor, the resulting membership functions tend to resemble characteristic functions of sets meaning that we are getting less elements with intermediate membership values. Simply, the results become localized around 0 or 1. The obtained fuzzy sets tend to resemble sets.

The context $\mathcal{A}$ has a profound effect on the performance of clustering. If **f** < **f'** then the population of the patterns involved in grouping and placed under context **f'** is lower. Similarly, the number of eventual clusters could be lowered as well. The above inclusion relation between the contexts holds if the context fuzzy sets are made more specific or if the contexts consist of more constraints (focal points). In the first case we get $\mathcal{A} \subset \mathcal{A}'$ where **f** is implied by $\mathcal{A}$ and **f'** by $\mathcal{A}'$. In the latter the ensuing **f** is associated with $A \times B \times C$ and **f'** comes with $A \times B$; here again $\mathcal{A} \subset \mathcal{A}'$.

Let us underline that the context of clustering plays an important role in discovering knowledge nuggets - rare yet essential pieces of information. Without any direction imposed by the user could be easily washed away in a mass of useless but frequent (and thus statistically meaningful) data. The filtering of data accomplished by the context prevents this from happening.

One should emphasize that the membership values of contexts do not sum up to 1; the similar phenomenon can be witnessed in possibilistic clustering (Krishnapuram and Keller, 1993) and clustering with noise cluster (Dave, 1992). One should stress, however, that the origin of these two departures from the original constraint is completely different.

5.2. Quantification of the associations between information granules.

The context-based clustering leaves us with the number of context s and induced clusters. The links (associations) between these entities are assumed by the method but not quantified at all. What we are left with is a structure depicted in Figure 4. The figure shows a web of links between the contexts (defined in the context space) and a series of induced clusters (those being located in the data space). Note, however, that these links have not been quantified. It could well be that some of them could be far more meaningful that the others.

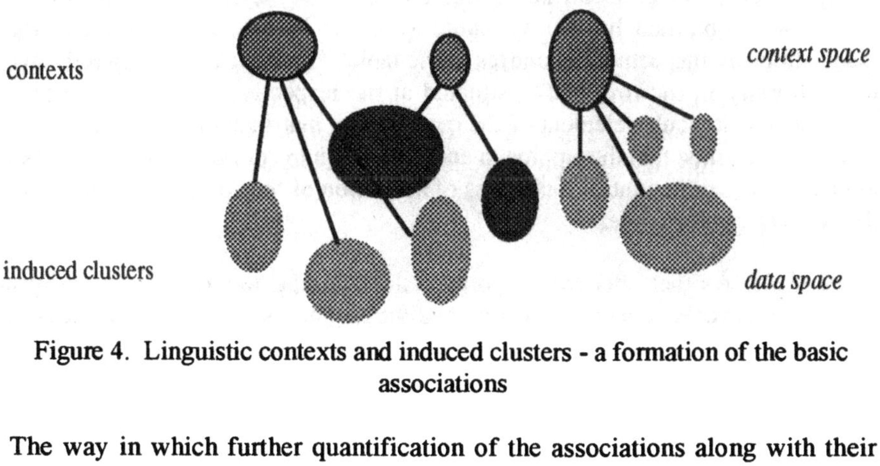

Figure 4. Linguistic contexts and induced clusters - a formation of the basic associations

The way in which further quantification of the associations along with their eventual modifications or even elimination is left for further developments. Two consecutive methods are anticipated:

- the use of the standard boolean confusion matrix in the development of the associations. In this case one admits a simple threshold criterion by assigning successive data to the induced clusters and the respective contexts by taking into consideration the highest membership grades. This is the simplest criterion possible that leads to the standard confusion matrix. Each row of the matrix denotes an induced cluster whereas the columns describe the contexts. The threshold criterion allocates the data across the matrix. The counting of the number of elements in each row provides a score to the association context-induced cluster. If the nonzero number of occurrences happens only in the single entry defined by this specific context and no otherwise then the association concerns only the context under consideration. It could well be that there are some other nonzero entries in this row meaning that the discussed induced cluster expanded to far and embraced some auxiliary contexts. By inspecting the entries of this contingency table one can order all the obtained associations.

While this method can be utilized as a basic vehicle aimed at the evaluation of the quality of the associations and produce some of their pruning, this approach does not discriminate between the data points being very close to the centers of the prototypes and those quite peripheral to the prototypes of the induced clusters or/and the contexts themselves. No matter where the data is located, it contributes to the same extent to the counting procedure applied to the contingency table. This, however, could be very restrictive, especially in light of the continuous boundaries between the resulting constructs. To alleviate this deficiency, we generalize the contingency table by counting the levels of strength of the respective induced clusters and the pertinent context. In the simplest case one can update the entries of the contingency table by updating them by the values of the products of the fuzzy sets or relations under consideration. The contingency table generalized in this way does not focus on the counting of the events (coincidences) but concentrates primarily upon the activation levels of the associations obtained by the available data. As before, one can order the associations by inspecting the entries of the table. The association with only one nonzero entry in the row that is situated at the respective context and a high value of this particular element of the contingency matrix assumes a high score. One may underline that this approach does not take into consideration the number of occurrences but counts a total mass of activation of the coincidences between the clusters and the contexts.

There is also another alternative approach that attempts to strike a compromise between the overall level of activation and the number of binary occurrences of the highest activations of the entities (clusters and context). One simple takes these two matrices and determine their ratio. More specifically, we divide the continuous version of the contingency table by its boolean counterpart. The entries of the new matrix formed in this way represented an average level of coincidence between the clusters and the respective context. As before, the associations can be easily ordered based on the distribution of the entries of the corresponding row of the matrix. More specifically, in spite of the form of the matrix, the following index can serve as an indicator of the relevance of the association

$$\kappa = \frac{\text{sum of entries of the rows corresponding to the context}}{\text{sum of all entries}}$$

If κ assumes high values, then the association is regarded highly relevant. This occurs when there are no other nonzero entries in this row (such nonzero entries tend to reduce the values of κ) and the respective entry is high enough. One could have a very focussed association with no activation of some other contexts but with very low values of the very entry and this also contributes to the overall low performance of the association.

Once the associations have been ordered the only most significant can be revealed as the result of mining of data set.

Finally, one should underline that the mining activities have been performed at a certain level of information granularity, and as such do not allow to introduce more details without further computations. In other words, what we have is a collection of meaning full associations, Figure 7, that can be treated as general patterns:

induced cluster - context

Any speculations about the internal details of this association are beyond discussion carried out in the conceptual realm discussed here. In fact, by imposing a certain level of granularity , our intent was to avoid getting into such details. Anyway, if at some point of further analysis the numerical details need to be revealed, one has to pursue numerically oriented computing of the relationships within the specific entities involved at this level of building the patterns within data.

The computations of their membership functions result directly from the assumed clustering model. Thus we derive

$$u_i = \frac{1}{\sum_{j=1}^{c}\left(\frac{\|\mathbf{x}-\mathbf{v}_i\|}{\|\mathbf{x}-\mathbf{v}_j\|}\right)^2}$$

j=1, 2, ..., c, with the same distance function as encountered in the original method.

Interestingly enough, the patterns have nothing to do with any specific direction - what has been revealed are just plain associations between the relations and the context.

5.3. Linguistic granules and associations as blueprints of numeric constructs

It is important to underline that linguistic granules deliver a useful and essential option of making sense of data by developing meaningful granules. The granules serve two important purposes:

- they help establish sound and meaningful chunks of information constructing a sound background for further refinements
- information granules support modularization of the data set that reduces a level of computing necessary to reveal detailed relationships at a numeric rather than linguistic level

Figure 5 contains a number of possible follow-ups dwelled on linguistic granules: they include correlation analysis, regression models, and neural networks.

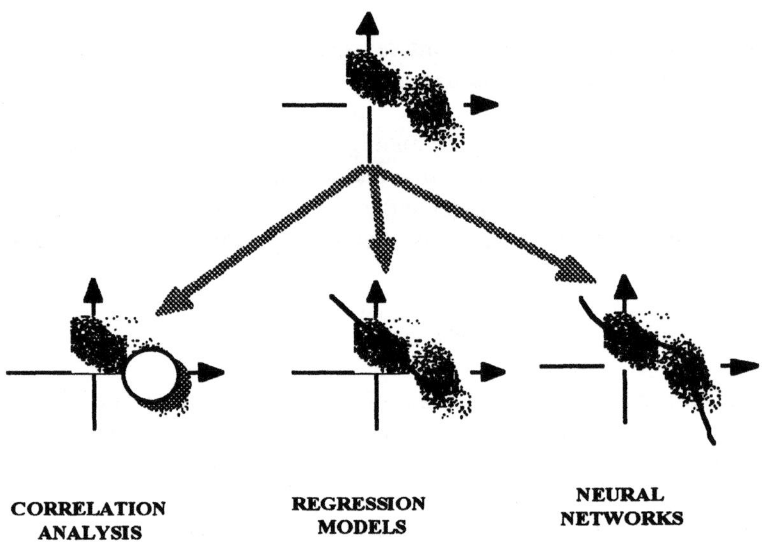

Figure 5. Refinements of associations between linguistic granules

5.4. Context-based clustering and databases

The context-based clustering carries some resemblances to standard queries in databases. Moreover, it rather generalizes the concept of a query that could be better described as a metaquery. In the standard querying process, one formulates a query and the database retrieves all pertinent records from the database that respond to the formulated request. Obviously, for the query of the type: "find all customers who have recently bought Ford Contour and are of middle age" the database retrieval mechanisms will produce a long (and perhaps in some cases useless) list of such individuals. The expectations are that we will be provided with a characterization (description) of this specific sector of the car market. This, in fact, what the discussed clustering method does, Figure 6. The generalized metaquery is just the imposed context while the characterization comes in the form of the induced clusters.

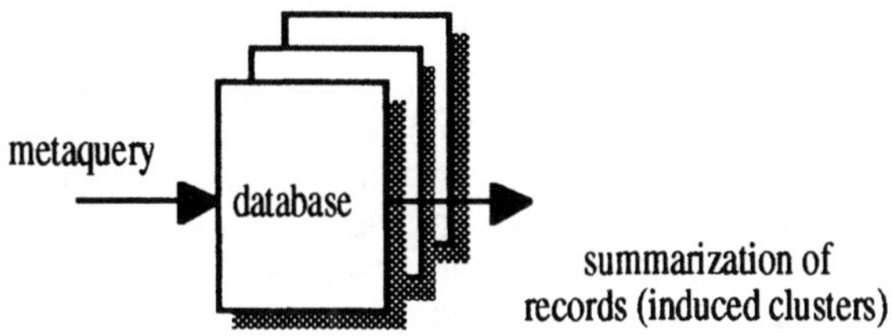

Figure 6. Context-based clustering as a process of summarization in a database

6. Numerical studies

In this section we concentrate on several selected examples and carry out a complete analysis highlighting the key features of the clustering approach to data mining.

6.1. Auto mpg example

The discussed data set, called auto mpg, comes from the repository of machine learning data sets situated at UC Irvine (http:// ftp.ics.edu/pub/machine-learning - databases/). The vehicles are characterized by 9 features such as fuel consumption (in miles per gallon), a number of cylinders, displacement, horse power, weight, acceleration, model year, and origin (USA, Europe, Japan), and the make of the vehicle. A short excerpt of this data set is shown in Figure 7. The origin of the vehicles are encoded as follows: 1-USA, 2-Europe, 3-Japan.

18.0	8	307.0	130.0	3504.	12.0	70	1	"chevrolet chevelle malibu"
15.0	8	350.0	165.0	3693.	11.5	70	1	"buick skylark 320"
18.0	8	318.0	150.0	3436.	11.0	70	1	"plymouth satellite"
16.0	8	304.0	150.0	3433.	12.0	70	1	"amc rebel sst"
17.0	8	302.0	140.0	3449.	10.5	70	1	"ford torino"
15.0	8	429.0	198.0	4341.	10.0	70	1	"ford galaxie 500"
14.0	8	454.0	220.0	4354.	9.0	70	1	"chevrolet impala"
14.0	8	440.0	215.0	4312.	8.5	70	1	"plymouth fury iii"
14.0	8	455.0	225.0	4425.	10.0	70	1	"pontiac catalina"
15.0	8	390.0	190.0	3850.	8.5	70	1	"amc ambassador dpl"
15.0	8	383.0	170.0	3563.	10.0	70	1	"dodge challenger se"
14.0	8	340.0	160.0	3609.	8.0	70	1	"plymouth 'cuda 340"
15.0	8	400.0	150.0	3761.	9.5	70	1	"chevrolet monte carlo"
14.0	8	455.0	225.0	3086.	10.0	70	1	"buick estate wagon (sw)"
24.0	4	113.0	95.00	2372.	15.0	70	3	"toyota corona mark ii"
22.0	6	198.0	95.00	2833.	15.5	70	1	"plymouth duster"
18.0	6	199.0	97.00	2774.	15.5	70	1	"amc hornet"
21.0	6	200.0	85.00	2587.	16.0	70	1	"ford maverick"
27.0	4	97.00	88.00	2130.	14.5	70	3	"datsun pl510"
26.0	4	97.00	46.00	1835.	20.5	70	2	"volkswagen 1131 deluxe sedan"

Figure 7. A excerpt from auto mpg dataset

For instance, take the first record (chevrolet). The features reads as:
- fuel consumption 18.0
- number of cylinders 8
- displacement 307.0
- horse power 130.0
- weight 3504
- acceleration 12.0
- model year 70
- origin USA

The first step is to formulate the point of view at the activity of data mining that is express a context variable and proceed with their granulation of interest. There are a number of possibilities. We choose the one that sounds quite useful: let us reveal relationships concerning vehicles of some categories of fuel efficiency. This naturally leads us to accepting the first variable as the context and work on clustering in the space of the remaining variables. The names of the cars are not used here. The granularity of the context variable is established via trapezoidal fuzzy sets with the membership functions of the form

T(y, -1 0 10 20)
T(y, 10 20 20 30)
T(y, 20 30 30 40)
T(y, 30 40 50 80)

where, as usual, the parameters standing there denote the characteristic points of the piecewise membership functions of these fuzzy sets, see Figure 8.

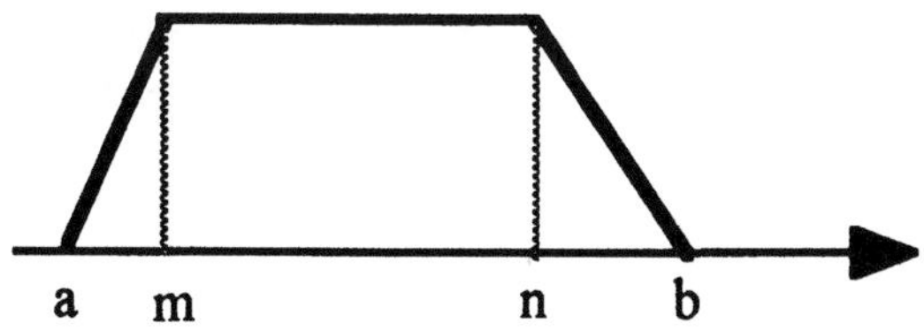

Figure 8. A class of trapezoidal fuzzy sets (fuzzy numbers) T(y, a, m, n, b)

In fact, as the two intermediate parameters are the same, we are dealing with triangular fuzzy sets. The first one can be regarded as a descriptor of vehicles of small efficiency while the last one characterizes vehicles of high fuel economy. The two intermediate categories deals with vehicles of medium fuel consumption. These linguistic fuzzy labels have been used to capture the meaning of the vehicles of some specific and meaningful nature. If necessary, these linguistic labels could be revised and modified according to the interest of the user. We should stress that the labels have not been optimized to meet some criteria discussed before (as, for instance, the equalization one). To illustrate that, the histogram of the context variable is shown in Figure 9.

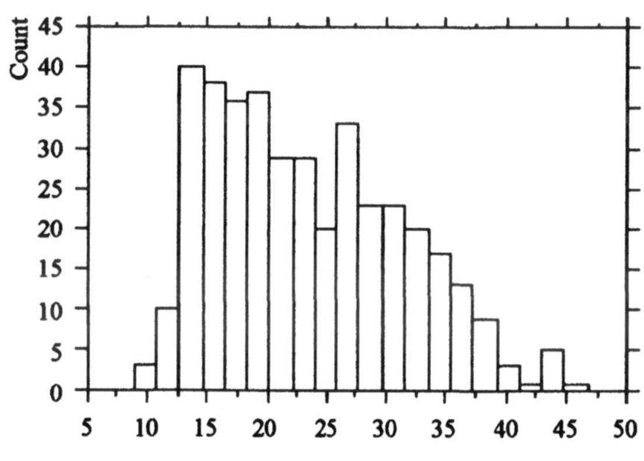

Figure 9. Distribution of the values of the context variable (mpg)

The calculations reveal the values of the σ-count of the respective fuzzy labels to be equal

$context_1$	64.8300
$context_2$	168.0400
$context_3$	118.9800
$context_4$	38.1500

so it becomes apparent, as expected by eyeballing the histogram that some linguistic terms are quite dominant. The clustering is carried out for five clusters per context so, finally, we end up with 20 different associations between the resulting linguistic granules. The fuzzification parameter was set to 2. The resulting prototypes are summarized below. Based on their values one can easily generate the corresponding membership functions of the linguistic terms; each row describes an individual prototype (5 per context)

first context

7.9597	324.0681	147.4904	4141.4565	13.8119	74.7960	1.0077
7.9935	421.9014	206.9132	4576.3774	11.0116	71.7837	1.0015
7.9754	338.9013	156.0435	4179.1138	13.1936	72.4731	1.0045
7.9851	364.9198	175.4141	4402.2515	12.4981	72.0487	1.0031
6.0845	246.5758	101.6843	3509.3506	17.7591	74.4538	1.0451

second context

4.0874	117.2117	95.2903	2561.4968	15.3389	74.0668	2.3533
7.9295	328.2322	149.5903	3978.1433	12.9293	75.3593	1.0127
5.6790	207.2347	99.2230	3134.1489	16.5716	75.9661	1.1594
5.7946	212.4101	98.3907	2967.3010	15.6952	72.7827	1.0960
5.9282	219.8767	99.9425	3295.7715	17.1119	77.6124	1.0705

third context

4.1583	113.9076	78.9360	2294.1370	15.7431	76.9066	1.5600
4.1166	135.1387	85.3163	2584.2524	16.1681	80.4332	1.0853
4.0465	93.6141	72.0283	2087.6772	17.5755	73.4383	2.4799
4.0475	105.1029	73.0323	2239.2920	16.8227	79.4058	2.8950
4.0955	105.7471	78.8554	2214.5576	15.3149	76.0530	1.9204

fourth context

4.0219	90.2672	65.1666	1979.7280	16.5085	80.6769	2.9150
4.0585	105.6941	69.6008	2095.6660	15.2831	80.6091	1.0754
4.0386	103.6010	75.0548	2111.0115	14.7648	80.5556	2.7140
4.0186	88.0564	65.0256	2063.3794	18.5730	79.6490	2.9457
4.0252	92.8853	49.6662	2170.7195	22.7944	80.0778	1.9977

But even at this numeric level one can reveal a series of interesting facts. For instance:
- when it comes to low fuel economy, large and heavy American cars dominate in this category
- Japanese cars are placed in the fourth category with horsepower in the range of 88-100, four cylinder engines and weight of *about* 2 tons

6.2. Computer performance dataset

This example concerns a performance of various models of computers. These

data describe various makes of computers using some basic hardware characteristics and summarize their performance through a single numeric index. The features of the patterns used therein are indicated below
MYCT: machine cycle time in nanoseconds
MMIN: minimum main memory in kilobytes
MMAX: maximum main memory in kilobytes
CACHE: cache memory in kilobytes
CHMIN: minimum channels in units
CHMAX: maximum channels in units
PERF: relative performance
To illustrate a variety of the computers under study, shown is an excerpt of this dataset

amdahl,470v/7,29,8000,32000,32,8,32,269
amdahl,470v/7a,29,8000,32000,32,8,32,220
amdahl,470v/7b,29,8000,32000,32,8,32,172
amdahl,470v/7c,29,8000,16000,32,8,16,132
amdahl,470v/b,26,8000,32000,64,8,32,318
amdahl,580-5840,23,16000,32000,64,16,32,367
...

sperry,80/6,180,512,4000,0,1,3,21,
sperry,80/8,124,1000,8000,0,1,8,42
sperry,90/80-model-3,98,1000,8000,32,2,8,46
sratus,32,125,2000,8000,0,2,14,52
wang,vs-100,480,512,8000,32,0,0,67

For instance, the first computer is characterized by the values of MYCT equal 29, MMIN 8000, MMAX 32000, etc. We complete the context-based clustering by defining contexts in the space of the relative performance. This allows us to discriminate between several linguistic categories of the computers as far as their performance is concerned and describe such categories of the machines. In the experiment we concentrate on four classes - context of the performance described by trapezoidal or triangular membership membership functions. They start with the computers of low performance, sweep through the machines of medium range and end up with the machines of high performance. More specifically, these corresponding membership functions are defined as

low performance	T(x, 0, 0, 10, 20)
...	T(x, 10, 20, 150, 250)
...	T(x, 150, 250, 400, 500)
high performance	T(x, 400, 500, 2000, 2100)

The experiments are carried out for three clusters per each context. Furthermore the fuzzification factor was set for 2, that is m = 2. First, we list the results by showing the prototypes of the individual contexts (note that we deal with a six-dimensional space of the parameters of the computers):

T(x, 0, 0, 10, 20)

prototype 1
223.43 555.56 1829.82 2.35 1.07 3.92
prototype 2
844.72 544.81 3624.26 0.16 0.99 2.64
prototype 3
1213.89 645.31 1491.56 0.00 0.70 0.72

T(x, 10, 20, 150, 250)

prototype 1
131.08 1634.28 7510.06 10.62 2.43 11.58
prototype 2
396.53 990.99 5571.41 5.93 1.80 9.35
prototype 3
88.20 3491.64 14788.85 34.78 5.24 19.96

T(x, 150, 250, 400, 500)

prototype 1
50.31 3071.15 31762.39 112.58 50.99 102.67
prototype 2
39.06 2377.62 9471.44 126.23 11.04 29.85
prototype 3
34.65 8113.07 30338.65 52.14 9.57 25.94

T(x, 400, 500, 2000, 2100)

prototype 1
29.94 8160.12 63610.66 113.23 12.08 173.02
prototype 2
28.95 15996.53 36633.18 105.92 15.15 29.27
prototype 3
23.36 30565.78 62270.66 132.00 30.56 60.71

The resulting linguistic labels in the space machine cycle and maximum main memory associated with the computers of low and high performance are shown in Figure 10.

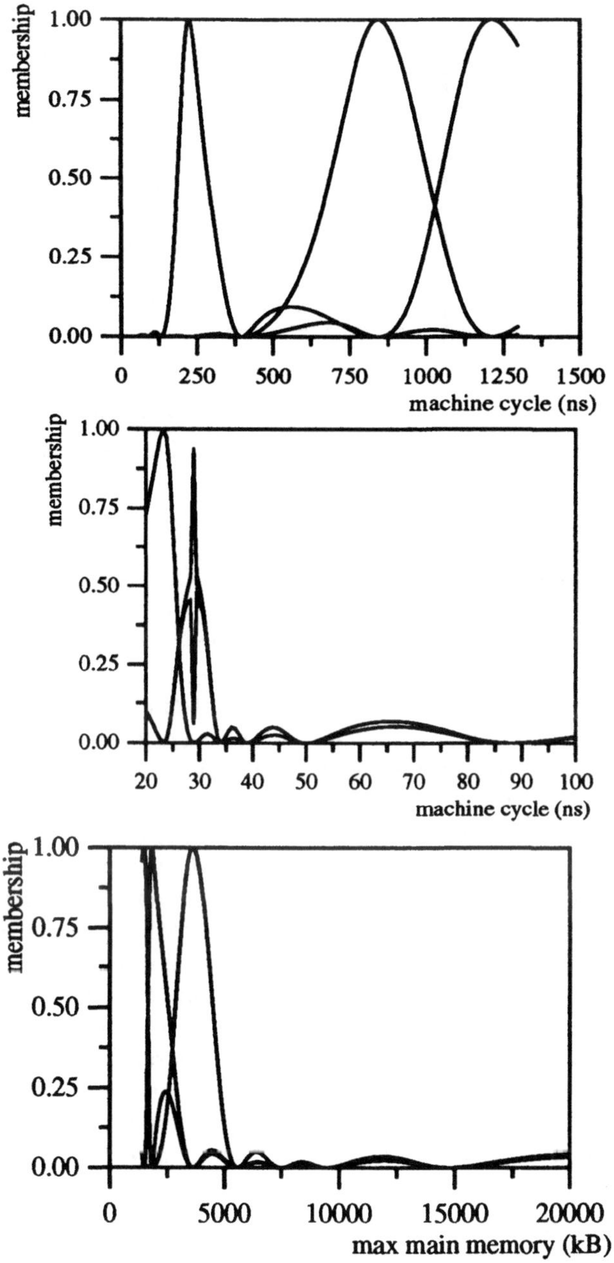

Figure 10. Linguistic terms associated with the computers of high and low performance

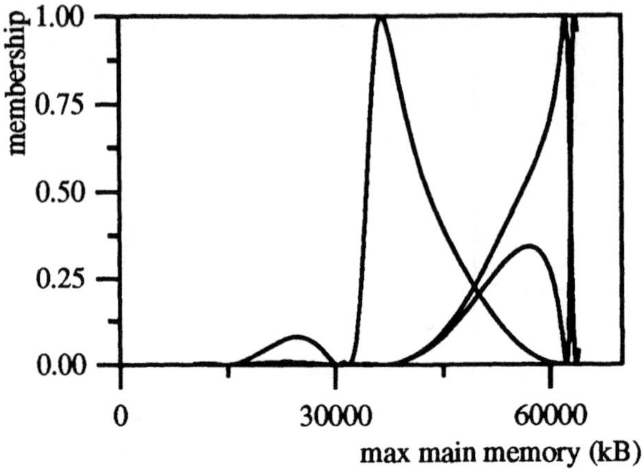

Figure 10(cont.) Linguistic terms associated with the computers of high and low performance

7. Conclusions

Making sense of data by searching for stable, meaningful, easily interpretable patterns is a genuine challenge all data mining techniques are confronted with. While data mining techniques may originate from different schools of thought and at the same time may adhere to some general methodological, such techniques need to seriously address the requirements stemming from the main requirement of data mining. This study has emphasized the role of granular computing as one of the cornerstones of data mining that realizes a quest for patterns that are transparent to the end user. Fuzzy sets appear to be one of the attractive alternatives in this regard: they focus on representing and modeling concepts with gradual boundaries (linguistic terms) that easily appeal to the end-user. We discussed the underlying principles in more detail by analyzing and quantifying the notions of information granularity as well as introducing some associated ideas of information generality and specificity. We have studied the ideas of unsupervised learning enriched by domain knowledge conveyed in terms of linguistic contexts that help focus on revealing the most essential relationships within the data sets. The resulting context-based clustering not only becomes a useful data mining tool but computationally is far efficient than the standard tools of fuzzy clustering. This efficiency comes with the modularization effect being introduced by the use of the linguistic contexts. The experimental studies using widely accessible data sets strongly justify the use of fuzzy sets as a suitable information granulation vehicle supporting data mining.

8. References

Anderberg, M. R. 1973. *Cluster Analysis for Applications*, Academic Press.
Backer, E. 1995. *Computer-assisted Reasoning in Cluster Analysis*, Prentice

Hall
Bezdek, J. C. 1981. *Pattern Recognition with Fuzzy Objective Function Algorithms*, Plenum Press
Communications of the ACM - a special issue on Data Mining, 11, 1996
Dave, R. 1992. Characterization and detection of noise in clustering, *Pattern Recognition Letters*, 12: 657 - 664
Everitt, B. S. 1974. *Cluster Analysis*, Heinemann
Fayyad, U. M., Piatetsky - Shapiro, G., Smyth, P.1996a. From data mining to knowledge discovery in databases, *AI Magazine*, 17:37 - 54
Fayyad, U.M., Piatetsky - Shapiro, G., Smyth, P., Uthurusamy, R (eds.) 1996b, *Advances in Knowledge Discovery and Data Mining*, AAAI Press
Frawley, W., G. Piatetsky - Shapiro, G., Matheus, C. 1991. Knowledge discovery in databases: an overview. In: *Knowledge Discovery in Databases*, G. Piatetsky - Shapiro and W. Frawley (eds.), AAAI Press, 1 -27
Hartigan, J. A. 1975. *Clustering Algorithms*, J. Wiley
Hirota, K. 1993. *Industrial Applications of Fuzzy Technology*, Springer Verlag
Hirota, K. 1995. *Industrial Applications of Fuzzy Technology in the World*, World Scientific Publishers
Int. J. Intelligent Systems - a special issue on Knowledge Discovery in Data - and Knowledge Bases. 1992, vol. 7, no. 7
Jain, A. K. and Dubes, R. C. 1988. *Algorithms for Clustering Data*, J. Wiley
Kandel, A. 1986. *Fuzzy Mathematical Techniques with Applications*, Addison-Wesley
Kaufman, L. and Rousseeuw, P. J. 1990. *Finding Groups in Data*, J. Wiley
Klir, G. J. and Folger, T. A. 1988. *Fuzzy Sets, Uncertainty and Information*, Prentice Hall
Krishnapuram, R. and Keller, J. M. 1993. A possibilistic approach to clustering, *IEEE Trans. on Fuzzy Systems*, 1: 98- 110
Moore, R. E. 1966. *Interval Analysis*, Prentice Hall
Pawlak, Z. 1982. Rough sets, *Int. J. of Computer and Information Sciences*, 11:341-356
Pedrycz, W. 1990. Fuzzy sets framework for development of perception perspective. *Fuzzy Sets and Systems*, 37:123-137
Pedrycz, W. 1992. Selected issues of frame of knowledge representation realized by means of linguistic labels. *Int. J. Intell. Syst.*, 7:155-170
Pedrycz, W. 1995. *Fuzzy Sets Engineering*, CRC Press
Pedrycz, W. 1996. Conditional Fuzzy C - Means, *Pattern Recognition Letters*, 17: 625 - 632
Pedrycz, W. 1997. *Computational Intelligence: An Introduction*, CRC Press
Pedrycz, W. and de Oliveira, J. V. 1993. Optimization of fuzzy relational models. In: *Proc. 5th IFSA World Congress*, Seoul, South Korea, vol 2: 1187-1190
Yager, R. R. 1982. Measuring tranquility and anxiety in decision making: An application of fuzzy sets. *Int. J. Gen. Syst.*, 8:139-146
Yager, R. R. 1983. Entropy and specificity in a mathematical theory of evidence. *Int. J. Gen. Syst.*, 9:249-260
Zadeh, L. A. 1965. Fuzzy sets, *Information and Control*, 8,:338-353

Zadeh, L.A. 1975. The concept of a linguistic variable and its application to approximate reasoning, *Information Sciences*, 8:199-249 (part I); 8:301-357 (part II); 9:43-80 (part III)

Zadeh, L. A. 1979. Fuzzy sets and information granularity, In: *Advances in Fuzzy Set Theory and Applications* (M. M. Gupta, R. K. Ragade, R. R. Yager, eds.) North Holland, 3- 18

Evolutionary Computation and Mathematical Programming

Fernando Jiménez[1] and José L. Verdegay[2]

[1] Dept. Informática, Inteligencia Artificial y Electrónica, Universidad de Murcia
[2] Dept. Ciencias de la Computación e Inteligencia Artificial
Universidad de Granada

Summary. A problem-independent evolutionary computation technique for general constrained optimization problems is proposed in this paper. Mathematical programming problems such as linear, nonlinear, integer, boolean and mixed programming problems can be solved by using this technique. Some important characteristics of the Evolutionary Algorithm are a natural representation of solutions, tournament selection, complete generational replacement and elitism strategy. Simulation results show a good performance by this method. An extension of this technique to find multiple nondominated solutions to constrained multiobjective optimization problems is also approached.
Keywords: Evolutionary algorithm; mathematical programming; constrained optimization; multiobjective optimization.

1. Introduction

Mathematical Programming is a broad discipline that has been concerned for many decades with *constrained optimization*, i.e. with the determination of solutions to problems that maximize or minimize a certain function and which are feasible within the limits of given constraints. This area has grown over the years and yielded very powerful theories and algorithms to find solutions to models of different mathematical structures, such as *linear programming*, *nonlinear programming*, *integer programming*, *boolean programming*, *goal programming*, *multiobjective programming*, *parametric programming*, or *fuzzy programming*. Mathematical programming has been applied to a great variety of theoretical and applied problems in a number of different areas such as Operations Research, Engineering, Artificial Intelligence, etc.

Here we consider an important subset of mathematical programming problems which include linear, nonlinear, integer, boolean and mixed programming problems. These problems can be represented by the following general mathematical formulation:

$$\begin{array}{ll} \text{Minimize} & f(\mathbf{x},\mathbf{y},\mathbf{z}) \\ \text{subject to} & \\ & g_j(\mathbf{x},\mathbf{y},\mathbf{z}) \leq 0, \quad j = 1,\ldots,m \end{array} \tag{1.1}$$

where:

- $\mathbf{x} = (x_1, \ldots, x_p) \in R^p$ is a p dimensional real-valued parameter vector, with $l_i^x \leq x_i \leq u_i^x$ ($l_i^x, u_i^x \in R$, $i = 1, \ldots, p$, $p \geq 0$), R stands for the real line, and no real-valued parameter is assumed when $p = 0$.
- $\mathbf{y} = (y_1, \ldots, y_q) \in Z^q$ is a q dimensional integer-valued parameter vector, with $l_i^y \leq y_i \leq u_i^y$ ($l_i^y, u_i^y \in Z$, $i = 1, \ldots, q$, $q \geq 0$), and Z represents the integer number set. No integer-valued parameter is assumed when $q = 0$.
- $\mathbf{z} = (z_1, \ldots, z_r) \in \{0, 1\}^r$ is an r dimensional boolean-valued parameter vector ($r \geq 0$). No boolean-valued parameter is assumed when $r = 0$.
- $f(\mathbf{x}, \mathbf{y}, \mathbf{z}), g_j(\mathbf{x}, \mathbf{y}, \mathbf{z})$ ($j = 1, \ldots, m$, $m \geq 0$) are linear or nonlinear arbitrary functions. No constraint is assumed when $m = 0$.

Note that we have not restricted ourselves to only considering minimization problems subject to less-than-or-equal-to-zero constraints, since:

- Maximization and minimization problems can be equivalently solved;
- A less-than-or-equal-to constraint $g_j(\mathbf{x}, \mathbf{y}, \mathbf{z}) \leq b_j$ can be rewritten as $g_j(\mathbf{x}, \mathbf{y}, \mathbf{z}) - b_j \leq 0$;
- A greater-than-or-equal-to constraint $g_j(\mathbf{x}, \mathbf{y}, \mathbf{z}) \geq b_j$ can be rewritten as $-g_j(\mathbf{x}, \mathbf{y}, \mathbf{z}) + b_j \leq 0$;
- An equality constraint $g_j(\mathbf{x}, \mathbf{y}, \mathbf{z}) = b_j$ can be represented by two inequality constraints $g_j(\mathbf{x}, \mathbf{y}, \mathbf{z}) - b_j \leq 0$ and $-g_j(\mathbf{x}, \mathbf{y}, \mathbf{z}) + b_j \leq 0$.

If all the functions f and g_j ($j = 1, \ldots, m$) are linear, then the problem simplifies to a linear program, which is the classical problem of mathematical programming and extremely efficient algorithms exist to obtain the optimal solution (simplex method and derived, for real-valued parameter optimization, and branch-and-bound technique, cutting methods, dynamic programming, etc., for integer, boolean and mixed programming). If one of the functions f or g_j ($j = 1, \ldots, m$) is nonlinear then we have a nonlinear programming problem. A nonlinear programming problem in which the objective function f and functions g_j ($j = 1, \ldots, m$) are arbitrary is, in general, intractable. It is unrealistic to expect to find a deterministic method for the general nonlinear programming problem in the global optimization category which would be better than an exhaustive search. Many optimization techniques based on gradient methods aim at local optimization only.

Evolutionary Algorithms (EA) [2, 7, 17] are global optimization methods that aim at complex objective functions and constraints. Most research into applications of EA to nonlinear programming problems has been concerned with complex objective functions but not with constraints, and only recently several approaches have extended evolutionary techniques by some constraint-handling methods. For particular constrained optimization problems, specialized EA have been developed by incorporating problem-specific knowledge into the EA, e.g. the transportation problem [12, 13, 14, 17], or the traveling salesman problem [8]. However, handling constraints by EA is not an easy task for general constrained optimization problems. The most usual technique in EA-based constrained optimization is the *penalty method*

[10], in which a constrained problem is transformed into a unconstrained one by associating a cost or penalty with all constraint violations. The success of this approach depends on the way in which the penalties are dealt with. The penalties, in order to prevent the premature convergence and divergence from the optimum result, must not be chosen either too large or too modest. Thus, the existence of nontrivial constraints produce a strong dependency between the problem and the EA. Other approaches such as decoders or repair algorithms [17] also suffer from the disadvantage of being tailored to the specific problem and are not sufficiently general to handle a variety of problems. An overview of EA for constrained parameter optimization problems is shown in [18].

With this background, we are interested in problem-independent evolutionary techniques to solve general constrained optimization problems such as linear programming problems, nonlinear programming problems, integer programming problems, boolean programming problems, and mixed programming problems. Obviously, the main interest is to solve problems with which existing methods have difficulties (complex nonlinear programming problems). Thus, the paper is organized as follows: Section 2 describes the structure and components of an EA to solve the considered mathematical programming problems. Some interesting test problems and simulation results are shown in section 3. Section 4 suggests an extension of the EA in order to consider multiobjective optimization, in which niche formation techniques have to be incorporated. Finally, section 5 indicates the main conclusions.

2. An Evolutionary Algorithm for Mathematical Programming Problems

Evolutionary Algorithms are adaptive procedures of optimization and search that find solutions to problems inspired by the mechanisms of natural evolution. They imitate, on an abstract level, biological principles such as a population based approach, the inheritance of information, the variation of information via crossover/mutation, and the selection of individuals based on fitness. EA start with an initial set (population) of alternative solutions (individuals) for the given problem which are evaluated in terms of solution quality (fitness). Then, the operators of selection, replication and variation are applied to obtain new individuals (offspring) that constitute a new population. The interplay of selection, replication and variation of the fittest, leads to solutions of increasing quality over the course of many iterations (generations). When finally a termination criterion is met, such as a maximum number of generations, the search process is terminated and the final solution is shown as output. Moreover, the algorithm uses a parameter set, such as population size, number of generations, crossing and mutation probabilities, to guide the evolutionary process. The structure of an EA can be as shown in figure 2.1.

```
procedure EA
begin
   initialize_population
   evaluate_population
   while (not termination-condition) do
   begin
      generate_new_population {selection, replication, variation
                               and generational replacement}
      evaluate_population
   end
end
```

Fig. 2.1. Structure of an EA.

Obviously, an appropriate *representation* of solutions to the problem is necessary. The most well-known class of EA is the *Genetic Algorithm* (GA) [9], which has received a lot of attention in the last few years. The classical GA use fixed-length binary strings to represent individuals and two basic genetic operators (binary mutation and binary crossover). Other variants of EA, such as *Genetic Programming* [16], *Evolution Strategies* [19], or *Evolutionary Programming* [4] are less popular, though very powerful too, and differences arise mainly in solution representation and importance of crossover/mutation. Nevertheless, the field of EA is characterised by high dynamics, and modifications and extensions of the technology are continuously being developed. Our EA for mathematical programming problems is basically a GA because of overall sequence of operations, but a "natural" representation of solutions is used (floating-point numbers to represent real-valued parameters, integer numbers to represent integer-valued parameters, and boolean values to represent boolean-valued parameters). Thus, an individual V of the population is represented as follows:

$$V = \{\mathbf{x}, \mathbf{y}, \mathbf{z}\}$$

where $\mathbf{x} = (x_1, \ldots, x_p)$, with $x_i \in R$ $(i = 1, \ldots, p)$, $\mathbf{y} = (y_1, \ldots, y_q)$, with $y_i \in Z$ $(i = 1, \ldots, q)$, and $\mathbf{z} = (z_1, \ldots, z_r)$, with $z_i \in \{0, 1\}$ $(i = 1, \ldots, r)$.

To handle constraints we consider the following general assumptions:

1. Populations are composed of feasible and unfeasible individuals.
2. Feasible individuals evolve towards optimality guided by an *optimality evaluation function.*
3. Unfeasible individuals evolve towards feasibility guided by a *feasibility evaluation function.*
4. Feasible individuals have greater probability of selection than unfeasible individuals.

According to these criteria, initialize_population, evaluate_population and generate_ new_population procedures can be designed as figures 2.2, 2.3 and 2.4 respectively show. In these algorithms:

- POP and NEW_POP represent the current population and the new population respectively.
- POP(s).IND represents the individual which is placed at the position s in the current population.
- POP(s).EVAL represents the evaluation of the individual which is placed at the position s in the current population.
- *popsize* is the population size.

```
procedure initialize_population
begin
   s ← 0
   while s ≤ popsize do
   begin
      s ← s + 1
      x_i ← random real value ∈ [l_i^x, u_i^x], for i = 1,...,p
      y_i ← random integer value ∈ [l_i^y, u_i^y], for i = 1,...,q
      z_i ← random value ∈ {0, 1}, for i = 1,...,r
      V ← {x, y, z}
      POP(s).IND ← V
   end
end
```

Fig. 2.2. A procedure to generate an initial population.

```
procedure evaluate_population
begin
   s ← 0
   while s ≤ popsize do
   begin
      s ← s + 1
      V ← POP(s).IND
      if feasible(V) then
         POP(s).EVAL ← f(x, y, z)
         {optimality evaluation function}
      else
         POP(s).EVAL ← max{g_j(x, y, z), j = 1...,m}
         {feasibility evaluation function}
   end
end
```

Fig. 2.3. Evaluation of individuals in a population.

Both optimality and feasibility evaluation functions have to be minimized. An individual $V = \{\mathbf{x}, \mathbf{y}, \mathbf{z}\}$ is feasible if $g_j(\mathbf{x}, \mathbf{y}, \mathbf{z}) \leq 0$ for all $j = 1, \ldots, m$. However, we allow a violation $\Delta \geq 0$ and then an individual $V = \{\mathbf{x}, \mathbf{y}, \mathbf{z}\}$ is feasible if $g_j(\mathbf{x}, \mathbf{y}, \mathbf{z}) \leq \Delta$ for all $j = 1, \ldots, m$. Note that there is a similarity between the feasibility evaluation function and the method of min-max formulation used in multiobjective optimization [3]. This method attempts to minimize the relative deviations of the single objective functions from the individual optimum, and it can yield the best possible compromise solution when objectives with equal priority are required to be optimized. Since constraints and objectives can be treated in a similar way, and equal priority is assumed for all constraints, the min-max formulation is also appropiate for constraint satisfaction.

The generate_new_population procedure can be designed in multiple ways. In our EA, *tournament selection*, *complete generational replacement* and *elitism strategy* are used. With the tournament selection (see figure 2.5), a group of *tourn* individuals is randomly sampled from the population and the best individual in the group is chosen for reproduction. Variation operators are applied to the selected individuals (with some probability) and the offspring are copied into the new population. This process is repeated until the whole new population is generated (complete generational replacement). Moreover, with the elitism strategy the best member of a population is always copied into the new population. Note that replication of individuals is achieved when no variation operator is applied.

```
procedure generate_new_population
begin
   s ← 1
   I ← {1,...,popsize}
   NEW_POP(s).IND ← best(I) {elitism strategy}
   while s < popsize do
   begin
      mate1 ← tournament_selection
      mate2 ← tournament_selection
      crossover(mate1,mate2,child1,child2)
      offspring1 ← mutation(child1)
      offspring2 ← mutation(child2)
      s ← s + 1
      NEW_POP(s).IND ← offspring1
      s ← s + 1
      if s ≤ popsize then
         NEW_POP(s).IND ← offspring2
   end
   POP ← NEW_POP
end
```

Fig. 2.4. A procedure to obtain a new population.

To obtain the best individual of a collection (see figure 2.6), the following criteria are assumed:

1. A feasible individual is better than another feasible individual if the evaluation of the first is smaller than the evaluation of the second.
2. A feasible individual is better than an unfeasible individual.

```
function tournament_selection
begin
   Set randomly J = {j_1, ..., j_tourn} ⊆ {1, ..., popsize}
   return(best(J))
end
```

Fig. 2.5. Tournament selection.

3. An unfeasible individual is better than another unfeasible individual if the evaluation of the first is smaller than the evaluation of the second.

```
function best
input: index set K = {k_1, ..., k_l} ⊆ {1, ..., popsize}
begin
   s ← 1
   V ← POP(k_s).IND
   while s ≤ l do
   begin
      s ← s + 1
      if (feasible(POP(k_s).IND) and feasible(V) and
      POP(k_s).EVAL<POP(V).EVAL) or
      (feasible(POP(k_s).IND) and unfeasible(V)) or
      (unfeasible(POP(k_s).IND) and unfeasible(V) and
      (POP(k_s).EVAL<POP(V).EVAL) then
            V ← POP(k_s).IND
   end
   return(V)
end
```

Fig. 2.6. A procedure to obtain the best individual of a collection.

Many variation operators have been proposed during the last 30 years. A discussion of these variation operators is shown in [18]. After a large experimentation process, we finally use *uniform crossover*, *nonuniform mutation* and *uniform mutation*.

Uniform crossover works as follows. With probability p_c, two parents $V_1 = \{\mathbf{x}_1, \mathbf{y}_1, \mathbf{z}_1\}$, with $\mathbf{x}_1 = (x_1^1, \ldots, x_p^1)$, $\mathbf{y}_1 = (y_1^1, \ldots, y_q^1)$, $\mathbf{z}_1 = (z_1^1, \ldots, z_r^1)$ and $V_2 = \{\mathbf{x}_2, \mathbf{y}_2, \mathbf{z}_2\}$, with $\mathbf{x}_2 = (x_1^2, \ldots, x_p^2)$, $\mathbf{y}_2 = (y_1^2, \ldots, y_q^2)$, $\mathbf{z}_2 = (z_1^2, \ldots, z_r^2)$, produce two children $V_3 = \{\mathbf{x}_3, \mathbf{y}_3, \mathbf{z}_3\}$, with $\mathbf{x}_3 = (x_1^3, \ldots, x_p^3)$, $\mathbf{y}_3 = (y_1^3, \ldots, y_q^3)$, $\mathbf{z}_3 = (z_1^3, \ldots, z_r^3)$ and $V_4 = \{\mathbf{x}_4, \mathbf{y}_4, \mathbf{z}_4\}$, with $\mathbf{x}_4 = (x_1^4, \ldots, x_p^4)$, $\mathbf{y}_4 = (y_1^4, \ldots, y_q^4)$, $\mathbf{z}_4 = (z_1^4, \ldots, z_r^4)$, where $x_i^3 = x_i^1$ or $x_i^3 = x_i^2$, with equal probability for all $i = 1, \ldots, p$, $y_i^3 = y_i^1$ or $y_i^3 = y_i^2$, with equal probability for all $i = 1, \ldots, q$, and $z_i^3 = z_i^1$ or $z_i^3 = z_i^2$, with equal probability for all $i = 1, \ldots, r$. Child V_4 is created by reversing decisions for all components.

The action of the nonuniform mutation, which is only applied to the components with floating-point representation, depends on the age of the population, and its effect is a fine local tuning in the last generations of the EA. Given an individual $V = \{\mathbf{x}, \mathbf{y}, \mathbf{z}\}$ with $\mathbf{x} = (x_1, \ldots, x_p)$, nonuniform mutation generates an offspring $V' = \{\mathbf{x}', \mathbf{y}, \mathbf{z}\}$ with $\mathbf{x}' = (x'_1, \ldots, x'_p)$ where x'_i $(i = 1, \ldots, p)$ has been mutated with probability p_m as follows:

$$x'_i = \begin{cases} x_i + (u^x_i - x_i) \cdot r \cdot (1 - \frac{t}{T})^c, & \text{if a random digit is 0} \\ x_i - (x_i - l^x_i) \cdot r \cdot (1 - \frac{t}{T})^c, & \text{if a random digit is 1} \end{cases}$$

As usual $[l^x_i, u^x_i]$ is the domain of the variable x_i, and r is a random number from [0, 1], T is the maximal generation number, t is the present generation, and c is a system parameter determining the degree of non-uniformity.

Uniform mutation is applied to the components with integer and boolean representation. Given an individual $V = \{\mathbf{x}, \mathbf{y}, \mathbf{z}\}$ with $\mathbf{y} = (y_1, \ldots, y_q)$, $\mathbf{z} = (z_1, \ldots, z_r)$, uniform mutation generates an offspring $V' = \{\mathbf{x}, \mathbf{y}', \mathbf{z}'\}$ with $\mathbf{y}' = (y'_1, \ldots, y'_q)$, $\mathbf{z}' = (z'_1, \ldots, z'_r)$, where y'_i $(i = 1, \ldots, q)$ and z'_j $(j = 1, \ldots, r)$ have been mutated with probability p_m as follows:

$$\begin{aligned} y'_i &= \text{random integer value} \in [l^y_i, u^y_i] \\ z'_j &= \text{random value} \in \{0, 1\} \end{aligned}$$

3. Simulation Results

In this section we show simulation results for the following mathematical programming problems:

1. Test case $G1$ reported by Michalewicz and Schoenauer [18], with 13 real-valued parameters, quadratic objective function, and 9 linear inequalities.
2. Test case $G7$ reported by Michalewicz and Schoenauer [18], with 10 real-valued parameters, quadratic objective function, 3 linear inequalities, and 5 nonlinear inequalities.
3. Test case $G9$ reported by Michalewicz and Schoenauer [18], with 7 real-valued parameters, polinomial objective function, and 4 nonlinear inequalities.
4. Test case $G10$ reported by Michalewicz and Schoenauer [18], with 8 real-valued parameters, linear objective function, 3 linear inequalities, and 3 nonlinear inequalities.

For these test cases, Michalewicz and Schoenauer [18] show some comparisons with several constraint-handling evolutionary methods (static penalties, dynamic penalties, annealing penalties, death penalty, behavioral memory, superiority of feasible points, and repair of unfeasible individuals). Moreover, for the sake of illustration we show simulation results for a linear integer programming problem and a linear mixed $\{0, 1\}$ programming problem, which have been reported by Taha [21]. The values of the EA parameters used in the experiments are shown in table 3.1. Although the maximal number of

Parameter	Value
Population size (*popsize*)	20
Maximal generation number (T)	problem-dependent (1.000 - 50.000)
Crossing probability (p_c)	0.4
Mutation probability (p_m)	0.4
Degree of non-uniformity (c)	2
Number of individuals in the comparison set for tournament selection (*tourn*)	4

Table 3.1. EA parameters used in the experiments.

generations is apparently high (50.000 generations in some problems), the real time of a run has been relatively short since the population size is small.

The test case G1 is:

$$\text{Minimize} \quad G1(\mathbf{x}) = 5x_1 + 5x_2 + 5x_3 + 5x_4 + 5\sum_{i=1}^{4} x_i^2 - \sum_{i=5}^{13} x_i$$

subject to:

$$\begin{aligned} 2x_1 + 2x_2 + x_{10} + x_{11} &\le 10, \\ 2x_1 + 2x_3 + x_{10} + x_{12} &\le 10, \\ 2x_2 + 2x_3 + x_{11} + x_{12} &\le 10, \\ -8x_1 + x_{10} &\le 0, \\ -8x_2 + x_{11} &\le 0, \\ -8x_3 + x_{12} &\le 0, \\ -2x_4 - x_5 + x_{10} &\le 0, \\ -2x_6 - x_7 + x_{11} &\le 0, \\ -2x_8 - x_9 + x_{12} &\le 0, \end{aligned}$$

and bounds:

$$\begin{aligned} &0 \le x_i \le 1, \ i = 1, \ldots, 9, \\ &0 \le x_i \le 100, \ i = 10, 11, 12, \\ &0 \le x_{13} \le 1. \end{aligned}$$

The problem has its global minimum at $G1(\mathbf{x}^*) = -15$. Several methods reported in [18] obtained the solution $G1(\mathbf{x}) = -15.000$ without violations by more than 0.001. We have obtained $G1(\mathbf{x}) = -15.000000032$, where

$$\begin{array}{lll} x_1 = 1.0, & x_2 = 1.0, & x_3 = 1.0, \\ x_4 = 1.0, & x_5 = 1.0, & x_6 = 1.0, \\ x_7 = 1.0, & x_8 = 1.0, & x_9 = 1.0, \\ x_{10} = 2.9999999801, & x_{11} = 2.9999999946, & x_{12} = 3.0000000576, \\ x_{13} = 1.0. & & \end{array}$$

Maximal violation allowed for solutions was $\Delta = 10^{-7}$. In the obtained solution all constraints are satisfied with maximal violation equal to $5.7618918525 \cdot 10^{-8}$.

The test case G7 is:

$$\begin{aligned}\text{Minimize}\quad G7(\mathbf{x}) = {} & x_1^2 + x_2^2 + x_1x_2 - 14x_1 - 16x_2 + (x_3 - 10)^2 \\ & +4(x_4 - 5)^2 + (x_5 - 3)^2 + 2(x_6 - 1)^2 + 5x_7^2 \\ & +7(x_8 - 11)^2 + 2(x_9 - 10)^2 + (x_{10} - 7)^2 + 45\end{aligned}$$

subject to:

$$\begin{aligned}105 - 4x_1 - 5x_2 + 3x_7 - 9x_8 &\geq 0, \\ -3(x_1 - 2)^2 - 4(x_2 - 3)^2 - 2x_3^2 + 7x_4 + 120 &\geq 0, \\ -10x_1 + 8x_2 + 17x_7 - 2x_8 &\geq 0, \\ -x_1^2 - 2(x_2 - 2)^2 + 2x_1x_2 - 14x_5 + 6x_6 &\geq 0, \\ 8x_1 - 2x_2 - 5x_9 + 2x_{10} + 12 &\geq 0, \\ -5x_1^2 - 8x_2 - (x_3 - 6)^2 + 2x_4 + 40 &\geq 0, \\ 3x_1 - 6x_2 - 12(x_9 - 8)^2 + 7x_{10} &\geq 0, \\ -0.5(x_1 - 8)^2 - 2(x_2 - 4)^2 - 3x_5^2 + x_6 + 30 &\geq 0,\end{aligned}$$

and bounds:

$$-10.0 \leq x_i \leq 10.0,\ i = 1, \ldots, 10.$$

The problem has its global minimum at $G7(\mathbf{x}^*) = 24.3062091$. The best result reported in [18] was obtained with the method of dynamic penalties at $G7(\mathbf{x}) = 25.486$ without violations by more than 0.001. We have obtained $G7(\mathbf{x}) = 25.012657345$, where

$$\begin{aligned}&x_1 = 2.2931284882, && x_2 = 2.2224845773, && x_3 = 8.4937676592, \\ &x_4 = 5.145537901, && x_5 = 0.98977059878, && x_6 = 1.5033402032, \\ &x_7 = 1.4679744246, && x_8 = 9.9021206132, && x_9 = 8.3676496816, \\ &x_{10} = 7.9690450647.\end{aligned}$$

Maximal violation allowed for solutions was $\Delta = 0.0001$. In the obtained solution all constraints are satisfied with maximal violation equal to $9.9527851766 \cdot 10^{-5}$.

The test case G9 is:

$$\begin{aligned}\text{Minimize}\quad G9(\mathbf{x}) = {} & (x_1 - 10)^2 + 5(x_2 - 12)^2 + x_3^4 + 3(x_4 - 11)^2 \\ & +10x_5^6 + 7x_6^2 + x_7^4 - 4x_6x_7 - 10x_6 - 8x_7\end{aligned}$$

subject to:

$$\begin{aligned}127 - 2x_1^2 - 3x_2^4 - x_3 - 4x_4^2 - 5x_5 &\geq 0, \\ 282 - 7x_1 - 3x_2 - 10x_3^2 - x_4 + x_5 &\geq 0, \\ 196 - 23x_1 - x_2^2 - 6x_6^2 + 8x_7 &\geq 0, \\ -4x_1^2 - x_2^2 + 3x_1x_2 - 2x_3^2 - 5x_6 + 11x_7 &\geq 0,\end{aligned}$$

and bounds:

$$-10.0 \le x_i \le 10.0, \ i = 1, \dots, 7.$$

The problem has its global minimum at $G9(\mathbf{x}^*) = 680.6300573$. The best result reported in [18] was obtained with Genocop III (repairing unfeasible solutions) at $G9(\mathbf{x}) = 680.640$ without violations by more than 0.001. We have obtained $G9(\mathbf{x}) = 680.63319807$, where

$$\begin{aligned} &x_1 = 2.3305563357, && x_2 = 1.9537226077, && x_3 = -0.45310296242, \\ &x_4 = 4.3581975196, && x_5 = -0.61872513858, && x_6 = 1.0543710376, \\ &x_7 = 1.596789505. \end{aligned}$$

Maximal violation allowed for solutions was $\Delta = 0.001$. In the obtained solution all constraints are satisfied with maximal violation equal to $9.9999148776 \cdot 10^{-4}$.

The test case G10 is:

$$\text{Minimize} \quad G10(\mathbf{x}) = x_1 + x_2 + x_3$$

subject to:

$$\begin{aligned} 1 - 0.0025(x_4 + x_6) &\ge 0, \\ x_1x_6 - 833.33252x_4 - 100x_1 + 83333.333 &\ge 0, \\ 1 - 0.0025(x_5 + x_7 - x_4) &\ge 0, \\ x_2x_7 - 1250x_5 - x_2x_4 + 1250x_4 &\ge 0, \\ 1 - 0.01(x_8 - x_5) &\ge 0, \\ x_3x_8 - 1250000 - x_3x_5 + 2500x_5 &\ge 0, \end{aligned}$$

and bounds:

$$\begin{aligned} &100 \le x_1 \le 10000, \\ &1000 \le x_i \le 10000, \ i = 2, 3, \\ &10 \le x_i \le 1000, \ i = 4, \dots, 8. \end{aligned}$$

The problem has its global minimum at $G10(\mathbf{x}^*) = 7049.330923$. The best result reported in [18] was obtained with Genocop III (repairing unfeasible solutions) at $G10(\mathbf{x}) = 7286.650$ without violations by more than 0.001. We have obtained $G10(\mathbf{x}) = 7088.9652637$, where

$$\begin{aligned} &x_1 = 720.37182162, && x_2 = 1638.7299328, && x_3 = 4729.8635093, \\ &x_4 = 192.91292275, && x_5 = 310.61648849, && x_6 = 207.48707226, \\ &x_7 = 282.69642022, && x_8 = 410.71646755. \end{aligned}$$

Maximal violation allowed for solutions was $\Delta = 0.001$. In the obtained solution all constraints are satisfied with maximal violation equal to $9.9998753935 \cdot 10^{-4}$.

Finally, for the sake of illustration we consider now the following two problems:

$$\text{Maximize} \quad f_1(\mathbf{y}) = y_1 - 3y_2 + 3y_3$$

subject to:

$$\begin{aligned} 2y_1 + y_2 - y_3 + y_4 &= 4, \\ 4y_1 - 3y_2 + y_5 &= 2, \\ -3y_1 + 2y_2 + y_3 + y_6 &= 3, \\ y_i \geq 0 \; \textit{and integer}, \; i &= 1, \ldots, 6 \end{aligned}$$

and

$$\text{Maximize} \quad f_2(\mathbf{x}, \mathbf{z}) = -3x_1 - 3x_2 - z_2 + 10$$

subject to:

$$\begin{aligned} -x_1 + x_2 + z_1 - 0.4z_2 &= 0.7, \\ x_i \geq 0, \; i &= 1, 2, \\ z_i \in \{0, 1\}, \; i &= 1, 2. \end{aligned}$$

These problems are solved in [21] by differents techniques. The optima are at $f_1(\mathbf{y}^*) = 11$, with $\mathbf{y}^* = (2, 2, 5, 3, 0, 0)$, and $f_2(\mathbf{x}^*, \mathbf{z}^*) = 9.1$, with $\mathbf{x}^* = (0.3, 0.0)$, $\mathbf{z}^* = (1, 0)$. We obtained the optimum solutions for the two problems in the first generations of the EA.

4. Extensions

In this section we describe an extension of the previous EA to solve *multiobjective programming problems.* A general constrained multiobjective optimization problem can be written as follows:

$$\begin{array}{lll} \text{Minimize} & f_i(\mathbf{x}, \mathbf{y}, \mathbf{z}), & i = 1, \ldots, n \\ \text{subject to} & & \\ & g_j(\mathbf{x}, \mathbf{y}, \mathbf{z}) \leq 0, & j = 1, \ldots, m \end{array} \tag{4.1}$$

where $f_i(\mathbf{x}, \mathbf{y}, \mathbf{z})$ $(i = 1, \ldots, n)$ are linear or nonlinear arbitrary functions. Solutions to multiobjective problems are expressed in terms of *nondominated solutions* (or *Pareto-optimal* points). A pareto-optimum offers the least objective conflict, i.e. a point in the search space which is optimally placed in relation to the individual optimum of each objective. These points cannot be improved for one objective without making it worse for another. Thus, a feasible solution $\{\mathbf{x}, \mathbf{y}, \mathbf{z}\}$ is said to be a nondominated solution if there is no other feasible solution $\{\overline{\mathbf{x}}, \overline{\mathbf{y}}, \overline{\mathbf{z}}\}$ such that:

$$\begin{gathered} f_i(\overline{\mathbf{x}}, \overline{\mathbf{y}}, \overline{\mathbf{z}}) \leq f_i(\mathbf{x}, \mathbf{y}, \mathbf{z}), \text{ for all } i = 1, \ldots, n, \\ \text{and} \\ f_i(\overline{\mathbf{x}}, \overline{\mathbf{y}}, \overline{\mathbf{z}}) < f_i(\mathbf{x}, \mathbf{y}, \mathbf{z}), \text{ for at least one } i. \end{gathered}$$

To solve these problems, the classical methods, by using some knowledge of the problem, combine all of the multiple objectives to form one only. A drawback of these methods however, is that a decision maker must have a thorough knowledge of the priority of each objective before the integration of all the objectives in a single objective. Thus, for different situations, different priorities need to be assigned, and consequently the same problem needs to be solved a number of times. A more realistic method would be one that could find multiple Pareto-optimal solutions simultaneously so that a decision maker would be able to choose the most appropriate solution for the current situation. Furthermore, the knowledge of many Pareto-optimal solutions is also useful for later use, when the current situation has changed and a new solution is required. Since EA deal with a population of points, multiple Pareto-optimal solutions can be captured in the population in a single run.

The idea of assigning an equal probability of reproduction to all the nondominated individuals in the population by means of a nondominated sorting procedure was first proposed by Goldberg [7]. This procedure is similar to the single-criterion ranking selection procedures [1], although the author suggested that it should be used in conjunction with the techniques of *niche formation* and *speciation* to maintain an appropriate diversity. Other authors [5, 11, 20] have developed variants based on this concept, and they have applied them successfully to some problems. An overview of EA in multiobjective optimization can be found in [6].

Jiménez and Verdegay [15] describe a Nondominated Sorting EA to find multiple nondominated solutions to constrained multiobjective problems. *Ranking selection* and a niche formation technique based on the *crowding factor model* are used to maintain diversity in the population. In this section we show how the EA described in the previous section can be modified to find multiple nondominated solutions to problems as in (4.1). The extended EA also uses tournament selection, complete generational replacement and elitism strategy. Modifications are as follows:

First, the evaluate_population procedure has to be changed to evaluate the feasible individuals in each of the objectives. Second, the tournament_selection procedure is now based in the nondominated concept, and an explicit niche formation technique is incorporated. In this nondominated tournament selection procedure, two individuals are picked at random from the population in order to select a winner in a tournament selection. The tournament is as follows:

- If both individuals are feasible, then they are compared to the feasible members of a comparison set which contains a specific number *tourn* of individuals picked at random from the population. If one of them is nondominated in the comparison set and the other is dominated, then the nondominated individual is selected. If both are either nondominated or dominated in the comparison set, a niche count is found for each individual in the entire population, and then the individual with the least niche count is selected.

- If one of them is feasible and the other is unfeasible, then the feasible individual is selected.
- If both individuals are unfeasible, then they are compared to the unfeasible members of a comparison set which contains a specific number *tourn* of individuals picked at random from the population. If one of them is better than the best unfeasible individual in the comparison set (according to the feasibility evaluation function) and the other is worse, then the first individual is selected. If both are either better or worse than the best unfeasible individual in the comparison set, a niche count is found for each individual in the entire population, and then the individual with the least niche count is selected.

The niche count NC for an individual V_i is calculated by adding the sharing function values for all individuals in the population as follows:

$$NC(V_i) = \sum_{j=1}^{popsize} SH(d_{ij})$$

with

$$SH(d_{ij}) \begin{cases} 1 - \left(\frac{d_{ij}}{\sigma_{share}}\right)^2, & if\ d_{ij} < \sigma_{share} \\ 0, & otherwise \end{cases}$$

where d_{ij} is the phenotypic distance between two individuals V_i and V_j in the population, and σ_{share} is the maximum phenotypic distance allowed between any two individuals for them to become members of a niche.

Third, elitism strategy now copies a random nondominated individual in the population into the new population.

This technique, already implemented, will be described in more detail with simulation results in future papers.

5. Conclusions

The main focus of this work has been to design a problem-independent evolutionary constraint-handling technique to find acceptable solutions to general constrained optimization problems. An important set of mathematical programming problems such as linear, nonlinear, integer, boolean and mixed programming problems can be solved by using this evolutionary computation technique. Simulation results for six test cases showed a good performance by the proposed EA. We have also shown the integration of this technique with other multiobjective optimization techniques to obtain an EA which finds multiple nondominated solutions to constrained multiobjective optimization problems. In this extended EA, an explicit niche formation technique has been incorporated to create stable subpopulations.

Acknowledgement

The authors thank the Comisión Interministerial de Ciencia y Tecnología (CICyT) for the support given to this work under the projects TIC97-1343-C02-02 and ESP97-1518-E.

References

1. Baker, J.E. (1985). Adaptive selection methods for genetic algorithms. In J.J. Grefenstette (Ed.). *Proc. of the First Intern. Conf. on Genetic Algorithms*, pp. 101-111. Lawrence Erlbaum Associates, Hillsdale, NJ.
2. Biethahn, J., Nissen, V. (1995), *Evolutionary Algorithms in Management Applications*. Springer-Verlag Berlin Heidelberg.
3. Chankong, V., Haimes, Y.Y. (1983). *Multiobjective Decision Making: Theory and Methodology*. North-Holland series in Systems Science and Engineering, Andrew P. Sage (Ed.).
4. Fogel, L.J., Owens, A.J., Walsh, M.J. (1966). *Artificial Intelligence through Simulated Evolution*. Wiley, New York.
5. Fonseca, C.M, Fleming, P.J. (1993). Genetic algorithms for multi-objective optimization: formulation, discussion and generalization. In S. Forrest (Ed.), *Proc. of the Fifth Intern. Conf. on Genetic Algorithms* (pp. 416-423). Morgan Kaufmann, San Mateo.
6. Fonseca, C.M., Fleming, P.J. (1995). An overview of avolutionary algorithms in multiobjective optimization. *Evolutionary Computation*, vol. 3, no. 1, pp 1-16.
7. Goldberg, D.E. (1989). *Genetic Algorithms in Search, Optimization, and Machine Learning*. Addison-Wesley.
8. Grefenstette, J.J., Gopal, R., Rosmaita, B.J., Van Gucht, D. (1985). Genetic algorithms for the traveling salesman problem. *Proc. of an International Conference on Genetic Algorithms and Their Applications*, pp. 160-168.
9. Holland, J.H. (1975). *Adaptation in Natural and Artificial Systems*. The University of Michigan Press, Ann Arbor.
10. Homaifar, A., Qi, C.X., Lai, S.H. (1994). Constrained optimization via Genetic Algorithms. *Simulation*, vol. 62, no. 4, pp. 242-254.
11. Horn, J., Nafpliotis, N. (1993). Multiobjective optimization using the niched Pareto Genetic Algorithm. IlliEAL Report no. 93005.
12. Jiménez, F., Cadenas, J.M. (1995). An evolutionary program for the multiobjective solid transportation problem with fuzzy goals. *Operations Research and Decision*, vol. 2, pp. 5-20.
13. Jiménez, F. (1996). *Genetic Algorithms based Heuristics to solve Transportation Problems*, Ph.D. thesis. Dpto. Informática y Sistemas, Facultad de Informática, Universidad de Murcia (in spanish).
14. Jiménez, F., Verdegay, J.L. (1996). Interval multiobjective solid transportation problem via genetic algorithms. *Procs. of the Sixth Intern. Conf. on Information Processing and Management of Uncertainty in Knowledge-Based Systems (IPMU'96)*, pp. 787-792. Granada, Spain.
15. Jiménez, F., Verdegay, J.L. (1998). Constrained multiobjective optimization by evolutionary algorithms. *Procs. of the International ICSC Symposium on Engineering of Intelligent Systems (EIS'98)*, pp. 266-271. University of La Laguna, Tenerife, Spain.

16. Koza, J.R. (1992). *Genetic Programming: On the Programming of Computers by Means of Natural Selection.* The MIT Press, Cambridge, Massachusetts.
17. Michalewicz, Z. (1992). *Genetic Algorithms + Data Structures = Evolution Programs.* Springer Verlag.
18. Michalewicz, Z., Schoenauer, M. (1996). Evolutionary Algorithms for constrained parameter optimization problems. *Evolutionary Computation*, vol. 4, no. 1, pp. 1-32.
19. Rechenberg, I. (1973). *Evolutionary Strategy: Optimization of Technical Systems According to the Priciples of Biological Evolution.* Frommann-Holzboog.
20. Srinivas, N., Deb, K. (1995). Multiobjective optimization using nondominated sorting in Genetic Algorithms. *Evolutionary Computation*, vol. 2, no. 3, pp. 221-248.
21. Taha, H.A. (1975). *Integer Programming. Theory, Applications and Computations.* Academic Press, New York.

Genetic Optimization of Fuzzy Classification Systems – A Case Study

Ulrich Bodenhofer* and Erich Peter Klement°

*Software Competence Center Hagenberg
A-4232 Hagenberg, Austria
°Fuzzy Logic Laboratorium Linz-Hagenberg
Institut für Algebra, Stochastik und wissensbasierte math. Systeme
Johannes Kepler Universität, A-4040 Linz, Austria

Abstract. This contribution presents a fuzzy method for a particular kind of pixel classification. It is one of the most important results of the development of an inspection system for a silk-screen printing process. The classification algorithm is applied to a reference image in the initial step of the printing process in order to obtain regions which are to be checked by applying different criteria. Tight limitations in terms of computation speed have necessitated very specific, efficient methods which operate locally. These methods are motivated and described in detail in the following. Furthermore, the optimization of the parameters of the classification system with genetic algorithms is discussed. Finally, the genetic approach is compared with other probabilistic optimization methods.

Keywords. Fuzzy system, genetic algorithm, pixel classification, print inspection.

1 Introduction

The main goal of this project was to design an automatic inspection system which does not sort out every print with defects, but only those with visible defects which are really unacceptable for the consumer. It is clear that the visibility of a defect depends on the structure of the print in its neighborhood. While little spots can hardly be recognized in very chaotic areas, they can be disturbing in rather homogeneous areas. So, the first step towards a sensitive inspection is to partition the print into areas of different sensitivity which, consequently, should be treated differently.

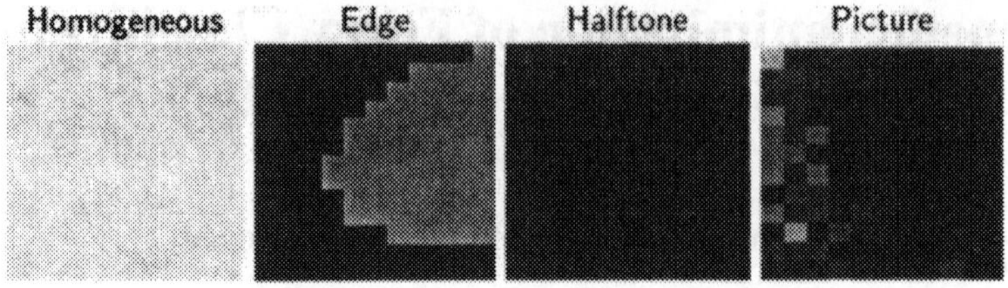

Fig. 1. Magnifications of typical representatives of the four types.

For certain reasons which can be explained with the special principles of this particular kind of silk-screen printing process it is sufficient to consider only the following four types:

Homogeneous area: uniformly colored area;
Edge area: pixels within or close to visually significant edges;
Halftone: area which looks rather homogeneous from a certain distance, although it is actually obtained by printing small raster dots of two or more colors;
Picture: rastered area with high, chaotic deviations, in particular small high-contrasted details.

The magnifications in Fig. 1 show how these areas typically look like at the pixel level. Of course, transitions between two or more of these areas are possible; hence, a fuzzy model is recommendable.

First of all, we should define precisely what, in our case, an image is:

Definition 1. An $N \times M$ matrix of the form

$$\Big((u_r(i,j), u_g(i,j), u_b(i,j))\Big)_{i=1,\ldots,N}^{j=1,\ldots,M}$$

with three-dimensional entries (additive RGB model)

$$(u_r(i,j), u_g(i,j), u_b(i,j)) \in \{0,\ldots,255\}^3$$

is a model of a *24 bit color image* of size $N \times M$. A coordinate pair (i,j) stands for a *pixel*, where i is the *row index* and j is the *column index*; the values $(u_r(i,j), u_g(i,j), u_b(i,j))$ are called the *gray values* of the pixel (i,j).

It is near at hand to use something like the variance of gray values in the neighborhood of the pixels or an other measure for deviations to distinguish between areas which show only low deviations, such as, homogeneous areas and halftone areas, and areas with rather high deviations, such as, edges or pictures.

On the contrary, it is intuitively clear that such a measure can never be used to separate edge areas from picture areas, because any geometrical information is ignored. Experiments have shown that well-known standard edge detectors, such as, the Laplacian or the Mexican Hat, but also many other locally operating filter masks [10], cannot distinguish sufficiently if deviations are chaotic or anisotropic. Another possibility we also took into consideration was to use wavelet transforms [3,13] or more sophisticated image segmentation methods [2,10]. Since we had to cope with serious restrictions in terms of computation speed, such highly advanced methods, although they are efficient, would require too much time. Finally, we found a fairly good alternative which is based on the discrepancy norm. This approach uses only, like the simplest filter masks, the closest neighborhood of a pixel. Figure 2 shows how the neighbors of pixel (i,j) are enumerated for the algorithm.

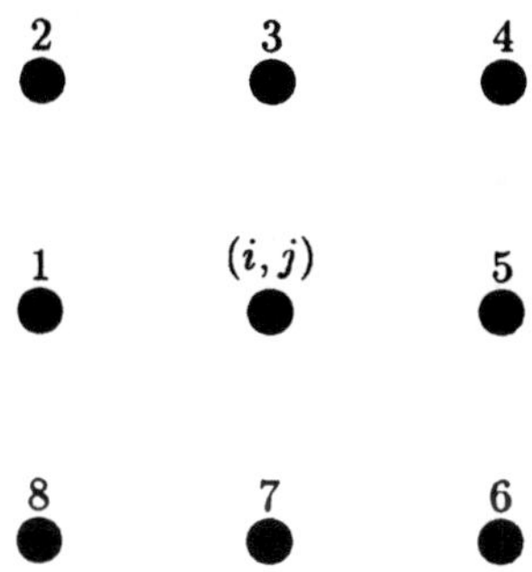

Fig. 2. Enumeration of the neighborhood of a pixel.

For an arbitrary but fixed pixel (i,j) we can define the enumeration mapping l as shown in Table 1. If we plot one color extraction of the eight neighbor pixels with respect to this enumeration, i.e $\left(u_x(l(k))\right)_{k\in\{1,\dots,8\}}$, where $x \in \{r,g,b\}$, we typically get curves like those shown in Fig. 3.

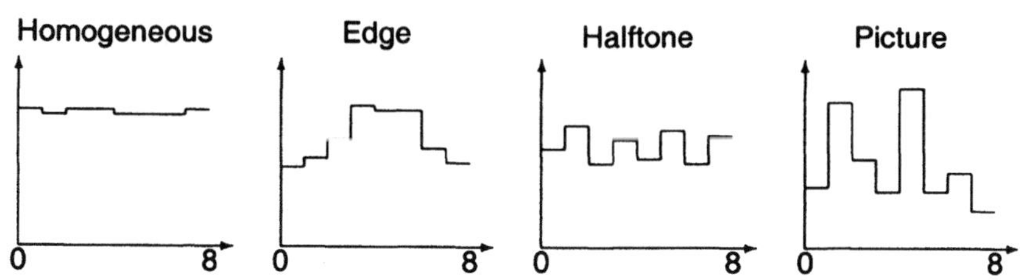

Fig. 3. Typical gray value curves of the form $u_x(l(.))$.

k	$l(k)$
1	$(i, j-1)$
2	$(i-1, j-1)$
3	$(i-1, j)$
4	$(i-1, j+1)$
5	$(i, j+1)$
6	$(i+1, j+1)$
7	$(i+1, j)$
8	$(i+1, j-1)$

Table 1. The enumeration mapping $l(.)$.

From these sketches, it can be seen easily that a measure for the deviations can be used to distinguish between homogeneous areas, halftones, and the other two types. On the other hand, the most eye-catching difference between the curves around pixels in pictures and edge areas is that, in the case of an edge pixel, the peaks appear to be more connected while they are mainly chaotic and narrow for a pixel in a picture area. So, a method which judges the shape of the peaks should be used in order to separate edge areas from pictures. A simple but effective method for this purpose is the so-called discrepancy norm.

2 The Discrepancy Norm

Definition 2. The mapping

$$\begin{aligned} \|.\|_D : \mathbb{R}^n &\longrightarrow \mathbb{R}^+ \\ x &\longmapsto \max_{1\leq\alpha\leq\beta\leq n} \left| \sum_{i=\alpha}^{\beta} x_i \right| \end{aligned}$$

is called *discrepancy norm* on $\mathbb{R}^n$.

In words, $\|x\|_D$ is the absolute value of the maximal sum of consecutive entries of the vector x. Obviously, unlike conventional norms, the signs and the order of the entries play an essential role. Nevertheless, one easily verifies that the mapping $\|.\|_D$ is a norm on $\mathbb{R}^n$.

The connection to the concept of discrepancy in measure theory can be motivated as follows: The discrepancy between two measures μ and ν on $\mathbb{R}$ is usually defined as

$$\mathcal{D}(\mu, \nu) = \sup_{a\leq b} |\mu([a, b]) - \nu([a, b])| .$$

If we have two discrete measures $\overline{\mu}$ and $\overline{\nu}$ on the set $\{1, \dots, n\}$ and if we write $x_i = \overline{\mu}(i)$ and $y_i = \overline{\nu}(i)$, then $\mathcal{D}(\overline{\mu}, \overline{\nu})$ equals $\|x - y\|_D$ [8,15]. Thus, it is reasonable to call $\|.\|_D$ a discrepancy norm in $\mathbb{R}^n$.

Obviously, the computation of $\|.\|_D$ by strictly using the definition requires $\mathcal{O}(n^2)$ operations. The following theorem allows us to compute $\|.\|_D$ with linear speed:

Theorem 1. *For all $x \in \mathbb{R}^n$ we have*

$$\|x\|_D = \max_{0 \leq \beta \leq n} X_\beta - \min_{0 \leq \alpha \leq n} X_\alpha,$$

where the values $X_j = \sum_{i=1}^{j} x_i$ denote the partial sums (with the additional setting $X_0 = 0$).

Proof. If we assign 0 to x_0 and x_{n+1} we obtain

$$\begin{aligned}
\|x\|_D &= \max_{1 \leq \alpha \leq \beta \leq n+1} \left| \sum_{i=\alpha}^{\beta} x_i \right| = \max_{1 \leq \beta \leq n+1} \max_{1 \leq \alpha \leq n+1} \left| \sum_{i=1}^{\beta} x_i - \sum_{i=1}^{\alpha-1} x_i \right| \\
&= \max_{1 \leq \beta \leq n} \max_{1 \leq \alpha \leq n} \left| \sum_{i=1}^{\beta} x_i - \sum_{i=1}^{\alpha} x_i \right| = \max_{1 \leq \beta \leq n} \max_{1 \leq \alpha \leq n} \left| X_\beta - X_\alpha \right| \\
&= \max_{1 \leq \beta \leq n} X_\beta - \min_{1 \leq \alpha \leq n} X_\alpha,
\end{aligned}$$

which completes the proof. □

The following theorem clarifies the relationship between the discrepancy norm and conventional l_p vector norms and, by this way, provides a motivation why the discrepancy norm can be useful for our classification problem.

Theorem 2. *For all $p \in [1, \infty)$ and for all $x \in \mathbb{R}^n$ we have*

$$n^{-\frac{1}{p}} \cdot \|x\|_p \leq \|x\|_D \leq n^{1-\frac{1}{p}} \cdot \|x\|_p, \tag{1}$$

where $\|x\|_p$ denotes the classical l_p-norm, i.e.,

$$\|x\|_p = \Big(\sum_{i=1}^{n} |x_i|^p \Big)^{\frac{1}{p}}.$$

In the case $p = \infty$, we obtain

$$\|x\|_\infty = \max_{1 \leq i \leq n} |x_i| \leq \|x\|_D \leq n \cdot \max_{1 \leq i \leq n} |x_i|. \tag{2}$$

Proof. Trivially,

$$\max_{1\leq i\leq n}|x_i| \leq \|x\|_D \leq \sum_{i=1}^{n}|x_i|.$$

Then the assertion follows from the relations

$$n^{-\frac{1}{p}} \cdot \|x\|_p \leq \|x\|_\infty,$$
$$n^{1-\frac{1}{p}} \cdot \|x\|_p \geq \|x\|_1,$$

which can be proved using the Hoelder inequality. □

For the vectors

$$x_1 = \big(1,-1,1,\dots,(-1)^{n-2},(-1)^{n-1}\big),$$
$$x_2 = \big(1,1,1,\dots,1\big),$$

we obtain the following:

$$\|x_1\|_p = n^{\frac{1}{p}} \qquad \|x_1\|_D = 1$$
$$\|x_2\|_p = n^{\frac{1}{p}} \qquad \|x_2\|_D = n$$

From these results, it can be seen easily that, for x_1 and x_2, in the inequalities (1) and (2), we indeed have equalities and that there is no monotonic relationship between the discrepancy norm and any l_p-norm with $p \in (1,\infty)$. Furthermore, it can be seen that the more entries with equal signs appear successively, the higher the discrepancy norm is. On the contrary, for sequences with alternating signs it is close to the supremum norm $\|.\|_\infty$. Therefore, $\|.\|_D$ can be used for judging the connectedness of the peaks with equal signs.

3 The Fuzzy System

For each pixel (i,j), we consider its nearest eight neighbors enumerated as defined in Table 1 which yields three vectors of gray values with 8 entries — one for each color extraction. If we denote the mean values of all three gray value curves as

$$\bar{r}(i,j) = \frac{1}{8}\cdot\sum_{k=1}^{8} u_r(l(k)),$$

$$\bar{g}(i,j) = \frac{1}{8}\cdot\sum_{k=1}^{8} u_g(l(k)),$$

$$\bar{b}(i,j) = \frac{1}{8}\cdot\sum_{k=1}^{8} u_b(l(k)),$$

the sums of quadratic deviations of the gray values can be computed as

$$v_r(i,j) = \sum_{k=1}^{8} (u_r(l(k)) - \bar{r}(i,j))^2,$$

$$v_g(i,j) = \sum_{k=1}^{8} (u_g(l(k)) - \bar{g}(i,j))^2,$$

$$v_b(i,j) = \sum_{k=1}^{8} (u_b(l(k)) - \bar{b}(i,j))^2.$$

Now we can take the sum of these three values as a measure for the size of the deviations in the neighborhood of the pixel:

$$v(i,j) = v_r(i,j) + v_g(i,j) + v_b(i,j)$$

On the other hand, the sum of the discrepancy norms of the vectors, where we subtract each entry by the mean value of all entries, can be used as a criterion whether the pixel is within or close to a visually significant edge:

$$\begin{aligned} e(i,j) =& \|u_r(l(.)) - (\bar{r},\dots,\bar{r})\|_D + \|u_g(l(.)) - (\bar{g},\dots,\bar{g})\|_D + \\ & \|u_b(l(.)) - (\bar{b},\dots,\bar{b})\|_D \end{aligned}$$

Of course, e itself can be used as an edge detector. Figure 4 shows how good it works compared with the commonly used Mexican Hat filter mask.

The fuzzy decision is then carried out for each pixel (i,j) independently: First of all, the characteristic values $v(i,j)$ and $e(i,j)$ are computed. These values are taken as the input of a small fuzzy system with two inputs and one output. Let us denote the linguistic variables on the input side with v and e. Since the position of the pixel is of no relevance for the decision in this specific application, indices can be omitted here. The input space of the variable v is covered by three fuzzy sets which are labeled "low", "med", and "high". Analogously, the input space of the variable e is covered by two fuzzy sets which are labeled "low" and "high". Experiments have shown that $[0,600]$ and $[0,200]$ are appropriate universes of discourse for v and e, respectively. For the decomposition of the input domains simple Ruspini partitions [11] consisting of trapezoidal fuzzy subsets were chosen, where a family of fuzzy subsets $(\mu_1,\dots,\mu_k)$ of a domain X is called *Ruspini partition* if and only if, for all $x \in X$, the equation

$$\sum_{i=1}^{k} \mu_i(x) = 1$$

holds. The typical shape of these partitions is shown in Fig. 5.

The output space is a set of linguistic labels, namely "Ho", "Ed", "Ha", and "Pi", which are, of course, just abbreviations of the names of the four

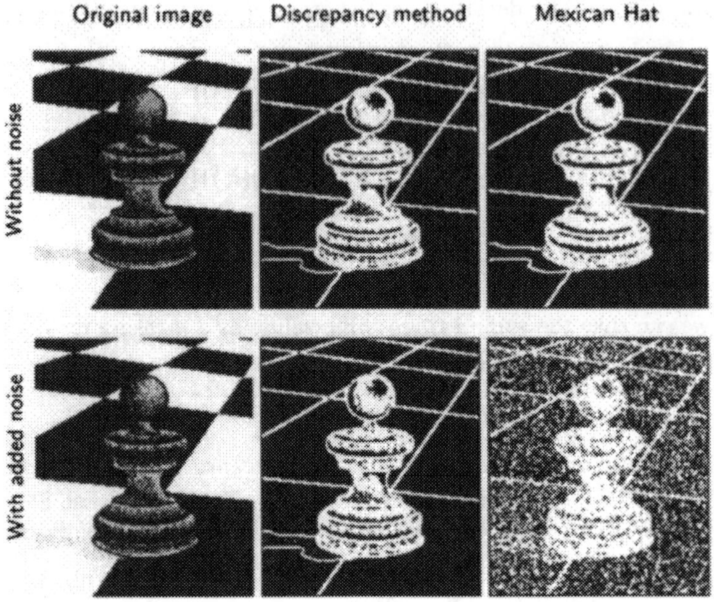

Fig. 4. Comparison between e and a standard 3×3 filter mask.

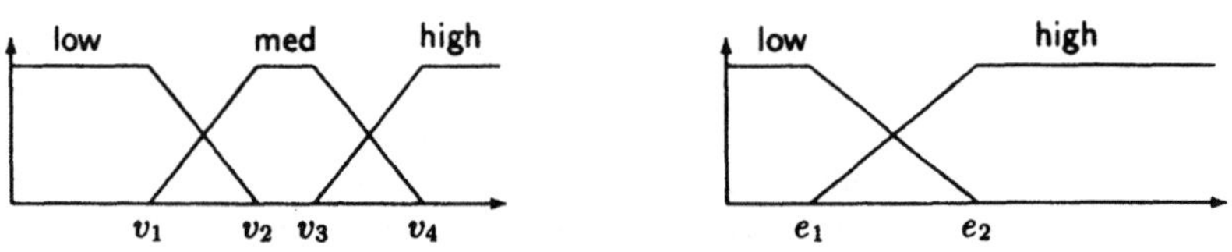

Fig. 5. The fuzzy variables v and e.

types. Let us denote the output variable itself with t. Finally, the output of the system for each pixel (i, j) is a fuzzy subset of {"Ho", "Ed", "Ha", "Pi"}. This output set is computed by processing the values $v(i, j)$ and $e(i, j)$ through a rule base with five rules, which cover all the possible combinations:

IF v is low	THEN t = Ho
IF v is med AND e is high	THEN t = Ed
IF v is high AND e is high	THEN t = Ed
IF v is med AND e is low	THEN t = Ha
IF v is high AND e is low	THEN t = Pi

In this application, ordinary Mamdani min/max-inference is used. Finally, the degree to which "Ho", "Ed", "Ha", or "Pi" belong to the output set can be regarded as the degree to which the particular pixel belongs to area Homogeneous, Edge, Halftone, or Picture, respectively.

In our application, the images are taken by an RGB video camera with a resolution of 720×576 pixels. We consider a clipping with approximately 250000 pixels. The A/D converter provides a resolution of 8 bit in each color channel (compare with Def. 1). For such an image, the classification takes at most two seconds on the hardware which had to be used (standard workstations with RISC CPUs, clock rates between 133MHz and 200MHz).

In this specific application, the raster dots and the pixels are of about equal size and the images are, due to expensive high-end camera equipment, remarkably sharp. If these conditions are not fulfilled, the performance of the algorithm in terms of the quality of the decision can be considerably weaker. The proposed methods are especially suited for the needs of this concrete application — the price to be paid for the applicability of the methods under such heavy time constraints is a certain loss of universality.

4 The Integration of the Classification System in the Inspection Procedure

The speed of the printing machine is approximately one print per second. The process can be stopped for at most four seconds. Our implementation takes the first four prints to compute a reference from them, then the machine is stopped for four cycles in order to have time for computing the classification and for doing the other preparatory work, where the purpose of the classification is twofold:

- It determines regions which can be interpreted with different criteria in the further printing process.
- The second purpose, which has not yet been mentioned at all, is that the classification of a pixel is used for computing a tolerance interval. Such a tolerance interval determines to which extent the gray values of a print image at a certain pixel may deviate from the reference image. If the difference between a gray value of the reference and the image, which should be checked, is bigger than the tolerance interval in at least one of the three colors, a pixel is marked as suspicious and has then to be looked at more carefully (by applying techniques which also take the classification into account).

For the first point, a fuzzy classification seems to be unnecessary. The reason why a fuzzy classification is used stems from the second point. The tolerance interval of a certain pixel $\sigma(i,j)$ is computed as the sum of predefined default intervals σ_{Ho}, σ_{Ed}, σ_{Ha}, and σ_{Pi} for the four types of areas weighted with the degree to which the pixel belongs to the respective area. Specifically,

$$\sigma(i,j) = \frac{\sum\limits_{X\in\{\text{Ho,Ed,Ha,Pi}\}} t_X(i,j)\cdot\sigma_X}{\sum\limits_{X\in\{\text{Ho,Ed,Ha,Pi}\}} t_X(i,j)} \tag{3}$$

which is, in some sense, a kind of Sugeno inference. Since Ruspini partitions are used for the decomposition of the input domains and since traditional Mamdani min/max inference is used for the evaluation of the rule base, the equation

$$\sum_{X\in\{\text{Ho,Ed,Ha,Pi}\}} t_X(i,j) = 1 \tag{4}$$

holds, and (3) simplifies to

$$\sigma(i,j) = \sum_{X\in\{\text{Ho,Ed,Ha,Pi}\}} t_X(i,j)\cdot\sigma_X.$$

Experiments have shown that, if crisp thresholds are used for the classification instead of the fuzzy transitions above, the quality of the decision can be unstable in transitional areas where at least one of the values $v(i,j)$ or $e(i,j)$ is close to a threshold value. Obviously, the tolerance intervals can flip abruptly in such areas. As a consequence, it can happen — in real printing, this is often the case — that pixels in transitional areas are either checked too tolerantly or too rigidly. In the fuzzy case, however, pixels in transitional areas are supplied with transitional tolerance intervals. From these considerations it might be clear that *the fuzzy model is indispensable.*

After computing the reference and its classification, the regular prints of the printing order are checked within the regular cycle time of one second mentioned above (see [1] for more details).

5 The Optimization of the Classification System

As apparent from Fig. 5, the behavior of the fuzzy system depends on six parameters, which determine the shape of the two fuzzy partitions. In the first step, these parameters were tuned manually. Of course, we have also taken into consideration the use of (semi)automatic methods for finding the optimal parameters.

The general problem is not to find an appropriate algorithm for doing that task, the difficulty is how to judge such a classification. Since the specification of the four types of areas is given in a vague, verbal form, no mathematical criterion is available for that. Hence, a model-based optimization process is, because of the lack of a model, not applicable. The alternative is a knowledge-based approach, which poses the question how to generate this knowledge — the examples from which the algorithm should learn.

Our optimization procedure consists of a painting program which offers tools, such as, a pencil, a rubber, a filling algorithm, and many more, which can be used to make a classification of a given representative image by hand. Then an optimization algorithm can be used to find that configuration of parameters which yields the maximal degree of matching between the desired result and the output actually obtained by the classification system.

Assume that we have N sample pixels for which the pairs of input values $(\tilde{v}_k, \tilde{e}_k)_{k\in\{1,\dots,N\}}$ are computed and that we already have a reference classification of these pixels

$$\tilde{t}(k) = (\tilde{t}_{\mathsf{Ho}}(k), \tilde{t}_{\mathsf{Ed}}(k), \tilde{t}_{\mathsf{Ha}}(k), \tilde{t}_{\mathsf{Pi}}(k)), \qquad k \in \{1,\dots,N\}.$$

Since, as soon as the values $\tilde{v}$ and $\tilde{e}$ are computed, the geometry of the image plays no role anymore, we can switch to one-dimensional indices here. Then one possibility to define the performance (fitness) of the fuzzy system would be

$$\frac{1}{N}\sum_{k=1}^{N} d(t(k), \tilde{t}(k)), \tag{5}$$

where

$$t(k) = (t_{\mathsf{Ho}}(k), t_{\mathsf{Ed}}(k), t_{\mathsf{Ha}}(k), t_{\mathsf{Pi}}(k))$$

are the classifications actually obtained by the fuzzy system for the input pairs $(\tilde{v}_k, \tilde{e}_k)$ with respect to the parameters v_1, v_2, v_3, v_4, e_1, and e_2; $d(.,.)$ is an arbitrary (pseudo-)metric on $[0,1]^4$. The problem of this brute force approach is that the output of the fuzzy system has to be evaluated for each pair (v_k, e_k), even if many of these values are similar or even equal. In order to keep the amount of computation low, we "simplified" the procedure by a "clustering process" as follows:

1. Choose a partition $(P_1,\dots,P_K)$ of the input space and count the number $(n_1,\dots,n_K)$ of sample points $\{p^i_1,\dots,p^i_{n_i}\}$ each part contains.
2. Then the desired classification of a certain part (cluster) can be defined as

   $$\tilde{t}_X(P_i) = \frac{1}{n_i}\sum_{j=1}^{n_i} \tilde{t}_X(p^i_j),$$

   where $X \in \{\mathsf{Ho}, \mathsf{Ed}, \mathsf{Ha}, \mathsf{Pi}\}$. Due to Eq. (4), we can conclude that, for all $i \in \{1,\dots,K\}$,

   $$\sum_{X\in\{\mathsf{Ho},\mathsf{Ed},\mathsf{Ha},\mathsf{Pi}\}} \tilde{t}_X(P_i) = 1. \tag{6}$$

3. If ϕ is a function which maps each cluster to a representative value (e.g., its center of gravity), we can define the fitness (objective) function as

$$f(v_1, \ldots, v_4, e_1, e_2) = \frac{100}{N} \sum_{i=1}^{K} n_i \cdot \left(1 - \frac{1}{2} \cdot d_i\right), \qquad (7)$$

with

$$d_i = \sum_{X \in \{\text{Ho,Ed,Ha,Pi}\}} \left(\tilde{t}_X(P_i) - t_X(\phi(P_i))\right)^2.$$

Note that, since Eqs. (4) and (6) hold, the value d_i always lies between 0 and 2.

If the number of parts is chosen moderately (e.g. a rectangular 64×32 net which yields $K = 2048$) the evaluation of the fitness function takes considerably less time than a direct application of Eq. (5).

In Eq. (7), the fitness is already transformed such that it can be regarded as a degree of matching between the desired and the actually obtained classification measured in percent. This value is always positive and has to be maximized.

Figure 6 shows cross sections of such a fitness function, where, in each case, five parameters are kept constant and only one is varied. From this figure it seems obvious that f is continuous but not necessarily differentiable — a fact which can proved easily — and that there can be a lot of local maxima. As a consequence, all conventional continuous optimization methods, which make fundamental use of derivatives, such as, gradient descent, Newton or Quasi-Newton methods, cannot be applied. So, it was near at hand to use a probabilistic optimization method. This, first of all, requires a (binary) coding of the parameters. We decided to use a coding which maps the parameters v_1, v_2, v_3, v_4, e_1, and e_2 to a string of six 8-bit integers $s_1, \ldots, s_6$ which range from 0 to 255. The following table shows how the encoding and decoding is done:

$$\begin{array}{ll}
s_1 = v_1 & v_1 = s_1 \\
s_2 = v_2 - v_1 & v_2 = s_1 + s_2 \\
s_3 = v_3 - v_2 & v_3 = s_1 + s_2 + s_3 \\
s_4 = v_4 - v_3 & v_4 = s_1 + s_2 + s_3 + s_4 \\
s_5 = e_1 & e_1 = s_5 \\
s_6 = e_2 - e_1 & e_2 = s_5 + s_6
\end{array}$$

If fuzzy sets of a more general shape are used, this coding is not applicable. Codings for such cases can be found for instance in [12] or [14].

A class of probabilistic optimization methods which has come into fashion in the last years are genetic algorithms (GAs). They can be regarded as simplified simulations of an evolution process, based on the principles of genetic

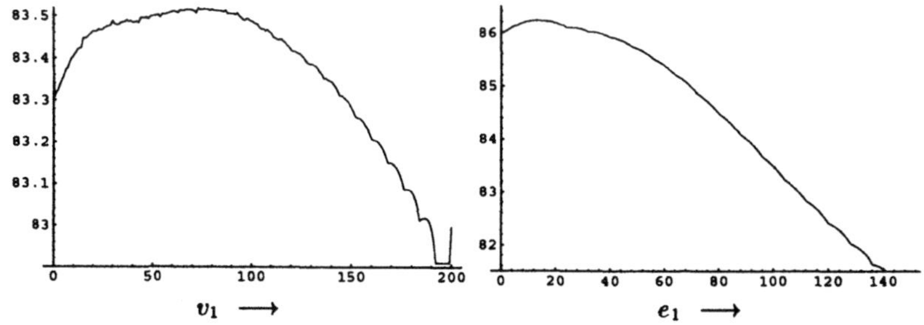

Fig. 6. Cross sections of functions of type (7).

reproduction employing mechanisms, such as, selection, mutation, and sexual reproduction. Another important difference between GAs and conventional optimization algorithms is that GAs do not operate on single points but on whole populations of points (which are, in this case, binary strings).

We first tried a standard GA [5,6] with proportional (standard roulette wheel) selection, one-point crossing over with uniform selection of the crossing point, bitwise mutation, and full replacement of the parent generation by its offsprings. The size of the population m was constant, the length of the strings was 48 (compare with the coding above, see [4] or [5] for an overview of more sophisticated variants of GAs). The following algorithm shows schematically how such a procedure works.

Algorithm 1.

$t := 0$;
Compute initial population $\mathcal{B}_0 = (b_{1,0}, \ldots, b_{m,0})$;

WHILE *stopping condition not fulfilled* **DO**
BEGIN
  FOR $i := 1$ **TO** m **DO**
    select an individual $b_{i,t+1}$ *from* $\mathcal{B}_t$;

  FOR $i := 1$ **TO** $m - 1$ **STEP** *2* **DO**
    IF Random[0, 1] $\leq p_C$ **THEN**
      cross $b_{i,t+1}$ *with* $b_{i+1,t+1}$;

  FOR $i := 1$ **TO** m **DO**
    eventually mutate $b_{i,t+1}$;

  $t := t + 1$
END

As apparent from Alg. 1, crossing over is only done with a probability p_C. Figure 7 shows graphically how standard one-point crossing over works. In the mutation step each bit is negated with a fixed, yet small, probability p_M.

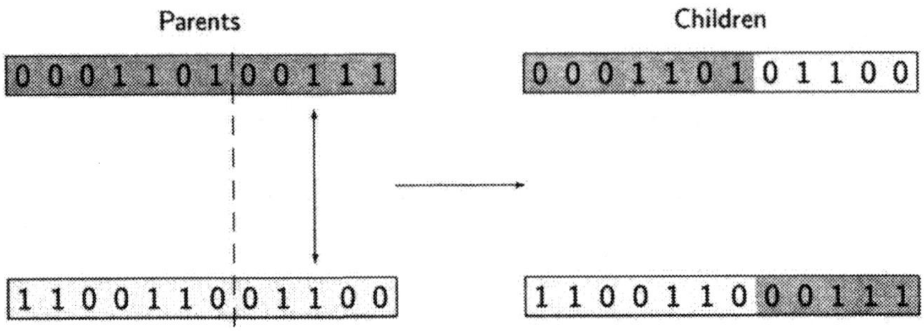

Fig. 7. One-point crossing over of binary strings.

Roulette wheel selection, more specifically, selects an individual with a probability proportional to its normalized fitness (i.e., the sum of fitness values of all individuals is scaled such that their sum is 1). This type of selection is, of course, only applicable if all fitness values are greater than zero, which is guaranteed in this application.

Algorithm 2.

$x := \mathsf{Random}[0,1]$;
$i := 1$

WHILE $i < m$ & $x < \sum_{j=1}^{i} f(b_{j,t}) / \sum_{j=1}^{m} f(b_{j,t})$ **DO**
  $i := i + 1$;

select $b_{i,t}$;

In order to compare the performance of the GAs with other well-known probabilistic optimization methods, we additionally considered the following methods:

Hill climbing: always moves to the best-fitted neighbor of the current string until a local maximum is reached; the initial string is generated randomly.

Simulated annealing: powerful, often used probabilistic method which is based on the imitation of the solidification of a crystal under slowly decreasing temperature (see [7,9] for a detailed description)

Each one of these methods requires only a few binary operations in each step. Most of the time is consumed by the evaluation of the fitness function. So, it is near at hand to take the number of evaluations as a measure for the speed of the algorithms.

Results

All these algorithms are probabilistic methods, therefore their results are not well-determined, they can differ randomly within certain boundaries. In order to get more information about their average behavior, we tried each one of them 20 times for one certain problem. For the given problem we found out that the maximal degree of matching between the reference classification and the classification actually obtained by the fuzzy system was 94.3776% . Table 2 shows the results in more detail, where $f_{\max}$ is the fitness of the best and $f_{\min}$ is the fitness of the worst solution; $\bar{f}$ denotes the average fitness of the 20 solutions, σ_f denotes the standard deviation of the fitness values of the 20 solutions, and # stands for the average number of evaluations of the fitness function which was necessary until the stopping criterion (i.e. that a local maximum is reached in case of hill climbing or that no further improvement can be observed for 100 iterations in case of simulated annealing or genetic algorithms) was fulfilled.

The hill climbing method with a random selection of the initial string converged rather quickly. Unfortunately, it was always trapped in a local maximum, but never reached the global solution (at least in these 20 trials).

The simulated annealing algorithm showed similar behavior at the very beginning. After tuning the parameters involved, the performance improved remarkably.

The raw genetic algorithm was implemented with a population size of 20; p_C was set to 0.15, p_M was 0.005. It behaved pretty well from the beginning, but it seemed inferior to the improved simulated annealing.

Next, we tried a hybrid GA, where we kept the genetic operations and parameters of the raw GA, but every 50th generation the best-fitted individual was taken as initial string for a hill climbing method. Although the performance increased slightly, the hybrid method still seemed to be worse than the improved simulated annealing algorithm. The reason, that the effects of this modification were not so dramatic, might be that the probability is rather high that the best individual is already a local maximum. So we modified the procedure again. This time, a ***randomly chosen individual*** of every 25th generation was used as initial solution of the hill climbing method. The result exceeded the expectations by far. The algorithm was, in all cases, nearer to the global solution than the improved simulated annealing was (compare with Table 2), but, surprisingly, sufficed with less invocations of the fitness function.

	$f_{\max}$	$f_{\min}$	$\bar{f}$	σ_f	#
Hill Climbing	94.3659	89.6629	93.5536	1.106	862
Simulated Annealing	94.3648	89.6625	93.5639	1.390	1510
Improved Simulated Annealing	94.3773	93.7056	94.2697	0.229	21968
GA	94.3760	93.5927	94.2485	0.218	9910
Hybrid GA (elite)	94.3760	93.6299	94.2775	0.207	7460
Hybrid GA (random)	94.3776	94.3362	94.3693	0.009	18631

Table 2. Some results

Figure 8 shows a graphical visualization of the results. Each line in this graph corresponds to one algorithm. The curve shows, for a given fitness value x, how many of the 20 different solutions had a fitness higher or equal to x. It can be seen easily from this graph that the hybrid GA with random selection led to the best results. Note that the x-axis is not a linear scale in this figure. It was transformed in order to make small differences visible.

6 Conclusion

In the first part of this paper, we demonstrated the synergy which lies in the combination of fuzzy systems with, more or less, conventional methods. This combination is in particular suitable for designing specific algorithms for time-critical problems. This specifity, however, often results in a loss of universality.

In the second part, we showed the suitability of genetic algorithms for finding the optimal parameters of a fuzzy system, especially if the analytical properties of the objective function are bad. Moreover, hybridization has been discovered as an enormous potential for improvements of genetic algorithms.

Acknowledgement

Ulrich Bodenhofer is working in the framework of the *Kplus Competence Center Program* which is funded by the Austrian Government, the Provincial Government of Upper Austria, and the Chamber of Commerce of Upper Austria.

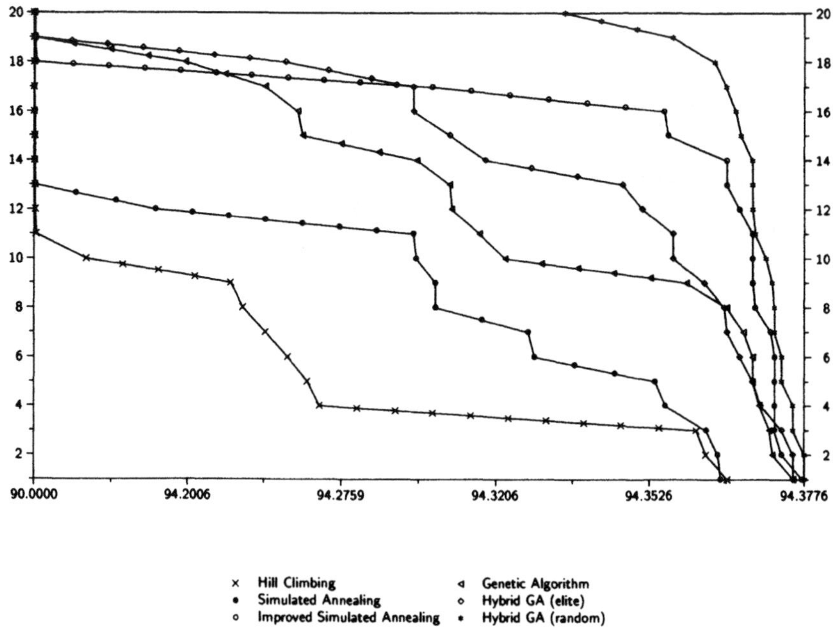

Fig. 8. A graphical representation of the results.

References

1. P. Bauer, U. Bodenhofer, and E. P. Klement. A fuzzy method for pixel classification and its application to print inspection. In *Proc. IPMU'96*, volume 3, pages 1301–1305, 1996.
2. J. C. Bezdek and S. K. Pal, editors. *Fuzzy Models for Pattern Recognition*. IEEE Press, New York, 1992.
3. I. Daubechies. Orthonormal bases of wavelets with finite support-connection with discrete filters. In J. M. Combes, A. Grossmann, and P. Tchamitchian, editors, *Wavelets*. Springer, Berlin, 1989.
4. A. Geyer-Schulz. *Fuzzy Rule-Based Expert Systems and Genetic Machine Learning*, volume 3 of *Studies in Fuzziness*. Physica Verlag, Heidelberg, 1995.
5. D. E. Goldberg. *Genetic Algorithms in Search, Optimization, and Machine Learning*. Addison-Wesley, Reading, MA, 1989.
6. J. H. Holland. *Adaptation in Natural and Artificial Systems*. The MIT Press, Cambridge, MA, first MIT Press edition, 1992. First edition: University of Michigan Press, 1975.
7. P. J. M. van Laarhoven and E. H. L. Aarts. *Simulated Annealing: Theory and Applications*. Kluwer Academic Publishers, Dordrecht, 1987.
8. H. Neunzert and B. Wetton. Pattern recognition using measure space metrics. Technical Report 28, Universität Kaiserslautern, Fachbereich Mathematik, November 1987.

9. R. H. J. M. Otten and L. P. P. P. van Ginneken. *The Annealing Algorithm.* Kluwer Academic Publishers, Boston, 1989.
10. A. Rosenfeld and A. C. Kak. *Digital Picture Processing*, volume II. Academic Press, San Diego, CA, second edition, 1982.
11. E. H. Ruspini. A new approach to clustering. *Inf. Control*, 15:22–32, 1969.
12. K. Shimojima, T. Fukuda, and Y. Hasegawa. Self-tuning fuzzy modeling with adaptive membership function, rules, and hierarchical structure based on genetic algorithm. *Fuzzy Sets and Systems*, 71(3):295–309, 1995.
13. H. G. Stark. Multiscale analysis, wavelets, and texture quality. Technical Report 41, Universität Kaiserslautern, Fachbereich Mathematik, January 1990.
14. H. Takagi and M. Lee. Neural networks and genetic algorithms to auto design of fuzzy systems. In E. P. Klement and W. Slany, editors, *Lecture Notes in Artificial Intelligence*, volume 695, pages 68–79. Springer, Berlin, 1993.
15. H. Weyl. Über die Gleichverteilung von Zahlen mod. Eins. *Math. Ann.*, 77:313–352, 1916.

Graduality and Databases: Some Contributions of Fuzzy Sets

Patrick Bosc

IRISA/ENSSAT, Technopole Anticipa
22300 Lannion Cedex, France

Abstract. Current commercial database management systems (DBMSs) are based solely on Boolean conditions which are used both for data retrieval and the expression of properties (or constraints). Possible contributions of fuzzy set theory are examined along these two lines. From a retrieval point of view, usual DBMSs do not allow for expressing preferences at the level of elementary conditions (over the acceptable values) and/or between the various conditions, and then to obtain discriminated answers. The concept of flexible (or gradual) query aims at compensating for this type of limitation. The characteristics of two query languages supporting flexible queries are presented. As to integrity constraints (ICs), one of the major roles of a DBMS is to guarantee that any visible state of the database agrees with the ICs that are declared. Among ICs are functional dependencies (FDs) which play a key role in capturing some forms of redundancy in the data. Regular FDs are extended by relaxing the strict equality, which enables to capture a new type of constraint interpreted as a gradual rule whose antecedent and consequent parts are fuzzy components.

Keywords. database management systems, relational databases, fuzzy-set theory, flexible queries, graded answers, integrity constraints, functional dependencies

1 Introduction

Database management systems (DBMSs) are components designed to store, retrieve, update and control large amounts of permanent data. Data retrieval (also called querying) and integrity constraints (i.e., properties that should be true at any observable time, especially when updates are performed) are two of the main aspects of DBMSs that might be concerned by fuzzy sets. As a consequence, this paper concentrates on these two points in the scope of relational DBMSs which are the most common database systems in use.

The querying component of a DBMS can benefit from fuzzy sets so as to relax the implicit hypothesis according to which queries are intended for the selection of elements fulfilling some more or less complex Boolean condition. This context may be very restrictive, especially if the user wants to express some preferences about elements to be selected, i.e., he does not consider only acceptable and unacceptable elements, but he wants to use a finer discrimination scale. Consider a person who uses a database system to find a "chinese" restaurant "close to" his residence with a "reasonable-priced" menu. The use of a regular DBMS imposes that the linguistic terms, "close to" and "reasonable-priced" are translated into Boolean (crisp) conditions, and then, the only possible discrimination is Boolean. On the contrary, the use of fuzzy sets to model the terms "close to" and "reasonable-priced" and more generally the fuzzification of queries will provide a natural way for expressing preferences over more or less acceptable values, and thus, getting graded answers.

The second point where fuzzy sets may contribute is data properties. In the context of databases, properties play an important role as integrity constraints (ICs) and one of the roles of a DBMS is to guarantee that any visible state of the database agrees with the ICs that are declared. Among ICs are functional dependencies (FDs) which play a key role in capturing some forms of redundancy in the data. For instance, in a universe describing employees, the functional dependency between experience and job on the one hand, and salary on the other hand expresses that all employees with the same experience and job must have the same salary. It is of interest to investigate the extent to which such a property can be fuzzified into "the closer the experiences and jobs, the closer the salaries". This example is often mentioned in the literature related to the area of the so-called fuzzy functional dependencies. At that point, it is worth mentioning that, as far as such statements play a role of constraint, they must return a Boolean truth value. We will see that such extended FDs can be modelled as gradual rules whose antecedent and consequent parts involve fuzzy components.

The remainder of this paper focuses on flexible queries on the one hand and an extension of functional dependencies on the other hand. In section 2, flexible querying is addressed and the extension of the usual relational query languages (algebra and SQL) is devised. The expressiveness of the fuzzy set framework is situated with respect to other approaches (e.g., distances). Section 3 is devoted to a specific type of integrity constraint that is based on an extension of a functional dependency where the usual equality is replaced by a (fuzzy) resemblance relation. The use and interest of such constraints is discussed, in particular with respect to the issue of redundancy.

2 Fuzzy Sets for Expressing Gradual Queries

In this section, the notion of a gradual query is introduced and its modeling thanks to fuzzy sets. Then, extensions of relational query languages are outlined.

2.1 Fuzzy (Gradual) Queries

Let us come back to the previous example of a person who wants to find a "chinese" restaurant, "close to" his residence, with a "reasonable-priced" menu. With a regular DBMS, two attitudes can be envisaged:

- to choose an "ideal-values" meaning ("chinese", ≤ 1 km, between 100 and 150 FF) with the risk of getting an empty answer,

- to give them only the meaning of "somewhat acceptable" values ("chinese" or "vietnamese" or "japanese", < 4 km, between 80 and 250 FF) and, in some cases, a huge number of answers may then be delivered.

In both cases, it is worth noticing that all the items delivered by the DBMS are "equivalent" in the sense that they comply with the required condition and the user is responsible for rank-ordering them if he wants a finer result. These drawbacks can be prevented (at least partly) if fuzzy conditions are used instead of Boolean ones, since by their very nature, such conditions return answers where each element is associated with a grade of satisfaction. In the introductory example, one may imagine that the fuzzy condition is: food-type = "chinese" **and** distance = "small" **and** price = "reasonable" where the fuzzy predicates are defined as follows:

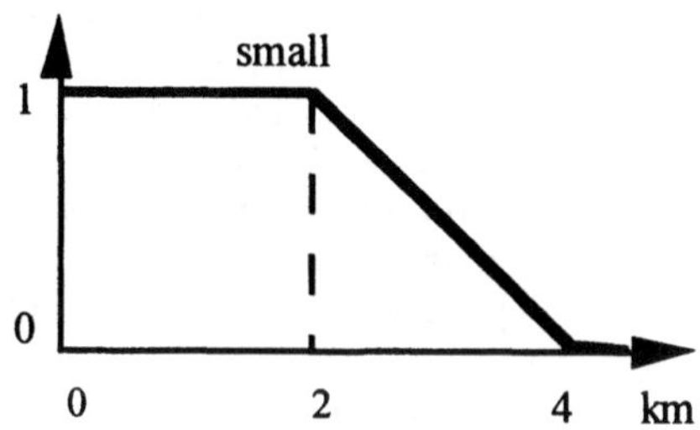

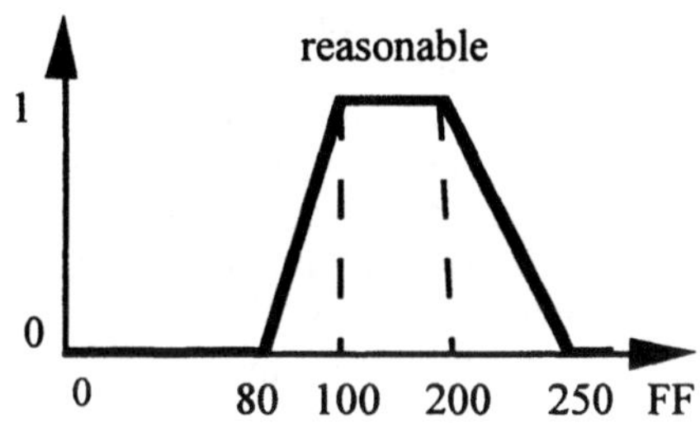

$\mu_{chinese}$(chinese) = 1, $\mu_{chinese}$(vietnamese) = .5, $\mu_{chinese}$(japanese) = .5.

More generally, a gradual condition is an expression involving base predicates, modified predicates, connectors and quantifiers. A base (or atomic) predicate is represented by a membership function over a set of domains. The predicates "young" and "around 40" correspond to adjectives and they illustrate the case where a single domain is used, whereas the fuzzy predicate "salary much greater than commission" is defined over a pair of domains.

Modified predicates appear by the adjunction of an adverb (e.g., very, relatively, fairly) intended for altering the initial meaning of the fuzzy predicate. Such a term is interpreted in a compositional way by a transformation of the membership function attached to the initial predicate. The following definitions are two examples:

- $\mu_{mod\,P}(x) = \mu_{p^n}(x) = (\mu_P(x))^n$ where n is greater (resp. smaller) than 1 if a strengthening (resp. weakening) is desired [Zade 72]; for instance, the modified predicate "extremely P" can be defined with n = 4 as: $\mu_{extremely\,P}(x) = (\mu_P(x))^4$,
- $\mu_{mod\,P}(x) = \mu_{p^n}(x) = (P\ \theta\ \ldots\ \theta\ P)(x)$ where θ is a non idempotent norm (resp. co-norm) for a strengthening (resp. weakening) and applies n times [Lako 73]; if n = 4 is still associated with "extremely" and $\theta(x, y) = \max(x + y - 1, 0)$, we will have: $\mu_{extremely\,P}(x) = \max(4 * \mu_P(x) - 3,\ 0)$.

A wide range of connectors can also be used to build compound fuzzy predicates. Fuzzy set theory offers a panoply of aggregation attitudes richer than the Boolean framework, including a variety of conjunctions and disjunctions, but also trade-off operations. As usual, the use of "min" (resp. "max") means that the grading of the least (resp. most) satisfied property will reflect the global level of satisfaction. This behavior can be modified considering that some elementary conditions are less important than others, which leads to weighted conjunctions and disjunctions [Dubo 86, Sanc 89]. Obviously, conjunction and disjunction operations, other than min and max, can be used. There also exist many trade-off operations between min and max (e.g., the arithmetic mean) which can model compensatory "and" for instance (a low degree of satisfaction for one elementary condition can be somewhat balanced by a high degree of satisfaction for another condition). An overview of fuzzy set aggregation connectives can be found in [Yage 91].

The last construct presented here concerns the use of linguistic quantifiers which allow for expressing quantified statements which are able to aggregate predicates in different ways. Linguistic quantifiers [Zade 83] model linguistic expressions such as **most of**, **around 3**, ... and express intermediate attitudes between the negation (**none**) and the generalized conjunction (**all**). Absolute quantifiers refer to an absolute number such as **about 3**, **at least 2**, ... while relative quantifiers refer to a proportion such as **about the half**, **at least a quarter**. The representation of an absolute quantifier is a fuzzy subset of the natural numbers and a relative quantifier is defined by a fuzzy subset of the unit interval [0, 1]. They can be used in the scope of predicates of the form "Q predicates among $\{P_1, \dots, P_n\}$ are fulfilled" as suggested initially in [Kacp 86], as well as for the selection of sets of tuples with statements of the form "Q Xs are A" (as illustrated in subsections 2.3.2 and 2.3.3).

Three main interpretations of such statements have been proposed. The first interpretation [Zade 83] is based on the cardinality of the (fuzzy) set $P_1(x), \dots, P_n(x)$ with respect to the quantifier Q and the truth value is then:

$$\mu_Q(\sum_{i=1}^{n} \mu_{P_i}(x)).$$

Since this approach has some shortcomings, alternate solutions founded on a relaxation mechanism have been suggested. The idea is to neglect (more or less) the less satisfactory elements (their "number" depending on Q) and then to assess the extent to which the remaining elements are satisfactory. In case of increasing quantifiers, R. Yager proposes two types of aggregation for the interpretation of "Q X are A". With an ordered weighted average (OWA) as it is defined in [Yage 88] one gets:

$$\sum_{i=1}^{n} (w_i * \mu_{P_i}(x))$$

where $\mu_{P_1}(x) \geq \dots \geq \mu_{P_n}(x)$ and $w_i = \mu_Q(i) - \mu_Q(i - 1)$ (resp. $\mu_Q(i/n) - \mu_Q((i - 1)/n)$) if Q is an absolute (resp. relative) quantifier. The weight w_i represents the increase of satisfaction when one moves from (i - 1) to i (resp. a proportion of (i - 1)/n to i/n) satisfactory elements. Using the competitive aggregation [Yage 84], the degree of satisfaction is obtained by:

$$\min_{1 \le i \le n} \max (1 - w_i, \mu_{P_i}(x))$$

where $w_i = 1 - \mu_Q(i-1)$ (resp. $1 - \mu_Q((i - 1)/n)$) is the importance given to the ith largest element when Q is an absolute (resp. relative) quantifier. It is worth mentioning that this approach can be extended to decreasing quantifiers (see [Bosc 93a], [Yage 93] for details).

2.2 Extending the Relational Algebra

The relational algebra provides a formal framework to manipulate relations so as to get answers to Boolean queries. Any operation takes one or two relations as input parameters and delivers a relation. The idea of the extension proposed here is to move from relations to gradual (or fuzzy) relations and to define the previous operators with such arguments.

2.2.1 Fuzzy Relations

A gradual (or fuzzy) relation R is made of weighted tuples, the weight associated to a tuple r ($\mu_R(r) \in [0, 1]$) indicating the extent to which r belongs to the fuzzy set represented by relation R. Such a relation R is formally defined as a fuzzy subset of the Cartesian product of ordinary domains $D_1, \ldots, D_n$. A usual relation is a particular case such that, for each r, $\mu_R(r)$ is equal to 1. Later, the fuzzy relations considered will be issued from usual relations by means of fuzzy predicates.

Example. Let us consider a database involving the usual relation EMP defined over the attributes {num, name, salary, age} and its extension:

EMP

num	name	salary	age
17	dupont	12000	38
76	martin	14500	40
26	durant	12000	37
12	dubois	12500	39

If the predicate "well-paid" whose characteristic function is given hereafter:

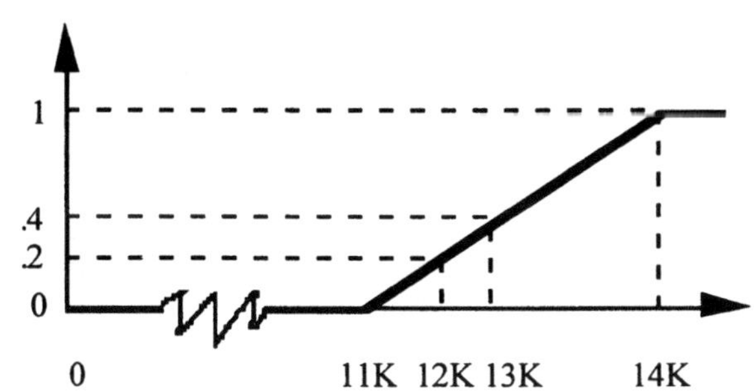

is applied on EMP, one obtains the relation WP-EMP:

WP-EMP

num	name	salary	age	degree
17	dupont	12000	38	.2
76	martin	14500	40	1
26	durant	12000	37	.2
12	dubois	12500	39	.3

describing "well-paid" employees♦

2.2.2 Set-Oriented Operators

Since relations derive from sets, the relational algebra involves set operators. Union, intersection and difference are defined according to the formulas used for fuzzy sets. If R and S represent two fuzzy relations defined over the same set of attributes X, one has:

- intersection: $\forall t,\ \mu_{R \cap S}(t) = T(\mu_R(t), \mu_S(t))$ where T is a triangular norm (min will be generally assumed later),
- union: $\forall t,\ \mu_{R \cup S}(t) = \perp(\mu_R(t), \mu_S(t))$ where $\perp$ is a triangular co-norm (max will be generally assumed later),
- difference: $\forall t,\ \mu_{R-S}(t) = \mu_{R \cap \overline{S}}(t) = T(\mu_R(t), 1 - \mu_S(t))$.

Moreover, if R is defined over the set of attributes X and S over Y, the Cartesian product of R and S is:

$$\forall r \in R, s \in S,\ \mu_{R \times S}(rs) = T(\mu_R(r), \mu_S(s)).$$

2.2.3 Relational Operators

On the other hand, relational operators take advantage of the structure of a relation in terms of attributes. Selection and projection are the two basic ones. The first one selects those tuples with a given property, whereas the second allows for retaining some of the initial attributes. In the context of our extension, they are defined in the following way:

- selection: $\forall r \in R,\ \mu_{R:\varphi}(r) = T(\mu_R(r), \mu_\varphi(r))$ where φ is a fuzzy predicate,
- projection: $\mu_{R[Y]}(y) = \perp_{r \mid r \in R \text{ and } r.Y = y}\mu_R(r)$ where Y is a subset of attributes of R (X).

In practice, there is a need for another operator, namely the join, which allows for establishing a connection between two relations on the basis of the satisfaction of a predicate linking a set of attributes A of R and a set of attributes B of S. Join is extended to fuzzy relations with a comparison predicate which may be a fuzzy one (i.e., θ may be a fuzzy comparison operator such as "much greater than") and its semantics stems from :

$$R[A\ \theta\ B]S = (R \times S) : (A\ \theta\ B).$$

Example. Let us consider the relations EMP(num, e-name, salary, age, dep) and DEP(dep, d-name, budget). The query aiming at retrieving the name of the high-budget departments where at least one old employee having a low salary works, can be expressed as:

(((DEP : budget = "high") [dep] $\cap$ (EMP : age = "old" and salary = "low") [dep]) [dep =dep] DEP) [d-name]

Using "min" for the conjunction and the following extension of EMP where the grade of membership of the predicates "old" (age) and "low" (salary) appear inside parentheses:

EMP	num	e-name	salary	age	dep
	47	dupont	12500 (1)	45 (0)	23
	76	martin	14500 (.1)	52 (.6)	23
	26	durant	13000 (.6)	57 (1)	23
	12	dubois	12500 (1)	50 (.5)	17

the intermediate relation resulting from the selection on age and salary is:

EMP	num	e-name	salary	age	dep	grade
	47	dupont	12500 (1)	45 (0)	23	0
	76	martin	14500 (.1)	52 (.6)	23	.1
	26	durant	13000 (.6)	57 (1)	23	.6
	12	dubois	12500 (1)	50 (.5)	17	.5

Similarly, a relation will be issued from the relation DEP:

DEP	dep	d-name	budget
	17	toy	200 (1)
	23	shoe	150 (.2)

when the condition on the budget applies. The intersection of the projections of these two intermediate fuzzy relations (on dep) yields: <.5/17>, <.2/23> and the final result (after an equi-join with DEP) is the pair of tuples: <.5/toy>, <.2/shoe>
♦

2.2.4 The Division of Fuzzy Relations

A last operation of the relational algebra is known as the division of two relations R(A, X) by S(B, Y) whose definition is:

$$R\,[A \div B]\,S = \{x \mid \forall a,\ a \in S[B] \Rightarrow \langle a, x\rangle \in R\}.$$

In other words, one looks for those X-values which are connected in R with at least all B-values appearing in S. A typical example occurs with the relations ORDER(#s, #p, qty) and PRODUCT(#p, p-name, price) and the query: "find the suppliers (number) who supply all products over $15 in a quantity under 100" that can be easily answered by the division of ((ORDER : qty < 100)[#s, #p]) by (PRODUCT : price > 15). If one imagines that the query becomes fuzzy by changing the Boolean predicates into fuzzy ones (for instance, moderate instead of less than 100 and expensive instead of greater than 15), the relations to be divided are fuzzy and it becomes necessary to define an extension of the division.

As proposed in [Dubo 96] and [Bosc 97], a natural extension of this formulation leads to:

- consider R[X] as a way for getting a referential of X-values and accordingly, this component is extended by the support operation and not by the projection,
- replace the universal quantifier by a generalized conjunction (a norm such as min),
- choose a fuzzy implication (denoted $\rightarrow$ hereafter),

which yields:

$$\forall x \in \text{support}(R[X]),\ \mu_{R[A \div B]S}(x) = \min_S \mu_S(b) \rightarrow \mu_R(b, x)$$

The semantics of the extended division depends strongly on the type of interaction between grades conveyed by the chosen implication. Two interpretations can be distinguished depending on whether an S-grade specifies the importance of the corresponding B-value or acts as a threshold to be attained.

In the first case, the higher $\mu_S(b)$ the more the grade $\mu_R(b, x)$ should be taken into account and influence the result. Kleene-Dienes implication is appropriate to model this behavior according to the rule: "the more b belongs to S, the more important the fact that the tuple <b, x> belongs to R". If $\mu_S(b) = 0$, the result is 1 since the grade $\mu_R(b, x)$ is completely ignored and the tuple <b, x> can even be absent from R. On the contrary, if $\mu_S(b) = 1$, the result is $\mu_R(b, x)$ since the tuple <b, x> is fully considered. Intermediary values of $\mu_S(b)$ provide a guaranteed satisfaction level equal to $1 - \mu_S(b)$. In this context, it is necessary to be provided with a complete scale of importances over [0, 1], which imposes that at least one value b is assigned the importance 1 (in other words, S must be normalized, i.e., $\exists b_0$ such that $\mu_S(b_0) = 1$). Since relation S is issued by a fuzzy condition, the preceding condition is not guaranteed and if necessary, S-grades are divided by the largest one (this procedure has the advantage of preserving the notion of relative importance between initial grades).

In the second case, the degree of membership to the result of the division corresponds to the satisfaction of the rule: "the higher $\mu_S(b)$, the higher $\mu_R(b, x)$ should be". A value x is fully satisfactory as soon as the required threshold $\mu_S(b)$ is less than (or equal to) $\mu_R(b, x)$ for every B-value of S. Otherwise, some penalty p applies and for the concerned B-value, the (local) result is (1 - p). Rescher-Gaines, Gödel, Goguen and Lukasiewicz implications fit this type of behavior.

Example. Let us come back to the query used in the introduction addressed to the base relations PRODUCT(#p, p-name, price) and ORDERS(#s, #p, qty). The fuzzy predicates qty = "moderate" and price = "expensive", give birth to the intermediate (fuzzy) relations MEDQ-ORD(#s, #p) and EXP-PRD(#p) which are involved in the division. If we consider the extensions hereafter:

ORD

#s	#p	qty	$\mu_{mod.}$
s1	p1	15	1
s1	p2	23	.3
s1	p3	17	.9
s1	p4	10	.5
s2	p1	13	1
s2	p2	24	.2
s2	p3	15	1

PRD

#p	pr	μ_{high}
p1	20	.6
p2	18	.4
p3	30	1
p4	8	0
p5	10	0

the following results are obtained with the five implications mentioned before (the first column corresponds to the interpretation in terms of importance, whereas the last four columns refer to the interpretation in terms of thresholds):

	Kleene-D.	Gödel	Goguen	Lukasiewicz	Rescher-G.
s1	.6	.3	.75	.9	0
s2	.6	.2	.5	.8	0

These two interpretations make sense since the relation EXP-PRD is normalized ♦

If most of the properties of the operators are preserved when they apply to fuzzy relations, it is worth mentioning that the expression of the division in terms of other algebraic operators is more tricky than in the usual case (see [Bosc 98b] for details).

2.3 An Overview of SQLf

SQL being "the" standard database query language, an extension of this language has been defined in order to allow for the formulation of gradual queries, thus generalizing the approach initially suggested by V. Tahani [Taha 77]. The principle underlying the extension consists in introducing graduality wherever it is relevant to do so. Some key points of the SQLf language are given hereafter and a more detailed review of the language can be found in [Bosc 95].

2.3.1 The Base Block in SQLf

In SQLf, the structure of the base block remains fundamentally the same as in SQL. The "from" clause is the same. The differences concern:

- the "select" clause where the calibration of the result can be expressed by a number of desired responses (denoted n) or a qualitative threshold (denoted t), or both,
- the "where" clause where fuzzy conditions are permitted.

Then, the formulation of the base block is:

select [distinct] [n | t | n, t] <attributes> **from** <relations>
where <fuzzy condition>

In the "where" clause, one can find different types of elements constituting a gradual condition as mentioned in subsection 2.1.

As in the usual case, there is a strong connection between the base block and relational operators since the base block is interpreted as a restriction (fuzzy in this case) of the Cartesian product of the relations involved, followed by a projection onto the attributes mentioned, and then by the calibration of the result. In the presence of the keyword "**distinct**", in case of duplicates, only the element with the highest degree is kept. The query:

select distinct R.A, S.B **from** R, S **where** fc_R **and** fc_S **and** (R.C θ S.D)

where fc_R (resp. fc_S) denotes a (fuzzy) condition over relation R (resp. S) and A, C (resp. B, D) are attributes of R (resp. S) leads to a resulting relation Res made of pairs <a, b> with the grade:

$$\mu_{Res}(a, b) = \max_{r \in R \text{ and } r.A = a \text{ and } s \in S \text{ and } s.B = b} \min(\mu_{fc_R}(r), \mu_{fc_S}(s), \mu_\theta(r.C, s.D)).$$

Example. Let us consider the relations EMP(num, e-name, salary, age, dep) and DEP(nd, d-name, budget). The query aiming at retrieving the pairs <department name, employee's name> where the employee has a high salary and works in this "high-budget" department can be expressed by:

select distinct e-name, d-name **from** EMP, DEP
where salary = 'high' **and** budget = 'important' **and** dep = nd.

With the extensions:

EMP

num	e-name	salary	μ_{high}	age	dep
17	dupont	15000	1	38	23
76	martin	13500	.5	42	23
26	durant	13000	.4	37	23
12	dubois	12500	.1	39	17

DEP

nd	d-name	budget	$\mu_{important}$
17	A	200	1
23	B	180	.7

the result obtained is composed of 4 tuples: {.7/<B, dupont>, .5/<B, martin>, .4/<B, durant>, .1/<A, dubois>} ♦

2.3.2 Subqueries in SQLf

Some SQL predicates are built by means of nested blocks, also called subqueries. Here, we just touch on two of them and other nested predicates (extended in a similar way) are discussed in [Bosc 95]. Hence, the "**in**" (resp. "**not in**") operator which, in SQL, expresses the membership (resp. non membership) to a set, expresses the membership (resp. non membership) to a fuzzy set in SQLf. More precisely, if a is the A-value of the current tuple of the outer block and SR denotes the nested (inner) block, the truth value of the predicate "A **in** SR" is:

$$\mu_{\text{A in SR}}(a) = \max_{b \in \text{support(SR)} \textbf{ and } b = a} \mu_{SR}(b).$$

In a similar way, in SQLf the "**exists**" (resp. "**not exists**") nesting evaluates the extent to which the (fuzzy) relation returned by the nested block is not empty (resp. empty) and we get the truth value:

$$\mu_{\text{exists}}(SR) = \max_{x \in \text{support(SR)}} \mu_{SR}(x).$$

A generalized form of this predicate is obtained by the use of an absolute quantifier instead of "**exists**" which, indeed, stands for the existential quantifier. The truth value of such a predicate expresses the extent to which the cardinality of the result returned by the nested block is compatible with the considered quantifier. Here, one has a statement of the form "Q X are A" where Q is an absolute quantifier, X is the set of tuples of Cartesian product of the relations involved in the "from" clause of the subquery and A is the vague condition appearing in the "where" clause of this subquery. Its truth value can be obtained using the approaches described in 2.1 (cardinality, OWA or competitive aggregation).

Example. The query "find the employees having a salary much greater than that of at least 2 employees from department #47" is formulated:

select #emp **from** EMP E **where** at least 2
    (**select** * **from** EMP **where** dep = 47 **and** >> (E.salary, salary))♦

It is worth mentioning that the "**not in**" and "**not exists**" nestings are used to express intersection and set difference. On the contrary, the union which delivers a superset of each input relation requires a specific construct in SQLf (as in SQL) for expressing queries of the form: (**select** ...) **union** (**select** ...).

2.3.3 Relation Partitioning and its Major Uses

The clause "group by" of SQL allows for the partitioning of a given relation (which may be a base or an intermediate one) depending on a set of attributes whose value is the same inside a given subset. In the following schema, A the partitioning attribute is supposed to take 3 distinct values (x, w and u) and the relation is split into three subsets:

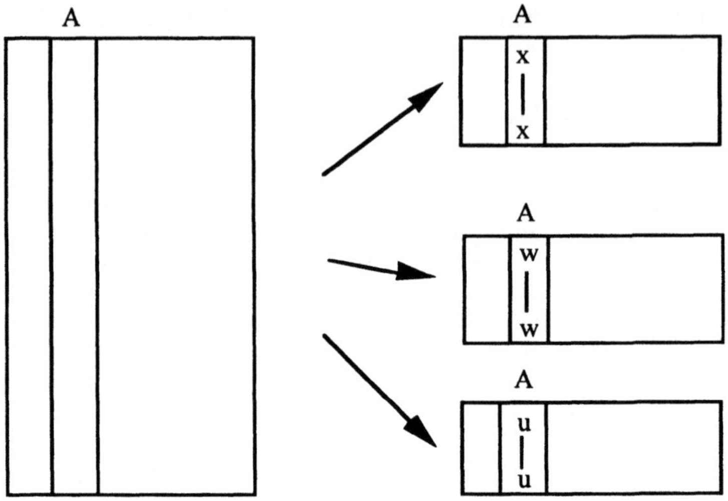

In this framework, it is then possible to select subsets and, in SQLf, two types of set-oriented conditions can be used:

- application of a fuzzy criterion to the result of an aggregate,
- use of quantified propositions.

Example. The query "find the (5 best) departments where the average of the salaries of the engineers is around $3000" can be written:

select 5 dep **from** EMP **where** job = "engineer"
group by #dep **having** avg (salary) ≈ 3000.

In this case, it is of special importance to notice that an aggregate function can apply only to a usual set, and then, the condition in the "where" clause can only be a Boolean one. If we now consider the query "retrieve the departments (number) where at least 2 employees are well-paid", it may be expressed:

select dep **from** EMP **group by** dep **having** at least 2 **are** salary = 'well-paid'

and the condition appearing in the "having" clause relies on a fuzzy quantified statement of the form "Q X's are A" where Q is the linguistic quantifier "at least", X represents the set of employees of a given department and A is the fuzzy predicate "well-paid". As it was mentioned earlier, such a statement has several interpretations (cf. 2.1)♦

SQL does not provide users with any feature allowing for a "direct" formulation of a division and it is then necessary to proceed to some transformations. This somewhat tricky process is still more difficult in SQLf for expressing the extended division presented in 2.2.4, since it would be necessary to use non commutative conjunctions and to introduce a new operation: the "support" (see [Bosc 98b] for details). That is why we suggest to use the partitioning mechanism which offers a more appropriate framework. The idea is to start from the division seen as an inclusion and then to write the division of the fuzzy relations R:fc_R by S:fc_S as:

select X **from** R **where** fc_R **group by** X
having set(A) **contains**$_i$ (**select** B **from** S **where** fc_S)

where "contains$_i$" stands for a gradual inclusion founded on the desired implication: Kleene-Dienes, Gödel, Goguen or Lukasiewicz. In so doing, all tuples of the fuzzy relation derived from R sharing a same X-value are gathered and the extent to which the corresponding set of A-values contains (according to the chosen implication) the set of B-values of the fuzzy relation stemming from S using fc_S, is computed.

Exemple. Let us consider the query: "retrieve the stores which ordered (at least) all expensive products in a moderate quantity" against the relations PRD(#p, pr) and ORD(#s, #p, qty). According to the previous SQLf pattern, it is written:

select #s **from** ORD **where** qty = 'moderate' **group by** #s
having set(#p) **contains**$_i$ (**selec #p from** PRD **where** pr = 'expensive').
With the extensions:

ORD

#s	#p	qty	$\mu_{mod.}$
s1	p1	15	1
s1	p2	23	.3
s1	p3	17	.9
s1	p4	10	.5
s2	p1	13	1
s2	p2	24	.2
s2	p3	15	1

PRD

#p	pr	$\mu_{exp.}$
p1	20	.6
p2	18	.4
p3	30	1
p4	8	0
p5	10	0

this query requires to compute the inclusion degree of {.6/p1, .4/p2, 1/p3} in {1/p1, .3/p2, .9/p3, .5/p4} (resp. {1/p1, .2/p2, 1/p3}) for s1 (resp. s2), which leads the same results as those given in the example at the end of subsection 2.2.4 ♦

2.4 Some Concluding Remarks on Gradual Queries

This section has shown that fuzzy sets provide a powerful sound framework for dealing with preferences which are the basis for the handling of graduality in user queries (i.e., gradual queries). A comparison with other approaches (e.g., distances) was carried out in [Bosc 92], which showed that the fuzzy set framework is general and may prevent some shortcomings appearing in these approaches which, indeed, are specific and offer a narrow range of preference mechanisms.

The regular relational algebra can be extended to fuzzy relations and most of the usual properties are maintained, in particular the compositionality principle. The most notable point concerns the division operator which can have two significantly different meanings depending on whether the grades attached to the divisor play a role of thresholds or importances. Moreover, from a primitivity point of view, these different meanings can only be reached by an algebraic expression involving other operators (as in the usual case), if a new one (the support) is introduced and various difference operations are available. Beyond these algebraic aspects, the extension of an SQL-like query language has been outlined, which would enable SQL programmers to write gradual queries in the same way as they write regular queries.

In fact, if the features of query languages and the bases are correctly mastered, a significant amount of work should be devoted to implementation of such systems, so as to pursue the works initiated in [Bosc 93b, Kacp 95, Bosc 98c]. This is clearly a key-point for the promotion of fuzzy querying and it is of prime importance to tackle performances and to assess the price to pay in terms of both software development and response time to make such systems come to maturity.

3 Fuzzy Sets and an Extended Functional Dependency

If fuzzy sets theory is useful for gradual queries, it may also be tempting to investigate whether they can enrich the range of properties (or constraints) that some data must fulfill. One interesting type of constraint in the database area is known as functional dependencies, which are strongly connected with redundancy and database schema design. One may think of different ways for introducing graduality in a functional dependency (FD) and one of them is described, where the idea is to relax the strict equality underlying FDs into a resemblance in order to model a new kind of property. The relationship between this new type of property (called here extended functional dependency, EFD), regular FDs and redundancy is discussed.

3.1 Some Reminders on Regular Functional Dependencies

Functional dependencies have been particularly studied in the 70s since they capture a type of property that appears frequently and that may generate redundancy in the database under design. The main idea is to remove data replication as far as possible at design time. This objective is motivated by the problems induced by redundancy when updates are performed. For example, when a value is updated, one must make sure that all the "copies" of this value are modified, otherwise the database might become inconsistent.

A functional dependency X $\rightarrow$ Y between the sets of attributes X and Y of a relation R expresses a constraint of the real world according to which one and only one value of Y is associated with each value of X (thus, there is a function between X and Y whose graph is given by the extension of R). It is clear that a functional dependency X $\rightarrow$ Y potentially carries some redundancy except in the case where the X-values are unique in R (X is then a key or a superkey). Depending on the functional dependencies which are valid, a relation R satisfies different normal forms. In the case where X is a key, the checking of this dependency does not necessitate any specific program (provided that the key is declared and the DBMS ensures the uniqueness of key values whenever database updates, i.e., insertion or modification of X and/or Y-value, are performed). This constitutes the major interest of the normalization theory from a practical point of view.

It has been shown that any universe can be modelled by:

- a set of relations in third normal form (in fact in EK normal form [Fagi 81]) without loss of dependencies (i.e., all the FDs are induced by the keys either directly or by transitivity),
- a set of relations in Boyce-Codd normal form (BCNF), but some dependencies can be lost.

This state of thing tells us that, in general, some FDs have to be checked by explicit (dedicated) programs. In practice, it is recommended to design a schema where each relation obeys 3NF.The transformation of a schema into another one is based on a decomposition theorem, stating that a relation R(X, Y, Z) where the functional dependency $X \rightarrow Y$ holds, can be replaced (in an equivalent way as far as data are concerned) by its two projections R[X, Y] and R[X, Z].

Example. Let us consider relation R(A, B, C) associated with the dependencies $A \rightarrow B$ and $\{B, C\} \rightarrow A$. This relation is 3NF since it owns two keys ({A, C}, {B, C}) and any attribute belongs to (at least) one key, but some redundancy can occur because of the dependency $A \rightarrow B$. If the schema R(A, B, C) is chosen, checking the validity of $A \rightarrow B$ requires a specific program (because A is not a key of R). The decomposition theorem allows to envisage the alternate schema R[A, B] and R[A, C], which satisfies Boyce-Codd normal form. However, in this case the dependency $\{B, C\} \rightarrow A$ is lost and its checking requires a specific program too♦

Functional dependencies have mainly been studied in the context of usual databases and in this section, the main objective is to point out one specific extension of functional dependencies having a clear semantics.

3.2 On the Relaxation of the Equality in Functional Dependencies

We do not discuss previous works on fuzzy functional dependencies, which, most often, have been carried out in the context of the so-called "fuzzy databases", i.e., where the database is pervaded with imprecision and/or uncertainty (the reader interested in this aspect can refer to [Bosc 98a] for a detailed review). The type of extension considered here relies on the relaxation of the strict equality underlying the definition of a usual FD into a resemblance. Intuitively, one wants to relax the constraint "employees having the same experience have the same salary" (FD: exp $\rightarrow$ sal) into a property like "employees having **similar** ages and experiences should have **similar** salaries", which semantics must be clearly explicited.

From the usual formula defining a functional dependency:

$$X \rightarrow Y \text{ holds on } R \Leftrightarrow \forall t1, t2 \in R, t1.X = t2.X \Rightarrow t1.Y = t2.Y,$$

relaxing the strict equality aims at imposing a constraint when the X-values are no longer equal, but "close" to each other. Thus, the constraint obtained is stronger when the choice made also leads to impose the equality on Y-values in case of equality on the X-values (functional relationship between X and Y). The idea is to define an extended FD X ~> Y according to:

$X \sim> Y$ holds over R $\Leftrightarrow \forall t1, t2 \in R,\ \mu_{\approx X}(t1.X, t2.X) \rightarrow_{R\text{-}G} \mu_{\approx Y}(t1.Y, t2.Y)$

where $\rightarrow_{R\text{-}G}$ denotes Rescher-Gaines implication ($a \rightarrow_{R\text{-}G} b = 1$ if $a \leq b$, 0 otherwise) and $\mu_{\approx D}$ denotes the truth value of a gradual resemblance function specific to the domain D, which is assumed to be reflexive and symmetric.

This view is similar to the definition suggested in [Raju 88] where imperfect data are taken into account. Moreover, this formula can be interpreted in a natural way as: the resemblance on Y is at least equal to the resemblance on X. It is based on a fuzzy rule of the type "the more ..., the more ..." which has a clear semantics [Dubo 92]. Variants could also be envisaged, in which the implication used conveys a semantics of a fuzzy rule, but has a non Boolean result (e.g., with Gödel, Goguen or Lukasiewicz fuzzy implications). Although interesting, this approach is not compatible with the idea of a constraint (which by its very nature is either true, or false) and it is not considered further.

The usual properties valid on FDs still hold on this type of EFD:

- reflexivity ($Y \subseteq X \Rightarrow X \sim> Y$),
- augmentation ($X \sim> Y \Rightarrow XZ \sim> YZ$),
- transitivity ($X \sim> Y$ and $Y \sim> Z \Rightarrow X \sim> Z$),
- union($X \sim> Y$ and $X \sim> Z \Rightarrow X \sim> YZ$),
- decomposition ($X \sim> YZ \Rightarrow X \sim> Y$ and $X \sim> Z$),
- pseudo-transitivity ($X \sim> Y$ and $YW \sim> Z \Rightarrow XW \sim> Z$).

In addition, if the strong reflexivity of the resemblance relation is assumed, i.e., $\mu_{\approx}(a, b) = 1 \Rightarrow a = b$, the validity of the EFD $X \sim> Y$ entails that of the regular FD $X \rightarrow Y$. Then, the usual decomposition theorem holds and a relation where the EFD $X \sim> Y$ holds, can be losslessly decomposed into its two projections R[X, Y] and R[X, Z].

Example. Let us consider the following extension:

EMPLOYEE

Name	Job	Experience	Salary
John	Engineer	6	4000
Jill	Engineer	6	4000
Peter	Technician	12	2000
Martin	Secretary	3	1500
Sue	Secretary	5	1200

If the resemblances on attributes Job, Experience and Salary are defined as:

$\mu_{\approx J}(j1, j2) = 1$ if $j1 = j2$, 0 otherwise; $\mu_{\approx S}(s1, s2) = 1/(1 + 1/300 * |s1 - s2|)$;
$\mu_{\approx E}(e1, e2) = 1 - |e1 - e2|/3)$ if $|e1 - e2| \leq 3$, 0 otherwise

the EFD {Job, Experience} ~> Salary is valid. In particular, the value of the implication for the last two tuples is:

$[\min(\mu_{\approx J}(\text{"Secretary"}, \text{"Secretary"}), \mu_{\approx E}(3, 5)) \rightarrow_{R\text{-}G} \mu_{\approx S}(1500, 1200)] =$
$[\min(1, 1/3) \Rightarrow_{R\text{-}G} 1/2] = 1.$

Because of the validity of the usual FD {Job, Experience} → Salary, one can use the schema EMP(Name, Job, Experience) and SAL(Job, Experience, Salary). The natural join between the extensions:

EMP

Name	Job	Experience
John	Engineer	6
Jill	Engineer	6
Peter	Technician	12
Martin	Secretary	3
Sue	Secretary	5

SAL

Job	Experience	Salary
Engineer	6	4000
Technician	12	2000
Secretary	3	1500
Secretary	5	1200

produces the initial extension♦

In fact, it appears that such an FD involves two parts, the regular FD which is concerned with redundancy and a constraint when X-values are somewhat resemblant which is not at all linked with redundancy. As a consequence, it turns out that update management loses the nice property of demanding no program when a tuple is inserted or theY-value associated with a given X is changed. It is clear that the aspect of an EFD tied to resemblance cannot be performed without programs and is far beyond the uniqueness of keys.

Example. Let us come back to the previous example and consider the insertion of the tuple t = <Bob, Engineer, 7, 4300> into the initial relation EMPLOYEE. The part of the EFD concerning the resemblances necessitates 5 comparisons to check if:

$$\forall t' \in R, [\min(\mu_{\approx J}(\text{"Engineer"}, t'.\text{Job}), \mu_{\approx E}(7, t'.\text{Exp})) \Rightarrow_{R\text{-}G} \mu_{\approx S}(4300, t'.\text{Sal})] = 1.$$

If with the schema resulting from the decomposition, the number of comparisons decreases (only 4 comparisons have to be performed), they cannot be eliminated. The same kind of comment could be made in case of the modification of the salary for 6 year experienced engineers♦

4 Conclusion

This paper has addressed two fairly distinct contributions of fuzzy sets to databases. The first one concerns queries and it has been shown that fuzzy sets provide a sound powerful framework for the expression of flexible queries, i.e., where preferences are introduced rather than purely acceptance/rejection mechanisms. This approach turns out to be more general than other techniques (e.g., distances). A general survey of the basic elements of an algebra extended to fuzzy relations has been given. This algebra is the partial basis of an SQL-like language allowing for flexible queries. It is important to notice that both languages concern usual databases, and the accounting for imperfect data is a completely orthogonal topic not directly related to fuzzy sets (except if possibility theory is used to model ill-known data). An important task is to prove that such systems can be implemented (and then marketed), which comprises experimental works to assess the performances of such systems with respect to those offered by presently commercial ones.

The second topic is connected with the extension of the notion of a functional dependency by the introduction of graduality thanks to the relaxation of the equality into a resemblance relation. The property obtained remains a constraint (i.e., it is either true or false) and its semantics is that of the fuzzy rule: "the more similar the X-values, the more similar the Y-values should be". It has been shown that a regular FD is encapsulated in this extended FD, which preserves some well-known results such as a decomposition theorem and establishes the actual connexion with redundancy. Moreover, update management can no longer get rid of explicit programs to check the validity of insertions of tuples and modification of Y-values. It turns out that such extended FDs are not appropriate for capturing redundancy (at least in the usual sense) and then are not really connected with database design. They can be viewed as constraints over the universe, i.e., statements whose truth value must be guaranteed by any extension.

References

[Bosc 92] Bosc P. and Pivert O., Some approaches for relational databases flexible querying, **Journal of Intelligent Information Systems**, 1, 323-354, 1992.

[Bosc 93a] Bosc P. and Liétard L., On the extension of the OWA operator to evaluate some quantifications, **Proc. 1st European Congress on Fuzzy and IntelligentTechnologies (EUFIT'93)**, Aachen (Germany), 332-338, 1993.

[Bosc 93b] Bosc P. and Pivert O., On the evaluation of simple fuzzy relational queries: principles and measures, *in* "**Fuzzy Logic - State of the Art**" (Lowen R., Roubens M., Eds.), 355-364, 1993, Kluwer Academic Publishers.

[Bosc 95] Bosc P. and Pivert O., SQLf: A relational database language for fuzzy querying, **IEEE Transactions on Fuzzy Systems**, 3, 1-17, 1995.

[Bosc 97] Bosc P., Dubois D., Pivert O. and Prade H., Flexible queries in relational databases - the example of the division operator, **Theoretical Computer Science**, 171, 281-302, 1997.

[Bosc 98a] Bosc P., Dubois D. and Prade H., Fuzzy functional dependencies and redundancy elimination, **Journal of the American Society for Information Science**, 49, 217-235, 1998.

[Bosc 98b] Bosc P., On the primitivity of the division of fuzzy relations, *to appear in* **Journal of Soft Computing**.

[Bosc 98c] Bosc P. and Pivert O., SQLf query functionality on top of a regular relational database management system, *to appear in* "**Knowledge Management in Fuzzy Databases**" (Pons O., Vila M.A., Kacprzyk J., Eds.), Physica Verlag.

[Dubo 86] Dubois D., Prade H., Weighted minimum and maximum operations in fuzzy set theory, **Information Sciences**, 39, 205-210, 1986.

[Dubo 92] Dubois D., Prade H., The semantics of fuzzy "if... then..." rules, *in*: **Fuzzy Approach to Reasoning and Decision Making** (Novák V., Ramík J., Cerny M., Nekola J., Eds.), 3-16, 1992, Kluwer Academic Publishers.

[Dubo 96] Dubois D. and Prade H., Semantics of quotient operators in fuzzy relational databases, **Fuzzy Sets and Systems**, 78, 89-94, 1996.

[Fagi 81] Fagin R., A normal form for relational databases that is based on domains and keys, **ACM Transactions on Database Systems**, 6, 387-415, 1981.

[Kacp 86] Kacprzyk J. and Ziolkowski A., Database queries with fuzzy linguistic quantifiers, **IEEE Transactions on Systems, Man and Cybernetics**, 16, 474-478, 1986.

[Kacp 95] Kacprzyk J. and Zadrozny S., FQUERY for ACCESS: fuzzy querying for a Windows-based DBMS. *In* "**Fuzziness in Database Management Systems**" (Bosc P., Kacprzyk J., Eds.), pp. 415-433, 1995, Physica Verlag.

[Lako 73] G. Lakoff, Hedges: a study in meaning criteria and the logic of fuzzy concepts, **Journal of Philosophical Logic**, 2, 458-508, 1973.

[Sanc 89] Sanchez E., Importance in knowledge systems, **Information Systems**, 14, 455-464, 1989.

[Taha 77] Tahani V., A conceptual framework for fuzzy query processing; a step toward very intelligent database systems, **Information Processing and Management**, 13, 289-303, 1977.

[Yage 84] Yager R.R., General multiple-objective decision functions and linguistically quantified statements, **Journal of Man-Machine Studies**, 21, 389-400, 1984.

[Yage 88] Yager R.R. , On ordered weighted averaging aggregation operators in multicriteria decisionmaking, **IEEE Transactions on Systems, Man and Cybernetics**, 18, 183-190, 1988.

[Yage 91] Yager R.R., Connectives and quantifiers in fuzzy sets, **Fuzzy Sets and Systems**, 40, 39-76, 1991.

[Yage 93] Yager R.R., Families of OWA operators, **Fuzzy Sets and Systems**, 59, 125-148, 1993.

[Zade 72] Zadeh L.A., A fuzzy-set theoretic interpretation of linguistic hedges, **Journal of Cybernetics**, 2, 4-34, 1972.

[Zade 83] Zadeh L.A., A computational approach to fuzzy quantifiers in natural languages, **Computational Mathematics with Applications**, 9, 149-183, 1983.

Fuzzy Retrieval of Object-Oriented Software Components

Ernesto Damiani

Università di Milano
Polo di Crema
edamiani@crema.unimi.it

Summary

The object selection problem requires the evaluation of the fitness of a *candidate server object* to a certain task on the basis of the information about its behaviour attached to it by a *classification model.* Many distributed O-O execution environments store such information in a *Trader* system which can be browsed or queried by client objects. In this paper a fuzzy data model is proposed as the basis of the design of a Trader system. A fuzzy query algebra is described, allowing for specifying operator definitions (and, therefore, query execution mechanisms) at run time, on the basis of user-selected semantics.

1 Introduction

The dynamic invocation of services in distributed O-O execution environments often requires evaluating the fitness of a *candidate object* with respect to a certain task on the basis of the information attached to it by a *classification model.* Indeed, this *object selection* problem is becoming crucial as a *network centric* computing model is gaining acceptance, where client objects explore an enterprise-wide Intranet or the global Net in order to access the services offered on a competitive basis by a number of distributed object oriented servers. In the network-centric model, client objects may select servers not only on the basis of their functional characteristics (i.e., the services they offer), but also taking into account non-functional, cost or performance-related requirements.

In this paper, we shall deal with the object selection problem in the context of the CORBA (Common Object Request Broker Architecture) object-oriented distributed software architecture proposed by the Object Management Group (OMG) [YD96]. Using CORBA, a client object can transparently invoke a method on a server object in two different ways: *static* or *dynamic* invocation. With dynamic invocation, the server is chosen at run time, according to the features of its interface. Thus, a CORBA-compliant execution environment should provide a Trading Service helping clients in identifying server objects on the basis of functional information; this service, also called *Trader* contains descriptions of services an provided by the servers, such as what servers exactly do, how and where they do it. But functional information is not enough, as the client may also want to consider non-functional information about the servers in order to make the correct choice, e.g., the server's price or performance, or its current load. Standard CORBA systems work on the basis of Boolean logic: a server either totally satisfies a client's needs, providing the desired services, or it does not. It seems then necessary to compensate this lack of flexibility taking into account the notion of *imprecise queries*.

Many approaches have been proposed to deal with imprecise queries in the database context; in this paper we adopt a model based on fuzzy sets theory [BP92], [BP95] which includes a fuzzy data model and a fuzzy query algebra and use it as the basis of the design of a CORBA Trader system.

In our approach, fuzzy selection techniques are transparent to client and servers alike. Servers periodically communicate their features to the Trader, also specifying crisp performance or cost values; clients associate crisp values to each functional or non-functional property they require from a server. Traders store linguistic variable definitions that are used to translate each server property in one or more triple constituted by a linguistic variable name, a fuzzy element and an associated numerical value, called *weight*. The same fuzzification is performed on user requests: the query constructed by the user is a list of desired properties associated to crisp values, associated with a semantics. These properties are translated by the Trader into a set of triples `<linguistic variable - fuzzy element-weight>`; after fuzzification, both the list of properties stored by the Trader and the user request can be considered as a fuzzy relations. Basically, our Trader executes an operation of fuzzy division on the basis of these relations, using the definition of the division operation that best matches the semantics requested by the user. This yields, for each available server, its degree of satisfaction relatively to the query with the intended semantics. Hence, the client is provided with a set of discriminated answers, and can choose the best fit among the available servers.

The paper is organized as follows: in Section 2, a quick overview of CORBA architecture is given, discussing how CORBA network centric conceptual model can be used as a reference architecture for the object selection problem. In Section 3, the fuzzy data model for a Trader, and the associated semantics, are presented. Section 4 discusses alternative definitions of the fuzzy division operation and their relationship with user-provided semantics for object selection. In Section 5 the architecture of a sample implementation of our fuzzy Trader is briefly outlined. Finally, in Section 6 conclusions and elements for a future development of this work are given.

2 CORBA Object Management Architecture

The Object Management Group has developed a conceptual model, known as the *core object model*, and a reference architecture, called the *Object Management Architecture (OMA)* upon which distributed applications can be constructed. OMA attempts to define, at a high level of abstraction, the various facilities necessary for distributed object-oriented computing. It consists of four components: an *Object Request Broker (ORB)*, *Object Services (OS)*, *Common Facilities (CF)*, and *Application Objects (AO)*.

Objects Services specifications define a set of objects that perform fundamental functions such as naming services, life cycle services, transaction services or trader services. Generally speaking, they augment and complement the functionality of the ORB, whereas CORBA Common Facilities provide services of direct use to application objects.

The core of the OMA is the ORB component, which is a transparent communication bus for objects that let them transparently make requests and receive responses from other objects located locally or remotely. In other words, the ORB intercepts calls and is responsible for finding an object that can execute them, pass it the parameters, invoke its methods and return the results. Moreover, operation invocations can be done either statically at compile time or dynamically at run time with a late binding of servers.

The client side is composed of IDL stubs, a *Dynamic Invocation Interface (DII)*, an *Interface Repository* and an *ORB Interface*. The client-side IDL stubs provide the static interfaces to object services and define how clients invoke corresponding services on the servers. On the other hand, the DII allows clients to construct and issue a request, whose signature is possibly unknown until run time, using information from the Interface Repository. As for the ORB interface (the only component of the architecture shared by both sides), it allows functions of the ORB to be accessed directly by the client code.

The implementation side interface consists of server IDL skeletons that provide static interfaces to each service exported by the server, a *Dynamic Skeleton Interface (DSI)*, an *Object Adapter*, an *Implementation Repository* and the ORB interface. The DSI (the server equivalent to the DII) looks at parameters values in an incoming message to determine a target object and method. The Object Adapter is on top of the ORB's core communication services and accepts requests on behalf of server objects. It provides the run time environment for creating instances of server objects, passing requests to them and registering their classes in the Implementation Repository.

As said previously, in addition to static method invocation, CORBA also provides a dynamic distributed invocation mechanism. Using CORBA's Dynamic Invocation Interface, Naming Services, Trader Services and the Interface Repository, a client application can discover new objects at run time and dynamically invoke their methods, with a late binding of servers. Clearly, the DII provides a very dynamic environment that allows systems to remain flexible and extensible. In CORBA, the dynamic identification system of an object is made in 4 steps:

1. The Trader identifies an object offering the needed service requested by the user on the basis of its functional properties.
2. Using the Interface Repository, the Trader Service retrieves the object interface, as well as a reference to it (an *IOR* or *Interoperable Object Reference*).
3. According to the description of the signature of the method (number and types of arguments), it constructs the invocation.
4. Finally, it invokes the object's method with adequate parameters and receives the results.

A CORBA Trader has a fundamental role in server object selection. We shall therefore discuss possible solution to the object selection problem with reference to Trader design and implementation techniques.

3 A Fuzzy Data Model For A Trader

In this Section, we outline the design a Trader which employs a repository storing a fuzzy descriptors of the network available services, in the line of [R91]. The problem of the availability of program databases for application development and maintenance has been explored in the context of the relational data model [SA96]. Our repository, henceforth called ***descriptor base***, is conceptually a structured collection of descriptors, each providing the description of an individual server. The issue of a hierarchy-aware descriptor base organization and management has been investigated in [DF97] and [BDF99]; here, this descriptor base is straightforwardly modeled as a fuzzy relational database.

As anticipated above, we shall use a model based on the concept of a ***fuzzy relation*** defined by applying imprecise criteria through a fuzzy predicate on a crisp relation [BP92], [BP95]. For such a fuzzy relation, built on a set of domains D_i, every t-uple is supplied with a membership degree μ_R from 0 to 1, interpreting how this t-uple satisfies a fuzzy predicate P applied to the relation R.

In our case, the Trader's descriptor base is a single fuzzy relation whose main attributes are: `object identification, offer property, fuzzy element, weight`. In CORBA conceptual model, offer properties are used as a policy-free mechanism; accordingly, we shall consider them simply as strings of a suitable ***domain-specific description language*** expressing server features. In other words, each offer property is mapped into a fuzzy ***linguistic variable***, and a weight is associated to each offer property-fuzzy element pair, describing to which extent the corresponding feature is offered by the object. The following example shows a fuzzy relation describing the properties of two audio/video servers.

OID	offer property	fuzzy element	weight
1	video service	good	.8
1	video service	average	.1
1	audio service	good	.4
2	video service	good	1
2	audio service	average	.5

In this example, the `video service` linguistic variable has three fuzzy elements, namely `poor`, `average` and `good`. The universe set used to define the linguistic variable could be, for instance, an interval called `frame rate`. Here, we assume that linguistic variables definitions are stored in the Trader private memory. Moreover, it is assumed that the Trader has access to a domain-specific Thesaurus allowing both functional and non-functional offer properties to be uniformed through a naming discipline, dealing with a standard context-dependent vocabulary. Fuzzy techniques for Thesaurus construction and management are presented in [DF95].

Clients need not be aware of the Trader's internal fuzzy model: they use strings of their domain specific description language, corresponding to linguistic variable names, to specify the offer properties that a server should possess. Moreover, they add to each property a crisp value chosen in its definition universe, which is again a part of the domain specific knowledge. According to stored linguistic variable definition, the Trader transforms all absolute values into weights. It is important to observe that this computation can take place both when the servers *sign up*, i.e. communicate to the Trader the availability of their services, and periodically, as a consequence of new load or network traffic conditions.

3.1 Object Selection Semantics

While looking for a server, clients can perform selection using different semantics. Our fuzzy Trader system proposes two main types of semantics: *importance* and *fulfillment*. The first one simply expresses the relative importance of offer properties: the user only has to give a percentage of importance for each desired property. As far as the semantics of fulfillment is concerned, we have two alternatives:

- Price fulfillment (or *ideal value vision*): the user expects a minimum distance between the values associated to the properties he specifies in the query and the ones held by the server proposed by the Trader.
- Performance fulfillment (or *threshold vision*): the values associated to the properties held by the server must be superior to those speciified by the user, while remaining as close as possible to them.

For both visions of fulfillment, the client can possibly ask for *absorption*. This means rejecting any server which does not offer even one of the desired properties. Considering the previous examples of descriptor base and fuzzy predicates, a user could for instance request a multimedia server having the following features: "a video service capable of 30 frames per second and an audio service with 16 Khz sampling rate", asking for a price fulfillment semantics with absorption.

This list of properties, after translation of absolute values according to the linguistic variables' definition, gives a list of triples `variable name - fuzzy predicate- weight` where weights have values between 0 and 1. Such a list defines the fuzzy request to the Trader, which is nothing but the following fuzzy relation:

offer property	fuzzy element	weight
video service	good	.1
video service	average	.5

The list of servers satisfying the requested properties can readily be achieved by computing the fuzzy relational division of the descriptor base by the query table [BP95], [DP94]. As we will see in the sequel, various fuzzy operators are available to compute this division.

4 Semantics of object selection and the fuzzy division operation

Before going dealing with the case of the division of fuzzy relations, we shortly recall the classical relational operation of division. Let us consider two relations $R(X, A)$ and $S(Y, A)$ where A, X, and Y point out sets of attributes. The division of R by S, denoted $R[A/A]S$ is a relation on X, which can be defined as follows:

$$x \in R[A/A]S$$

if $\forall a \in S[A], (x, a) \in R$

Following [BDPP97], we are now ready to examine the extension of the division to fuzzy relations. The operation of division of R by S can be defined in terms of set inclusion:

$$x \in R[A/A]S \iff S[A] \subseteq \Gamma^{-1}(x)$$

where $\Gamma^{-1}(x) = \{a, (x, a) \in R\}$. This inclusion, in the case of the extension of the division to fuzzy relations, can be interpreted either using the cardinality of (finite) fuzzy sets:

$$Incl(S \subseteq R) = \frac{\sum_{x \in X} op(\mu_S(a), \mu_R(x, a))}{\sum \mu_S(a)}$$

where the operation denoted op is a triangular norm.

Otherwise, inclusion can be defined in terms of a fuzzy implication:

$$Inc(S \subseteq R) = min_S(\mu_S(a) \rightarrow \mu_R(x, a))$$

Using the gradual inclusion based on set cardinality, we obtain a purely set-oriented vision, loosing the logic aspect of the division in which we are interested. As a consequence, we shall only deal with the definition of division operation based on fuzzy implication.

Among fuzzy implication connectives, we focus on three families which seem appropriate as a basis for the definition of fuzzy division in our case:

- R-implications, denoted $a \to b = sup\{c \in [0,1], T(a,c) \leq b\}$. Namely, we have *Goguen implication* $a \to b = 1 if a \leq b, b/a$ otherwise, if we associate T with the multiplication operation, and *Gödel implication* $a \to b = 1 if a \leq b, b$ otherwise, if we associate T with minimum.
- S-implications, namely $a \to b = n(T(a, n(b)))$, where n is an involutive order reversing negation operator, and T is a conjunction operation modeled by a triangular norm. We get Dienes implication $a \to b = max(1-a, b)$, if T is the minimum. Gödel reciprocal $n(b) \to n(a) = 1 if a \leq b, 1-a = n(a)$ otherwise.
- RS-implications such as Lukasiewicz implication, defined by: $a \to b = 1 if a \leq b, 1-a+b$ otherwise, obtained with Lukasiewicz norm $T = max(a+b-1, 0)$.

Ultimately, the "right" choice for the implication to be used in division operation definition depends on the semantics the user wants to give to μ_S membership values. In fact, $\mu_S(a)$ degrees can be considered either as importance degrees or as fulfillment degrees. If $\mu_S(a)$ degrees must express relative importance, any element x will completely satisfy the query if, for each element $a \in S \neq 0$, we have a maximum membership degree for the corresponding tuple $(x, a) \in R$.

$$\mu_{R[A/A]S}(x) = 1 \iff (\forall a, \mu_S(a) > 0 \iff \mu_R(x,a) = 1)$$

In the same way, an element x will not satisfy at all a condition if there is any element a of S such that the tuple (x, a) has membership degree equal to 0

$$\mu_{R[A/A]S}(x) = 0 \iff \exists a, \mu_S(a) = 1 \wedge \mu_R(x,a) = 0$$

This desired behavior leads to define the division operation by using Dienes implication. Then, we have:

$$\mu_{R[A/A]S}(x) = min_S(\mu_S(a) \to \mu_R(x,a)) = min_S(max(1-\mu_S(a), \mu_R(x,a)))$$

where S is a fuzzy normalized relation (i.e. $\exists a \in S, \mu_S(a) = 1$) in order to have a complete scale of importance levels. Moreover, Dienes implication ensures a sort of pseudo-absorption since it guarantees weaker results when μ_S is high and μ_R is not.

In the case of performance fulfillment semantics, μ_S degrees are specified by the user as degrees to be reached, that is to say thresholds. For this semantics, we may want to have:

$$\mu_{R[A/A]S}(x) = 0 \iff \exists a, \mu_S(a) > 0 \wedge \mu_R(x,a) = 0$$

and

$$\mu_{R[A/A]S}(x) = 1 \iff \forall a, \mu_S(a) \leq \mu_R(x,a)$$

It is interesting to consider what can be done when a tuple (x, a) exists which satisfies the desired property to a degree which is less than the required one (i.e. if $\exists a, \mu_S(a) > \mu_R(x, a)$). One could take Gödel implication, ensuring that an element x will be retrieved with a degree as high as $\mu_R(x, a)$ whenever $\mu_S(a)$ is larger than $\mu_R(x, a)$. Obviously, in this case, the result does not depend at all on $\mu_S(a)$. As an alternative, we could take Goguen implication, that gives the ratio between $\mu_R(x, a)$ and $\mu_S(a)$, and yields a relative level of fulfillment of the considered property. It is obvious that the R-implications like Gödel and Goguen implications ensure the absorption property. Indeed, if $\mu_R(x, a) = 0$, Gödel implication yields $\mu_S(a) \rightarrow \mu_R(x, a) = \mu_R(x, a) = 0$, and Goguen implication gives $\mu_S(a) \rightarrow \mu_R(x, a) = \mu_R(x, a)/\mu_S(a) = 0$. For this reason, S-implications should be used when non-absorption is required; for the fulfillment semantics, the use of Lukasiewicz implication would be improper since it yields a non-zero degree of inclusion of S into R even if R is empty, provided that S is not normalized. Since both Gödel and Goguen implications yield 1 when $\mu_S \leq \mu_R$, it is interesting to study their behavior when the query membership value is above the offer value. Consider the following example:

$\mu_S(a)$	$\mu_R(x,a)$	Gödel	Goguen
.9	.8	.8	.88
.9	.7	.7	.77
.9	.2	.2	.22
.7	.6	.6	.85
.7	.3	.3	.42
.5	.4	.4	.8
.5	.2	.2	.4
.3	.2	.2	.66
.3	.1	.1	.33

If we consider μ_S values as thresholds to be reached, we notice that Gödel implication gives a lower result when μ_S is small, whereas Goguen implication does not penalize much the result when μ_R is close to the threshold value μ_S. If the distance between the two values is high, it gives anyway a small result. In addition, Gödel implication always gives a lower value than Goguen's if μ_R is beneath μ_S. This suggests to adopt Gödel implication for performance semantics and Goguen's for the price one.

In order to provide fulfillment semantics without absorption we may follow the same empiric reasoning, discussing the behavior of Gödel reciprocal and Lukasiewicz implications through an example:

$\mu_S(a)$	$\mu_R(x,a)$	Gödel reciprocal	Lukasiewicz
.9	.8	.1	.9
.9	.7	.1	.8
.9	.2	.1	.3
.7	.6	.3	.9
.7	.3	.3	.6
.5	.4	.5	.9
.5	.2	.5	.7
.3	.2	.7	.9
.3	.1	.7	.8

We note that, using Lukasiewicz implication, the closer μ_R is to μ_S, the higher the result. On the contrary, if μ_R does not reach the threshold value μ_S, Gödel reciprocal gives a substantially lower result. Then, it seems obvious that Gödel reciprocal implication expresses the threshold semantics better than Lukasiewicz implication.

In conclusion, we have the following summary:

	Absorption	**Non-Absorption**
Importance	Dienes	Dienes
Price Fulfillment	Goguen	Lukasiewicz
Performance Fulfillment	Gödel	Gödel reciprocal

It is worthwhile observing that, whenever classical implications do not exactly fit the user-provided semantics, one could be tempted to define ad-hoc implications that completely match with them. But this temptation should indeed be resisted. For example, one could define an "implication" for performance fulfillment as follows:
$a \to b = 1$ if $a = b$, 0 if $a > b$ (or $b = 0$ in case of absorption), $1 + a - b$ otherwise
and for price fulfillment:
$a \to b = 0$ if $b = 0$ (in case of absorption), $1 - |a - b|$ otherwise.
At first sight, this latter implication could seem an ad hoc S-implication underlain by the norm $T(a,b) = |a + b - 1|$. Nevertheless, even if 1 is the neutral element and the commutativity property is respected, we would loose associativity and monotonicity properties. These properties turn out to be essential to preserve Trader system consistency and extendability.

4.1 A Naïve Algorithm

Whatever implication is used to perform the division, we can give the following naive algorithm, that sequentially seeks for each element x of the divided relation R, the tuple (x, a) for each element a of the relation S.

```
for each x of R do
μR/S(x) := 1.0;
for each a of S do
seek sequentially (x,a) in R;
if found then
```

```
μ_current(x) := μ_S(a) → μ_R(x,a);
else
μ_current(x) := μ_S(a) → 0;
end;
μ_R/S(x) := min(μ_R/S(x), μ_current(x));
done;
done;
```

Obviously, this naïve algorithm is very costly in matter of memory accesses (even if the tuple (x, a) does not exist the algorithm examines the whole relation R). Though optimization is not the purpose of this paper, it is clear that improvements based on heuristics are necessary.

Supposing the existence of a threshold l that the servers final weights must reach in order to be selected, we can give the following heuristics:

- The first heuristic is a *heuristic of failure* valid for any implication: the element x will not be retrieved if $\exists a \in S, \mu_S(a) \rightarrow \mu_R(x, a) < l$, since the division computes a minimum value.
- The second one concerns Dienes and Lukasiewicz implications, as well as the reciprocal of Gödel implication. If we assume that S is sorted on decreasing μ_S membership values, one can stop the computation as soon as the current degree $\mu_{R/S}(x)$ is inferior to $1 - \mu_S(a)$. Indeed, in this case, if the values $1 - \mu_S(a)$ are increasing then the degree of satisfaction for the element x considered cannot decrease anymore.
- Finally, dealing with Gödel and Goguen implications, for a given element x, if there exists an element a in S such as the tuple (x, a) does not exist in R, then we have $\mu_R(x, a) = 0$, and $\mu_S(a) \rightarrow \mu_R(x, a) = 0$. This heuristic is used whenever the number of t-uples of any partition of the relation R is inferior to the number of t-uples of the relation S.

5 The architecture of a Fuzzy Trading System

In this section we briefly discuss some design and implementation issues of a Fuzzy trader System; extensive presentations of this material, including a complete description of our current CORBA-compliant Trader prototype, can be found in [D98]. Our whole architecture is composed of four main components:

1. A *client* connected to Internet from a certain machine, who requires a service from the trading system. Again without dealing with classification issues, we could assume that the client has previously contacted a "Trader of Traders", which contains lists of various URL of known Traders in the domain under consideration. The client's Web browser automatically downloads and executes the GUI interface of the Trader.
2. A *Trader site* where all classes defining the GUI interface are stored, together with the Trader System itself and a database storing the features

of the servers, and the characteristic values of the various fuzzy predicates. The Trader receives fuzzy requests from users, and on the basis of this information, performs the division (according to the fuzzy predicates) on the descriptor base and returns the best matching server to the user.

3. An *Adapter site* whose role is to peep into picture servers information and maintain definitions of fuzzy predicates according to servers properties. Whenever one server's features change, the Adapter updates the descriptor base of the Trader (adding or removing a server, or partially updating its properties) and, if necessary, it also updates the functions defining the fuzzy predicates.
4. Several *object servers* that actually provide the services described in the Trader base. These servers need not be aware of the fuzzy trader model: the server programmer or installer needs only to specify the absolute values of properties (e.g., the current price of a service) that will then be interpreted by the Adapter.

6 Conclusions and Future Work

On the basis of the fuzzy data model presented in Section 3, the retrieval mechanism of servers can be enlarged to take into account features the servers should *not* have, in order to further discriminate between those that would have a same level of fitness after the division. Indeed, the division searches the descriptor base for servers that have the more possible of the desired requirements. A subsequent, optional phase of differentiation should compute a similarity or a dissimilarity measure to eliminate servers that have properties the user did not ask for. Since this treatment of differentiation is semantically different from the division, a complete retrieval will consist in several phases.

- First, fuzzy division is computed with regard to a query based on functional properties only. It seems natural to begin the retrieval taking functional information into account, since this information describes the services actually provided by a server. This division, whose definition has been chosen according to the semantics selected by the user, yields a first set $S1$ of candidate servers.
- Second, an optional phase of *differentiation* is performed which is particularly aimed to functional properties. In fact, according to the list of properties used for the previous division, we implicitly have defined a secondary list containing all functional properties that the user did not mention, all weighted 0. Considering servers and their properties as objects, this phase is nothing but a comparison of description of objects, where the fuzzy table (whose t-uples correspond to secondary properties) is considered as a *reference object*. This second phase compares all objects from $S1$ with the reference and yields a second set $S2$ constituted of the n best servers with respect to the differentiation.
- Finally, the computation of the division of the descriptor base represented by $S2$ with respect to a fuzzy relation obtained from a fuzzy query this time dealing with non-functional properties

Many measures of comparison of descriptions of objects have been proposed and studied in given frameworks or domains of applications. B. Bouchon-Meunier, M. Rifqi and S. Bothorel [BRB96] proposed a general classification consisting in four main kinds of measures of comparison, depending on the purpose of their utilization; they define measures of ***satisfiability***, ***resemblance*** and ***comparison***. Satisfiability corresponds to a situation where we consider a reference object and decide whether a new object is compatible with its class or not. Generally speaking, the measure of resemblance and the measure of inclusion also take into account the closeness of a candidate to a reference object, but tend to enhance "important" common points between candidate and reference. In a future release of our Trader, a general measure of dissimilarity will be used to evaluate to which extent an object is different from the reference, helping the user to choose objects that are closer to the desired reference than the others. As far as the design of the architecture is concerned, we are currently working on the servers-to-Trader dialogue in order to support intelligent load balancing techniques [D99]. Finally, though in this paper we did not deal with classification issues, it is interesting to note that linguistic variable definitions used by the Trader for computing the fuzzy offer properties can also be uploaded by servers themselves when signing up to the Trader. Moreover, client query could also be expressed directly in fuzzy form, allowing for fuzzy specification of components behavior [DDT98]. We intend to explore this subject in a future paper.

Acknowledgements
The background of this paper is largely based on joint work with MariaGrazia Fugini amd on Patrick Bosc's seminal papers on fuzzy relational division semantics. The author wishes to thank Gianni Degli Antoni, Daniele Mundici and David Rine for many useful discussions on the subject. Thanks are also due to Laurent Le Nedelec for developing the first fuzzy Trader prototype during his stage at the Milan University's Crema campus in 1997.

References

[BP92] P. Bosc and O. Pivert, "Some Approaches For Relational Databases Flexible Querying", Journal of Intelligent Information Systems, (2)1, 1992

[BP95] P. Bosc and O. Pivert "SQLf: A Relational Database Language For Fuzzy Querying", IEEE Transactions on Fuzzy Systems, 3 (1), 1995

[BDPP97] P. Bosc, D. Dubois, O. Pivert and H. Prade "Flexible Queries In Relational Databases - The Example of The Division Operator", Theoretical Computer Science 171, 1997

[BDF98] P. Bosc, E. Damiani and M.G.. Fugini "Dynamic Service Identification in a CORBA-like Environment", Proceedings of CAISE '98 Post-Conference Workshop on Internet Information Systems, Pisa 1998

[BRB96] B. Bouchon-Meunier, M. Rifqi and S. Bothorel "Towards General Measures of Comparison of Objects", Fuzzy Sets and Systems 84, 1996.

[D98] E. Damiani, "The Design of a Fuzzy Trader System", Proceedings of the ICAIE Conf. on Intelligent Systems, Wuhan, China, 1998.

[D99] E. Damiani, "A Fuzzy Stateless Approach to Load Distribution for O-O Distributed Environments" Intl. Jour. of Knowledge-Based Eng. Sys., (3) 4, 1999

[DF95] E. Damiani and M.G. Fugini "Automatic Thesaurus Construction Supporting Fuzzy Retrieval of Reusable Components", Proceedings of the ACM Symposium on Applied Computing (SAC'95) Nashville, US, 1995

[DF97] E. Damiani, M.G. Fugini and E. Fusaschi "A Descriptor-Based Approach to O-O Code Reuse", IEEE Computer, Special Issue on O-O Development and Reuse, (30) 10, 1997

[BDF99] C. Bellettini, E. Damiani and M.G. Fugini "A Hierarchy Aware Approach to Faceted Classification of O-O Components", ACM Trans. on Softw. Eng. Meth., (3) 8, 1999

[DDT98] E. Damiani, G. Degli Antoni and A. Tettamanzi "DEE: A Tool for Genetic Tuning of Software Components on a Distributed Network of Workstations", International Journal of Applied Software Technology, Special Issue on Reusable Software and Adaptive Fuzzy Controller Architectures, (3) 3, 1998

[DP94] D. Dubois and H. Prade "Quotient Operators in Fuzzy Relational Databases", Proceedings of the European Congress on Fuzzy and Intelligent Techniques (EUFIT'94), Aachen, Germany, 1994.

[R91] D. Rine, "Design of Fuzzy Object-Oriented Software Components Databases", Cybernetics and Systems 22, 1991.

[SA96] P. Santanu and P. Atul "A Query Algebra for Program Databases", IEEE Transactions On Software Engineering 22, 1996

[YD96] Z. Yang and K. Duddy "CORBA: A Platform for Distributed Object Computing", ACM Operating Systems Review, 30, 1996.

Using Fuzzy Quering over the Internet to Browse through Information Resources

Janusz Kacprzyk and Slawomir Zadrożny

Systems Research Institute, Polish Academy of Sciences, ul. Newelska 6
01-447 Warsaw, Poland
{kacprzyk, zadrozny}@ibspan.waw.pl

Abstract. We present, first, how to construct and implement the FQUERY for Access system, a fuzzy querying user-friendly interface to Microsoft Access, which accommodates fuzzy (imprecise) terms and linguistic quantifiers allowing for more human-consistent queries. Then, we show how implement this fuzzy querying system for querying databases over the Internet (WWW) to browse through vast information resources available.

Keywords: database querying, flexible querying, fuzzy querying, fuzzy logic, fuzzy linguistic quantifiers, Microsoft Access, Internet, WWW.

1 Introduction

The motivation for this paper is manifold. First, due to advances in computing technology which have happened in recent years, characterized by lower and lower prices and sharply rising capacities of computing equipment, users have tended to maintain larger and larger databases.

On the other hand, computer systems less and less often work alone, and are in virtually all cases connected in networks, local on the one extreme, and global (Internet) on the other extreme.

Therefore, the users have access to vast information resources, stored in various databases scattered over the whole world. In fact, it is often said that everything can be found in the Internet, provided that we know how to browse.

Browsing a database either over the Internet or locally is however not easy using conventional tools. First, the users can rarely precisely formulate what they are interested in, and the conventional querying tools and techniques, which could eventually be employed for that purpose, need in general very strict and precise formulation of queries. This is a good example of an inherent discrepancy between a "soft" human being and a "hard" machine. For the former, natural language, with its inherent imprecision and vagueness, is the only fully natural communication means, hence the most preferable, while for the latter natural language is strange and difficult to grasp and manipulate. This discrepancy is one of more serious difficulties in the use and proliferation of all kinds of information systems, and hence has been a subject of intensive research and development that has led to more human consistent interfaces which makes the use of (quasi) natural language possible.

Fuzzy logic has played here a crucial role making it possible to considerably improve those interfaces by providing formal means to handle vagueness resulting from the use of natural language. In this paper we will show how fuzzy logic can provide new qualities to database querying. We will present some linguistic, fuzzy-logic-based interfaces to DBMSs, meant for the browsing via the Internet and WWW. First, however, we will discuss the topic for standalone applications as they are the points of departure.

This paper is based, first of all, on our previous works on fuzzy querying for a standalone DBMS (Kacprzyk and Ziółkowski, 1986a, b; Kacprzyk and Zadrożny, 1994a - 1997c, Zadrożny and Kacprzyk, 1995, 1996).

We assume a conventional (non-fuzzy) DBMS (Microsoft Access® 97), and construct an add-on to it which may help the human operator (e.g., decision maker) retrieve information related to some highly aggregated and vaguely defined concepts or relations.

Basically, our querying system allows for queries of the type ``find (all) records such that *most* (almost all, much more than a half,...) of the *important* attributes are as specified (e.g., equal to 5, much less than 100, low, etc.)''.

First, we discuss the use of fuzzy sets (logic) in standalone database querying showing where such fuzzy elements may be employed, exemplified by our implementation in FQUERY for Access.

In next parts we describe how this querying concept can be implemented using a WWW browser (Netscape Navigator® and Microsoft Explorer®) as interface as proposed and implemented by Kacprzyk and Zadrożny (1996, 1997d).

2 A Fuzzy Querying Interface to a DBMS

In querying the users are often interested in answers to imprecisely specified questions exemplified by retrieve "all *younger much_better_than_average* paid employees" which is inconsistent with conventional (precise) querying languages.

The extension of a query language of an existing DBMS to allow for the use of such linguistic (fuzzy) terms involves four issues to be dealt with:

- the extension of the syntax of a query language,
- the semantics of an extended language,
- the elicitation and manipulation of linguistic (fuzzy) terms and queries and
- the embedding of fuzzy querying in a native querying engine of a DBMS.

In what follows, we assume Microsoft Access as the host DBMS. Internally, Access represents a query using SQL, hence we focus on the simple query of the type:

SELECT <list of fields> FROM <list of tables> WHERE <condition>

and propose the following extension to the syntax of its WHERE clause:

```
<condition> ::=  <linguistic quantifier>
                 <sequence of subconditions> ;
<sequence of subconditions> ::=
        <subcondition> |
        <subcondition> OR <sequence of subconditions>
<subcondition> ::=
        <linguistic quantifier><importance coefficient>
        <sequence of atomic conditions>
<sequence of atomic conditions> ::=
        <atomic condition> |
        <atomic condition> AND <sequence of atomic conditions>
<atomic condition> ::=
        <attribute> = <fuzzy value> |
        <attribute> <classical relational operator><numerical-attribute> |
        <attribute> <fuzzy relation> <attribute> |
        <attribute> <fuzzy relation> <number> |
        <single-valued-attribute> IN <fuzzy-set constant> |
        <multi-valued-attribute><compatibility operator><fuzzy-set constant>
<attribute> ::= <numeric field>
<linguistic quantifier> ::= <OWA-tag> <quantifier name>
<OWA-tag> ::= OWA |
<classical relational operator> ::= < | <= | > | >= | =
```

The main entities used in the system, their linguistic (fuzzy) representation, elicitation and handling are:

- **Attributes**

For each attribute the user specifies: the lower limit (LL) and upper limit (UL) which determine the value interval of the field's values. This interval is used for scaling the values of the attributes for the particular records while calculating the degree of matching with a linguistic (fuzzy) value, or the degree of membership in a fuzzy relation. In fact, they need not describe the real value intervals.

- **Single-Valued Attributes, Multi-Valued Attributes**

A single-valued attribute may clearly be considered as a special case of a multi-valued attribute. For the former, only special compatibility operators (IN) are meaningful, and various compatibility indices may be employed for the latter.

The matching degree for an atomic condition involving a single-valued attribute (*at*) and a fuzzy set (*FS*) is calculated for each record as the value of the membership function of *FS* for the value of the attribute *at* in a given record.

The calculation of matching degree for multi-valued attributes is discussed in what follows with regards to the compatibility operator.

- **Linguistic (Fuzzy) Values**

The imprecise linguistic terms as, e.g., *large* in "salary is *large*", are defined by trapezoid membership functions on [-10, +10] shown in Figure 1, to allow for context-independent definitions.

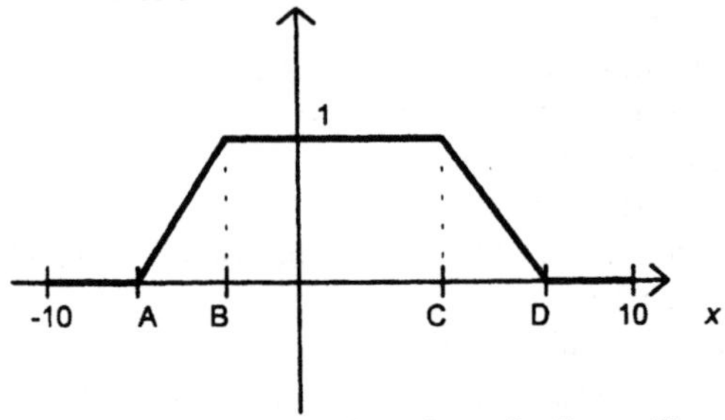

Figure 1. Trapezoidal membership function of a fuzzy (linguistic) value

Thus, to define a fuzzy value the four points A, B, C, and D are needed, and their interpretation is obvious.

The matching degree, $md(\cdot,\cdot)$, of an *atomic condition* AT = FV and a record R is

$$md(\text{AT} = \text{FV}, \text{R}) = \mu_{\text{FV}}(\tau(\text{R}(\text{AT})) \tag{1}$$

where: R(AT) is the value of attribute AT in record R, μ_{FV} is the membership function of the fuzzy value FV, and τ: $[\text{LL}_{\text{AT}},\text{UL}_{\text{AT}}] \rightarrow [-10,10]$ is the mapping from the variability interval of the attribute AT onto the unified [-10,10] interval.

- **Fuzzy (Linguistic) Relations**

Fuzzy (linguistic) relations, exemplified by "Amount_in_Stock Is MUCH_GREATER_THAN Amount_on_Orders", is represented similarly as a fuzzy value though two attributes are involved, i.e. we have atomic conditions as

$$\text{FR}(\text{AT1},\text{AT2}) \tag{2}$$

We assume the universe of discourse to be the set of possible values of difference of the values of attributes, $[\text{LL}_{\text{AT1}}\text{-UL}_{\text{AT2}}, \text{UL}_{\text{AT1}}\text{-LL}_{\text{AT2}}]$. Then, a fuzzy relation, FR, may be equated with a fuzzy set, FRS, defined on this interval, i.e., $\mu_{FR}(x, y) = \mu_{FRS}(x - y)$; thus again four points: A, B, C and D are needed for the definition as in Figure 1.

The matching degree, $md(\cdot,\cdot)$, of an *atomic condition* (2), and a record R is

$$md(\text{FR}(\text{AT1},\text{AT2}),\text{R}) = \mu_{\text{FRS}}(\tau(\text{R}(\text{AT1}) - \text{R}(\text{AT2}))) \tag{3}$$

where: R(AT1), R(AT2) are the values of attributes AT1 and AT2, in R, μ_{FR} is the membership function of FR, and τ is the mapping τ: [LL_{AT1}-UL_{AT2}, UL_{AT1}-LL_{AT2}] → [-10, 10].

- **Linguistic Quantifiers**

In the FQUERY for Access system the fuzzy linguistic quantifiers are defined in the sense of Zadeh (1983), with the [0.0, 10.0] interval assumed for technical reasons. On the other hand, they may be interpreted either using original Zadeh's approach or via the ordered weighted averaging (OWA) operators (cf. Yager, 1988, Yager and Kacprzyk, 1997). We assume that the membership function of the fuzzy linguistic quantifier is piecewise linear as sketched in Figure 2.

To define a fuzzy linguistic quantifier it is therefore needed to provide two numbers corresponding to A and B meant similarly as for a fuzzy value.

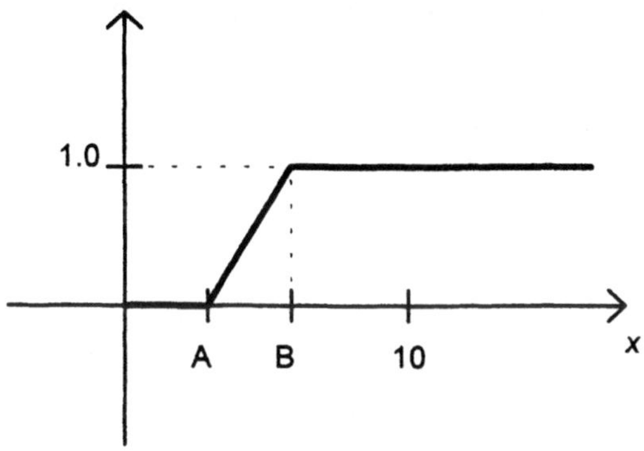

Figure 2. The membership function of a fuzzy linguistic quantifier

Thus, the matching degree, $md(\cdot,\cdot)$, for the query „Q of N clauses are satisfied" for record R is equal to

$$md(Q\{\text{clause}_{i=1,..N}\},\mathrm{R}) = \mu_Q(\tau(\sum_i md(\text{clause}_i,\mathrm{R}))/10) \tag{4}$$

where: md(clause$_i$,R) is the matching degree for clause i, for record R, μ_Q is the membership function of the linguistic quantifier Q, and τ: [0,N]→[0,10].

The above formula may be extended to the case with the importances of particular clauses (cf. Zadeh, 1983 for tools). Moreover, the OWA operator interpretation of a linguistic quantifier may also be employed [cf. Yager and Kacprzyk's (1997) volume].

- **Fuzzy Set Constant**

A fuzzy set constant represents the user's requirement as to the value of a single-valued or a multi-valued attribute. For instance:

1.COUNTRY IN	1.0/Bulgaria
2.COUNTRY IN	1.0/Belarus + 1.0/Russia + 1.0/Ukraine
3.COUNTRY IN	1.0/CzechRepublic + 1.0/Hungary + 1.0/Poland + 1.0/Slovakia + 0.8/Belarus + ...

where IN is a compatibility operator corresponding to the classic set theory operator $\in$.

The user, e.g., looking for a customer from Bulgaria only, will employ the first condition. If a few countries are relevant, the second condition may be used. Finally, if the choice of a customer's country of origin refers to a vague concept like, e.g., the Central Europe, the third form should be employed.

- **Compatibility Operators**

Compatibility operators make possible to express a relation that should be met by a single-valued attribute or a multi-valued attribute and a fuzzy set constant in an atomic condition.

The matching degree of an atomic condition involving a single-valued attribute (AT) and a fuzzy set (*FS*) is calculated as equal to $\mu_{FS}(\mathrm{R(AT)})$, where $\mathrm{R(AT)}$ is the value of the attribute AT in a given record R.

Let *FS* (in a query) and *D* (in a database record) be two fuzzy sets in *U*, i.e., $FS, D \in F(U)$, and *md(FS,D)* be a compatibility operator to be defined. Then the following definitions may be employed:

1. Degree of possibility of matching

$$md(FS,D) = \Pi(FS \mid D) = \sup_{u \in U} \min(\mu_{FS}(u), \mu_D(u)) \tag{5}$$

2. Degree of necessity of matching

$$md(FS,D) = \mathrm{N}(FS \mid D) = \inf_{u \in U} \max(1 - \mu_{FS}(u), \mu_D(u)) \tag{6}$$

3. Generalized Jaccard coefficient

$$md(FS,D) = \mid FS \cap D \mid / \mid FS \cup D \mid \tag{7}$$

The matching degree for an atomic condition involving a multi-valued-attribute (AT) and a fuzzy set (*FS*) is calculated for each record as the value of the selected compatibility operator for *FS* and the value of AT in the record.

2.1. Declaration of Attributes and Definitions of Fuzzy Terms

FQUERY for Access is implemented as a kind of a library database, so-called add-in in Access terminology. It contains code and tables. The code is responsible for the proper manipulation of particular fuzzy terms and a query as a whole. The tables store definitions of attributes and fuzzy terms. The user declares attributes and defines fuzzy terms in the special toolbar (Exhibit 1) by an interactive specification of a number of parameters.

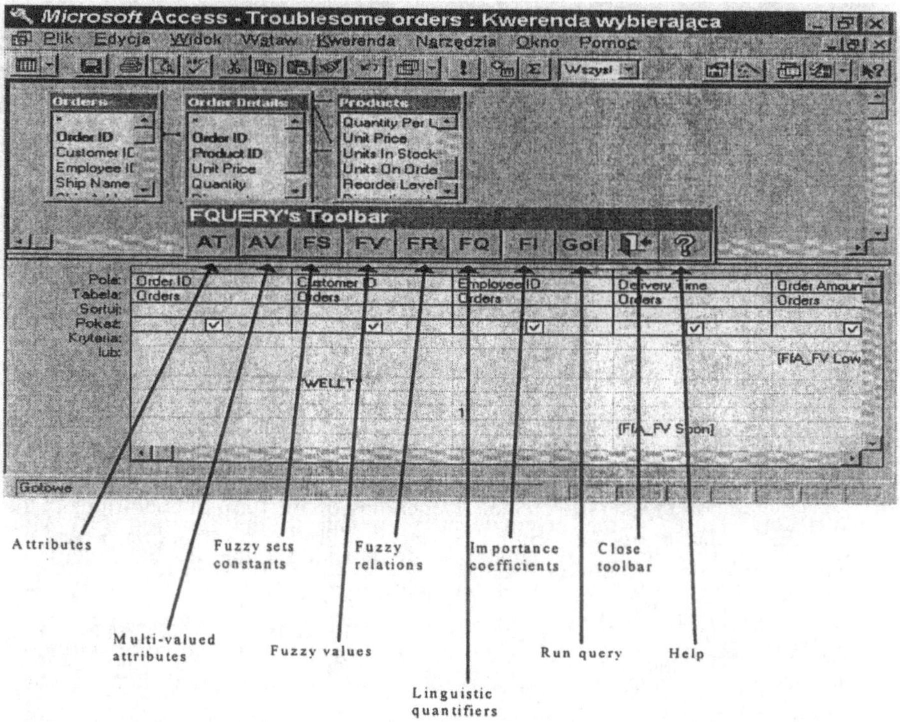

Exhibit 1. FQUERY for Access's toolbar

In the case of fuzzy values, relations and linguistic quantifiers interaction with the user is quite similar. Appropriate records have to be added to appropriate library database tables. The fuzzy terms defined are illustrated by graphs corresponding to the Figures 1 and 2 - see Exhibit 2 for fuzzy relations, and similarly for a fuzzy value and quantifier.

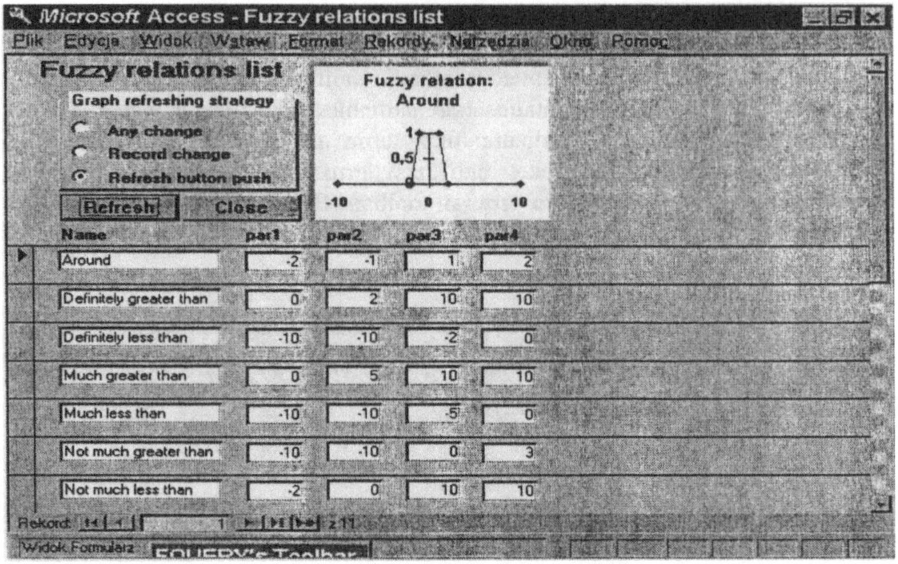

Exhibit 2. Definition of fuzzy relations

Finally, after the GO button is pressed, the query is automatically transformed, and then run as a native (legitimate) query of Access. The transformation is done in two main steps:

I. A new temporary query is created. Depending on the form of conditions in the WHERE clause of the original query, a call to the function FfA_MD, implemented by the library database code, is added to the SELECT clause of the new query with the list of all fields used in the original query. The arguments in FfA_MD call correspond to particular conditions appearing in the WHERE clause of the original query. Together with the composition of the query - recorded by FQUERY for Access' in its internal data structure while parsing the original query - this allows to compute a matching degree. Thus, this temporary query takes the form:

   SELECT list_of_fields, FfA_MD(parameter) As MD INTO newTable

   and is executed in the background.

II. The original query is transformed as follows: all condition in the WHERE clause are replaced with MD > threshold, where threshold is a value defined by the user. This means that the query will display only records matching its conditions to the degree higher than the threshold specified. The FROM clause is replaced with FROM newTable. The ORDER BY MD clause is added. Thus, the transformed query looks like follows:

SELECT list_of_fields, MD FROM newTable ORDER BY MD

As a result, each record displayed by the query is accompanied with the value of its matching degree (all fields selected originally are preserved in the SELECT clause).

So, after pressing the GO button the new, temporary query (I) is executed and then the SQL string of the original query is replaced by the modified one (II). Then, the query is run by Access as usually. Records matching the query to a degree higher than a prespecified threshold are displayed with the value of their matching degree. The SQL string in its original form is restored into the query, so that the user cannot even see its modified form on which the currently displayed information is based.

2.3. Example

Suppose we have a database of a small trading company and we wish to retrieve a list of *troublesome* order items requiring special attention, those characterized by:

1. since the company is based in the USA, orders coming from abroad may require more attention (transportation formalities, customs duties, etc.),
1. a *short* delivery time,
2. a *low profitability* of the order due to: a *low* amount of ordered product, *high* freight charges, and *high* discount rates,
3. the ordered amount is *much greater than* that now available in stock,
4. the order is placed by a customer (e.g., Wellt) with whom we have experienced some problems in the past,
5. an employee responsible for the order (e.g., labeled 1) has recently had a few unsuccessful transactions.

A requirement that *all* of the above difficulties (conditions) should occur in full scale is often unreasonable, and the fulfilling of, e.g., *most* of the conditions listed above may surely be treated as potentially troublesome.

One can easily recognize in the above formulation several linguistic (fuzzy) concepts supported by FQUERY for Access: fuzzy values (*short*, *low*, *high*), a fuzzy relation (*much greater than*) and a linguistic quantifier (*most*).

Let the following database tables and fields convey information required (similarly as in Microsoft Access exemplary database nwind.mdb):

- in the table Orders information about all the orders is stored,
- in the table [Order Details] information on the particular items (ordered products) of each order is stored,
- in the table Products information about particular products is stored.

We need to define attributes, fuzzy values, fuzzy relations and fuzzy linguistic quantifiers as shown in Exhibit 2.

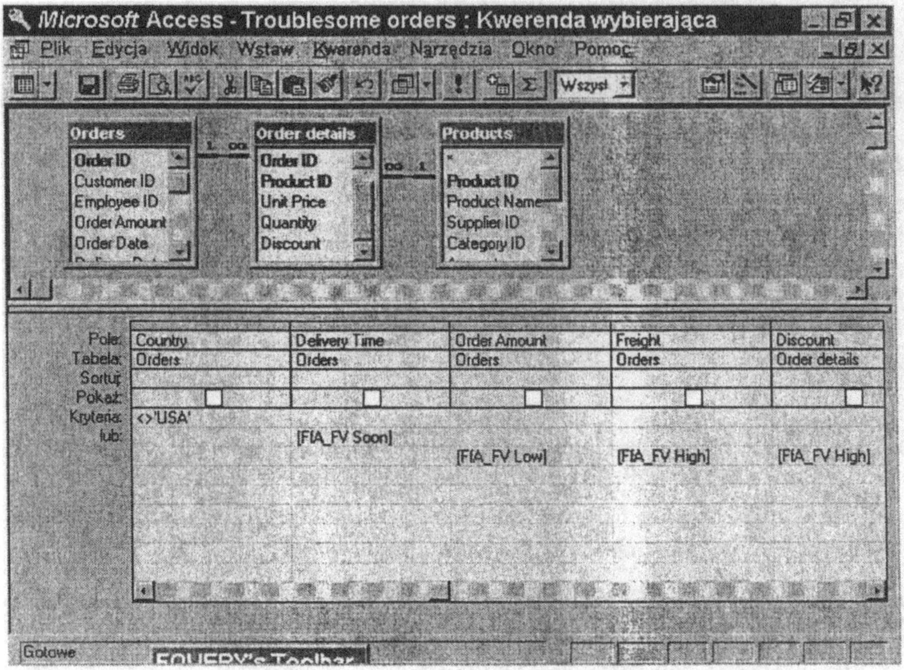

Exhibit 3. Composition of a query in the Query by Example grid

The query considered may be expressed in SQL of Microsoft Access as:

```
SELECT DISTINCTROW
Orders.[Order ID], Orders.[Customer ID],
Orders.[Employee ID], Orders.[Delivery Time],
Orders.Amount, Orders.Freight,
[Order Details].Discount, [Order Details].Quantity,
Products.[Units In Stock], Products.[Units On Order]
FROM
(Orders INNER JOIN [Order Details] ON
Orders.[Order ID] = [Order Details].[Order ID])
INNER JOIN Products ON
[Order Details].[Product ID] = Products.[Product ID]
WHERE
((Orders.[Ship Country]<>'USA')) OR
((Orders.[Delivery Time]=[FfA_FV Soon])) OR
((Orders.[Order Amount]=[FfA_FV Low]) AND
(Orders.Freight=[FfA_FV High]) AND
```

([Order Details].Discount=[FfA_FV High]) AND
([Order Details].Quantity=[FfA_FQ Most])) OR
((Products.[Units On Order]=[FfA_FR Much greater than|Products:Units In Stock])) OR
((Orders.[Customer ID]="WELLT")) OR
(([Order Details].Discount=[FfA_FQ A Lot of])) OR
((Orders.[Employee ID]=1));

In the QBE window of Access this query looks as shown in Exhibit 3 (only a part of it is visible).

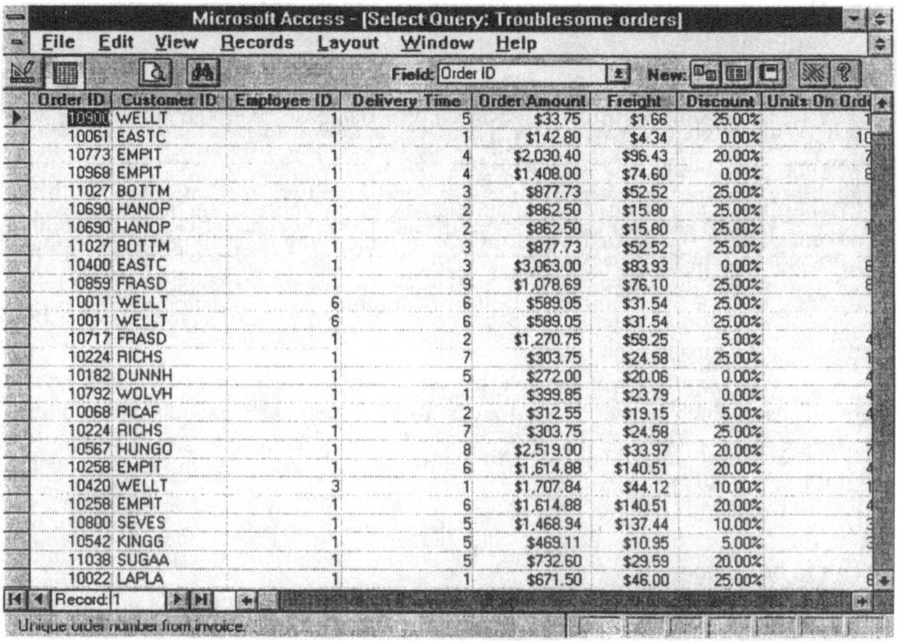

Order ID	Customer ID	Employee ID	Delivery Time	Order Amount	Freight	Discount	Units On Ord
10900	WELLT	1	5	$33.75	$1.66	25.00%	
10061	EASTC	1	1	$142.80	$4.34	0.00%	
10773	EMPIT	1	4	$2,030.40	$96.43	20.00%	
10968	EMPIT	1	4	$1,408.00	$74.60	0.00%	
11027	BOTTM	1	3	$877.73	$52.52	25.00%	
10690	HANOP	1	2	$862.50	$15.80	25.00%	
10690	HANOP	1	2	$862.50	$15.80	25.00%	
11027	BOTTM	1	3	$877.73	$52.52	25.00%	
10400	EASTC	1	3	$3,063.00	$83.93	0.00%	
10859	FRASD	1	9	$1,078.69	$76.10	25.00%	
10011	WELLT	6	6	$589.05	$31.54	25.00%	
10011	WELLT	6	6	$589.05	$31.54	25.00%	
10717	FRASD	1	2	$1,270.75	$59.25	5.00%	
10224	RICHS	1	7	$303.75	$24.58	25.00%	
10182	DUNNH	1	5	$272.00	$20.06	0.00%	
10792	WOLVH	1	1	$399.85	$23.79	0.00%	
10068	PICAF	1	2	$312.55	$19.15	5.00%	
10224	RICHS	1	7	$303.75	$24.58	25.00%	
10567	HUNGO	1	8	$2,519.00	$33.97	20.00%	
10258	EMPIT	1	6	$1,614.88	$140.51	20.00%	
10420	WELLT	3	1	$1,707.84	$44.12	10.00%	
10258	EMPIT	1	6	$1,614.88	$140.51	20.00%	
10800	SEVES	1	5	$1,468.94	$137.44	10.00%	
10542	KINGG	1	5	$469.11	$10.95	5.00%	
11038	SUGAA	1	5	$732.60	$29.59	20.00%	
10022	LAPLA	1	1	$671.50	$46.00	25.00%	

Exhibit 4. Results of the query

After pressing the GO button (and selecting the ordering according to the matching degree value and the threshold equal to 0.4) the above query is transformed ("behind the scene") according to the rules presented earlier.

As a result we obtain the list of records shown in Exhibit 4.

This concludes our brief description of FQUERY for Access, an add-on to Microsoft Access, which makes it possible to effectively and efficiently handle imprecise and vague linguistic terms in database querying.

Now we will show how the idea and solutions employed there can be used for devising a fuzzy querying interface for querying over the Internet.

3 Fuzzy Querying over the Internet

The FQUERY for Access is a standalone application. The same concept of fuzzy querying may be also implemented so as to be used via a WWW browser, as proposed and implemented by Dobrzyński, Kacprzyk and Zadrożny (1997). This will hopefully be a first step in a more human-consistent and human friendly use of vast information resources available worldwide.

We will start with some general remarks, and this part is based on Kacprzyk and Zadrożny (1997e), and then present two implementations proposed in Kacprzyk and Zadrożny (1997d) and Dobrzyński, Kacprzyk and Zadrożny (1997).

3.1. General Remarks on Fuzzy Querying over the Internet and its Implementation

The most popular solution for accessing a database over the Internet is via the World Wide Web (WWW). WWW creates a new framework for applications following the client-server paradigm. This features, e.g. a cross-platform availability, cheaper software maintenance and a unified user interface. With the advent of WWW and fast development of underlying technologies, the population of potential database users has grown to an unprecedented scale. A fast development of telecommunication infrastructure and sophisticated, but relatively cheap software tools, notably Web browsers, implied an easier and easier access and navigation through the Internet.

A growing popularity of the Internet inevitably changes the profile of a typical network user. Such a user is no longer an IT expert, and expects more human consistent user interfaces to communicate with information servers using, in addition to graphical controls, also flexible terms from natural language. As DBMSs will surely still be workhorses of many WWW-based applications, the need for simple, highly flexible and human-consistent interfaces to databases seems to be obvious.

The WWW service follows the client-server architecture, i.e. there are basically two types of WWW-related applications: the WWW server and the WWW client. The WWW (HTTP) server may be regarded as a kind of a file server providing on request various files (documents or pages), primarily written in HTML, the native format of WWW.

Currently available implementations of the WWW servers provide a much more extended functionality. The most important feature is the ability to execute other applications and deliver to the user appropriately encoded results (e.g., by using HTML). Thus, the WWW server may also be treated as an application server what is attained by different techniques. Most of the servers support a *Common Gateway Interface* (CGI). This approach is standard, but rather not effective in terms of the host computer's resources usage. The proposed replacements are on the other hand specific for particular products.

The WWW browser is a client application for this Internet service. The user initiates the connection providing the browser with the address of a required document, an Uniform Resource Locator (URL), and the browser forms and sends to the WWW server a request for this document. The communication is regulated by the HTTP protocol. Then, the server checks if a required document exists, and if so, delivers it to the browser. The browser renders the document to the required form by, e.g., interpreting HTML commands (tags) contained in the text, and displays the document on the user's screen. HTML allows to mark selected parts of a document text so as to inform the browser that this parts should be emphasized, underlined etc. The most characteristic feature of the HTML are hyperlinks allowing the user to quickly "jump" from a given document to other related documents, somewhere on the WWW.

To provide for a more dynamic communication in the WWW environment, some enhancements were introduced to the basic request-and-display rules. First of all, to make the CGI protocol really useful, some means of sending input data for server-based CGI-compliant applications have to be provided. This may be done through an extension to HTML, so-called *forms*. The browser displays a HTML form using Microsoft Windows' *controls* or X-windows' *widgets*, such as a push button, listbox etc. The data entered using these controls will be sent to the server with the request for a document - usually referring to some CGI application. Then, the server will execute this application setting the data provided by the user as an input. Such data may be, e.g., a query, which is used by the above CGI-compliant program to fetch matching records from a database. The server catches the output and sends it back to the browser.

Thus, the supporting of HTML forms provides a basic level of interaction which may be sufficient for the implementation of a database querying interface including fuzzy extensions - see, e.g., Kacprzyk and Zadrożny (1996), but still lacks some important features. For example, a browser-side verification of the data introduced by the user is not assumed in this approach. In consequence, e.g., the user's spelling errors may be discovered only at the server-side and their correction will be connected with some extra network transmissions.

Forms have become part of the HTML standard soon after its introduction and are now widely recognized by different browser implementations, even in a non-GUI environment (cf. the Lynx browser). Recently proposed enhancements are much more sophisticated though much less standardized. Three most important of them should be discussed here. All of them allow embedding in an HTML page a code, which is to be executed on the browser-side rather than on the server-side, as it is the case of CGI-compliant applications. The simplest technique consists in the use of scripting languages, such as Microsoft's Visual Basic Script or Netscape's Javascript. The routines written in these languages and embedded in the HTML text, although rather restricted in their capabilities, are powerful enough to serve as a glue between all elements of the user interface provided by a browser. For example, they allow checking data entered by the user and signal potential mistakes already at the browser-side, thus avoiding unnecessary network transmissions.

The second novel technique is connected with the Java language. It is a general purpose programming language designed to meet the requirements of a distributed environment such as the Internet. Thus, specially prepared Java programs, so-called *Java applets*, may be embedded in the HTML text. They are more powerful than the script routines, however still somehow limited in comparison to standalone Java programs, for security reasons. Anyway, using Java applets a developer can create advanced user interfaces still taking advantages of working within the WWW environment. Java is designed to be platform independent and is supported by leading software vendors.

Finally, the third hot Internet solution is referred to as *ActiveX controls*. Functionally, they are similar to Java applets in that ActiveX are small programs, which may be embedded in an HTML page. On the other hand, from the software engineering point of view, they are quite different. The ActiveX controls are sent over the network in the binary ready-to-execute form, thus are faster in execution than applets which have to be interpreted by a Java machine (or at least initially compiled at the browser side). However, the ActiveX controls are currently limited to the Microsoft Windows platform, while Java applets are also working on other platforms, notably UNIX.

Basically, the HTTP protocol used for communication between WWW agents is state-less making it possible to keep the protocol simple. On the other hand, there does not exist built-in mechanism allowing to employ the concept of a session which is quite important for some applications, including database querying. Some remedy for this drawback is offered by *cookies*. A cookie is a piece of text, which may be sent by a server with the document requested by a browser. Whenever the browser requests a related page from the same server, it adds to the request the cookie previously received. This makes possible to maintain the state of a session.

While the core of the HTML language is pretty well standardized and recognized by all WWW browsers, it is unfortunately no longer true for the extensions mentioned above.

3.2. Integration of a DBMS with WWW

The diversity of existing WWW-related software and protocols implies diverse solutions for the integration of a database with a WWW service. A WWW browser might be considered as an attractive alternative for specialized database clients as mentioned in Section 3.1. We can expect that this way of accessing a database over the Internet (or Intranet) will gain more and more popularity. Before looking for opportunities and challenges provided by a fuzzy logic based approach in this respect, we will first try to classify the existing solutions for the integration of WWW and DBMS. Basically, the criteria for this classification will refer to the way the data flow is arranged between all the agents involved, i.e. the WWW server and browser, DBMS software and other intervening pieces of software. We will trace the flow of information starting from the browser side.

First, we can differentiate the solutions taking into account the division of work done at the browser and server sides. Thus, we can distinguish the approaches where:

- the browser side processing of data is kept at the minimal level, or
- a preliminary processing is already done at the browser side.

The former approach allows for full independence of the type of browser used by the end users. Only a basic level of interaction with the user is maintained at the browser side, usually through the HTML forms. The data is checked and processed only at the server side. Thus, some additional data transmissions may be required in case of errors in input data or if a more complex user interaction is necessary (cf. Kacprzyk and Zadrożny, 1996). Anyway, this solution may be adequate when the targeted population of the end users is large and/or spatially and organizationally distributed, i.e. no assumptions may be made about the type of browsers used. The latter approach requires the use of, e.g., scripting languages routines, which will carry out some preliminary data checking and maybe also provide some more advanced functionality as, e.g., operations on cookies - see Kacprzyk and Zadrożny (1997d).

Second, the access to a database may be accomplished as follows:

- within the regular communication between the WWW server and the client, or
- using a separate connection specifically arranged for that purpose.

The first solution would usually consist in using an HTML form on the browser side and some additional application executed by the server. An advantage of such an approach is its portability - virtually all browsers and WWW servers support forms and some ways to execute external applications, respectively. The second solution may be accomplished using a Java applet or an ActiveX control communicating directly over the network with a target DBMS. It may be much more efficient but there are also some aspects to be carefully considered. For example, from the viewpoint of security, applets and ActiveX controls in particular are considered potentially dangerous. Obviously, the question of security is more general and there are tremendous efforts to solve it so that we can expect some satisfactory solutions fairly soon. On the other hand, this approach has little to do with a real integration of WWW and DBMS. In fact, the WWW browser plays here a rather marginal role and may be substituted by, e.g., a standalone Java application.

The third solution is related to how a WWW server cooperates with some "middle-ware" usually sitting between the server and DBMS. Here, two main classes may be distinguished:

- Using the CGI protocol,
- Using specialized Application Programming Interfaces (APIs).

The former solution is supported by virtually all WWW server software (in Microsoft Windows environment its variant, *called WinCGI*, is sometimes employed). CGI-compliant applications may be written using popular languages, like C, Perl, script languages, etc. but this way of executing an external application by the WWW server is considered inefficient. The latter solution extends the WWW server dynamically so as to provide a required functionality - in this case to make possible an access to the database. This is a more efficient solution but the standard for APIs does not exist.

Many commercial DBMS packages offer now some means for the integration of their products with the Internet. On the other hand, some WWW server software vendors include in their products some tools essentially facilitating the integration with a database (see, e.g., the Microsoft Internet Information Server and Active Server Pages mechanism, or the AOL server with its SQL Server or Illustra DBMSs connectivity).

3.3. Processing of Linguistic Data via Fuzzy Logic over the Internet

In this paper fuzzy querying is meant in the spirit of the previous works of the authors exemplified by Kacprzyk and Zadrożny (1995a, 1997a) and discussed in the previous sections. Basically, the vocabulary of querying languages is extended with linguistic (fuzzy) terms to allow for query conditions to contain clauses like: 'temperature *is high*', 'income *is much greater than* expenditures', '*most* of subconditions are met', etc. Then, these terms are to be interpreted during the query evaluation against subsequent records from a database. As a result we obtain *a matching degree* stating how well a given record meets conditions specified in the query. Hence, we need some methods for the modelling, definition and maintenance of fuzzy terms. The former issue is dealt with extensively in the previous sections. Basically, fuzzy sets, fuzzy relations and linguistic quantifiers are used to represent particular linguistic terms. This approach may be directly applied also in the Internet environment. On the other hand, the ways particular fuzzy entities are defined and stored depends on the user interface capabilities and general structure of the querying system. Thus, in case of an Internet-based querying application we have to devise appropriate procedures fitting the specifics of the WWW, notably those discussed in the previous sections. Following the criteria used for the aforementioned classifications of the WWW-DBMS integration approaches, we will now briefly look how the processing of fuzzy terms may be accomplished.

Obviously, the maintenance of fuzzy terms, i.e. their definition, storage and interpretation, requires some additional measures to be undertaken in comparison to a non-fuzzy querying system. It may be advantageous to have a more sophisticated user interface provided already on the browser side. For example, the definition of a fuzzy set representing a fuzzy value or linguistic quantifier requires a membership function to be defined. It may be rather cumbersome to create a sufficiently flexible user interface for that purpose using the HTML forms only.

Certainly, this is the only solution if full independence of the browser software capabilities is sought. On the other hand, using, e.g., a Java applet may make the interface more user friendly, cf. Kacprzyk and Zadrozny (1997d) for an example.

The definitions of linguistic (fuzzy) terms may be stored on the server or browser side. The first solution is more consistent with the WWW standards. The parameters of particular fuzzy terms may be stored in the same database as the data to be retrieved, in a separate database or even in flat files. It should be relatively easy for a CGI- or API-compliant application to handle this information at the server side. It may be a little bit cumbersome to achieve personalization of fuzzy terms in this approach. All definitions have to be stored at the server side so that, in case of multiple users, this may require an essential amount of extra disk space. Thus, the storing of this information at the browser side would solve the question of personalization. Unfortunately, the manipulating of data on the local disk at the browser side is considered as risky for security. Presently, this may be achieved by using the ActiveX controls or cookies. The first option provides a full access to a local file system and may become acceptable in the future when security problems will be solved. The second option is fairly secure but local data handling is rather limited and even here standards do not exist.

Anyway, the parameters of available fuzzy terms, predefined or defined by current and/or other users, have to be embedded in the user's querying interface. This may be done through HTML form controls or Java applets and ActiveX controls parameters. In case of HTML forms, it may be convenient to store definitions of fuzzy terms in cookies and/or so-called control properties. They are not visible to the user but their content may be easily manipulated by, e.g., a JavaScript script.

The actual database search and calculation of matching degrees for the particular records against a query containing fuzzy terms may take place at the browser or server side. The former alternative results in a solution rather loosely connected with the WWW services and we will omit it here. The latter approach may be implemented using a CGI-compliant application [see, e.g., Kacprzyk and Zadrożny (1996)] or a WWW server extensions using API (see, e.g., Dobrzyński, Kacprzyk and Zadrożny, 1997). From the viewpoint of functionality of this "middle-ware" (gateway) application, the following classification may be proposed:

- the gateway fetches the rows from the database and only then evaluates the query against them,
- the handling of fuzziness is built into the DBMS, and the gateway just forwards the query and its results,
- the gateway itself manages the database, and the handling of fuzziness is a part of its regular query processing.

The first approach may be applied for virtually any DBMS. The whole fuzzy querying has to be implemented in the gateway. The second approach would be definitely most efficient though commercial DBMSs accepting fuzzy queries are not available yet. For example of such a solution, see Dobrzyński, Kacprzyk and Zadrożny (1997). The third approach may be well suited for simple databases as, e.g., an XBase file (see Kacprzyk and Zadrożny, 1997d).

Finally, results of the query are to be displayed. Here, the features of the HTML perfectly fit the needs. The results may be a list where each line consists of a value of a key field of the record with its matching degree. Each such a line contains a hyperlink that brings to the screen the content of the whole record.

We will now present an implementation of fuzzy querying over the Internet, and some WWW-related tools and techniques mentioned above.

4 Implementation of Fuzzy Querying over the Internet

Now, we will briefly describe two linguistic (fuzzy) querying interfaces based on the WWW. We will show how tools available in WWW, in particular Java applets and JavaScript, may be effectively and efficiently employed for implementing advanced, multi-platform and user-friendly fuzzy-logic-based querying and other applications following general remarks provided, and solutions adopted in our FQUERY for Access.

The first interface, employing advanced client-side techniques will be illustrated on a WWW-based fuzzy querying interface for a database of Research, Technology and Development (RTD) institutions from Central and Eastern Europe (cf. Kacprzyk and Zadrożny, 1996,1997d). The second interface makes it possible to submit a query over the Internet to the fuzzy querying engine implemented by the FQUERY for Access add-on, and to display the results back on the user screen in the window of a WWW browser (cf. Dobrzyński, Kacprzyk and Zadrożny, 1997).

Obviously, the DBMS is still the main element of such a system. It may be a full-fledged, network-based product like Oracle, Sybase, Microsoft SQL Server etc. This will be the best choice for large systems serving many customers. For intranet-oriented systems, smaller DBMSs may be sufficient as, e.g., Microsoft Access. Most of the existing commercial DBMSs offer now means of the integration with the Internet. For our implementation we use a relatively simple database consisting of a set of Xbase format and text files.

The second element of our fuzzy querying system is a WWW server that follows a simple CGI-based scheme in order to access the database. More precisely, a CGI-compliant C program performs the actual querying of a Xbase file, including the processing of fuzzy terms. Obviously, it has to be provided by a WWW server with a query formulated by a user and sent to the server using the next component, a WWW browser.

In our first pilot implementation we have chosen the Netscape Navigator but a similar functionality may be attained by using the Microsoft Explorer which was also used in further cases. As the processing of fuzzy terms essentially increases the scope of interaction with a user, limitations of the standard HTML pose serious obstacles for creation of an effective and efficient WWW-based fuzzy querying interface. Thus, we will employ some new enhancements of the standard HTML mentioned earlier.

4.1. The Database Component

The core of the system is here a relatively simple database, an XBase file, which contains descriptions of some Research, Technology and Development (RTD) institutions from Central and Eastern Europe. This database has been constructed as a result of a research project for the support of cooperation between the scientific communities of the European Union and other European countries. Each organization in the database is described by many attributes (fields).

For the purposes of fuzzy querying we selected the following attributes:

1. number of employees (*numerical*),
2. country (*single-valued*),
3. subjects of activity related to RTD (*multi-valued*),
4. specific topics/know-how (*textual*).

The first field is numerical. Regular (non-fuzzy) queries referring to this field would use it with a classical relational operator as <, >, = etc. Our fuzzy querying scheme extends them with fuzzy values and fuzzy relations, and then fuzzy linguistic quantifiers. Here we will only illustrate them with examples of simple queries exemplified by: "Number of employees IS *small*", "Number of employees IS *much greater than* 100".

The second field is a text (string). Typically, a non-fuzzy query may contain a test for equality with some fixed text (here: the name of a selected country of origin of the RTD organization sought). However, very often (also here) it may be natural to pose a question like: "Country IS IN *Central Europe*". The concept of "Central Europe" should be represented by a set, preferably fuzzy, as one can claim that, e.g., Slovenia belongs to this set but only to some degree.

The third field is a virtual one, represented by a set of logical (Yes/No) fields. More precisely, there is a separate field corresponding to each possible subject of activity related to RTD in a given organization. A query may refer collectively to all these fields. Thus, we propose to treat all this fields as one, virtual multi-valued field. Then, its value would be a set of subjects of activity and, consequently, in a query it may be compared to a, possibly fuzzy, set. Dealing with a set of values, both in a record and a query, calls for soft measures of matching as the requirement that both sets are exactly equal is usually too rigid.

Finally, the fourth field is typical for information retrieval, i.e. it contains purely textual data. We do not propose any fuzzy extensions in this respect. Approaches with fuzzy thesauri to enhance querying capabilities may be applied.

4.2. The Browser Side Processing

A WWW browser provides a framework for the user interface of our querying system. Basically, we use the following features:

- HTML forms,
- Java applets,
- JavaScript scripting,
- frames, and
- cookies.

Frames make possible to divide the screen into more or less independent parts that may display different documents. At the same time, the script code embedded in a document in one frame may manipulate other frames, i.e. make them display some documents or even dynamically create new documents in other frames. This is very convenient for our purposes.

The main screen of our system is shown in Exhibit 5. There are three frames:

- the main frame, at the left, for specifying query criteria,
- the second frame for specifying membership functions for a fuzzy set employed in a query and for displaying help information,
- the third frame, at the bottom, for quickly moving around the first frame.

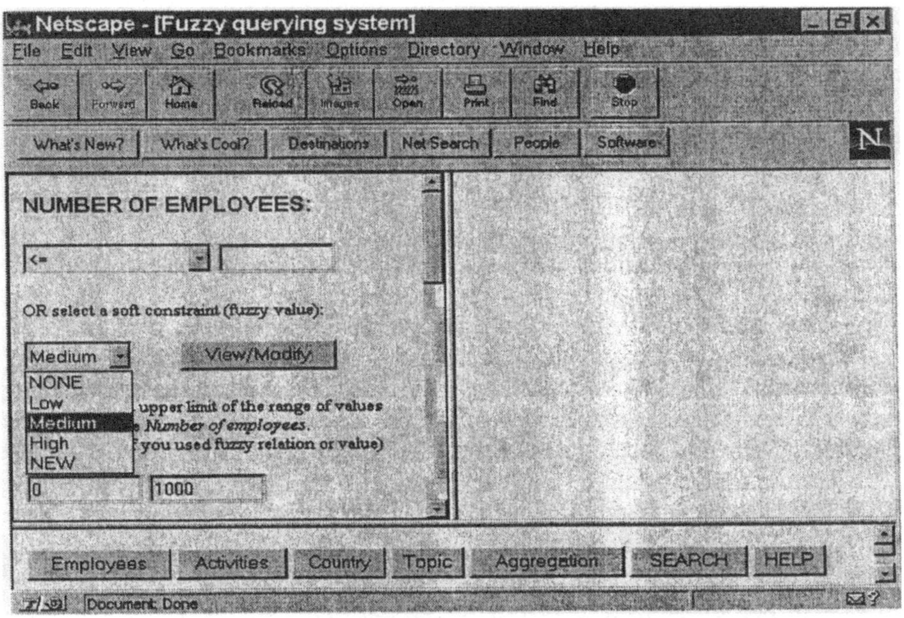

Exhibit 5. The main screen of the interface

In the main frame there is an HTML form with separate controls corresponding to particular fields. Now we will briefly discuss how they may be associated with various fuzzy terms.

The numerical field „Number of employees" may be used in a query with fuzzy values or fuzzy relations. Exhibit 5 shows how a fuzzy value may be introduced into a query. Thus, the user may select a fuzzy value from a list that may be easily manipulated via a GUI. The content of the list depends on the history of previous interactions with the system. If a user contacts the system for the first time - what manifests itself with the lack of the cookie at the client side - the list is short as in Exhibit 5. The user can also define "own" fuzzy values stored at the browser side within the cookie and available during next sessions. The definition is initiated by selecting the "NEW" option and is supported by a graphical interface shown in Exhibit 6. This is implemented as a Java applet.

The definitions of fuzzy values, relations and quantifiers are stored and defined similarly using cookies and Java applets, respectively. Thus, a Java applet used to modify the parameters of an existing fuzzy term will fetch its parameters from the cookie and store them after modification at the same place. Hence, definitions of fuzzy terms will always go to the server with the query.

The single-valued attribute "Country" may be manipulated by the user in a similar way as the multi-valued „Subjects of activity". (cf. Exhibit 8). As the latter requires more user-interaction, we will focus on it. The user looking for an RTD organization active in some areas should select names of these areas in the main frame. Then, if the user is interested in various areas to a different degree, he or she may fuzzify the set of selected activities. For doing this, an appropriate button is to be pressed and the list of earlier selected activities will be displayed in the right frame along with the textboxes for changing the membership degree value from 1.0 (assumed initially) to a chosen one. Then, after the "OK" button is pressed, values assigned to particular members of the set are stored "inside" the HTML form displayed in the main frame. The VALUE property of the HTML's SELECT control is employed to store these values and send them back to the server with the query.

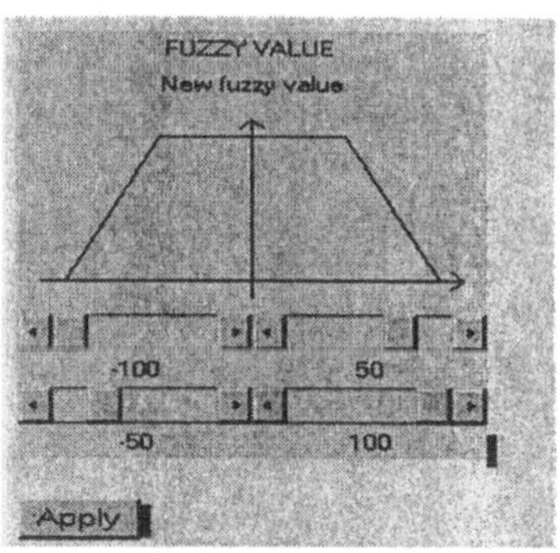

Exhibit 6. A Java applet for the definition of a fuzzy value

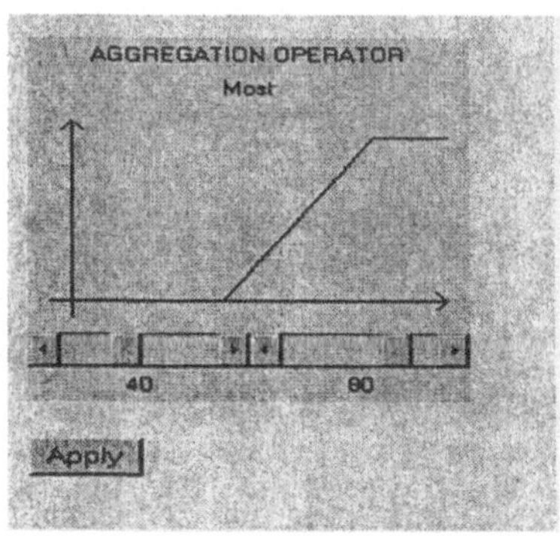

Exhibit 7. A Java applet for the definition of a linguistic quantifier

This type of fields requires some compatibility indices. The following indices are currently available in the system:

1. degree of possibility of matching,
2. degree of necessity of matching 1,
3. degree of necessity of matching 2,
4. generalized Jaccard coefficient.

Basically, the first should be used when looking for an organization dealing with at least one subject of activity specified in a query, the second - when looking for an organization dealing with all activities specified in a query (and maybe some more), the third - for the search of an organization dealing only with activities specified in the query, not necessarily all, and the fourth -when looking for an organization dealing with most activities specified in the query and not many other.

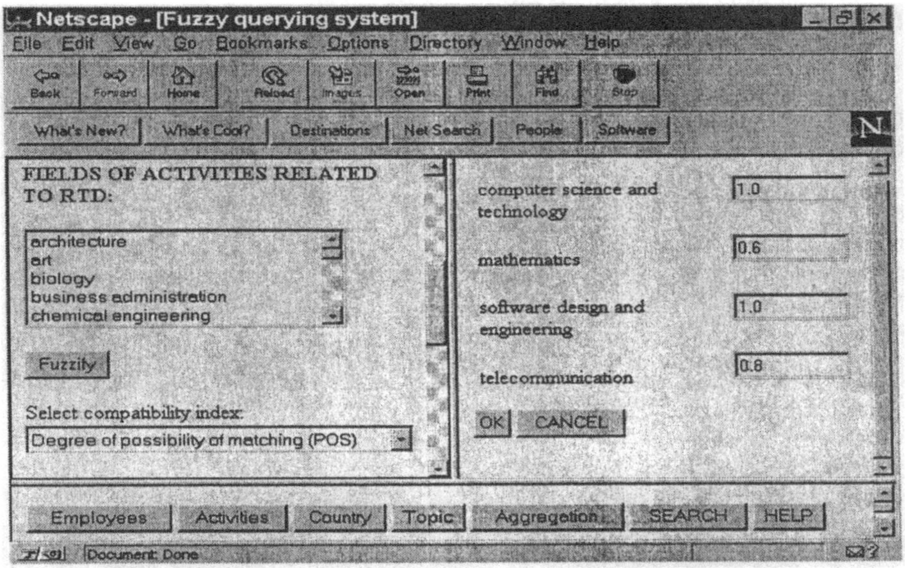

Exhibit 8. A multi-valued attribute and a fuzzy set constant

The last field, i.e. "Special topic (of activity)/know-how" does not require any special treatment. The user just enters some keywords in a textbox which need no preprocessing or manipulation at the browser side.

Classically, all conditions specified for the particular fields mentioned would be combined using the AND and OR logical connectives. Here we allow for more flexible aggregation operators, representing linguistic quantifiers. Thus, the user may request that, e.g., "most" of the conditions are met. These linguistic quantifiers are meant due to Zadeh (cf. Section 2), and the user may interactively define "own" quantifiers using a Java applet - cf. Exhibit 7.

4.3 The Server Side Processing

At the server side we can distinguish two types of operations:

- a regular communication with a WWW browser due to the HTTP protocol done by the WWW server, and
- the generation of dynamic HTML documents and processing of a query by a set of CGI-compliant programs.

The whole processing is initiated by a browser requesting the "main document" of our querying system containing the query form, as shown in Exhibit 9. The browser request may be accompanied by the cookie comprising the definitions of user-specific fuzzy terms. The server simply sends the query form to the browser together with the cookie if one was present in the request. Now the browser side processing takes place, as described in the previous section. Finally, the user presses the "SEARCH" button and all information entered by the user is transmitted to the server. Then, the server initially processes the data according to the CGI specification and calls our main C program which makes the actual query processing and database search.

In fact, all information about fuzzy terms possibly used in the query is contained in the data forwarded to this program by the WWW server. Thus, it has only to extract particular pieces of data and place them in its internal data structures and then start the search of the database. It fetches subsequent records and computes the matching degree. A partial fulfillment of the criteria by a record is possible. We start with the matching of particular conditions against the values of the attributes in a record. Then, the partial matching degrees are combined using an aggregation operator and we obtain an overall matching degree sought. Then, the records are ordered according to their matching degrees, and finally an HTML document containing the list of hyperlinks to the particular records is produced. More precisely, each hyperlink consists of the matching degree and the content of a pre-specified field of the record. All these hyperlinks lead to another C program that delivers the full content of the records selected (cf. Exhibit 9).

To summarize, at the server side we have the following components of our fuzzy querying system:

- a database file in the XBase format,
- HTML pages for: query form (enhanced with JavaScript functions and applets), list of records and the contents of a selected record,
- the searching program, and
- the program displaying (reporting) records.

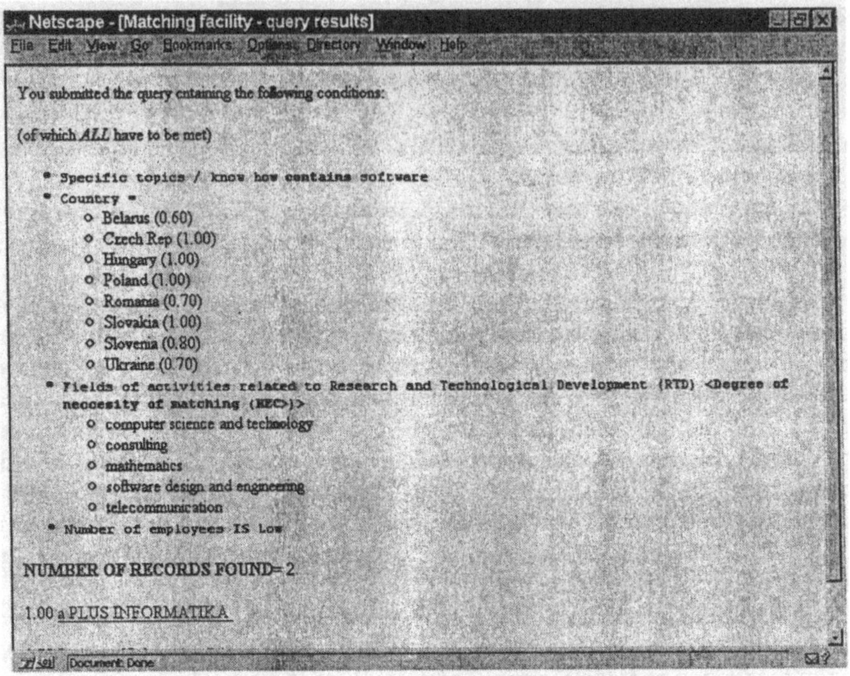

Exhibit 9. Example of querying results

4.4. A WWW-Based Interface to FQUERY for Access

The WWW based interface presented in this section allows to form a query containing fuzzy elements and submit a query over the Internet to the fuzzy querying engine implemented by the FQUERY for Access add-on. Then, the query is processed in exactly the same way as in the standalone case. The results of the query are sent back to the client and displayed by the browser.

The process of query formation and processing may be described using an example for querying a database of houses for sale in a real estate agency. Basically, in that kind of application virtually all customers' requirements are imprecise as, e.g., "*possibly low* price", "*more or less* two bedrooms", "*in the city center*", etc. Here we will just present a simple example of how a single imprecise condition "price should be *low*" is formulated using the Microsoft Explorer based user-interface. We will also show how the results of such a query, i.e. the addresses of apartments and or houses with their major descriptions and the values of a matching degree, are displayed via the Explorer's window.

Firstly, the user, using a WWW browser, opens the main document of the querying system shown in Exhibit 10. It contains a simple query form, making it possible to define a SQL query. Such a query may contain fuzzy elements, which are put there as query parameters. The same syntax and semantics applies as presented in Section 2.

When the query is created, the user sends it to the WWW server pressing the SEND button. After receiving the request with the query definition data, the server starts a script, written in VBScript, embedded in the requested document. Notice that the script is run at the server side rather than at the client side as in the previous case. This script opens an appropriate database, and then executes the query submitted over the Internet. The execution is initiated through a call to FQUERY for Access routines securing proper interpretation of all fuzzy terms. The results of the query are captured by the script and used to create an HTML page which is then send back to the browser - see, e.g., Exhibit 11.

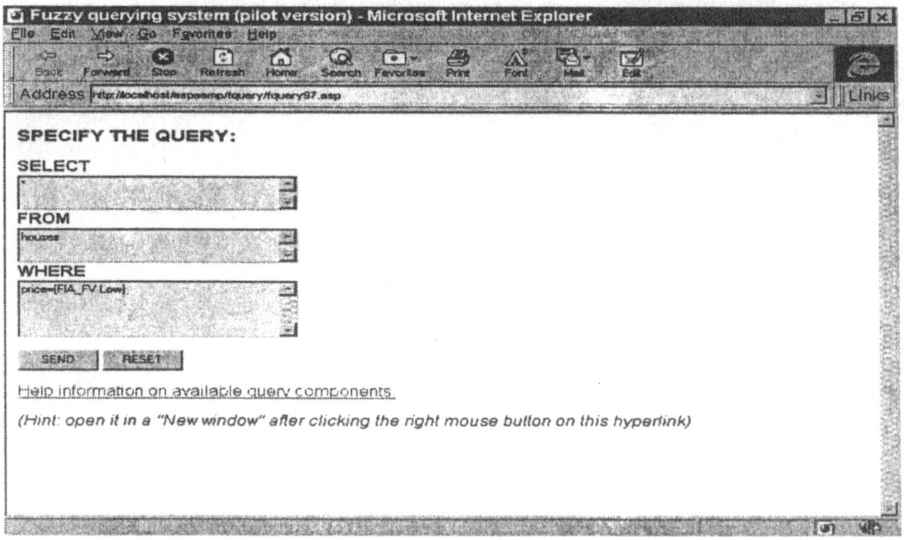

Exhibit 10. Formulation of a simple condition in a query using the Microsoft Explorer

Therefore, the same fuzzy querying tool, FQUERY for Access, may be used in the standalone (desktop) and Internet environments.

This completes our brief description of implementations of linguistic (fuzzy) querying over the Internet by employing two major WWW browsers, the Netscape Navigator and Microsoft Explorer. We have only mentioned here some implementation-specific elements and solutions since the other ones are implemented analogously as for the standalone application described earlier.

We hope that the Internet is a challenge for fuzzy querying and, at the same time, may give momentum to a further research in this relevant field.

5 Concluding Remarks

We presented, first, our FQUERY for Access, an add-on for the implementation of fuzzy querying, and then showed how fuzzy querying over the Internet can be implemented using a WWW browser. This should help an average user browse vast information resources available through the Internet.

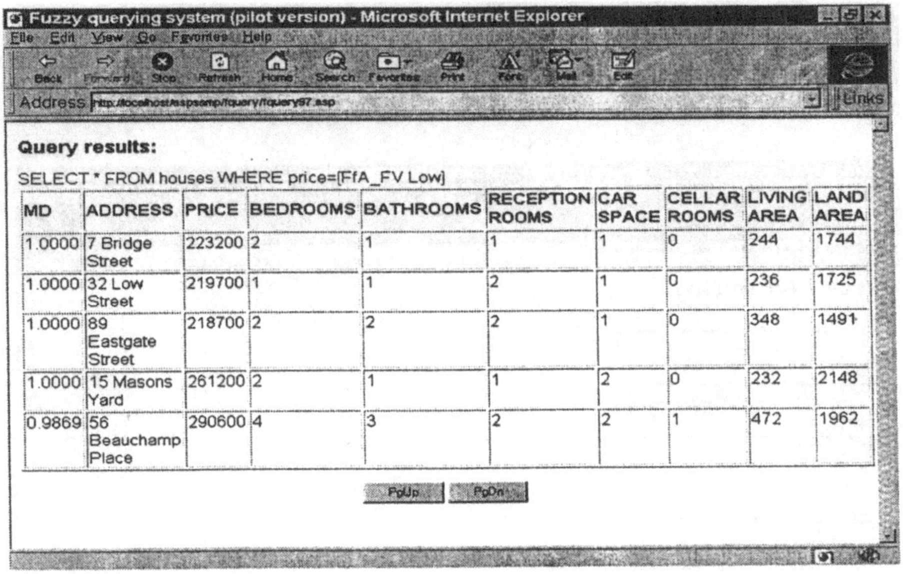

MD	ADDRESS	PRICE	BEDROOMS	BATHROOMS	RECEPTION ROOMS	CAR SPACE	CELLAR ROOMS	LIVING AREA	LAND AREA
1.0000	7 Bridge Street	223200	2	1	1	1	0	244	1744
1.0000	32 Low Street	219700	1	1	2	1	0	236	1725
1.0000	89 Eastgate Street	218700	2	2	2	1	0	348	1491
1.0000	15 Masons Yard	261200	2	1	1	2	0	232	2148
0.9869	56 Beauchamp Place	290600	4	3	2	2	1	472	1962

Exhibit 11. Results of fuzzy querying over the Internet using the Microsoft Explorer

Literature

Bosc P. and J. Kacprzyk, Eds. (1995) Fuzziness in Database Management Systems. Physica-Verlag, Heidleberg,

Bosc P. and O. Pivert (1992) Fuzzy querying in conventional databases. In L.A. Zadeh and J. Kacprzyk (Eds.): Fuzzy Logic for the Management of Uncertainty. Wiley, New York, pp. 645-671.

Chen G.Q. (1998) Fuzzy Logic in Data Modeling - Semantics, Constraints and Database Design. Kluwer, Boston.

Dobrzyński W., Kacprzyk J. and S. Zadrożny (1997) An example of fuzzy querying using Microsoft' Active Server Pages tools. Proceedings of Fifth European Congress on Intelligent Techniques and Soft Computing - EUFIT'97 (Aachen, Germany), 1997, vol. 2, pp. 1181-1185.

Kacprzyk J. (1995) Fuzzy logic in DBMSs and querying, in N.K. Kasabov and G. Coghill (Eds.): Proceedings of Second New Zealand International Two-Stream Conference on Artificial Neural Networks and Expert Systems (Dunedin, New Zealand), IEEE Computer Society Press, Los Alamitos, CA, USA, pp. 106 - 109.

Kacprzyk J. and S. Zadrożny (1994a) Fuzzy querying for Microsoft Access. Proceedings of the Third IEEE Conference on Fuzzy Systems (Orlando, USA), Vol. 1, pp. 167-171.

Kacprzyk J. and S. Zadrożny (1994b) Fuzzy queries in Microsoft Access: toward a 'more intelligent' use of Microsoft Windows based DBMSs, Proceedings of the 1994 Second Australian and New Zealand Conference on Intelligent Information Systems - ANZIIS'94 (Brisbane, Australia), pp. 492 - 496.

Kacprzyk J. and S. Zadrożny (1995a) FQUERY for Access: fuzzy querying for a Windows-based DBMS. In: P. Bosc and J. Kacprzyk (Eds.) Fuzziness in Database Management Systems, Physica-Verlag, Heidelberg, pp. 415 - 433.

Kacprzyk J. and S. Zadrożny (1995b) Fuzzy queries in Microsoft Access v. 2, Proceedings of 6th International Fuzzy Systems Association World Congress (Sao Paolo, Brazil), Vol. II, pp. 341 - 344.

Kacprzyk J. and S. Zadrożny (1996) A fuzzy querying interface for a WWW-server-based relational DBMS, Proceedings of IPMU'96 - 6th International Conference on Information Processing and Management of Uncertainty in Knowledge-Based Systems (Granada, Spain), 1996, vol. 1, pp. 19 - 24.

Kacprzyk J. and S. Zadrożny (1997a) Fuzzy queries in Microsoft Access v. 2, in D. Dubois, H. Prade and R.R. Yager (Eds.): Fuzzy Information Engineering - A Guided Tour of Applications, Wiley, New York, 1997, pp. 223 - 232.

Kacprzyk J. and S. Zadrożny (1997b) Implementation of OWA operators in fuzzy querying for Microsoft Access. In: R.R. Yager and J. Kacprzyk (Eds.) The Ordered Weighted Averaging Operators: Theory and Applications, Kluwer, Bostonn 1997, pp. 293 - 306.

Kacprzyk and S. Zadrożny (1997c) Flexible querying using fuzzy logic: An implementation for Microsoft Access, in T. Andreasen, H. Christiansen and H.L. Larsen (eds.): Flexible Query Answering Systems, Kluwer, Boston, 1997, pp. 247-275.

Kacprzyk and S. Zadrożny (1997d) A fuzzy querying interface for a WWW environment, Proceedings of IFSA'97 - Seventh International Fuzzy Systems Association World Congress (Prague, Czech Rep.), Academia, Prague, Vol. IV, pp. 285 - 290.

Kacprzyk J. and S. Zadrożny (1997e) Issues and solutions for fuzzy database querying over Internet. Proceedings of Fifth European Congress on Intelligent Techniques and Soft Computing - EUFIT'97 (Aachen, Germany), 1997, vol. 2, pp. 1191-1195.

Kacprzyk J., Zadrożny S. and Ziółkowski A. (1989) FQUERY III+: a 'human consistent` database querying system based on fuzzy logic with linguistic quantifiers. Information Systems 6, 443 - 453.

Kacprzyk J. and Ziółkowski A. (1986a) Retrieval from databases using queries with fuzzy linguistic quantifiers. In H. Prade and C.V. Negoita (Eds.) Fuzzy Logics in Knowledge Engineering. Verlag TÜV Rheinland, Cologne, pp. 46-57.

Kacprzyk J. and Ziółkowski A. (1986b) Database queries with fuzzy linguistic quantifiers. IEEE Transactions on Systems, Man and Cybernetics SMC - 16, 474 - 479.

Kim P.-C. (1996) A taxonomy on the architecture of database gateways for the Web. [URL:http://grigg.chungnam.ac.kr/~uniweb/documents/taxonomy/text.html]

Petry F.E. (1996) Fuzzy Databases: Principles and Applications. Kluwer, Boston.

Yager R.R. (1988) On ordered weighted averaging aggregation operators in multicriteria decision making. IEEE Transactions on Systems, Man and Cybernetics, 18, 183-190.

Yager R.R. and Kacprzyk J., Eds. (1997) The Ordered Weighted Averaging Operators: Theory and Applications. Kluwer, Boston.

Yazici A. and R. George (1999) Fuzzy Database Modeling. Physica-Verlag, Heidelberg and New York.

Yazici A., R. George, B.P. Buckles and F.E. Petry (1992) A survey of conceptual and logical data models for uncertainty management. In L.A. Zadeh and J. Kacprzyk (Eds.): Fuzzy Logic for the Management of Uncertainty. Wiley, New York, pp. 607-643.

Zadeh L.A. (1983) A computational approach to fuzzy quantifiers in natural languages. Computers and Maths. with Appls. 9, 149 - 184.

Zadrożny S. and J. Kacprzyk (1995) Fuzzy querying using the 'query-by-example' option in a Windows-based DBMS", Proceedings of Third European Congress on Intelligent Techniques and Soft Computing - EUFIT'95 (Aachen, Germany), vol. 2, pp. 733-736.

Zadrożny S. and J. Kacprzyk (1996) Multi-valued fields and values in fuzzy querying via FQUERY for Access, Proceedings of FUZZ–IEEE'96 - Fifth International Conference on Fuzzy Systems (New Orleans, USA), vol. 2, pp. 1351 - 1357.

Zadrożny, J. Kacprzyk and K. Floisand (1997) Internet and WWW - new opportunities for information technology and soft computing, Proceedings of IFSA'97 - Seventh International Fuzzy Systems Association World Congress (Prague, Czech Rep.), Academia, Prague, Vol. IV, pp. 316 - 319.

Zemankova M. and J. Kacprzyk (1993) The roles of fuzzy logic and management of uncertainty in building intelligent information systems, Journal of Intelligent Information Systems 2, 311-317.

Zemankova-Leech M. and Kandel A. (1984) Fuzzy Relational Databases - a Key to Expert Systems. Verlag TÜV Rheinland, Cologne.

GPSR Compliance

The European Union's (EU) General Product Safety Regulation (GPSR) is a set of rules that requires consumer products to be safe and our obligations to ensure this.

If you have any concerns about our products, you can contact us on ProductSafety@springernature.com

In case Publisher is established outside the EU, the EU authorized representative is:

Springer Nature Customer Service Center GmbH
Europaplatz 3
69115 Heidelberg, Germany

Batch number: 10577876

Printed by Printforce, the Netherlands